THE UNITED STATES AIR FORCE
IN SOUTHEAST ASIA

Development and Employment of Fixed-Wing Gunships 1962-1972

by

Jack S. Ballard

OFFICE OF AIR FORCE HISTORY
UNITED STATES AIR FORCE
WASHINGTON, D.C., 1982

Library of Congress Cataloging in Publication Data

Ballard, Jack S
  The Development and Employment of Fixed-wing Gunships, 1962–1972.

  (The United States Air Force in Southeast Asia series)
  Bibliography
  Includes index.
  1. Vietnamese Conflict, 1961–1975—Aerial operations, American. 2. United States. Air Force—History—Vietnamese Conflict, 1961–1975. 3. Gunships (Military aircraft)—United States. I. Title. II. Series: United States Air Force in Southeast Asia series.
  DS558.8.B35   959.704'348   80-25422

For sale by the Superintendent of Documents, U.S. Government Printing Office
Washington, D.C. 20402

Foreword

One of the more striking aspects of the war in Southeast Asia was the adaptation of existing weapons in the American arsenal to the peculiar needs of an unconventional war. Total air superiority presented to the United States great opportunities to support ground operations. Very early some in the Air Force saw the need for a system that could saturate the ground with fire for interdicting enemy reinforcements, for supporting ground troops in contact with the enemy, and for defending isolated hamlets and outposts under attack. Such a weapons system had to be able to hit small, often fleeting targets in difficult terrain, at night, and in bad weather, through thick jungle cover. It had to be flexible and survivable, to linger for a protracted time over targets, and above all it had to possess great firepower. Nothing in the inventory could do all of this, so the Air Force developed the fixed-wing gunship. This volume, written by Lt. Col. Jack S. Ballard during his assignment to the Office of Air Force History, traces the gunship's history from initial conception in the early 1960s through deployment and operations to the end of American combat involvement in early 1973.

Gunship theory—flying an airplane in a pylon turn to aim side-mounted guns at a fixed point on the ground—had been known for years. But it took men of vision and persistence to mate the theory with modern technology, and then sell the idea to higher authorities. Once the concept had been accepted, the resulting family of gunships was designed to meet specific requirements, then modified as requirements changed. The result was one of the most innovative and successful weapons used in the war.

As impressive as was the hardware, the author does not ignore the human element. The gunship program had its share of high-level indecision, production snarls, and equipment failure; but these were overcome by sound management and determination. Sometimes tactics were faulty, even dangerous, and had to be adjusted to the realities of combat. Gunship crews enjoyed a relatively wide latitude in methods of attacking individual targets; not infrequently they found themselves acting as airborne commanders directing the employment of other strike aircraft. Most of the tactical decisions and a large number of key management decisions were made by officers of surprisingly junior rank. The gunship story shows that the individual still makes a difference in modern war, no matter what the dependence on technology.

One of the most instructive aspects of Ballard's volume is the relationship between theory and experience. Theory drove the initial design concept and employment, but experience in combat drove modification of the aircraft and execution of tactics throughout the war. While the evolution of the gunship and the changing character of its use were not always smooth processes, the gunship worked successfully. The goal of meeting mission requirements always remained paramount.

Lt. Col. Ballard interviewed many key participants involved in this story and gathered extensive data relating to this unique weapon. His principal sources include official letters, messages, memoranda, reports, and minutes of meetings. Most of his research was conducted in the Office of Air Force History, the Albert F. Simpson Historical Reseach Center and Air University Library, Maxwell Air Force Base, Ala., in the records of the Air Staff, and Offices of the Secretary of the Air Force.

Lt. Col. Ballard's work is one of a series of books dealing with the war in Southeast Asia which is being published by the Office of Air Force History.

RICHARD H. KOHN
Chief, Office of Air Force History

Preface

In an age of supersonic jet aircraft, megaton atomic weapons, and sophisticated electronic devices, nothing seemed quite so incongruous as a lumbering C-47 transport evolving into a potent weapon system. Counterinsurgency warfare, as exemplified by the Southeast Asian war, had generated modern air weaponry paradoxes such as old T-28 trainers serving as attack aircraft. The gunship* joined this group as an improvisation that surprised nearly everyone. From a humble modification of the apparently ageless C-47 (DC-3), the gunship grew into a highly complex weapon system. In doing so, it pioneered new research developments and revolutionized aerial counterinsurgency tactics.

Basically, in the case of the fixed-wing gunship, the U.S. Air Force installed side-firing guns in available aircraft (mostly transports) and employed them tactically while in an orbiting maneuver. This unlikely conversion of relatively slow, large-cabin aircraft into heavily armed aerial firing platforms filled the need for an air weapon system that could direct saturating, extremely accurate firepower on generally small—even fleeting—targets in difficult terrain, varying weather, and particularly during hours of darkness. Very simply, the Air Force's combat aircraft of the early 1960s often could not find nor accurately strike enemy targets at night or under cover of the great jungle canopy. The urgent need for such a capability became dramatically obvious as guerilla warfare expanded in South Vietnam.

From the outset, the AC-47 gunship and its successors—the AC-130 and AC-119—were inseparably linked to the war in Southeast Asia (SEA). More and more, the enemy used the cover of darkness and jungle to mask his supply movements and attacks on South Vietnamese forts, hamlets, and forces. Because the gunship could orbit, lock on a target with special sensors, and carefully apply firepower, it became a vital weapon in the overall U.S.-South Vietnamese war strategy. It quickly proved its worth as a night protector of friendly villages, bases, and forces. Its matchless effectiveness in night operations helped strip away the enemy's "shield of darkness."† Of the three principal types of gunships the Air Force employed, the powerful AC-130 became the preeminent truck-killer of the war. As a primary interdiction weapon, it was employed to try to choke off North Vietnamese support of communist insurgent forces infiltrating into South Vietnam.

---

*In this study "gunship" refers to the fixed-wing, side-firing aircraft of the U.S. Air Force or allied air forces.

†Maj William R. Casey, "AC-119; USAF's Flying Battleship," *Air Force/Space Digest,* Feb 1970, pp 48-50.

Gunship successes sparked enemy countermeasures, especially along the Ho Chi Minh Trail in Laos. The struggle to keep ahead of the enemy's defenses and to impede his largely seasonal combat and resupply surges is a recurring theme of this history. During the wet summer months when enemy logistics movement all but ceased, the Air Force undertook crash programs to refurbish and improve the gunships in anticipation of the end of the monsoons and a new enemy surge of personnel and supplies down the trail. These USAF efforts had one goal—to return a more effective and less vulnerable gunship to combat in the dry winter months to counter the stepped-up enemy activity. Also, the Air Force steadily refined its combat tactics to better cope with enemy defenses. The gunship was teamed with other aircraft over strongly defended areas. Thus its tactics grew more complex. The story of these cyclical equipment changes and the effect of changing combat missions takes up a large but essential part of this narrative.

Besides spotlighting various combat activities in Southeast Asia, a significant and engrossing story about Air Force research and development is contained in the chapters that follow. The gunship evolved dynamically through modification of several cargo aircraft—C–47s, C–130s, and C–119s—with serious consideration also given from time to time to other aircraft, such as light planes. Colorful names—Spooky, Spectre, Shadow, and Stinger—kept pace with major aircraft changes. Moreover, this pluralistic gunship development became multinational by way of the U.S. Military Assistance Program, with several types of gunships turned over to the Vietnamese and other allied air force. The following account chronologically traces the story of these unique weapon systems in terms of the models of aircraft used, their numbers, and their operational performance.

The gunship's rapid progression toward greater sophistication touches and illuminates many of the problems associated with weapon system advancement. Thus, this study covers such matters as Air Force management, contractor relations, technical problems, funding, and high-level debate and decisions concerning the size, character, and effectiveness of the gunship force. Especially at the beginning, the labor pains incident to the birth, acceptance, and employment of a relatively new idea prove noteworthy. The solutions to some development problems and issues carry lessons far transcending the gunship program.

An outstanding theme of the gunship story was the Air Force's constant improvisation and tinkering as the system evolved. The weapon system did not spring out of the think tanks, move from the drawing boards to the wind tunnels, or undergo exacting scientific-engineering analysis. Instead, its growth largely stemmed from the Air Force making do with basic equipment already in the inventory. It consisted of molding parts from various systems and blending operational concepts from widely different sources. While most technological advances involve borrowed ideas and hardware, the gunship development reflects this to an unusual degree.

People are crucial in any program but a relatively small group of key men determined the gunship's progress. Facing opposition and skepticism, these men battled first for a concept and then for a weapon system employing it. The gunship's success and eventual acceptance hinged chiefly on their personal effect. This, then, is a history of men as well as machines.

The text traces gunship developments through 1972 to the early 1973 truce that closed the American combat role in South Vietnam and Laos. Though fighting in Cambodia continued into 1973 and gunships took part, the gunship combat story had largely been told. Still ahead were interesting and important equipment additions or modifications. However, these and the final events in Cambodia merit a separate account.

Much of this study could not have been written without the prior historical work of others and the kind assistance to the author by numerous individuals and organizations. Their contributions can be seen in the sources cited.

The author wishes to express his appreciation to the people in the Office of Air Force History for their support, assistance, and advice: to the past chiefs in the Office of Air Force History: Brig. Gen. Brian S. Gunderson, Brig. Gen. Earl G. Peck, Dr. Stanley L. Falk, and Maj. Gen. John W. Huston, who supported this project for an earlier edition and encouraged its broad publication; to Dr. Richard H. Kohn, the present chief, his deputy, Col. John Schlight, and to Max Rosenberg and Carl Berger. Mr. Eugene P. Sagstetter, Mary F. Loughlin, and Vanessa D. Allen edited, proofread, and purged the manuscript of the typographical errors and misprints that elude the closest checking. Special acknowledgement goes to Mr. Lawrence J. Paszek, Senior Editor, for his work in selecting photography, designing the arrangement, and managing the publication through various stages of production. Dave Haddock, U.S. Government Printing Office, deserves particular credit for his assistance in correcting serious typographical deficiencies.

Photographs were selected predominantly from the Defense Audiovisual Agency, where considerable assistance came from Ada Scott and Dana Bell, now with Smithsonian's National Air and Space Museum. Mr. Bell's incisive knowledge in aviation photography helped immensely in defining visual material presented in this work.

Jack S. Ballard

Contents

Illustrations and Photographs

Maps and Charts

Tables

The Author

Dr. Jack S. Ballard wrote the *Fixed-Wing Gunship* study while assigned to the Office of Air Force History in Washington, D.C., during the period 1970–1974. He had a varied Air Force career, including assignments as a personnel administrative officer and AFROTC instructor at Occidental College, a senior military training advisor to a Korean Air Force training wing, Assistant Professor in the history department at the Air Force Academy, and chief of the Plans and Requirements Division of the Lowry Technical Training Center. He retired from the latter position and the Air Force in 1980 to join the Denver Aerospace Division of the Martin Marietta Corp. He holds a BSE degree from the University of Arkansas, an MA from the University of Southern California, and a PhD in history from UCLA. He has written a number of historical articles related to military-aviation history and has authored *The Shock of Peace: Demobilization Following World War II*. He also serves on the history staff at the University of Colorado, Colorado Springs.

Development and Employment
of Fixed-Wing Gunships
1962–1972

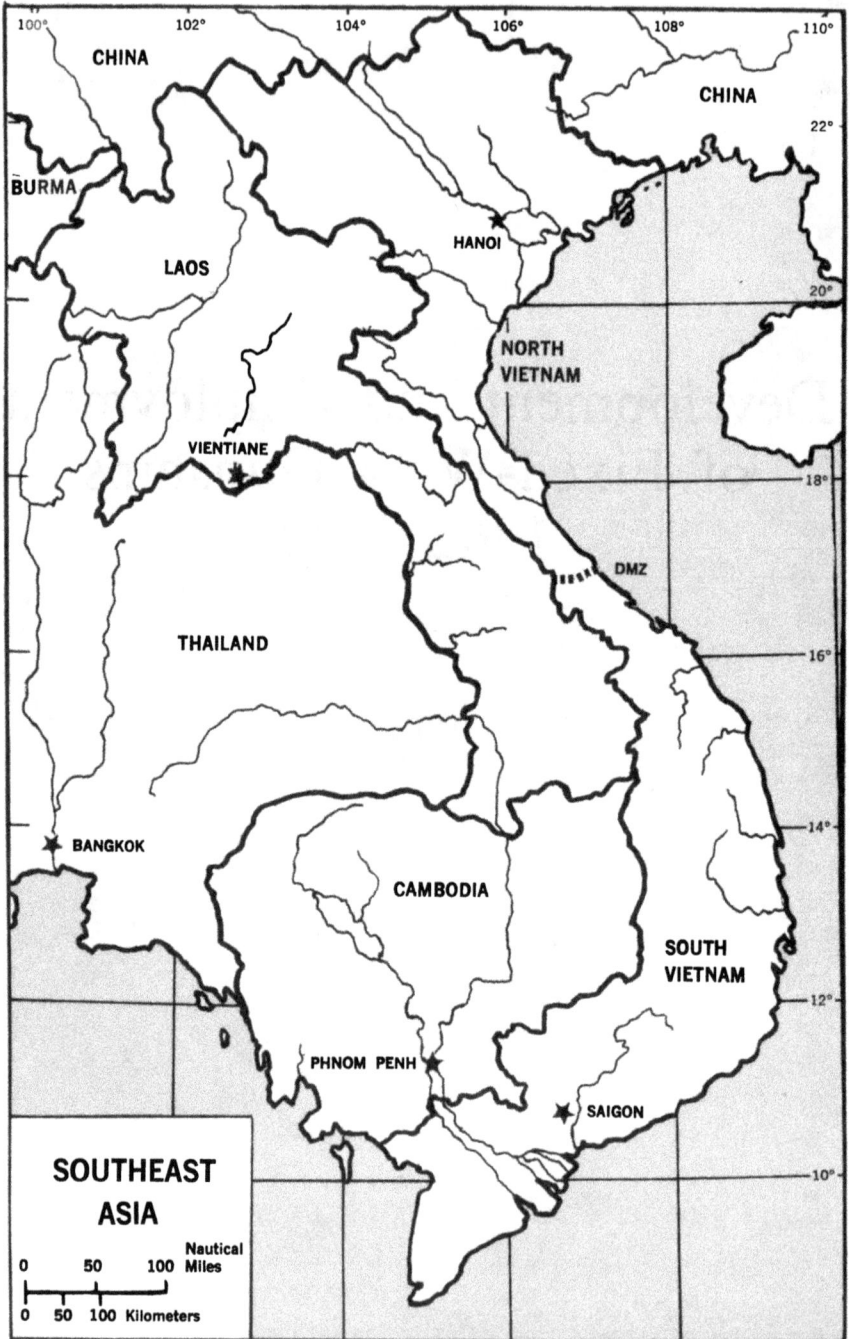

SOUTHEAST
ASIA

Nautical
0   50   100 Miles

0   50   100 Kilometers

I. Origin and Early Development

The genesis of the gunship is relatively obscure, even though the idea was tested as early as 1926–27 and appeared in various proposals during 1939 and 1942. The concept, in its simplest form, combined a long-known aerial maneuver with previously employed weapons. Nonetheless, nearly two decades passed before firing laterally from an aircraft in a pylon turn caught on as a useful combat tactic. Its development stemmed directly from battlefield needs of the war in Southeast Asia. Like many new ideas, this one nearly succumbed in infancy. That the gunship eventually evolved into an effective and impressive weapon system was due mainly to a handful of men who early saw its potential and doggedly urged its adoption.

One of the strong proponents of the gunship idea was Ralph E. Flexman, an Assistant Chief Engineer with Bell Aerosystems Company, Buffalo, N.Y. In early 1962 he became intrigued with the problems of limited war and counterinsurgency operations. Bell had received several contracts to work on hardware associated with limited war, coincident with rising American involvement in the Vietnamese guerrilla war. From this focus of concern came a proposal for a gunship. On December 27, 1962, Flexman submitted to Dr. Gordon A. Eckstrand, Behavioral Sciences Laboratory, Wright-Patterson AFB, Ohio, several ideas that he and his Bell associates were working on. He wrote that:

> . . . with respect to aircraft, we believe that lateral firing, while making a pylon turn, will prove effective in controlling ground fire from many AA [antiaircraft] units. In theory at least, this should more than triple the efficiency of conventional aircraft on reconnaissance and destructive missions.[1]

Of course, the idea of firing a weapon from the side of an aircraft was not new. Swivel-mounted machineguns on World War I aircraft fired laterally at air and ground targets. In 1926–27, 1st Lt. Fred Nelson, a supervisor of one phase of an air training program at Brooks Field, San Antonio, Texas, successfully experimented with a DH–4, equipped with a fixed-mounted, side-firing .30-caliber machinegun. Nelson flew in a pylon turn, sighted through an aiming device on a wing strut, and scored accurate hits on a ground point marked with lime. In 1939 Capt. Carl J. Crane, recalling the Nelson exploits, proposed a side-firing pursuit aircraft in an Air Corps Tactical School thesis. The famed Flying Fortresses and Liberators of World War II relied on waist gunners to help ward off attacks of German and Japanese interceptors. Several C–47 transports of the 443d Troop Carrier Group—in support of British Brigadier Orde Charles Wingate's operations against Japanese-held Burma—carried .50-caliber machineguns that fired from both sides of the aircraft.[2] These historical precedents, however, were largely forgotten.

The pylon turn harked back to the air races and flying training of early aviation. A unique recent use, however, stuck in Flexman's mind. He had read an account of a South American missionary, Nate Saint, who executed the maneuver with a long rope extending from the aircraft to the ground. This had permitted amazingly accurate delivery of mail and other objects to remote villages.[3] In addition, Flexman recalled his experiences as a flight instructor, when he had pivoted his plane over a fencepost and held the post in view at the tip of the wing. He therefore believed it reasonable that with a very small sight one could fire ammunition along the sight path to a target. All this pointed to possible counterinsurgency applications.[4]

Perhaps most influential to the development of Flexman's proposal was his contact with Gilmour Craig MacDonald of Ames, Iowa. In fact, this inventive and imaginative individual should be credited with the first formulation of the gunship concept. On April 27, 1942, as a first lieutenant in the 95th Coast Artillery (AA), he had suggested a way to increase the effectiveness of civilian aircraft on submarine patrol:

> With a view of providing means for continuous fire upon submarines forced to the surface, it is proposed that a fixed machine gun be mounted transversely in the aircraft so that by flying a continually banked circle the pilot may keep the underseacraft under continuous fire if necessary.

MacDonald further pointed out the advantage of the side-firing pylon-turn maneuver, in keeping the submarine crew from bringing its own antiaircraft guns into action. He contrasted this with the normal forward-firing aircraft, that might make one pass at the submarine, then lose precious minutes in positioning for another.[5] Nothing came of the proposal.

MacDonald wrote on May 2, 1945, to the Research and Development Service Sub-Office at Dover Army Air Base, Dover, Del., suggesting a transverse-firing T–59 Superbazooka be installed in a liaison-type aircraft. He visualized that a plane so armed, flying a pylon turn, could pin down enemy soldiers in their foxholes and strike tanks effectively. World War II was waning, however, and the proposal died.[6]

Sixteen years later, with President John F. Kennedy's new administration emphasizing counterinsurgency operations, MacDonald resurrected his old ideas. On September 14, 1961, he (then an Air Force lieutenant colonel) submitted a recommendation, "Transverse Firing of Rockets and Guns," to a Tactical Air Command (TAC) panel on limited war problems. To his way of thinking, lateral firing could offer some real benefits to spotter and liaison aircraft.[7] In a follow-up submission to the panel on September 19, 1961, he declared: "By flying a banked circle, the airplane can keep the gun pointed continuously at a target, and by flying along with one wing low, limited longitudinal strafing can be done without worrying about pullout." His proposed project would "investigate launch, fire control, and ballistic problems," cost an estimated $100,000, last about six months, and take one hundred hours of test time on a liaison-type aircraft using the Eglin AFB, Fla., land and water ranges.[8] But again the MacDonald proposal failed to arouse a response.

During a reserve active duty tour in late 1961 at Eglin AFB, Ralph Flexman first met Gilmour MacDonald. From the latter he learned of MacDonald's proposal to the TAC Limited War Committee and of the flying missionary's feats.[9] Back at Bell Aerosystems, Flexman mulled over the pylon-turn/lateral-firing concept and introduced it at a Bell brainstorming session in late 1962.[10] This led to his letter to Dr. Eckstrand.

Flexman had concluded by April 16, 1963, that lateral firing from a pylon turn was definitely feasible. He reported to his Air Force professional colleagues the concept's advantages in limited war operations. Aircraft often lost guerrilla-war targets between first sighting and the time of the second pass. In contrast, an aircraft rolling immediately into a pylon turn could sweep a target with instant effective fire from a fixed aiming point. Flexman further foresaw that lateral fire from a low-flying, slow-speed aircraft could provide wider coverage, a high angle of fire, and a capability for pinning down enemy troops.

Nevertheless, the concept contained three major questionable areas: ballistics of the projectiles as they were fired and their dispersion, ability of the pilot to aim his lateral weapon and hold the target, and the reaction time necessary to change from straight-and-level flight to an on-pylon turn. Flexman suggested to Capt. John C. Simons that a test program examine these points and at the same time demonstrate the validity of the concept.[11]

Captain Simons had known Ralph Flexman for several years as a result of their mutual interests in aeronautically related human factors research. Flexman had sent him a copy of the 1962 letter containing the idea of a pylon-turning side-firing gunship. Additionally, Simons was familiar with the South American missionary's long-rope delivery techniques while flying a pylon turn.[12] Simons carefully weighed the informal proposal for testing, discussed it with Flexman by phone, and became an advocate.[13] He strongly supported the concept, viewing it as opening up a profitable new research area, and would "bet anyone a case of beer it will be much larger than 'lateral firing' as its only use."[14]

On April 26, 1963, Captain Simons forwarded Flexman's tentative test proposal to several offices of the Aerospace Medical Research Laboratory (AMRL) and Wright-Patterson AFB offices interested in limited war and counterinsurgency development.[15] Replies to this referral for comment and support, however, did not reflect Captain Simons' complete confidence in the concept. A May 8, 1963, response, for instance, named general areas needing investigation (reminiscent of Flexman's concerns): "What is the dispersion due to sighting wander? Under what conditions can a pilot sight a 'pop up' target and convert to an 'on pylon' attack against the target?"

3

Again, would the lateral gun firing be an "operationally useful technique" and would a gunner-operated waist gun have advantages over a pilot-aimed one? There was the suggestion some of the questions might be answered by using cameras rather than actual gunfire and by consulting on ballistic matters with Eglin AFB units.[16]

Meantime, one of Captain Simons' supervisors referred the concept to two different Aeronautical Systems Division (ASD) review boards of weapon and ballistics experts. Both boards evaluated the idea, raised serious doubts about the ballistics associated with side-fired weapons, then rejected the concept as technically unsound. This was in marked contrast to Flexman's position when he wrote Simons on April 16, 1963, commenting on questions involving the ballistics of laterally-fired weapons. He cited the published work of Dr. W. H. T. Loh, Associate Chief Engineer of Bell Aerosystems. Dr. Loh had developed equations that could be computer-programmed to define the trajectory of weapons fired from aircraft in an on-pylon turn. Flexman estimated that for about $200,000 a computer study would verify the concept's feasibility, provided the weapons used were of high muzzle velocity such as .30-caliber or above.[17]

Captain Simons firmly believed only an actual firing test would clear away all concern with ballistic problems. So in May 1963, he proposed to sidestep local flight-support requirements and request the United States Army Laboratory, Ft. Rucker, Ala., to determine the dispersal patterns of the side-firing guns. This effort collapsed, however, when supervisors told him he "should not get involved with the weapons aspect."[18] Even though success of the concept might hinge on live-firing test results, they considered dabbling in weapon trajectories as stretching a research psychologist's duties a bit too far.

Nevertheless, Captain Simons persisted in his search for support. An important factor was the encouragement of his immediate supervisor, Dr. Julian Christensen, who did not want to see the idea die without a test.[19] On May 20, 1963, Simons submitted to the Deputy for Engineering, ASD, a "Request for Support of Limited War Study." It proposed a nine-month study: six months to check dispersal patterns by sightings from an unarmed aircraft in an on-pylon maneuver; two months for testing a weapon mounted in a T–28 aircraft; and one month of operational analysis to weigh such factors as vulnerability, time-over-target, and ultimate design. Some of the groundwork for this request grew out of Simons' discussions with two interested pilots of the ASD office, Capts. J. D. Boren and J. A Birt. Already the proposed air-to-ground firing study bore the tentative nickname, "Project Tailchaser."[20]

Meanwhile, Captain Simons diligently pursued test arrangements. In June he prepared a flight-test plan for his branch to establish skill and display requirements and to develop sighting techniques. Rejection of the concept by the ASD review boards had seemingly blocked support from the flight-test section. Simons therefore sought permission to fly some of the sighting tests in conjunction with other projects. One of his superiors gave him under-the-table approval for a few test flights.[21]

Later that same month, Simons flew a T–28 at Wright-Patterson AFB, accompanied by a test pilot Capt. Harley Johnson. He executed the pylon turn and visually tracked a target from the left cockpit window. A grease-penciled horizontal line on the glass served as a rudimentary sight. Target-tracking continued for ten minutes under varying lateral distance, airspeed (110–220 knots), altitude (500–3,000 feet), and pitch angle. On a second T–28 flight that took off after dusk, Simons found that by turning up the cockpit lights he could track a light on the ground with is makeshift sight.[22]

Both these flights added convincing evidence that an aircraft could track line, point, and area targets while in a pylon turn. A prime case in point was Captain Simons' holding a truck in the sight as the vehicle drove from a route parallel to the aircraft to one at right angles—a portent of the tracking that was to make the gunship justly famous. Simons observed that on-pylon tracking in low-speed aircraft was free of the "yaw rigidity and changing control forces" that often degrade the performance of high-speed planes. He marveled at the pylon turn's simplicity and the ease with which a target could be acquired and held in the sight.[23]

Near the end of June, Simons and Captain Boren flew a C–131 for three hours to check lateral-sighting techniques in a cargo aircraft. Flying low over southern Ohio, the pilot banked the aircraft about ten degrees and with rudder control followed a road, keeping it in view with the single horizontal line on the left-side cockpit window. Tracking this continuous target proved easy both from the standpoint of flying and sighting. Next the pilot singled out silos, barns, moving horses, and even fighting geese as point targets. The aircraft rolled into a pylon turn around the object selected. Finally, he changed the horizontal line on the window to a vertical one. This did not affect case of tracking but precise sighting along a line was lost. From this flight Simons concluded that cargo aircraft could acquire and keep targets in the sight during a pylon turn, and saturate them with assumed ballistic dispersion patterns.[24]

The first T–28 test flight had convinced Captain Simons that the concept's ballistic problems could be overcome. A ballistic expert agreed they might be ironed out provided there was a fixed-mounted gun.[25] Advocating ever more strongly the air-to-ground study. Simons started to improve the gunship apparatus. Working from Simons' suggestions, SSgt. Estell P. Bunch, also of the medical research laboratory, prepared the plans and supervised the fabrication of a holder into which gunsight reticles could be inserted.[26] Reticle designs included a horizontal line, a vertical line, concentric circles, a cross, and combinations of these.[27]

Plans to verify sight and gun alignments followed. In June 1963 one of the C–131Bs at Wright-Patterson was fitted with a new sight, mounted at the pilot's left cockpit window. The sight's optical axis was perpendicular to the aircraft's flight path. Next, three synchronized cameras were installed. One 16-mm motion-picture camera was positioned to record the sight

Camera Installation for Lateral Sighting

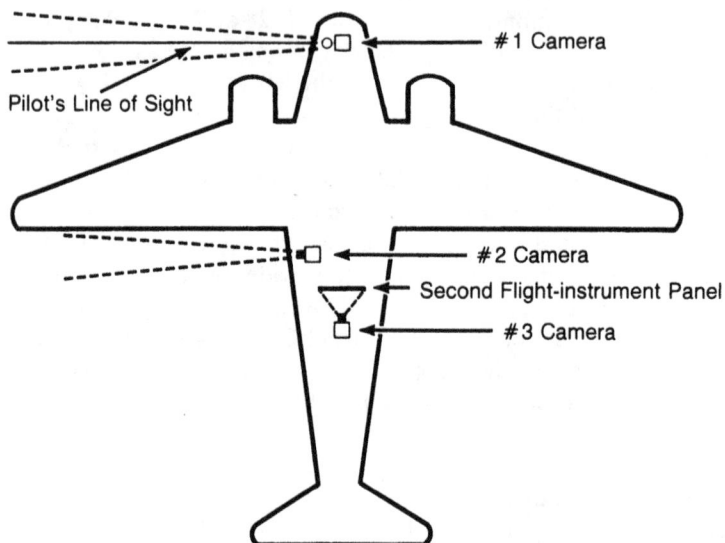

alignment. Another, in the cargo compartment back of the wing, aimed through a window where a gun might be positioned. A third camera was placed to photograph the special flight instrument panel in the cargo compartment. The panel showed altitude, airspeed, turn and bank, and attitude factors. From this test equipment Simons hoped to obtain enough data to plot pilot error involving altitude, line-of-sight distance, wind, indicated airspeed, and to secure realistic inputs for computing the firing geometry.[28] Later, a second version of a camera installation was prepared including one camera to record the pilot's sight alignment and three cameras to represent guns. This concept was presented to the Aeronautical Systems Division flight test organization but was delayed indefinitely because of lack of priority.

In July 1963 Captain Simons gave his supervisor a progress report on test flights and preparation of test equipment. He highlighted his success in tracking various targets and urged that the next step be turnover of the C–131 to ASD cargo flight-test personnel. Suggested test equipment was installed in this aircraft. Flexman believed two flights should supply ample data to analyze the essential firing functions before actual firing tests. Looking to the future, he foresaw ASD research into minimum and maximum tumbling characteristics of ammunition fired from the waist gun, the prospect of using the on-pylon technique for pickup and delivery, and possible use of a laser beam to designate targets, or side-looking infrared equipment to acquire night targets during the pylon turn.[29] That these three areas had significant development later establishes Simons as farsighted indeed.

As a fallout from the Simons proposal of May 20, 1963, a meeting was held on July 1. Attending were Captain Simons, Lt. Col. James L.

Hight and Captains Birt and Boren, the latter three from ASD's Directorate of Crew Subsystems Engineering. On July 3 this group officially supported testing the concept.[30] By August Captain Simons had the part-time services of Captains Birt and Boren to help set up sighting-definition flights. On October 28 a new flight-test plan changed Project Tailchaser from a lateral-firing to a lateral-sighting project because of resistance to the firing phase. The plan prescribed use of a C-131 and later a T-28 in flights from Wright-Patterson AFB, possibly Ft. Rucker, Ala., and Eglin AFB. Captain Boren became project manager, with Captains Birt and Simons and Sergeant Bunch designated engineers. Capt. Edwin J. Hatzenbuehler was named project pilot.[31]

The plan projected three hundred testing hours spread over one year. It allotted two weeks for installing test apparatus, followed by twenty-five flying hours in a C-131 to select targets, check out equipment, and develop pilot techniques. A second phase specified that flight-test pilots validate experimental designs and techniques. The final phase stipulated that a C-131 evaluate designs by tactical pilot subjects. After analysis of these C-131 flights, a T-28 would fly a pattern similar to the initial flight tests but keep adaptation to a particular counterinsurgency aircraft in mind. Flight tests were expected to include simulated firing passes at point, line, or area targets, and at varying altitudes and airspeeds. All tests were to be recorded on film.[32] At last it appeared a firm test plan was ready.

Heartened by the latest flight-test plan, Captain Simons reported to Ralph Flexman on November 13 that all test equipment had been installed in the C-131B aircraft and checked out. The first flight was set for November 15 but Simons cautioned that problems persisted—chief among them a need for funds to sustain a complete flight-test program.[33]

Crablike progress ensued and the C-131B camera test equipment stood idle. The part-time officers, Captains Birt and Boren, were recalled by their units for higher-priority duties. Project Tailchaser was virtually at the bottom of the list of priorities and was likely to stay there, in view of the increased attention given Vietnam-related counterinsurgency developments. Test flight were hard to arrange. In seven months the C-131B made just two flights and these were preliminary procedure checkouts.[34] Not a single actual or camera-verified firing test had taken place. People remained skeptical of the whole concept. Frustrations mounted with the seemingly endless delays.

With undimmed enthusiasm, Captain Simons, Sergeant Bunch, and other pioneers of the concept's early testing, remained convinced of Tailchaser's potential. On February 10, 1964, they were cheered by news from Captains Boren and Birt of a flight set for the near future, "hopefully in February." Technicians reinstalled the cameras (they had been removed from the C-131B) and boresighted them like guns.* Test pilots scanned aerial photos of Ohio's Clinton County seeking test targets. But over this

---

*A boresight line is an optical reference line used in harmonizing guns, rockets, or other weapon launchers.

7

activity loomed the priorities problem, a roadblock to the tests. At one point ASD returned the sighting-project files to the medical research laboratory, commenting the project deserved total attention of several people whom it could not provide and admitting "limited surveillance and informal management of the project" had fostered delays.[35] Again the planned flights failed to take place.

Finally a few flights were made in the summer of 1964. By this time, however, the press of his other duties forced Captain Simons to give up his gunship responsibilities. He picked 1st Lt. Edwin Sasaki, a fellow medical laboratory researcher interested in the project, to act in his stead as human performance engineer on the lateral-firing team.[36] In addition, the project pilot, Captain Hatzenbuehler, was replaced by Maj. Richard M. Gough and he in turn by Capt. Ronald W. Terry. Despite these changes, Simons kept up his interest in Project Tailchaser's development, reiterating that the concept's acceptance hinged on live-firing tests.[37]

The appearance of Captain Terry as a project pilot proved a propitious development. His personality projected a subtle blending of tact and tenacity, self-confidence and openness, intelligence and common sense, and, most significant for the progress of the gunship, an uncommonly convincing salesmanship. Also, his past mental conditioning made him keenly receptive to the gunship's possibilities. In the spring of 1963 he had served on an Air Force Systems Command (AFSC) team in South Vietnam. Its job was to assess problems in the field and suggest hardware developments to deal with them, the overall goal being a five-year development program to satisfy Southeast Asia requirements. The team probed for almost six weeks, visiting bases and talking with the men who worked alongside of and advised the South Vietnamese.[38] Combined with this firsthand knowledge was Terry's fighter pilot experience. He knew how hard it was to place ordnance on a target in bad weather, at night, and in tight tactical situations.[39]

Captain Terry first came across Project Tailchaser while perusing the files in Flight Test Operations at ASD. Obviously, the project had been dormant for some time. Yet as he read, Terry was intrigued by the potential of the idea for development and use in Vietnam. Disregarding the ballistic skeptics who branded the concept unworkable, he obtained permission to work on Tailchaser. Immersed in the project, Terry's interest heightened and he gained approval at several points to evaluate the idea further. Finally, he drafted a scenario for a tactical operation employing a side-firing weapon system, mainly in defense of hamlets and forts. He viewed this system as performing a policeman-on-the-corner or prowl-car role, prepared for anything and able to respond anywhere at most anytime. ASD's Limited War Office warmly welcomed the scenario and promised to sponsor it.[40] This achievement, together with Terry's first C–131 flight where he practiced lateral-firing techniques, fueled his enthusiasm.[41] He became primarily responsible for restoring momentum to the gunship idea.

In August 1964 the ASD Limited War Office and Flight Test Operations, together with the Aerospace Medical Research Laboratory, took a significant step in the testing of the lateral-sighting study. An amendment to the flight-test plan specified that one or two small-caliber guns, remotely fired by the pilot, be installed in the cargo doorway of a C–131 "to determine the feasibility of firing guns with the lateral sighting system." Eglin AFB would help install the guns and conduct the ground tests, firing blanks to determine if the mounts could stand the recoil. The amendment also prescribed preflight boresighting and safety precautions.[42] Groundwork had been laid for the long-awaited firing test.

The C–131 was flown to Eglin to become the testbed for the firing. A relatively new weapon was selected and installed on the left side of the aircraft's cargo compartment. The General Electric SUU–11A, 7.62-mm gun pod (Gatling gun) could fire 6,000 rounds-per-minute.[43] Sergeant Bunch, who worked on fabricating the sight and other test equipment, played a key part in mounting the Gatling gun.[44]

The first live-firing tests occurred in late summer. The pilot flew the C–131 with line-of-sight distance to the target varying from 1,750 to 9,000 feet. Altitudes ranged from 500 to 3,000 feet and airspeed from 115 to 250 knots. On Eglin's water range a one-second firing burst scored twenty-five hits on a minimum ten-foot-square raft and seventy-five hits on a maximum fifty-foot-square one.[45] A testing phase on the land range saw twenty-five manikins scattered in different positions over three-quarters of an acre. A three-second firing run on this area target hit nineteen manikins, ten of them considered "killed."[46] The test results exceeded expectations.[47] As Captain Simons had long predicted, they adequately confirmed the concept's feasibility and convinced many of the skeptics that this was indeed a worthwhile weapon system. At this point ASD assumed management of the program.

The C–131 test results aroused the interest of 1st Combat Application Group personnel at Eglin AFB. They asked Captain Terry, Sergeant Bunch, and other Tailchaser crewmembers if a gun kit in side-firing mode could be built into other aircraft. Specifically, they wanted to modify a C–47 or C–123, since Air Force Special Forces units in South Vietnam were using these aircraft.[48] Captain Terry jumped at this opportunity, and in short order three of the Gatling guns (called miniguns) were installed in a C–47 cargo compartment.[49] The C–47 side-firing tests in September 1964 repeated the successes of the C–131 tests.

The Air Force carefully weighed the combat advantages and disadvantages of this C–47 with laterally-firing guns. The aircraft was available as were the crews to fly it. The plane could carry a large volume of ammunition and flares and could be used for cargo, troop, and reconnaissance missions. It possessed two-engine safety, long alert capability, lengthy time-over-target, and the capability to loiter for flaredropping. In flight the crew could select ordnance; choose varied

Top left: Lt. Col. Ronald W. Terry.

Top right: Lt. Col. John C. Simons.

Bottom: SUU–11A Gatling (miniguns).

weapon dispersion patterns; arm, disarm, maintain, and repair weapons; and carry out immediate bomb damage assessment (BDA).* Some of these things any slow-mover could do, others only could be done in large cabin aircraft.[50] Admittedly one major disadvantage did exist—the C–47's vulnerability to ground fire and aerial intercept. Critics swiftly seized upon this weakness and argued that it was formidable enough to cancel out all the aircraft's advantages and nullify its usefulness.

Captain Terry was articulate in pointing up the advantages of the side-armed C–47 in a Vietnam-like setting. He considered the Gooney Bird a Johnny-on-the-spot that could cover a hamlet with continuous fire, holding off the enemy until arrival of additional air or ground support. Terry knew his fighter operations and pictured the serious problem of precise ordnance delivery in tight situations involving rugged terrain, bad weather, night flying, hard-to-detect targets, and exact location of friendly forces. The fighter pilot relied mainly on a forward air controller (FAC) for target acquisition and location of friendly forces. Once on his own, the pilot faced a sea of green jungle that often thwarted his efforts to acquire or reacquire targets.[51]

On the other hand, the C–47 could fly over the terrain and spot friendly forces and the probable location of the enemy. Then, after acquiring and locking on a target in a pylon turn it could deliver continuous fire with the near-surgical precision of artillery. If the first bursts missed the target, instructions quickly furnished by an observer on the ground or in the aircraft put the fire on the mark. Moreover, the accuracy of the side-firing miniguns allowed wider discretion in attacking within basically friendly territory. In contrast, use of napalm, bombs, and rockets could, and did break up attacks on hamlets but might require an aid program later to rebuild these same villages.[52] As to the C–47's vulnerability, Captain Terry felt the aircraft could be effective flying above the range of small-arms fire expected in South Vietnam. Certainly it should be less vulnerable than the helicopters already being used extensively as gunships. Arguments on the gunship went on in a similar vein at various Air Force command levels.

Captain Terry kept talking to different people about the potential of the modified C–47 and briefings moved steadily up the command chain. These efforts culminated with a presentation on November 2, 1964, by Captain Terry and Lieutenant Sasaki to Gen. Curtis E. LeMay, Air Force Chief of Staff, and other Air Staff members. General LeMay reacted favorably and directed that a team go to Vietnam, modify a C–47 and test it in combat.†

---

*This term encompasses the determination of the effect of all air attacks on targets (e.g., bombs, rockets, or strafe); also referred to as "*battle* damage assessment."

† Later General LeMay spoke of gunships with less favor: "It's not a very good platform and you can't carry the load. You don't have the range, staying capacity, or anything else. They're too vulnerable both on the ground and in the air." Despite these sentiments the General was the one who first committed the Air Force to the aircraft. [Intvw Dr. Thomas G. Belden, Chief Historian, Ofc AF Hist. with Gen. Curtis E. LeMay, March 29, 1972.]

Six miniguns were also to be installed in aircraft there. Sergeant Bunch's projected assignment to Turkey was deferred while he prepared another gunsight for the test.[53] The administrative machine moved to high gear to support the overseas combat test.

At this time American concern over Vietnam mounted, as South Vietnamese ability to repel Viet Cong (VC) and North Vietnamese attacks appeared to be deteriorating rapidly. By the spring of 1964 the initiative had passed to the communists; 200 of 2,500 villages lay in enemy hands, and "incidents" surged to 1,800 per month. South Vietnamese forces faced serious recruiting problems. Troop morale was low, losses of weapons and desertions were high.

Increased Viet Cong activity in the Mekong River Delta area climaxed with a major defeat of the South Vietnamese in July 1964. In August the Tonkin Gulf incident and attacks on U.S. facilities deepened American concern and involvement. On the night of October 31/November 1 the Viet Cong attacked Bien Hoa AB, inflicted serious damage, and cast serious doubt on airbase security. Seven U.S. and Vietnamese Air Force (VNAF) aircraft were destroyed, sixteen U.S. and two VNAF aircraft damaged. In addition, the political turmoil in Saigon grew.[54] These events generated a need for greater U.S. aid and air power if the country was to be saved. In beefing up Vietnam units, the Air Force eagerly sought new ways to bolster counterinsurgency operations.[55]

The Air Staff prepared the way for the C–47 combat tests by telling the Commander in Chief, Pacific Air Forces (CINCPACAF) of the side-firing aircraft's advantages. The plane could loiter around targets, change firing patterns, correct malfunctions in flight, and deliver great quantities of ordnance accurately on the target. While best fitted for night and counter-insurgency operations, its great slant range* might enable it to strike targets on steep mountain slopes or in other previously inaccessible spots.[56]

CINCPACAF notified both the Commander in Chief, Pacific Command (CINCPAC) and the Commander, United States Military Assistance Command, Vietnam (COMUSMACV). The latter requested the program be stepped up, estimating that effective test and evaluation should take from sixty to ninety days.[57] On November 12, 1964, Lt. Gen. James Ferguson, Air Force Deputy Chief of Staff for Research and Development, wrote to Maj. Gen. Joseph H. Moore, Jr., 2d Air Division commander in Vietnam. He asked General Moore to personally evaluate the system, chiefly from the standpoint of its value on night missions. He added that tests at Eglin had shown it "highly effective against troops in wooded terrain," and stressed that the upcoming C–47 test and 7.62-mm minigun evaluation reflected the swing of research and development (R&D) application to counterinsurgency requirements.[58]

The testing decision posed a dilemma to the Air Staff for it had begun to oppose unrestricted evaluation of equipment in South Vietnam. The

---

*Slant range: the line-of-sight distance between two points not at the same elevation.

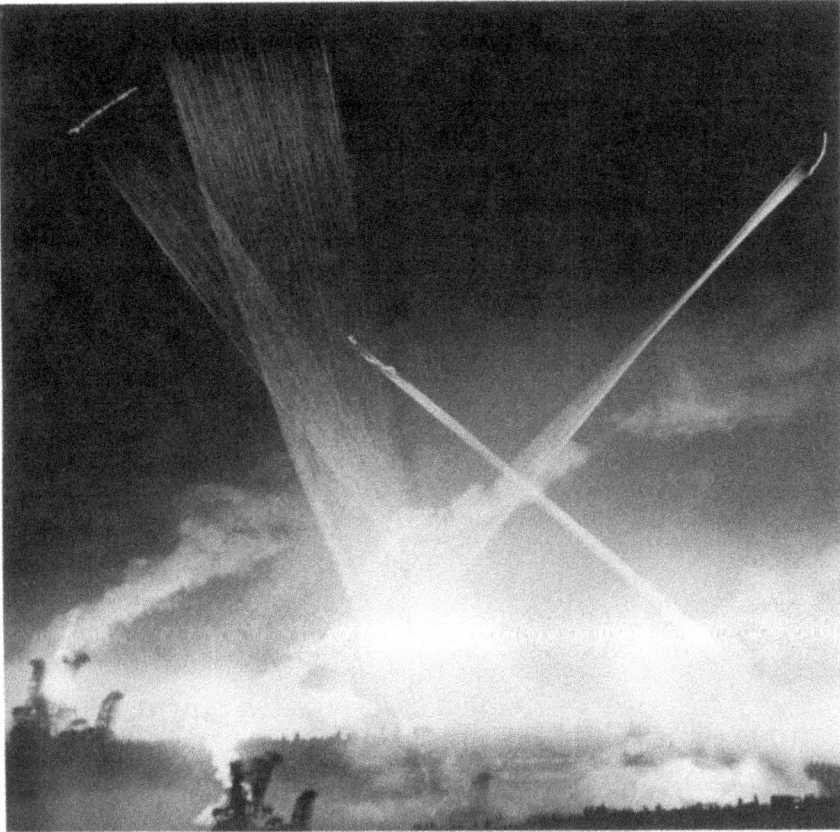

Streams of tracer fire pour on an illuminated target from a circling C-47.

opposition sprang mainly from a feeling that the U.S. Army had used such tests to support its case on service roles and missions. Nevertheless, the gunship needed some kind of combat trial to prove its validity. The Air Staff therefore steered a middle course by considering the gunship a "unique" R&D item to be closely controlled as to roles and missions controversies.[59] It told the Military Assistance Command, Vietnam (MACV) that interest in the gunship test was primarily on "operational use of this equipment in RVN [Republic of Vietnam] rather than a test of the equipment."[60] Walking this fine line between operational and hardware evaluation would not be easy.

Meanwhile, Gen. Walter C. Sweeney, Jr., head of the Tactical Air Command, doubted that the gunship could survive the gunfire expected in Vietnam and fulfill its mission. He flatly said, "This concept will place a highly vulnerable aircraft in a battlefield environment in which I believe the results will not compensate for the losses of Air Force personnel and aircraft." He further saw a successful gunship test weakening the Air Force in its battle with the Army over use of helicopters in offensive fire-support

Basic Gunship Principle

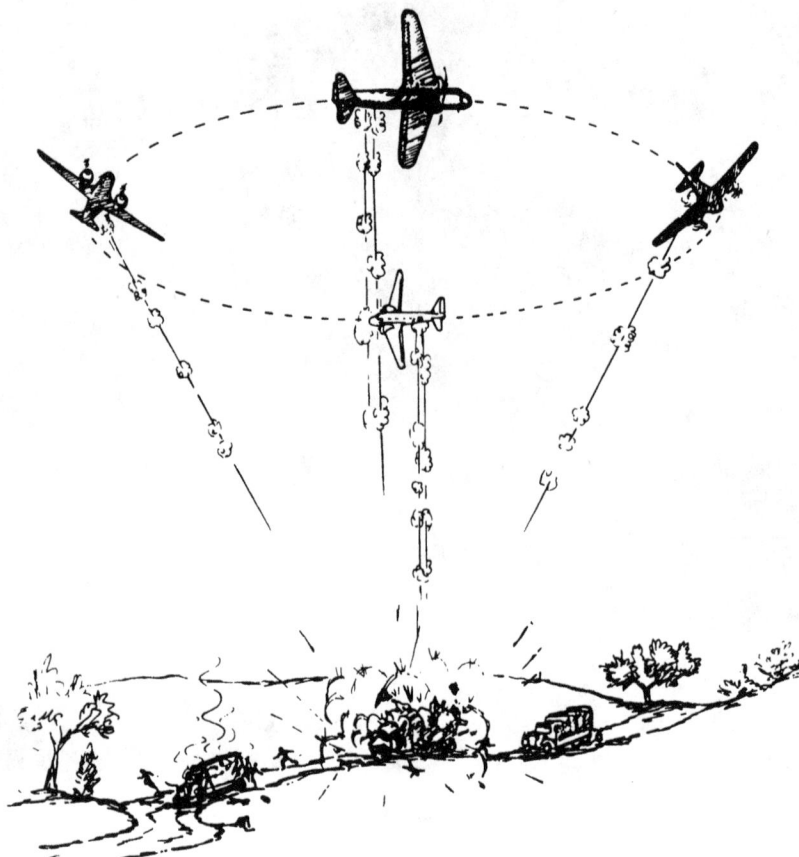

missions. Conceivably, it might encourage the Army to use transports in a ground-support role. What's more, if the gunship was made a permanent weapon system, its use might be "disastrous in some future conflict." [He seemingly had in mind a more conventional war such as a North Atlantic Treaty Organization (NATO)-Soviet conflict in Europe.] General Sweeney could only conclude " . . . we should continue to vigorously oppose the offensive . . . employment of all such highly vulnerable aircraft."[61] His criticism presaged an enduring opposition among many people in the Tactical Air Command. Significantly, TAC was the command charged with employing the gunship!

The Air Force Chief of Staff rejected the TAC commander's position on gunships. Gen. John P. McConnell, Vice Chief of Staff, explained the Air Force position to General Sweeney. He pointed out that the side-firing C–47 was to be evaluated for specific counterinsurgency missions, and gave

**Procedure To Decrease
Lateral Distance to
Target**

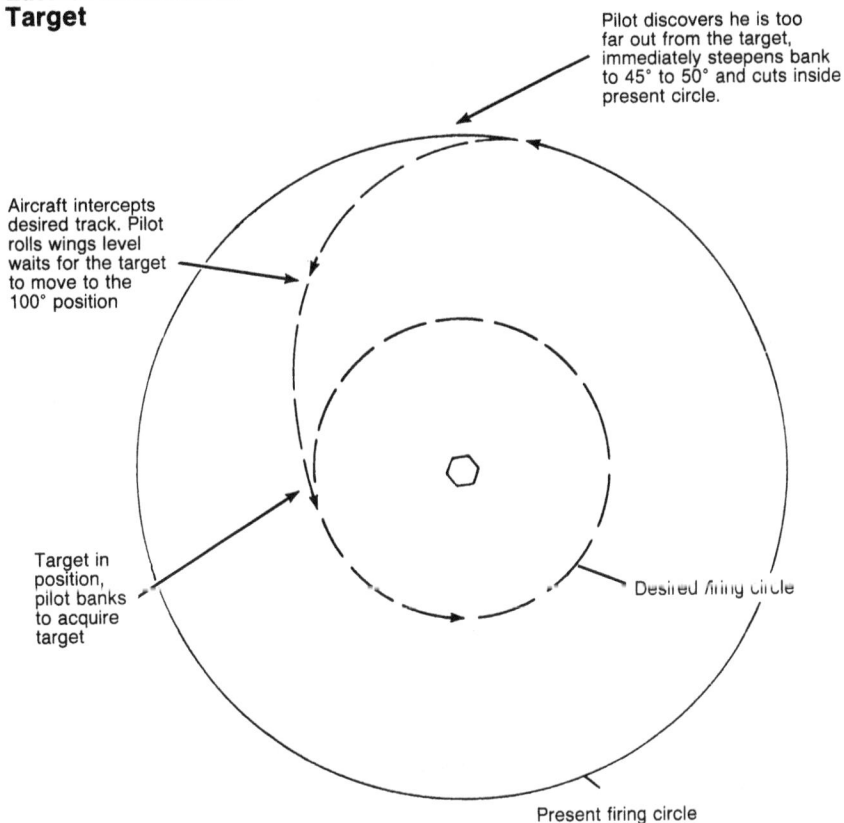

Pilot discovers he is too
far out from the target,
immediately steepens bank
to 45° to 50° and cuts inside
present circle.

Aircraft intercepts
desired track. Pilot
rolls wings level
waits for the target
to move to the
100° position

Target in
position,
pilot banks
to acquire
target

Desired firing circle

Present firing circle

every appearance of being well suited for the Southeast Asian environment. He accented the gunship's anticipated role of defending hamlets and outposts under night attack. Thus he indirectly fingered an alarming weakness in tactical air's night operation capabilities and strike aircraft responsiveness. There were too few strike aircraft for airborne alert. Furthermore, those on ground alert could not react quickly enough to prevent the enemy from overrunning outposts and villages. At least the armed C–47 might be able to hold off the enemy until strike aircraft arrived. General McConnell admitted the survivability problem of transport aircraft but deemed it most desirable to test the concept in counterinsurgency situations.[62]

The test team headed by Captain Terry arrived in South Vietnam on December 2, 1964. Gun kits for modifying two C–47s, gunsights, and ammunition arrived on December 9.[63] Bien Hoa Air Base, near Saigon, became the staging base since it was the center of C–47 operations. As personnel and equipment arrived, the whole operation fell under the

Procedure To Increase Lateral Distance to Target

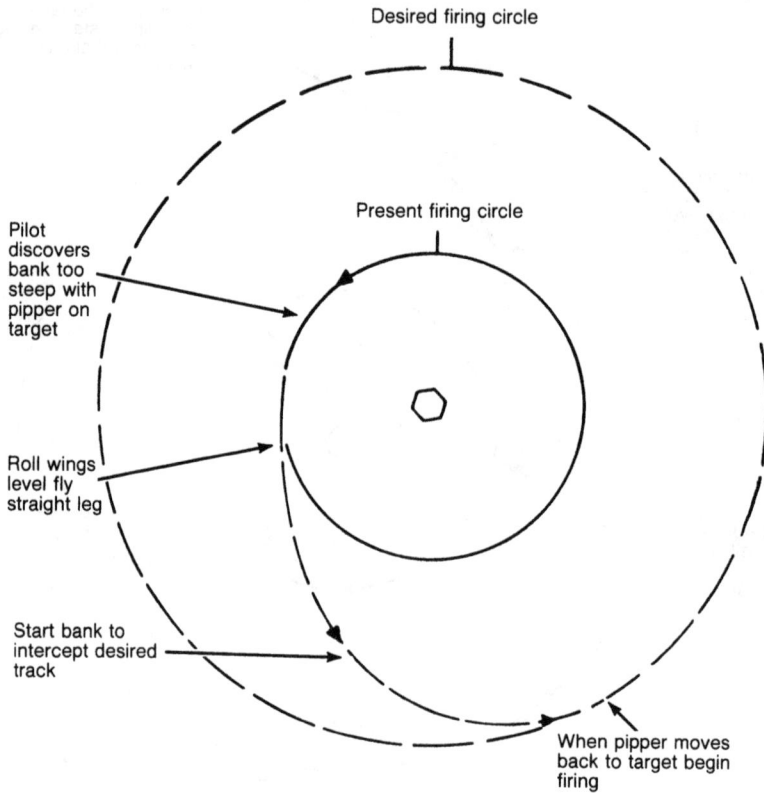

Desired firing circle

Present firing circle

Pilot discovers bank too steep with pipper on target

Roll wings level fly straight leg

Start bank to intercept desired track

When pipper moves back to target begin firing

supervision of the Joint Research and Test Activity (JRATA).*[64] In quick order the team installed the gunsight (a converted 16-mm camera reflex viewfinder with cross-hair reticle),[65] guns, and other ancillary equipment in C–47s made available.[66] The team had modified the first aircraft by December 11, the second by December 15, but did not modify the third because two guns had failed during early operation of the first aircraft.[67] Simple, reliable, manually-operated flare dispensers for night tests were installed in the cargo-compartment doors. These modified aircraft were first known officially as FC–47s due to their tactical role and for want of a better designation.[68]

Captain Terry set about introducing the gunship concept to the C–47 crews assigned to the project from the 1st Air Commando Squadron

---

*In February 1964 the Joint Chiefs of Staff ordered all Vietnam research and test agencies combined in one command. COMUSMACV therefore established JRATA on April 23, 1964, consisting of representatives from the U.S. Army, the Air Force, and Office of the Secretary of Defense/Advanced Research Project Agency. The Commander, JRATA, advised COMUSMACV on research development, testing, and evaluation.

(ACSq).[69] He especially stressed boresighting the miniguns because firing was anticipated near friendly troops. Rough boresighting was done by depressing the guns about 10 degrees and aiming at a target some 2,500 feet away. For inflight boresighting the pilot flew a 20-degree bank at 2,000 feet above mean sea level around a flare dropped in the sea. After making an approximate setting in the gunsight he flew parallel to the direction of the flare's smoke. While in the twenty-degree bank he kept the gunsight pipper on the head of the smoke and fired a three-second burst from one gun—watching with the other observers as the rounds kicked up the water. Next he executed upwind and downwind passes to negate wind effect, then adjusted the gunsight for windage.[70]

The pilot also made checks for proper elevation, using the setting determined for one gun to adjust the other guns. This setting was valid for only a single given slant range. An altitude to angle-of-bank relationship had to be established for computing settings of other slant ranges. As a rule of thumb, compensation for range was set at about ten mils for each 500 feet of altitude. In sum, these boresighting tests produced mil settings accurate enough for tactical use. Above 2,500 feet, however, observers could scarcely see the rounds hit the water unless weather and sea conditions were excellent. The basic mil setting for each aircraft was posted near the gunsight but most pilots had no trouble remembering it under battle stress. Finally, to keep things simple and insure firing accuracy, it was decided to fly firing passes at a constant altitude.[71]

Additionally, Captain Terry used these over-water flights to teach the C-47 pilots how to acquire a target (the Mk-6 flare), roll in on it and fire. Approaching the target area the pilot would position the FC-47 to keep the target off the left wing, banking the instant it passed under the left-engine nacelle. This dropped the left wing and permitted the gunsight pipper to pick up the target. There followed just a few seconds of tracking before the pilot fired a three- to five-second burst while in the pylon turn. Most firing passes were made at 3,000 feet, a slant range of 5,000 feet, and an airspeed of about 120 knots. During the tracking and firing pass, the copilot warned the pilot if he was exceeding any of these established limits. If so, the pass would be discontinued at once. The training progressed smoothly. After a few flights, the C-47 pilots mastered the proper angle of bank and other maneuvers involved in attacking a target with a side-armed aircraft.[72]

The FC-47 carried a crew of seven Air Force personnel plus one Vietnamese observer. The pilot (aircraft commander) fired the guns while controlling the aircraft as the copilot monitored instruments and coordinated crew activities. A flight mechanic kept an eye on the various aircraft systems. The navigator checked the aircraft's position, and in the target area worked with the Vietnamese observer to verify target information and establish liaison with ground forces. Two gunners were assigned to load and troubleshoot inflight operations of the miniguns. A loadmaster armed and dropped flares from the rear cargo door.[73]

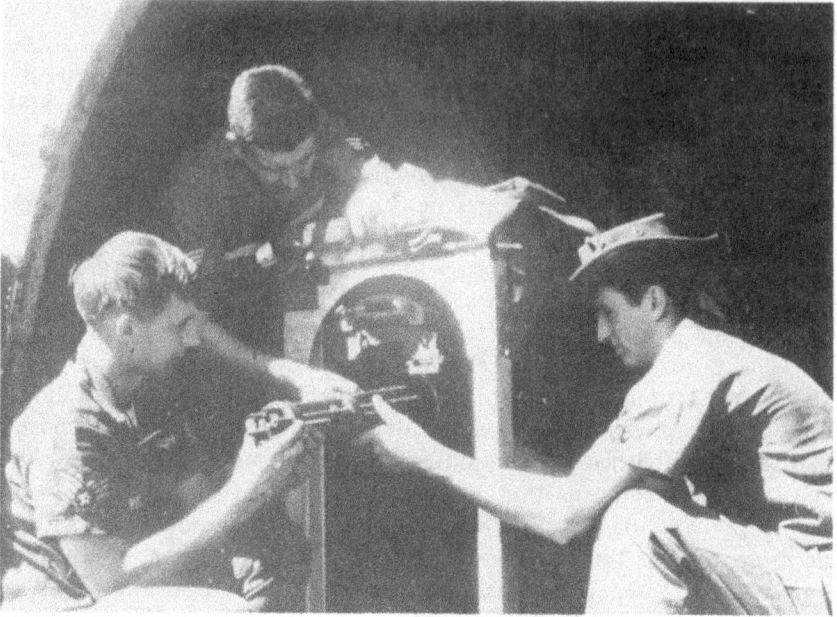

P. 18 (top): Installing minigun in AC-47; bottom: Members of one of the first AC-47 teams.

P. 19 (top left): A 7.62 minigun in the doorway of an AC-47; top right: AC-47 gunsight mounted at the left side of cockpit; bottom: Loading ammunition into a Spooky.

Additional observers frequently accompanied this crew during the test and evaluation period.

The FC-47 flew the first of several day combat missions on December 15, 1964.[74] On this sortie Captain Terry and the crew worked with a forward air controller, seeking targets of opportunity and trying to become familiar with counterinsurgency operations and theater rules of engagements.[75] The gunship fired accurately on enemy sampans, buildings, trails, and suspected jungle staging areas. On the afternoon of December 21, an FAC called on the FC-47 to attack a large structure into which fourteen Viet Cong had reportedly run. Shortly after the strike, friendly forces found the building "looking like a sieve" and twenty-one bodies scattered about.[76]

The FC-47's first night mission on December 23/24 went equally well. While on airborne alert, the gunship was directed toward Thanh Yend (west of Can Tho in the Mekong River Delta area), where the Viet Cong had the outpost under heavy attack. The FC-47 dropped seventeen flares and expended 4,500 rounds of 7.62 ammunition. The outpost defenders reported the Viet Cong broke off their assault. Next the aircraft was diverted to aid Trung Hung, an outpost twenty miles farther west. A Vietnamese Air Force C-47 had already dropped seventy flares over the area but the Viet Cong continued their onslaught. The gunship used eight flares and 4,500 rounds of ammunition. Trung Hung defenders announced that the Viet Cong offensive ceased with the first burst of fire from the skies.[77] This performance marked the FC-47 as a night operator. As Captain Terry put it, saving forts or hamlets at night "was the only thing we ever got to do."[78]

The sudden significance of the gunship's night role was easy to understand. Since 1963, night attacks on South Vietnam outposts and hamlets had soared alarmingly. During the first half of 1964 these assaults spotlighted the need for a much greater night air effort. At stake was the entire Republic of Vietnam's pacification program, as the Viet Cong under the cover of darkness assaulted and overran forts and strategic hamlets in government-designated "safe areas." Continued enemy successes would lay bare the RVN's incapability to protect these villages and outposts and effectively stifle its attempts to reestablish control over vast areas.[79]

June 1963 saw a sharp upswing in Air Force night flare and strike-support missions.[80] By September C-123s had joined Vietnamese flareships on airborne alert.[81] No longer did the mere dispensing of flares from a C-47 or C-123 intimidate the enemy in night attacks.[82] Now the Viet Cong adopted more aggressive tactics. When the flareship (or attack aircraft) arrived, they stopped the attack only to renew it when the plane left. After these softening-up forays, the fort or village would be overrun.[83] Small wonder the Air Force hurried the gunship into night operations, putting it on airborne alert to compensate for its slow reaction speed and to enlarge its coverage. By December 26, 1964—eleven days after its first combat mission—the gunship had flown seven training and sixteen combat sorties, expending 179,710 rounds and experiencing thirty-three mal-functions.[84]

Brig. Gen. John K. Boles, Jr., USA, Director of the Joint Research and Test Activity, flew as observer on the gunship mission of December 28. Captain Terry piloted the FC-47 to Ngai Giao, a district capital thirty-seven miles from Bien Hoa. The Viet Cong were attacking the town and its fort. Arriving over the area at 2030, the aircraft found each corner of the small triangular fort outlined with flarepots and designated by a fire arrow.* The gunship dropped Mk-6 flares and swept the embattled fort's perimeter with gunfire. To prolong support Captain Terry fired the guns singly. In more than one hour and twenty minutes, eighteen flares were dropped and seven thousand rounds fired—the miniguns were reloaded once.[85] Viet Cong tracer fire failed to hit the gunship. General Boles noted: "At the end of the mission the personnel at the post reported that due to the air support the VC attack had been broken off and they were extremely grateful for this support."[86] As the aircraft departed Ngai Giao for its orbiting station over Saigon, the crew reloaded the guns. At about 2230 the FC-47 was directed to support another outpost, but the Viet Cong ended the assault before the aircraft could fire a shot. At midnight this airborne alert mission ended. It had demonstrated once more the gunship's unique capability in night operations.

A still more dramatic demonstration of gunship power unfolded on the night of February 8, 1965. The aircraft was sent to the Bong Son area to help blunt a Viet Cong offensive in the Vietnamese highlands. From 1850 to 2310 the miniguns blazed, pouring 20,500 rounds onto a hilltop where the enemy had dug in. This strike killed about three hundred Viet Cong.[87]

Gunship techniques were essentially the same in day and night operations with adjustments to accommodate flares. Few targets, for example, required a lateral pass (flying parallel to a target). Hence the pilot attacked in a pylon turn and returned to "his most advantageous flare drop position in a minimum of time."[88] Nonetheless, night operations did disclose problems. General Boles highlighted one—dropped flares started fires in woods, rice stacks, or houses. He cited the Ngai Giao support mission with six or eight confusing fires started near flare markers on the corners of the fort. This made it difficult for the gunship crew to find the fort as operations progressed, and location might have become impossible had one of the fort's corner flares burned out. General Boles suggested that Tiara† replace flares for marking enemy targets and use of an airborne floodlight be considered.[89]

---

*The fire arrow could be made of many materials; metal gas cans filled with gasoline-soaked sand were often used. Ignited, it was easy to see at night. Hamlet defenders relayed to strike aircraft the enemy's position with reference to the fire arrow.

†Nickname for a chemiluminescent material which the Army tested for possible use in bombs or mortar projectiles. When released in the air, Tiara glowed rather than flamed and gave off little light. It worked poorly in humid and hot weather. For these reasons the Army did not put Tiara in bombs or other projectiles.

In response to General Boles' suggestion, the Air Force mounted a large searchlight in the doorway of an unarmed C–47 and tested it. From the normal operating altitude of 3,000 feet above ground level the searchlight's intensity was too weak on the ground for easy target identification. With the C–47 simulating the gunship, tests showed the searchlight when fixed-mounted for level flight lost effectiveness as the plane banked to fire. If aligned with the gunsight, it likewise detected few targets. Seemingly, the best answer would be to install an improved lighting system in a separate aircraft which would work with the gunship.[90]

While the Air Force sought an effective airborne lighting system, the gunship relied on flares for illumination. The most commonly used flare, the Mk–24 Mod 3, could illuminate an area with two-million candle-power for three minutes. The Mk–24 would not completely burn out in the air if released below 2,500 feet. Most crews therefore dropped it at 3,000 feet on a crosswind heading upwind from the suspected target. After dropping the flare the pilot held the same heading for fifteen seconds, meanwhile trying to avoid having the gunship illuminated with its own flares and attracting ground fire. This interval also gave the flares time to ignite and permitted the pilot to survey the area before executing a pylon turn and acquiring the target. An attack technique evolved whereby the pilot would dip the left wing, fire, level out, dip the left wing again, fire, and level out again. After two to four firings and 2½ to 3 minutes, the pilot would have returned to the original flaredrop position. Then by dropping more flares, constant illumination could be maintained over the target area. At times the flares alone discouraged enemy night attacks or halted those in progress.[91]

Two or three flights were usually required to check out the pilot and other gunship crew members in combined flare and firing operations. This presupposed, however, a crew experienced in day firing and night flare drops. The dive, bank, and climbing-turn maneuver was quickly discarded as too complex and not needed. Its varying air speed and angle of bank proved far more dangerous at night than the pylon turn and hampered target acquisition and firing accuracy as well.[92] Most of these gunship test missions were flown over the flat Mekong River Delta area where terrain problems were few.[93]

The gunship fired tracer ammunition on night missions to see where the minigun rounds were hitting. The gun's rapid fire appeared as tongues of flame spewing from the black sky accompanied by a distinctive sound. An impressive sight, it boosted the morale of fort and hamlet defenders but terrorized the enemy. It didn't take long for the FC–47 to earn the nicknames of "Puff, the Magic Dragon" and "dragonship."*

FC–47 missions, particularly night ones, highlighted the language difficulties and equipment problems in air-to-ground communication.

---

*Stories differ on the nickname's origin. Captain Terry believed it derived from a mix of 1964 being the Chinese Year of the Dragon, stories from captured enemy prisoners about tongues of fire from the gunship and recollections of the fairy tale, *Puff the Magic Dragon.* Others trace its origin to the children's song, popular in late 1964, regarding a magic dragon.

Adequate communication was crucial to precision firing during close support of a besieged post. Few American advisors were in the many forts and villages. Most contact was therefore with Vietnamese and the gunship carried a Vietnamese observer to facilitate conversations. The navigator's task was to determine what support the ground personnel needed. To eliminate confusion this sometimes involved a painstaking exchange of notes with the observer. General Boles considered the Ngai Giao mission of December 28 "quite successful in that the communications worked fine and the man on the ground was able to speak and be understood by us and by our Vietnamese Air Force officer aboard." Nevertheless, the general noted that inadequate communication was a common deficiency.[94]

Additionally, the gunship test accented the difficulty of bomb damage assessment, a problem common to all combat air operations in South Vietnam. Ground teams frequently found it too risky to penetrate enemy territory to assess results of an FC-47 attack. Furthermore, the Viet Cong carefully removed their casualties under cover of darkness. Having no BDA capability of their own, the gunship crew turned to the man on the ground who had to report what had happened. Playback on the aircraft's tape recorder produced little more than "number one"; "more, more, same thing"; "good shooting"; until that sure indicator of success "OK enemy go away now" was heard. Added to this was a trickle of intelligence on some strikes that filtered to the test team via American advisors. Despite this dearth of BDA detail, the gunship attacks did keep forts and villages out of enemy hands.[95] General McConnell and other top Air Staff members had followed the combat test with intense interest. Even without the specifics, they warmly greeted the FC-47's tactical success and foresaw its efficiency in outpost defense, freeing fighters from some night commitments.[96]

The minigun was a key component of the test gunship and its performance was closely evaluated in combat operations. The final evaluation report on the gun was not published until February 1965. But in late January, Headquarters, Pacific Air Forces (PACAF) notified Air Force headquarters it had ample information and could project the number of pods needed for future operations. It said the tests had shown the pod "easy to load, maintain, and capable of quick turn-around." The malfunction rate was low and the maintenance personnel needed no extensive special training. PACAF concluded that "a high degree of accuracy and reliability has been demonstrated," making the minigun an effective weapon for both day and night missions in Vietnam. It requested 126 guns to equip up to fifty aircraft.[97] The Air Staff had been pressing for this figure because of an established one-year lead time for procurement.[98] It notified PACAF a few days later that procurement action was under way, with a $4.3 million authorization in fiscal year 1965 funds for the first eighty-two guns.[99]

The Air Force test team's final report considered the minigun an excellent weapon for the side-firing aircraft but not entirely trouble free. At times the locking lug on the gun rotor service would break. This

Top: Machinegun-equipped gunship attacks target; bottom: .30-caliber machinegun in early AC–47.

allowed the gun to overspend because no provisions were incorporated to interrupt power when all ammunition had been expended. Life of the gun was thereby reduced. There was also a need for greater cooling of the gun. The report recommended modifications to correct these deficiencies and develop a more compact and accessible pod.[100]

While the combat tests failed to silence critics who deemed the gunship vulnerable to ground fire, they did demonstrate the FC–47's capability to operate in South Vietnam at the 1965 counterinsurgency level. During the missions the aircraft met with small-arms fire (mostly .30-caliber) but took few hits. Due to the gunship's orbiting altitude most of the rounds arrived nearly spent. In one case a round penetrated the cabin, hit the navigator in the heel, but caused no injury.[101] Such incidents were enough, however, to generate recommendations for armor to protect the FC–47 during close-range strike operations. The test team's report concluded that the gunship could hit the majority of targets yet be relatively invulnerable to ground fire.[102]

Commanders found it unnecessary to await completion of the combat evaluation before charting the gunship's future course. Interim test results so intrigued General Moore, 2d Air Division commander, that he asked for a squadron of FC–47s as quickly as possible.[103] On February 23, 1965, General Ferguson, then serving as Commander, Air Force Systems Command, strongly seconded the request to Air Force headquarters. He noted that:

> . . . the reports which have been received indicate spectacular success in killing Viet Cong and in stopping attacks together with concurrent great psychological factor way out of proportion to effectiveness of other aircraft strike efforts and ground force efforts.[104]

Ferguson urged prompt production of gunpods and planning for conversion of a better transport aircraft to a gunship. He called for a "highest Air Force and Department of Defense level" review, so that every possible channel can be cut in producing this needed capability.[105] On March 2 the Air Staff requested the PACAF commander's requirement for gunships, stressing the special significance of the associated minigun requirement.[106] Study of the type and extent of the gunship force had begun.

The Air Force test team's report noted that the FC–47's size kept it from realizing its full potential in night strike operations. For future gunships, the report recommended an aircraft having more cargo compartment space and greater payload.[107] A PACAF capabilities study of March 12, 1965, suggested the Air Force use the C–131 (or its T–29 counterpart) as the gunship airframe and that a squadron of sixteen aircraft be sent to South Vietnam. On March 20 the PACAF commander proposed adopting the C–131 for its advantage of speed and double payload over the aging C–47.[108] After reviewing the test team's and PACAF's recommendations, the Air Staff ordered a feasibility study on April 20 to weigh these recommendations against the availability of aircraft.[109] On May 12 the Air Staff decided to utilize the C–47 as the gunship for Southeast Asia.[110] No serious questions were raised regarding the suggested size of the gunship force.

On June 18 PACAF formally proposed a sixteen-plane FC–47 squadron to Air Force headquarters. Foreseeing difficulties in minigun production, the proposal specified four C–47s should be modified with .30-caliber machineguns at once. The twelve minigun-equipped aircraft were to follow as soon as possible. When their supply permitted, miniguns would replace the interim .30-caliber guns. Aircraft, aircrew, support personnel, and equipment were to be provided in one package from outside PACAF. Of the 329 personnel (79 officers and 250 airmen) projected, about one-fourth were to be in place for the first four gunships. Upon Air Staff approval of this proposal, PACAF would seek CINCPAC and COMUSMACV concurrence in the deployment.[111] On July 13, 1965, Air Force headquarters directed that a gunship squadron be sent to South Vietnam, the move to be completed by November 9.[112]

After the Air Force completed FC–47 combat testing and the study of a future gunship force, many essential items fell into place. Operational tactics were defined, problem areas pinpointed, the need for the gunship capability established, available airframes and equipment determined (the minigun remaining a trouble spot), and the first gunship squadron ordered deployed. A new weapon system moved into the Air Force inventory.[113]

In retrospect, several significant points of the gunship's early history stand out. One thread throughout the entire story of gunship development is the part played by improvisation. Captain Simons first tested the concept in the old T–28 and later in the C–131. Combat evaluation took place in the C–47, one of the oldest planes in the Air Force. A camera viewfinder initially served as the gunsight. The miniguns, although new, just happened to be available at Eglin Air Force Base where the gunship tests were held. Assembling gunship components was largely a matter of tapping local shop resources and ingenuity. Improvisations seemed endless and contrasted sharply with the long slow stages of engineering, test, and manufacturing required for most modern weapon systems. Likewise, the gunship tactic of side firing from the pylon turn synthesized old aerial maneuvers and weaponry ideas. This make-do-with-what-you've got attitude gave the gunship system rare economy and availability that would continue to spur its future evolution and sophisticated development.

A related factor was the tortuous path the side-firing concept traveled before being accepted as a valid basis for a combat weapon. At several critical junctures the proposal almost died. It faced bureaucratic oblivion, burial in government files, rejection by ballistic experts, plus the usual delaying problems of time, manpower, and money. Some critics doubted an aircraft employing the concept could survive in combat, and some believed the idea violated Air Force doctrine. Only the dogged persistence of key individuals enabled the concept to emerge from such a deadly thicket.

The role of four imaginative and determined men was outstanding. Most Air Force developments involve team effort with credit for improvements and changes broadly shared. The gunship was no exception. Nevertheless, in evaluating the gunship's origin, one is struck with the singular results produced by MacDonald, Flexman, Simons, and Terry. Each of these men focused on problems of counterinsurgency warfare. Each studied the Vietnam war with intense interest and saw new combat challenges. Each pushed the gunship concept to help meet counterinsurgency requirements after he discovered that current Air Force aircraft, tactics, and weapons could not. MacDonald's inventive mind seized upon the old pylon turn, merged it with a laterally-fired weapon, and introduced a new concept. Flexman pursued and transmitted the idea, stressing all the while its value in the Vietnam war. A pilot in three wars, Simons recognized the problems in placing munitions on targets with the precision called for in guerrilla warfare. Since the side-firing aircraft could help attain this accuracy, Simons refused to let the idea die. On his Southeast Asian trip in 1963, Terry learned firsthand what was needed to deal with attacks of insurgents. He therefore felt the concept had to be tried. In the tenacious attack on the problems at hand, each of the four men served in a distinctive yet overlapping role. MacDonald can be tabbed the "originator," Flexman the "catalyst," Simons the "tester," and Terry the "seller." Their evolutionary efforts combined to create the unique weapon system employed in Southeast Asia—the gunship.

II. Gunship I (AC–47)

The selection of the C–47 as the first Air Force gunship put the new 7.62-mm minigun into one of the Air Force's oldest operational aircraft. In fact, it was not unusual for gunship crewmembers to discover that their aircraft had been built before they were born. The first flight of the Douglas Aircraft DC–3 (in military guise, the C–47) took place on December 18, 1935, and only a few years thereafter it became the most widely used transport in the world. The armed forces ultimately received 10,123 production models, most of them during World War II.[1] But despite its age and apparent obsolescence, the aircraft's great versatility, reliability, and all-around ruggedness kept it in use. These characteristics prompted the Air Force to rely heavily upon it during the Korean War and to deploy it in Vietnam during the escalating counterinsurgency warfare of 1961.[2]

The first Air Force commitment of four C–47s occurred with the arrival of the Farm Gate detachment* in November 1961. By this time the South Vietnamese already had two squadrons of U.S.-supplied aircraft and were using them in a variety of roles. Both American and South Vietnamese C–47s flew extensive airdrop, medical evacuation, and transport-type missions. Gradually they moved into flareship operations in support of besieged hamlets and forts. In late 1965 the arrival of the first squadron of gunship-configured C–47s added still another operational dimension. These armed C–47s began one more chapter in the illustrious and seemingly endless history of the old Gooney Bird.

One FC–47 continued operations in Vietnam after the Air Force test team completed its work and returned to the United States. This gunship was soon pressed into service to counter a serious enemy threat to cut Vietnam in half through the highlands. Gen. William C. Westmoreland, COMUSMACV, ordered all-out air support for a large-scale troop deployment to block the enemy push. During this operation the FC–47 flew two interdiction strikes between 1850 and 2310 on the night of February 8, 1965. It fired 20,500 rounds of 7.62-mm ammunition, and ground observers reported one hundred Viet Cong killed by strikes. On the afternoon of the 8th the Viet Cong captured a sergeant of the Army of the Republic of Vietnam (ARVN). After the gunship attacks, the sergeant escaped and told of helping carry away 80 or 90 enemy bodies of the 250 he believed had been killed. He cited the confusion of enemy troops as to the source of the firepower. Some thought they had been hit by a heavy ground attack, while others thought it was a new gun of some kind. An impressed U.S. Army advisor in the II Corps area requested the FC–47 be permanently committed to support operations there.[3]

---

*Detachment 2, 4400th Combat Crew Training Squadron, Tactical Air Command.

Other C–47s were available for possible gunship missions in various parts of Vietnam, but the limiting factor was the shortage of guns, particularly replacement gun barrels. Captain Terry felt interim weapons might be used and began scouting the Air Force inventory to see what might be available. At McClellan AFB, Calif., he found some old World War II .30-caliber machineguns about to be salvaged. A personal appeal to Gen. Mark E. Bradley, Jr., Commander, Air Force Logistics Command (AFLC), resulted in all .30-caliber guns being allocated for the gunships. Captain Terry and other members of an Air Force Systems Command team designed a kit using ten of the .30-caliber guns. The team flew to Vietnam and by June 1965 had modified four more C–47s with this interim arsenal. The machinegun-equipped aircraft proved successful but the guns wore out rapidly. Nonetheless, the three hundred guns, extra barrels, and spare parts kept the aircraft going until the arrival of the first gunship squadron.[4]

A number of steps, preliminary to a gunship squadron deployment, began soon after the first FC–47's combat success. As previously noted, Air Force headquarters weighed proposals for utilizing other aircraft for the gunship role but elected to go with the C–47, largely on the basis of its availability. Hence the Air Staff directed the Air Force Logistics Command in May 1965 to prepare a feasibility study on installation of GAU 2/A guns in twenty C–47s. Warner Robins Air Materiel Area (WRAMA) completed the study on July 2, 1965, and submitted it to the logistics command and Air Force headquarters for review.[5] The Air Staff then asked AFLC and AFSC to coordinate all plans for the aircraft modifications as the gunship squadron moved closer to reality.

Logistics Command headquarters assigned modification number 1729, "Install GAU–2/A gun," to the gunship program. WRAMA and the Aeronautical Systems Division worked together on the modification proposal and specified these items in each aircraft: three GAU–2/A miniguns; a gunsight; a ballistic cloth; associated racks, controls, and wiring; communication and navigation equipment. Projected cost for modifying twenty aircraft totaled $4,288,975. This included the new General Electric module, the GAU–2/A gun, and more than $2 million for spare items.[6]

Still another addition to the gunship equipment was a flare launcher. Interest in a flare-launch capability for the gunship developed almost at the very beginning of the tests at Eglin. The Special Air Warfare Center (SAWC) had asked Air Force headquarters for such a capability, and on August 13, 1965, the Air Staff directed that flare launchers be installed. Warner Robins awarded a contract to the Gary Corporation, San Antonio, Texas, to manufacture the launchers and install an actuator mechanism obtained from Navy excess. Although officials knew these actuators differed from those used at Eglin, they were considered suitable. Tests showed, however, that the slightly faster firing time kicked rather than pushed the flare. WRAMA and the Special Air Warfare Center adjusted the actuator mechanisms (called Pogo Sticks) to the original production model configuration. The contractor then completed this further modification by the end of November 1965. By mid-April 1966 SAWC had completed extensive and successful tests of the flare launcher.[7]

During the early planning for the gunship program, the Air Force decided to modify a total of twenty-six C–47s with a side-firing capability. Sixteen gunships would be assigned to PACAF, six to TAC for training purposes, and four would be used for command support and attrition.[8] On July 16, 1965, AFLC set the modification program into motion. All aircraft were to be completed and ready to depart by November 7.[9]

The early departure date meant a tight modification schedule. To speed the program, C–47s would be taken from storage (most of them from Davis-Monthan AFB) and modified concurrently with IRAN (inspection and repair as necessary). On July 20, a prototype C–47 would begin IRAN and modification with all other aircraft beginning by August 15. A forty-day flow time was planned.[10] On August 12 Air Force headquarters amended the modification requirement to include more specifics on electronics equipment.[11] (It allowed acceptable substitute items to prevent any delay in the delivery schedule.) The modification program was assigned a high priority, the contract being let on July 28, 1965.

The program moved along rapidly. All other IRAN inputs were suspended in order to concentrate on the C–47s. Contractor and Warner Robins personnel, virtually working as one team, completed the prototype's IRAN and modification on September 1. Production of the other C–47s started September 16 with the last one finished on October 25 ahead of the deadline. Twenty of the modified aircraft had been delivered to Forbes AFB, Kans., by October 19. One week later, the remaining six were sent to Eglin AFB for use in training.[12]

The modification of the C–47s called for three GAU–2B/A gun pods on each aircraft. The Air Force recognized that these pods would not likely be available since they were just entering production. It therefore ordered the separately procured SUU–11A gun pods installed until the GAU–2B/As arrived. Even the supply of SUU–11As, however, proved inadequate as the modification progressed.

In line with the C–47 modification effort, Air Force headquarters ordered TAC on July 13, 1965, to organize and train an FC–47 squadron for deployment. Within TAC the Special Air Warfare Center and its 1st Air Commando Wing had the main responsibility for readying the unit.[13] TAC headquarters requested SAWC to submit an aircrew training schedule, suggest locations for squadron activation and training, and specify help needed beyond the center's resources. It stipulated that SAWC personnel would support the project, but aircraft and aircrews would come from other Air Force sources.[14]

Selection of a base for squadron activation and gunship training posed an immediate problem. TAC headquarters directed the Special Air Warfare Center to survey the Eglin AFB complex for an available auxiliary field.[15] The excellent Eglin land and water ranges were naturally a prime consideration. Hurlburt Field and the entire Eglin area, however,

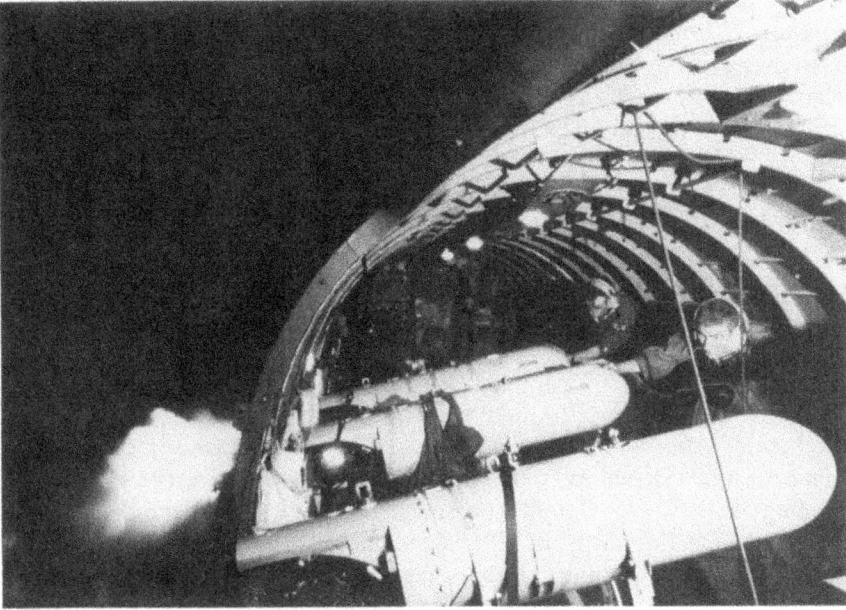

Top: 7.62 minigun pods: bottom: SSgt. William C. Ohlig checks miniguns before takeoff.

were already overtaxed for aircraft space and transient quarters for personnel. After much discussion, message traffic, and consideration of such bases as Tyndall, Maxwell, MacDill, and Cannon, Forbes AFB, Kans., was selected as the training location.[16] A conference at TAC headquarters on July 22, attended by representatives from various TAC and SAWC agencies, hammered out a concept of operation.[17] One decision was to establish Training Detachment 8 of the 1st Air Commando Wing (ACWg) at Forbes AFB to administer the program. On July 27–28 a SAWC/1st ACWg staff team visited Forbes to survey support facilities and to coordinate range training with Headquarters, 838th Air Division.[18]

Activation of Detachment 8 took place on August 9 with a small advance party on hand.[19] The SAWC listed the detachment's training requirements as 11 C–47 and 4 FC–47 aircraft plus a cadre of instructors: 15 pilots, 15 navigators, 10 flight engineers, 10 loadmasters, and 5 weapons mechanics. Additional manning included 44 officers and 115 airmen.[20] Some of the instructors were also expected to support the concurrent training of the 5th Air Commando Squadron, a newly formed psychological warfare unit at Forbes. Most of the detachment's cadre came on temporary duty from other TAC units and was in place by August 15. Lt. Col. William C. Thomas, former commander of the 319th ACSq at Hurlburt Field, was chosen to command Detachment 8. The entire program was now labeled Big Shoot* and the FC–47 unit designated the 4th ACSq.[21] Arrival of the men to be trained wrapped up the major preliminaries. Rigorous training got under way on August 29.[22]

Major problems quickly turned up in the Forbes program. Only one FC–47 was equipped with miniguns due to the shortage of gun pods. To meet the pressing need for firing training, M–2 .30-caliber machineguns were mounted in the other three FC–47s. Use of the M–2 caused maintenance trouble for armament personnel unfamiliar with the weapon. Assistance was obtained from U.S. Army personnel at Ft. Riley, Kans., to resolve some of the difficulties.[23] It was first assumed M–2-equipped aircraft would provide enough firing training. The Special Air Warfare Center noted, however, "debriefs of FC–47 crews returning from SEA [Southeast Asia] indicated that training with the .30-caliber guns would not be sufficient because of the dispersal pattern and lateral thrust of the SUU–11A guns." Hence training was revised to include maximum possible time in the one minigun-equippd FC–47.[24]

Modification problems likewise came to light that required correction by contractor personnel. Detachment personnel discovered during October a serious deficiency in ferry-tank installation on FC–47s destined for Vietnam. The two 500-gallon auxiliary ferry tanks had been installed backwards in the cabin thereby permitting fuel to siphon in flight. Furthermore, the navigator had little working room because the loran set had been placed on his table instead of on brackets above it. These

_____

*The 5th ACSq training program was designated Quick Speak.

contractor difficulties, the pressure to use every possible flying hour, and the extensive maintenance required on some of the C-47s exacted long hours from maintenance personnel to keep an acceptable in-commission rate.[25]

Big Shoot created singular supply problems as well. Besides the usual complications caused by dispersal of SAWC operations, a critical shortage existed in survival equipment such as parachutes, radios, individual survival kits, and flareguns. These were eventually secured from SAWC or TAC. Use of .30-caliber guns on the FC-47s for training entailed special procurement of ammunition, a successful but slow task.[26]

A number of training hitches developed and were resolved as the program progressed. Approximately fifty percent of the men who arrived for training had never attended survival school at Stead AFB, Nev. Lack of time now prevented their attendance so TAC formed a mobile training team of survival specialists who administered the training at Forbes. Likewise, a Ft. Bragg Special Warfare School team arrived and gave the men the field training necessary for defending forward operating bases in Vietnam.[27] Capt. Ronald R. Ellis, who had flown one of the original FC-47s in Vietnam, was diverted to Forbes enroute to a new stateside assignment. This afforded the trainees an opportunity to talk with someone having combat experience.[28] Thus, in many cases, unusual effort was essential to insure members of the squadron were operationally ready by the November deadline.

The FC-47-equipped 4th Air Commando Squadron faced the many problems that beset any unit preparing for a combat theater. Yet it moved steadily toward operational status and its November departure date. The advantages in the unit's utilization of an old, but reliable, aircraft like the C-47 had been offset by complications arising from the unique gunship modifications and the new pylon-turn, side-firing training. Nevertheless, these challenges had been met. On November 1, Big Shoot came to an end with the inactivation of Detachment 8 and return of its personnel to Hurlburt and other TAC bases. Deployment of aircraft and personnel of the 4th Air Commando Squadron to Vietnam also began under code name Operation Sixteen Buck.[29]

While the 4th Air Commando Squadron was still at Forbes AFB, a test project, called Red Sea, had commenced in Vietnam. Forward-looking infrared (FLIR) was installed in an FC-47 based at Bien Hoa AB to determine if it would enhance the gunship's night effectiveness. Red Sea represented part of a major Air Force drive to improve night operations capability. The need for an improved capability was clear since analysts estimated in 1964 and 1965 that eighty percent of Viet Cong logistics support moved during darkness. In July 1965 the Air Force Chief of Staff ordered a FLIR test program. On July 28 an infrared system developed by Texas Instruments was tested at Eglin AFB using a company DC-3. The plane flew over simulated Viet Cong targets such as small boats, huts, personnel, and trucks.[30] Next came the Red Sea tests in Vietnam with the FC-47 trying the FLIR system during different climatic conditions and over various terrain features. The many variables, the moisture, and the equipment's inadequate sensitivity created many problems. The FLIR operator was unable to distinguish village perimeters but could spot markers such as a fire arrow.[31] The scant success of these tests led the Air Force to return the equipment to Texas Instruments for further development. General Boles, Director of the Joint Research and Test Activity, recommended that development of aerial infrared systems be pushed despite these discouraging test results.[32] Although Red Sea was not successful, it was a forerunner of future attempts to give the gunship better night eyes.

Deployment to the Republic of Vietnam of the 4th Air Commando Squadron with its twenty AC-47s* (sixteen plus four for command support and attrition) was part of a hurried attempt by the United States to shore up the crumbling South Vietnamese government and its slipping control over the countryside. The threat of a communist victory in the South had been growing more serious month by month. Looking back from 1971 the Air Force Chief of Staff, Gen. John D. Ryan, commented:

> In 1965 such a takeover seemed inevitable. Communist forces controlled most of the country. South Vietnamese morale was low and the fall of the government was imminent unless the Vietnamese were given substantial assistance. Air power was the only way of providing assistance quickly in amounts large enough to take the initiative and victory away from the Viet Cong.[33]

It was into this situation that the 4th ACSq arrived at Tan Son Nhut AB, outside Saigon, on November 14, 1965. The squadron was assigned to the 2d Air Division and placed under the operational control of the 6250th Combat Support Group.[34] The gunships were welcomed because the test of interim FC-47s in Vietnam had proved extremely effective for night close air support. Furthermore, a Viet Cong summer offensive had underlined the urgent need for more gunships, especially for outpost and village defense.[35] Air Force headquarters now officially took the wraps off the AC-47 gunship. A 2d Air Division news release of November 23 (November 22 in Washington) discussed the aircraft and the 4th's move to Vietnam.[36] For the first time the American public had official information on this new weapon system.

Bringing aircrews to operationally ready status was the 4th ACSq's first order of business. Pilots, copilots, navigators, and flight mechanics had come with the aircraft. Loadmasters and weapons mechanics, however, did not arrive until December 1965. Cross-training of the loadmasters and weapons mechanics began at once so enough fully qualified crews would be available

---

*The "FC 47" designation for the 4th ACSq's gunships had been questioned in September 1965. A review led to the new designation "AC-47D." Henceforth, all transport aircraft modified into a gunship configuration were to carry the modified mission symbol "A."

without delay. Training was conducted between missions. By May 1, 1966, twenty-six crews had become combat qualified which actually exceeded the 1.5 aircrews allotted for each authorized aircraft.[37]

The long-standing armament problem remained an early operational headache. To cut weight for the long overwater flights,* the miniguns had been removed at Forbes. From November 20 to December 17, 1965—pending arrival of the gun pods in South Vietnam—the AC-47s flew fifty-eight courrier and cargo missions.[38] The aircraft also carried out flare-drop sorties and provided familiarization for aircrews.[39] By December 17, the ground crews had enough miniguns to install one or two in each AC-47. None of the gunships received its full complement of three miniguns in 1965. Nevertheless, the existing armament enabled the squadron to operate on a full-time basis.[40]

Seventh Air Force Operations Order 411-65 stated that the 4th Air Commando Squadron's mission in Vietnam was "to respond with flares and firepower in support of hamlets under night attack, supplement strike aircraft in the defense of friendly forces, and provide long endurance escort for convoys."[41] Given the Vietnam situation of 1965, these were demanding tasks. The gunship's versatility, however, attracted special assignments: search and rescue, forward air control, and reconnaissance.[42] The squadron faced unexpected challenges almost at once. In June 1965 the 2d Air Division had drawn up a proposal for gunship operations which CINCPACAF later backed. One-fourth of the proposed sixteen-plane squadron would be used in each of Vietnam's four military corps areas. For better combat support in the corps areas, Tan Son Nhut would become the main operating base, with forward operating locations at Da Nang, Pleiku, Nha Trang, and Binh Thuy.[43]

In line with the proposal and shortly after the 4th ACSq's gunships touched down at Tan Son Nhut, a contingent of the unit moved to Da Nang. There followed, however, an unanticipated shift of four AC-47s from Tan Son Nhut to Udorn Royal Thai Air Force Base (RTAFB), Thailand, to support the war lapping over into Laos. These gunships began flying day armed reconnaissance in late December 1965 over the Steel Tiger† area of Laos. It was the Laotian dry season and the AC-47s were to strike at enemy traffic moving down the Ho Chi Minh Trail complex to South Vietnam or to help control strikes of other aircraft on the trail targets. This interdiction role required development of new tactics and techniques, partly because operations over Laos proved far more hazardous than over South Vietnam. Antiaircraft fire was heavy, the Laotian terrain mountainous, maps poor, and weather conditions difficult.[44] No one foresaw at this time that the gunship would become famous in Laos and that its effectiveness in an interdiction role would have far-reaching impact.

---

*To avoid adding cold-weather equipment for the northern route, the AC-47s crossed the Pacific via Hawaii.

† Steel Tiger, initiated in April 1965, was the code name given to an operational area south of the 17th parallel in Laos where strikes were made against enemy infiltration routes.

35

The heavy gunship commitment both in South Vietnam and Laos produced notable records within a short time. In the remaining days of 1965, the 4th Air Commando Squadron flew 1,441 hours and 277 combat missions, mostly during the hours of darkness in support of fort and village defense. The gunships expended 137,136 rounds of 7.62-mm ammunition and 2,548 flares and received credit for 105 Viet Cong killed.[45] This was a remarkable effort from a recently organized unit, a new weapon system, and rookie crew personnel, fighting a unique war in an unfamiliar environment. Two AC-47s were lost, however. Enemy ground fire downed one on December 17 as it flew cross-country from Tan Son Nhut to Phan Rang.[46] Its wreckage, with no survivors, was spotted on December 23. The next day a gunship on a mission over Laos was heard transmitting "mayday" and "Spooky 21" as it neared the target area. This ended all contact with the aircraft, and the crew was officially listed as missing.[47] Thus the squadron's debut in Southeast Asia was not without its grim moments.

The appearance of a complete gunship squadron in Southeast Asia during late 1965 reflected the fast-changing face of the war. The year saw the United States give up its restricted advisory-type role for a clear air-and-ground combat commitment. This switch saved South Vietnam from almost certain collapse, but the survival struggle had just begun. Strong Viet Cong and North Vietnam forces, estimated at 230,000, remained undefeated. Allied strength consisting of 651,885 Vietnamese (regular and paramilitary), 184,314 Americans, 20,000 Koreans, 1,500 Australians, and 100 New Zealanders was still increasing. Phase I of U.S. air and ground deployments— of which the 4th Air Commando Squadron was a part—ended in the last half of 1965 with Phase II set for 1966. Air Force strength in Southeast Asia had already mushroomed to more than 20,000 men and 514 aircraft in South Vietnam and 9,000 men and 207 aircraft in Thailand. The U.S. buildup was to continue in step with the intensified air and ground effort.[48]

AC-47 gunship operations and deployments in 1966 reflected the rising American involvement in Southeast Asian fighting. Some deployment adjustments were made to improve command or strengthen operational responses. In May 1966 the 4th Air Commando Squadron shifted its headquarters from Tan Son Nhut to Nha Trang[49] where its newly formed parent unit, the 14th Air Commando Wing,* was based. In June, AC-47s were sent to Bien Hoa AB (III Corps area). These aircraft were in addition to those previously placed at the bases of Da Nang (I Corps area), Pleiku (II Corps area), and Binh Thuy (IV Corps area).[50] The missions of this dispersed gunship force expanded in number and variety. Most fell into these main categories: hamlet and fort defense, close air support for ground combat units, convoy escort, control of air strikes, armed reconnaissance, and

---

*Activated on March 8, 1966.

interdiction. Often gunships flew with other aircraft and several types of missions might be combined in a single evening's operations. Missions were not limited to the hours of darkness but the majority of them took place at night.

Defense of hamlets and forts was a key gunship mission that often began with a relay of a call for help to a Spooky* on airborne alert. This was the case when the Viet Cong attacked a hamlet in Phu Yen Province on the night of January 8. Arriving over the village, the gunship fired 13,000 rounds of 7.62-mm ammunition within a hundred meters of friendly positions. The fire silenced one .50-caliber machinegun and the Viet Cong broke off their attack.[51] During the night of April 9, Majs. Jack Haller and Jack Graden, pilots of Spooky 23, were called to defend a special forces camp close to the Cambodian border. The nearness of the border and heavy antiaircraft fire passing within feet of the plane severely hampered the pilots. They nevertheless pressed their attack, then provided flares and fire suppression for an F–100 flight that followed. Finally, with ammunition exhausted and fuel low, Spooky 23 returned to base. The commander of Detachment B–41 of the Special Forces Group reported, "The superb airmanship and aggressiveness displayed by the AC–47 was the major determining factor in preventing the fort from being overrun." United States personnel counted 168 Viet Cong killed by the air strikes. Many weapons were captured including the first Viet Cong flamethrower found in the IV Corps (Delta) area.[52] On July 15 a company of Viet Cong assaulted a thirty-two man Popular Force outpost in Phong Dinh Province. The attackers proclaimed by loudspeaker, "We are not afraid of your firepower." Thereupon, four AC–47s dropped seventy-five flares and expended 48,800 rounds. Two F–100s next dropped napalm on the enemy positions and the Viet Cong stopped the attack.[53] During the night of October 11, a record was set for the most 7.62-mm rounds fired in a single night by an AC–47. The gunship expended 43,500 rounds and ninety-six flares to aid a besieged outpost in Kien Phong Province. After using up its entire flare and ammunition load, the aircraft landed, reloaded, and returned to the attack. The outpost commander credited the AC–47 with saving the fort.[54]

Hamlet defense was not entirely restricted to South Vietnam. On March 4 six enemy battalions attacked the strategic city of Attopeu, Laos, defended by outnumbered Royal Laotian troops. Two AC–47s, commanded by Maj. George W. Jensen and Capt. Theodore M. Faurer, helped rout the enemy forces. Major Jensen's Spooky 41 used a starlight scope, which intensified light reflected from the moon or stars, to locate the enemy. With the dawn of March 5 a forward air controller reported spotting twenty-six enemy dead. General Thao Ma, commander of the Royal Laotian Air Force, was highly pleased with the gunship strike results. Later, Spooky 41 sighted three hundred of the enemy and the regional commander

---

*The designations of the AC–47 gunship, "Spooky", "Puff", and "Dragonship", are used interchangeably in this chapter. Puff was once used as a call sign when the 1st Air Commando Squadron had the first of the gunships. The 4th Air Commando Squadron began using Spooky as their radio call sign, based on their night flying in camouflaged aircraft.

Viet Cong Infiltration Systems

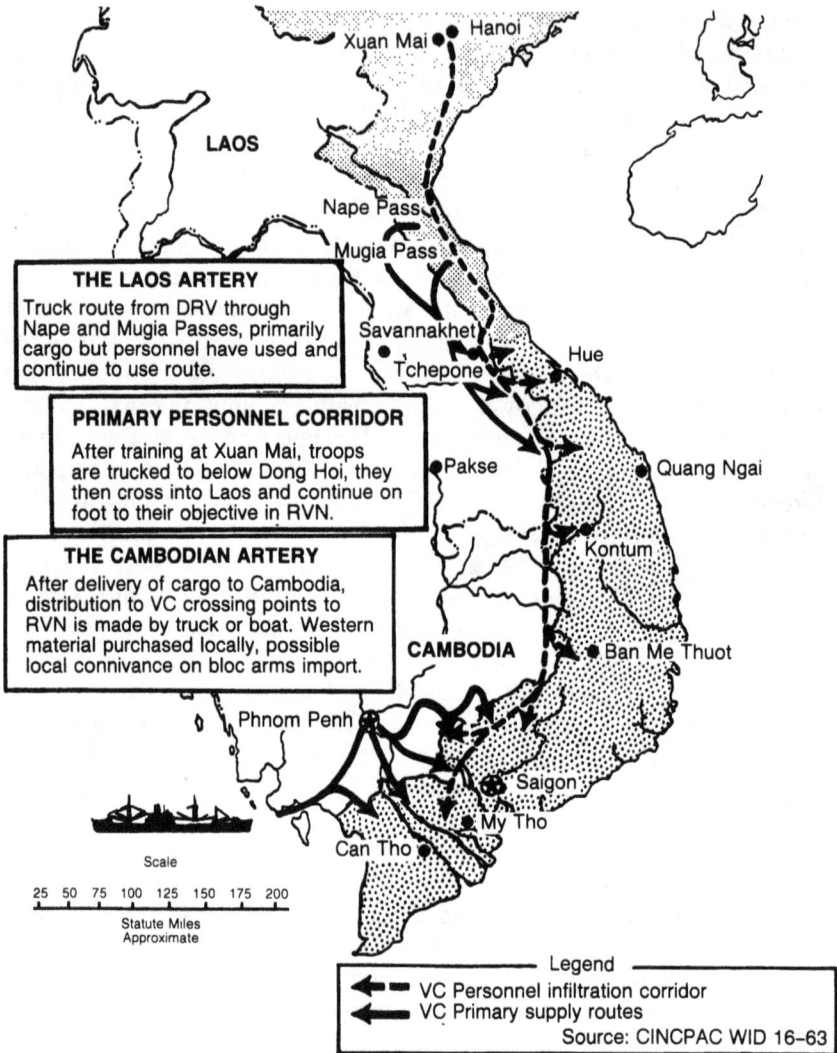

LAOS

Xuan Mai • Hanoi

Nape Pass

Mugia Pass

THE LAOS ARTERY
Truck route from DRV through
Nape and Mugia Passes, primarily
cargo but personnel have used and
continue to use route.

Savannakhet

Tchepone

Hue

PRIMARY PERSONNEL CORRIDOR
After training at Xuan Mai, troops
are trucked to below Dong Hoi, they
then cross into Laos and continue on
foot to their objective in RVN.

Pakse

Quang Ngai

THE CAMBODIAN ARTERY
After delivery of cargo to Cambodia,
distribution to VC crossing points to
RVN is made by truck or boat. Western
material purchased locally, possible
local connivance on bloc arms import.

Kontum

CAMBODIA

Ban Me Thuot

Phnom Penh

Saigon

My Tho

Can Tho

Scale

25 50 75 100 125 150 175 200

Statute Miles
Approximate

Legend

VC Personnel infiltration corridor
VC Primary supply routes

Source: CINCPAC WID 16–63

Major Interdiction Areas (Southeast Asia)

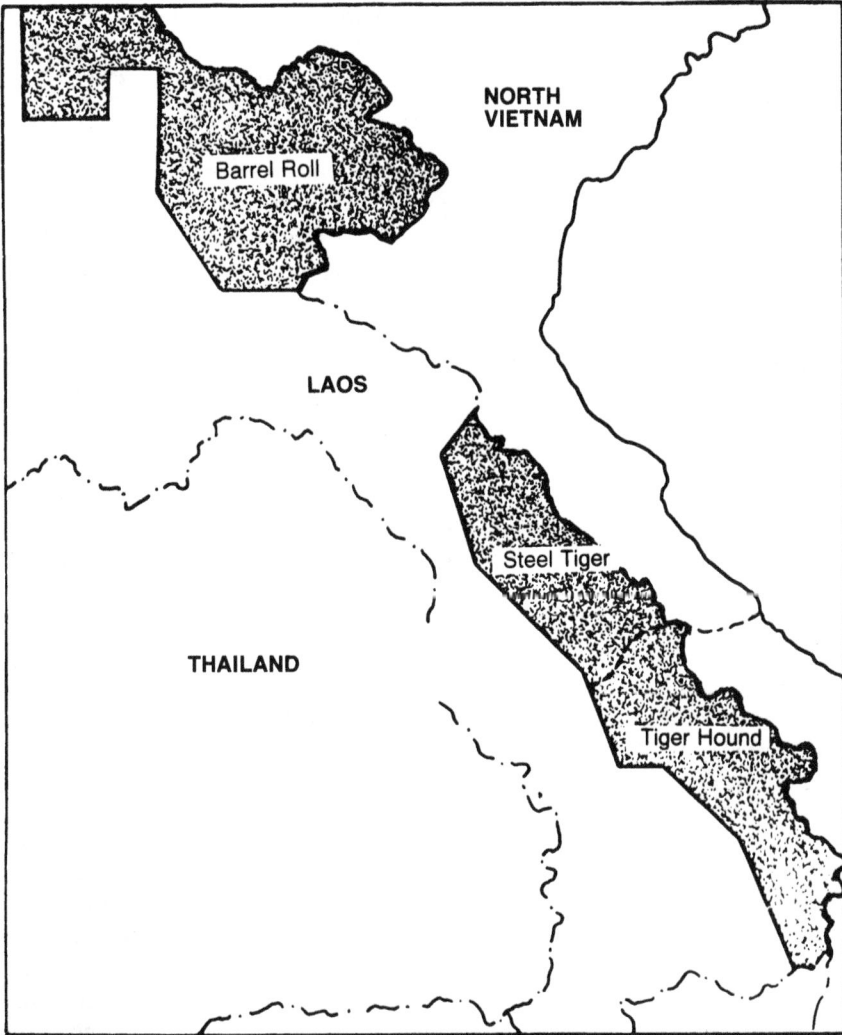

gave permission to strike. The outcome was a body count of fifty-two in groups of six to twenty.[55] The Deputy Commander, 2d Air Division/ Thirteenth Air Force, commended this action:

> Outstanding airmanship, personal bravery and hard work of your AC–47 crews (Spooky 41 and 43) no doubt saved Attopeu from possible capture the night of March 4, 1966 and dealt a devastating blow to attacking enemy battalions. A review of the reports of the action indicates a minimum of 100 killed by air, an actual number probably over 250, with many more wounded. My congratulations on a most effective display of tactical air power.[56]

The case of the fort of Thanh Anh best illustrates the importance of these many gunship missions in defense of hamlets and outposts. This fortification was part of the "oilspot" concept for dealing with counter-insurgency, which called for providing the people and villages protection and physical security. From these fortified areas, a circle of "strategic" and "defended" villages was to expand outwards to eventually extend the Republic of Vietnam's rule to the borders of Cambodia and Laos. Such a fortified ring was begun in the Mekong Delta (IV Corps) area of Vietnam, circling Binh Thuy AB and the provincial capital of Can Tho. Thanh Anh, eight miles south-southeast of Binh Thuy AB, defended a point where the Bassac River meets a canal. It denied the Viet Cong use of an excellent waterway into the more secure interior area and was also the first fort of the next larger circle. Thanh Anh's significance made it a prime Viet Cong target. In July 1966 Viet Cong bullhorns blared: "Leave the fort. Leave now and you will live. Stay until the next dark of the moon and you will be killed. No one will be spared."[57]

Firing on Thanh Anh intensified as the no-moon period neared. The fort's twenty-six defenders were besieged by an estimated two companies of Viet Cong. Nightly the enemy dug narrow zig-zag trenches that eventually edged to within 250 yards of the triangular fort's perimeter. The Popular Forces men at Thanh Anh filled the trenches by day only to find them booby trapped and redug during the night. Nightly, it became routine for a single gunship to keep the Viet Cong close to their trenches. During the darkness of July 13, however, four gunships fired almost 50,000 rounds of 7.62-mm ammunition and about ninety flares to repulse mass attacks. The 4th Air Commando Squadron responded so frequently to aid this beleaguered fort that pilots concluded Thanh Anh was the only tiny Vietnamese village with its own private air force.[58]

Thus, the gunships' role developed as a key element in the Vietnamese government's reassertion of control over the countryside. The outposts might be small and seemingly insignificant. Notwithstanding, for the first time effective and long-sustained night air support meant the difference for survival of many remote fortified points. In the eyes of most observers, this could steel the will to resist the Viet Cong and bolster support for the government.

Despite considerable success in defending hamlets and forts, the gunships could not avert the fall of the A Shau Special Forces camp in early March. The camp nestled at the base of a narrow valley about 20 miles southwest of Hue and 2½ miles from the Laotian border. The triangular-shaped fort with its adjoining 2,300-foot airstrip was a watchpost on an enemy infiltration route. At 0200, March 9, 1966, the fort came under heavy Viet Cong and North Vietnamese attack. Fire barrages from mortars, 75-mm recoilless rifles, and automatic weapons killed two Americans and eight Vietnamese. Another thirty Americans and thirty Vietnamese were wounded. A low cloud ceiling made air strikes prohibitive. The Viet Cong pressed this advantage until dawn and resumed the assault that night. C–123 flareships dropped 377 flares trying to keep the area illuminated for the defenders.[59]

At 1120 on March 9 an AC–47 was dispatched to A Shau. The camp had reported it was in immediate danger of being overrun. Despite a ceiling near 400 feet, the pilot, Capt. Willard M. Collins, and the copilot, 1st Lt. Delbert R. Peterson, tried to get under the clouds and aid the camp defenders. On the third attempt the plane reached the fort and made a firing pass at the besiegers. During a second pass, intense ground fire tore the gunship's right engine from its mount and silenced the other engine only seconds later. The Spooky crash-landed on a mountain slope and one crewmember had his legs broken. The uninjured crewmembers prepared for an expected enemy attack. Barely fifteen minutes after the crash, the crew repulsed the first enemy probe but a second one killed the pilot and the injured airman.[60]

An Air Force HH–43 rescue helicopter dropped through the clouds to pick up the remainder of the crew just as another enemy assault began. Using an M–16 rifle and a .38-caliber pistol, Lieutenant Peterson charged an enemy .50-caliber machinegun position. This permitted rescue of three survivors[61] but prevented his own evacuation. Later, A–1E strike aircraft were directed to destroy the downed AC–47, if possible, during their missions in support of the camp.[62] At the same time, U.S. Marine jets, employing radar bombing, and other aircraft attempted to penetrate the cloud cover. Nevertheless, abandoning the camp during the day was considered the wisest course in the face of the estimated two thousand attackers. The fall of A Shau on March 10 showed the enemy's awareness of the value of nighttime attacks during weather that restricted air operations.[63] In spite of Spooky's heroic defense efforts, a gunship had fallen victim to that awareness.

Another gunship mission—assisting defenders of U.S. air bases—was closely related to that of supporting village and outpost defense. The rapid American buildup had brought more hit-and-run attacks on U.S. installations, particularly air bases. An orbiting gunship on airborne alert apparently deterred some base assaults. At times, however, Spooky defended bases with firepower. For instance, the enemy launched a mortar attack on Binh Thuy AB on February 20, 1966. In spite of incoming mortar rounds, Captain Faurer and his crew took off in an AC–47 and struck the mortar positions, helping break up the attack.[64] A like action took place at Pleiku AB on April 22. Capt. Albert Haddad and his crew were having a weather briefing when the mortar attack began. They rushed to their gunship while others ran to shelters. Fuel flooded the ramp area. Debris and dud mortar rounds littered both the ramp and runway. Ignoring their own safety, the aircrew saved the AC–47 by getting it airborne and later assisted in silencing the Viet Cong fire.[65] Another mortar attack on Binh Thuy took place on the night of July 8. Two gunships responded within three minutes and their firepower ended the bombardment. Again, squadron gunships flew a special orbit nightly for two weeks around a Saigon petroleum, oil, and lubricants (POL) tank farm. It was feared the enemy would retaliate for the initial bombing strikes on POL dumps in the Hanoi and Haiphong areas.[66] Spooky's success in helping deter and quell attacks on bases led the Commander, 14th Air Commando Wing, to remark: "I think we're going to find that the 4th Air Commando Squadron is the greatest thing since sex, so far as protecting a base is concerned."[67]

Several spectacular 1966 actions typified another gunship mission—the close air support of ground combat units. On April 15 such a unit trapped an estimated battalion-size Viet Cong force at night in the crook of a river near Tan An. Helicopters sprayed the river with bullets to cut off escape in that direction. Six AC–47 sorties were flown, led by Lt. Col. Max L. Barker, 4th Air Commando Squadron commander. The gunship attack was pushed until all ammunition was gone. Flares were dropped to light up the area for ground troops and other air strikes. By American count, air action killed 470 Viet Cong that night. Close air support involving the AC–47s also recorded high enemy casualties later in the month. During daylight of the 23rd, elements of the 21st ARVN Division, engaged in Operation Dan Chi 219, closed with the Viet Cong. The fight lasted into the night. Three dragonships dropped sixty-eight flares and fired 23,000 rounds into enemy positions. Six A–1H and nineteen F–100 strikes supplemented the gunship fire. At dawn 228 Viet Cong dead were confirmed with an estimated 170 carried away. The air liaison officer of the 21st ARVN Division stated that "the application of TAC air during the period of heavy contact probably saved the friendlies from being overrun and prevented heavier friendly casualties from being inflicted."[68]

On the afternoon of August 2, a two-platoon task force of the 2d Battalion, 35th Infantry, U.S. Army, came upon a communist base camp. In the ensuing fight the American task force was surrounded and suffered heavy casualties including the company commander and first sergeant. The enemy also surrounded a company-size relief force and dealt it severe blows by mortars from high ground. At about 2200, whistles, bugles, and screams seemed to signal a communist pep rally prior to a full-scale assault. The ground commander requested air support, and a gunship was directed to provide cover. Rays of a single flashlight through a tiny hole in the jungle canopy marked the task force's defensive position. Working via radio with this force, the gunship poured gunfire around the position. Aided by Spooky both encircled forces beat off the enemy's attacks. The

Geography of Control

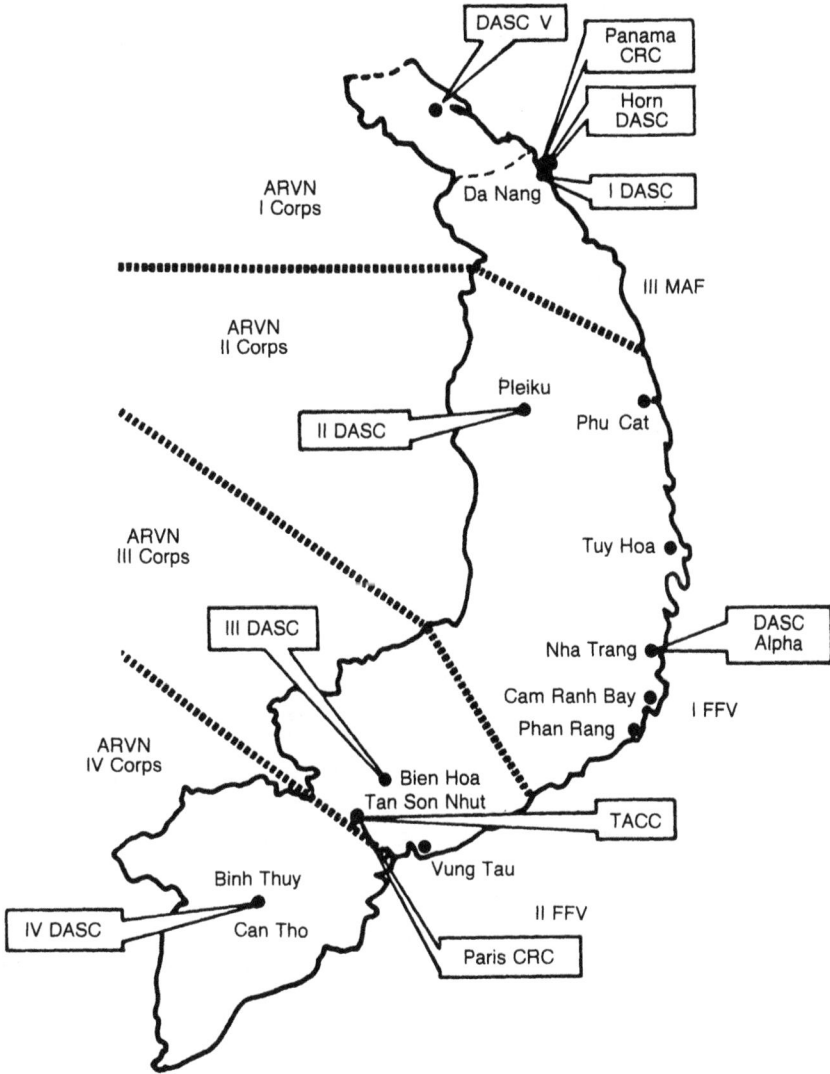

DASC V

Panama CRC

Horn DASC

I DASC

ARVN I Corps

Da Nang

III MAF

ARVN II Corps

Pleiku

II DASC

Phu Cat

ARVN III Corps

Tuy Hoa

DASC Alpha

III DASC

Nha Trang

Cam Ranh Bay

I FFV

Phan Rang

ARVN IV Corps

Bien Hoa
Tan Son Nhut

TACC

Vung Tau

Binh Thuy

II FFV

IV DASC

Can Tho

Paris CRC

DASC—Direct Air Support Centers

Paris CRC—Call sign of the control and reporting center at Tan Son Nhut

Panama CRC—Call sign of the center at Da Nang Air Base

43

next morning U.S. patrols counted 106 enemy bodies and found evidence that others had been removed. The 2d Battalion commander commended the 4th Air Commando Squadron, stating that "the men of this battalion have great appreciation for and full confidence in the United States Air Force and point to this particular action as an outstanding example of interservice cooperation at its finest."[69]

The gunships played an increasingly significant role in major ground combat operations. These included Operations Hawthorne (a search-and-destroy mission in II Corps), Masher, Paul Revere (a long operation to intercept enemy forces crossing into South Vietnam from Cambodia), and Prairie (a search-and-destroy operation along the demilitarized zone).[70] Close air support missions were chiefly in the northern half of South Vietnam due to the American counterstrategy of blocking the enemy's infiltration and any drive to cut the country in two. To support American Marine operations near the Demilitarized Zone, one gunship based at Da Nang was placed on special ground alert at Dong Hoa on August 25. The short narrow runway (3,900 ft x 56 ft) of pierced aluminum planking over sod and the lack of maintenance, refueling, and armament resupply facilities made operations doubly difficult in this area.[71] As additional U.S. Army and Marine troops arrived, the support sorties for ground units steadily rose.

In 1965 the 2d Air Division had begun to emphasize night aerial armed reconnaissance of South Vietnam's rivers, coasts, and roads. Nicknamed Snipe Hunt, the surveillance carried over into 1966 and involved U.S. Army OV-1 aircraft, forward air controllers in O-1 aircraft, and C-123s or AC 47s using flares.[72] During the night of January 8, 1966, a Spooky detected and rolled in to attack a Viet Cong junk along the South Vietnamese coast. The gunship forced the craft aground, then flew cover as Vietnamese naval units boarded it and took off ammunition and equipment.[73] A like operation occurred on June 20. An AC–47 on alert at Binh Thuy was ordered to assist the U.S. Coast Guard cutter *Point League* in apprehending a Viet Cong supply vessel moving up the coast to a Mekong River outlet. The gunship silenced a machinegun on the ship, dropped flares, and squelched fire from the shore. This air-sea action resulted in the capture of a steel-hulled vessel and more than 7,000 weapons.[74]

The great versatility of the AC–47s became clearer as the months went by. It could be a deadly strike aircraft or protective mother hen. In February, for example, the gunship flew cover for an American ship lying helplessly offshore after an enemy attack. In March it attacked forty Viet Cong sampans. In April it resumed its protective role of flying escort for a truck convoy—ready to strike in case of ambush.[75] Spooky's flare capability, loitering time, and firepower combined to give it a flexibility that military commanders in Vietnam quickly grasped.

At times gunships acted as forward air controllers in the Tiger Hound area of Laos and within Vietnam. All pilots of the 4th Air Commando

Squadron took an abbreviated course in this kind of mission. Overcoming poor cockpit visibility,[76] the gunship crews competently controlled strikes by most aircraft in Vietnam: A-1Es, B-57s, F-100s, F-4Cs, F-5s, and a number of Navy aircraft. In some cases the AC-47s supplemented the firepower of the strike aircraft they were controlling by suppressing ground fire with the miniguns.[77]

Of all gunship interdiction missions, perhaps the most telling ones were flown outside South Vietnam. U.S. Ambassador to Laos William H. Sullivan requested that gunships be committed to support a major American attempt to locate and destroy enemy supplies and equipment moving along infiltration routes in southern Laos. The AC-47s were to be part of interdiction operations designated by the code name Cricket, flown in the Tiger Hound geographical area of Laos bordering on South Vietnam. In response to Ambassador Sullivan's request, American officials in Vientiane, Laos, urged on January 10, 1966, that the 2d Air Division send six to eight gunships to Nakhon Phanom RTAFB for operations over Laos. On February 5 the 2d Air Division set up the requirement for these gunships. Twelve days later, however, attention was momentarily diverted from the Laotian interdiction mission by urgent phone calls from the deputy commander of the Thailand-based headquarters of the 2d Air Division/Thirteenth Air Force. The calls asked for AC-47s to help defend the Air America airstrip in northern Laos (Lima Site 36) which was under heavy enemy pressure. The two gunships were sent immediately to Udorn RTAFB, performed well, but failed to save Lima Site 36. Nevertheless, the Ambassador to Laos and the Air Attache were sufficiently impressed with the gunships' capability that they requested the AC-47s be left at Udorn permanently.[78]

Meantime, Adm. Ulysses S. Grant Sharp, Jr., CINCPAC, approved on February 19 the original request to position AC-47s at Nakhon Phanom. Then, after Thailand gave the go-ahead on February 25, the 2d Air Division sent four AC-47s and five aircrews to Udorn RTAFB for 179 days temporary duty.[79] The gunships were sent to Udorn in lieu of Nakhon Phanom since two of the gunships were already there. Also, it was believed they could better fulfill Ambassador Sullivan's requirements for both site defense and interdiction missions from that base. Subsequently, the AC-47s were shifted to Ubon RTAFB in April because the arrival of A-1E aircraft at Udorn overcrowded the ramps.[80]

Two major types of AC-47 interdiction missions emerged in Laos: (1) armed reconnaissance over the intricate network of roads and trails known collectively as the Ho Chi Minh Trail, and (2) assisting in interdiction of trail traffic by controlling strikes of other aircraft.[81] Thailand-based gunships as well as Spookies from Pleiku and Da Nang flew Tiger Hound area missions.[82] The busy gunships averaged two armed reconnaissance sorties a night with each sortie lasting about six hours.[83] These were pioneer flights over a rugged and inadequately charted mountainous area where the enemy had long been skillful in concealing trail development. Col. John F.

Three Phases of the Gunship Interdiction Task

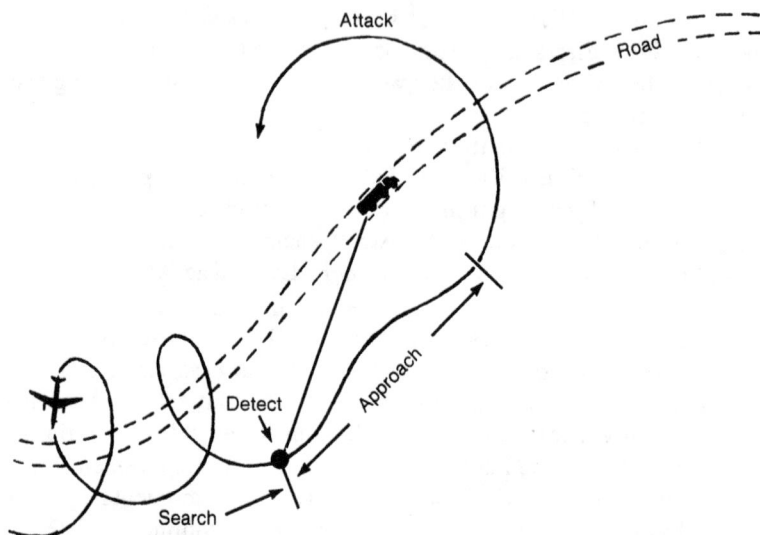

Groom, Tiger Hound Task Force commander, sized up the Spooky interdiction effort: "We put them over known roads and trails when we were sure there was truck traffic, and with their own flare capability and side-firing guns, they have done exceptionally well in the Tiger Hound area."[84]

The roadwatch "truck-busting" mission on the night of February 23 was typical. Capt. William Pratt and his AC–47 crew spotted a truck convoy halted where a bomb crater gutted the road. Working in a valley with sheer cliffs, the gunship first struck the rear truck setting it afire. Next the aircraft began an orbiting strike maneuver around the trapped trucks. The convoy replied to the attack with intense small arms fire. The gunship stayed on the target, destroying eleven trucks and damaging many more.[85]

As the number of AC–47 interdiction sorties rose, a system of truck-busting began to take shape. Two Spooky gunships from Udorn were scheduled to fly continuous coverage at night over the Cricket area and part of the Steel Tiger area of Laos. One aircraft took off at 1800, the other at midnight. The gunships flew a planned schedule that allowed at least four contacts per night with each of the roadwatch teams operating clandestinely around the Ho Chi Minh Trail network. After flying to the designated area, a Lao observer on board the gunship radioed the roadwatch team. If a target was indicated in the area the gunship would drop flares along a road or trail in an effort to acquire the target. Once a truck was spotted, the gunship went into its strike orbit and fired away. At times it would call for additional strike aircraft. This system was first employed on March 21 and proved effective. The success in striking and harassing trucks at night was tempered by the enemy's dogged persistence in strengthening his air defenses and in using hundreds of troops and coolies to repair roads quickly, build new ones, and remove damaged or destroyed vehicles from the roads.[86]

The AC-47 gunships also flew reconnaissance and forward air control missions at night to complete the twenty-four hour roadwatch begun by O-1E aircraft during the day. The gunships covered the Tiger Hound area toward the south end of the Laotian panhandle and Cricket operations were flown in the north portion. Hence for the first time effective around-the-clock capability seemed possible. In addition, the gunships shared airborne battlefield command and control center (ABCCC) functions with C-130A aircraft, thus providing on-the-scene coordination, target validation by Laotian authority, and forward air controlling.[87]

The interdiction success of the gunships attracted trouble. The enemy responded with more and better air defense. Communist forces were equipped with various antiaircraft weapons including 37-mm guns, which outstripped the range of Spooky's miniguns. As a result, by June 30, 1966, four gunships were lost to ground fire, three of them downed over Laos.[88] This was nearly one-fourth of the entire Southeast Asia gunship force and triggered a reassessment of gunship utilization in the more hostile environment of Laos. The 4th Air Commando Squadron had replaced half the losses with aircraft based in South Vietnam. Nevertheless, the squadron commander recommended to the 14th Air Commando Wing that the gunships be returned to close air support in South Vietnam.[89] His recommendation was based on improved enemy defenses, the AC-47's vulnerability due to slow speed and aerial tactics used, the difficulty in operating over the rugged terrain, combat exposure time (about 800 hours of night combat per crew in a twelve-month period), the questionable suitability of the gunship for the forward air controller mission, and the need for more air support in South Vietnam for hamlet and outpost defense. The wing commander, Seventh Air Force,[90] PACAF, and Pacific Command (PACOM), agreed with the proposed redeployment. On July 20 the 4th Air Commando Squadron flew its last Tiger Hound mission.[91] By the end of August all gunships had departed Thailand.[92]

The withdrawal of the AC-47s from Thailand tied in with other plans and actions. A case in point was the deployment of A-26s for interdiction missions over Laos. When the Air Force first directed that AC-47s be sent to Thailand, Gen. Hunter Harris, Jr., Commander in Chief, PACAF, doubted the gunships could survive the hostile environment over Laos. He expressed some of his reservations to General McConnell, Air Force Chief of Staff. The latter noted that the gunships would have to operate within range of enemy ground weapons in Laos. He proposed A-26 aircraft as a possible alternative to the gunship and offered eight of them for evaluation.[93] General Harris accepted this substitution for the AC-47s with the concurrence of Ambassador Sullivan and the Thai government. In June 1966 the A-26s began interdiction sorties over southern Laos.[94] Also reinforcing the AC-47 withdrawal decision was the urgent need to relieve C-123s of their Vietnam night flare duties so they could return to an airlift role. It was felt the AC–47s returned from Thailand could probably handle the flare requirements.[95]

Previous to the decision to withdraw the AC–47s, the Air Force had planned to send eight more AC–47s and aircrews from the United States to Thailand to support a full-fledged interdiction effort over Laos. In January 1966 Ambassador Sullivan had asked for aircraft suitable for Operation Cricket, and the gunship was considered as part of the force to meet this requirement.[96] The Air Staff and Joint Chiefs of Staff approved the proposed additional AC–47s. The Secretary of Defense, however, was a bit reluctant to proceed, stating that he wanted to "limit Thailand deployment to those which are essential to fulfill mission requirements."[97] On May 25 General McConnell requested CINCPACAF to furnish further information in support of the deployment request.[98]

Based on this extra information provided by Air Force headquarters, the Office of the Secretary of Defense approved the AC–47 deployment. A date of October 1, 1966, was set for the aircraft to be in Thailand.[99] In the meantime, to make up for the loss of gunships, A–26 Counter Invaders assumed the interdiction role over Laos. This led the Seventh Air Force to request in September (with PACAF's concurrence) diversion of the additional AC–47s to South Vietnam for the defense of military bases.[100] When the Pacific Command concurred and forwarded this request to the Joint Chiefs on October 22, 1966, the supplemental AC–47s had already touched down at Clark AB, Philippines, on the way to Thailand.[101] The gunships were ordered held at Clark until the JCS approved the diversion. This approval was not received until December 22, and the additional AC–47s did not arrive at South Vietnamese bases until January of 1967.[102]

Col. Gordon F. Bradburn, Commander, 14th Air Commando Wing, had coupled his proposal for withdrawing AC–47s from Thailand with anticipated improvements in South Vietnam gunship operations. He pictured one AC/C–47 flying airborne alert from one-half hour before sunset to one-half hour beyond sunrise at each of the bases in the four corps areas of Vietnam. One more AC/C–47 would be put on fifteen minute ground alert at each base. Colonel Bradburn expected these actions to enhance gunship support in the corps areas, strengthen command control, and better centralize flare requirements. He estimated a seventy-eight percent in-commission rate could be maintained under his proposed schedule. Accepted by the Seventh Air Force, this airborne/ground alert program commenced on July 22, 1966.[103]

While most attention focused on combat operations in South Vietnam and Laos, the United States set in motion a major effort to shore up counter-insurgency forces in Thailand and Laos. Northern Thailand and Laos, so close to the central area of conflict, appeared marked for "national liberation" movements as South Vietnam had been in the late 1950s. In both countries the ingredients were there—poor transportation and communication networks, an economy at bare subsistence level, friction among ethnic groups, rugged isolated terrain suited for guerrilla bases, an inadequately trained and equipped constabulary, and inequitable distribution of land and resources. To thwart this growing threat the United States launched an extensive assistance and training program along with large base construction projects. Since mid-1964 the U.S. Air Force had assumed a large role in the effort by setting up a counterinsurgency training detachment, called Water Pump, at Udorn RTAFB in northern Thailand. By late 1965 another project (encompassing Water Pump) saw the formation of the composite 606th Air Commando Squadron at Nakhon Phanom RTAFB. The squadron and augmented operation bore the name of Lucky Tiger. The 606th was to have C-123s, T-28Bs, U-10Bs, and CH-3s. In early June 1966 it was decided to also add to the AC-47s because of their operational success. Eight AC-47s and 214 personnel were to be sent to Nakhon Phanom in September 1966.[104]

Air Force headquarters designated Warner Robins Air Materiel Area as weapon system control point for AC-47s destined for the 606th Air Commando Squadron. The contract with Air International of Miami specified that modification of four Gooney Birds into AC-47s begin by July 15, four more by August 1, with the first four due to go to Southeast Asia in early September. When September arrived, however, the gunships were not ready and the deployment date was slipped to October.[105] PACAF then revised the 606th's target date for full operational readiness to November 1.[106] Arrival of the AC-47s in late 1966 introduced the gunship concept to the Thais and Laotians. Spooky's utility as a counterinsurgency weapon was spreading.

The first full year of gunship operations had already demonstrated the weapon system's versatility and value. The gunship had successfully flown a wide range of missions, from protective cover for friendly convoys to the destruction of those of the enemy. Its around-the-clock operations extended over all areas of South Vietnam and Laos. Its airborne command and control and forward air controller functions became a valuable adjunct to other air operations. Most important, it helped fill the crucial void in night air operations, a void the enemy had been so skillfully exploiting both in South Vietnam and Laos. In early December 1965, for instance, only twenty-five percent of armed reconnaissance missions had taken place at night while eighty percent of the enemy traffic moved during darkness.[107] The gunship had a major part in the effort to correct this imbalance.

Impressive statistics for 1966 pointed to the extent of AC-47 operations and the gunship's effect on the enemy. The 4th Air Commando Squadron, the sole gunship unit, claimed successful defense of its 500th fort on the last day of 1966. Three more forts were added that night to end the year officially with a total of 503.[108] Men of the squadron were very proud of their role in helping defend outposts and hamlets, and running totals (the Spooky Count) were kept of the successes.[109] In all, during 1966 they dropped 81,700 flares and expended 13,616,643 rounds of 7.62-mm ammunition. In January more than 2,500 flares and 611,600 rounds were used, compared to a peak in December of 10,451 flares dropped and more than two million rounds expended. The squadron flew 5,584 sorties, which consumed about 25,000 hours of flying time, all accident-free. As for interdiction, the gunships were credited with 204 enemy trucks damaged or destroyed by the time they withdrew from Laotian operations in midyear.[110] Only an estimate could be made of total enemy killed by gunship strikes, but it was conservatively placed at well over 4,000.[111] In sum, the statistics show the scope of operations. However, it was often the letters and messages expressing the gratitude of embattled defenders—"if it had not been for the Spooky Birds . . ."—that most heartened the men of the 4th.[112] Lt. Col. Robert E. Gibson, the new squadron commander, summed up 1966: "We're proud of our record and hope to meet the challenge of 1967 with the same success."[113]

The compilation of operational statistics often does not reveal the extent of a unit's problems. As might be expected, the gunship squadron wrestled with some notable ones during its full year of combat operations. Most critical, of course, was the loss of four AC-47s during the first six months of 1966 (six gunships lost since November 1965). Projecting this loss rate over a year would have meant an 80 percent attrition rate for aircraft and 61.5 percent for personnel.[114] These figures graphically highlighted the AC-47's vulnerability in areas heavily defended by antiaircraft weapons as in Laos and led to the decision to commit the gunships exclusively to South Vietnam operations. The 4th also had difficulties with command control of its widely dispersed operating locations (aggravated by inadequate communications),[115] turnover of personnel,[116] a high dud rate in flares,[117] and inadequate facilities.[118] Inasmuch as the squadron had deployed in late 1965, most of its experienced personnel wound up the one-year Vietnam tour around the same time. Hence, the personnel turnover in October 1966 hit the unit far harder than a normal rotation would have. An investigation of the rise in flare duds looked into "kicker"* practices and moisture problems of outside flare storage. It turned up no specific cause for the many flare duds, but investigators did recommend better protection of the flares from the Vietnamese weather.[119]

Almost from the moment the gunship arrived in the combat theater, efforts got under way to improve its capability. Gunners of the 4th Air Commando Squadron recommended an important change—declination of the miniguns 12°. Under direction of SSgt. Wayman E. Hicks, gunner on the 4th's standardization crew, the guns were declined in 3° increments and 12° was found most desirable. In March advantages and disadvantages of the 12° declination were analyzed and the modification was approved. The first gun mounts entered the machine shop on April 1 and the new mounts were installed in twelve gunships by June 30.[120] Capts. Russel R. Young and Robert K. Stein, with Sergeant Hicks, further researched and tested the 12° declination, then published a new squadron manual on minigun operations.[121] The Air Force Armament Research and Technology Division at Eglin analyzed the squadron test results and published its findings in a brochure.[122] Adoption of the 12° declination decreased the angle of bank

---

*A "kicker" was the gunship crewmember charged with dropping the flares.

required, making it easier for the pilot to roll onto the target. It added stability to the gunship, permitting easier flare-handling and gunnery operations, decreased the slant range of the guns allowing for an increase in altitude, and raised the minigun's impact velocity.[123]

Two communication modifications and a flareholder improvement were likewise completed. All the gunships were equipped with a dual headset capability at the navigator position. This allowed the Vietnamese observer and the crew navigator to simultaneously monitor aircraft-ground communications, thereby saving time in this critical operation. In addition, an improved multichannel radio was installed.[124] Construction and installation of steelplated flare boxes by the rear cargo door allayed a nagging fear of crews that ground fire might set off a flare. The new boxes also kept flares from shifting in flight.[125]

Though not entirely successful, the tests made of the starlight scope and the .50-caliber machineguns in the AC-47s had great portent for the future. The Army-developed starlight scope enabled troops to see in the dark by intensifying reflected moonlight or starlight. On March 4, 1966, Major Jensen piloted a gunship that used a starlight scope over Attopeu with huge success in locating enemy troops. Tests of the scope on other occasions were inconclusive. Seeking a better truck-busting weapon, gunship crews evaluated the .50-caliber machinegun as a possible substitute for the 7.62-mm minigun. Both equipment tests were delayed after the Ubon-based test gunship was shot down over Laos. Aboard were the squadron and Seventh Air Force test project officers—Major Jensen and Maj. Joe Reilly. Some armament tests continued on gunships out of Da Nang but the results were inconclusive.[126] Despite problems, this testing pointed the way to major future development of gunship sensors and armament.

The momentum and success of 1966 gunship operations carried over into 1967. A major gunship augmentation got under way, reflecting the still-rising intensity of the fighting in South Vietnam and an even greater commitment of U.S. forces. Gunship operations roughly followed the 1966 pattern. Close air support missions predominated in the north of the country; and outpost and hamlet defense in the south. In the middle, or highland region, it was mostly air support but mixed with sorties to defend forts, U.S. Army Special Forces camps, or to assist in base defense.

Heavy fighting in South Vietnam's midsection led the 4th Air Commando Squadron to replace C-47 flareships assigned to C Flight at Nha Trang with AC-47s in January. C Flight and also B Flight at Pleiku now operated in the II Corps area but no formal division of the tactical area of responsibility existed for either flight. B Flight normally covered the area mainly to the north and west of Pleiku, C Flight from Bong Son south to Qui Nhon.[127] Locations of other 4th Air Commando Squadron flights remained the same: A Flight (Da Nang), I Corps; D Flight (Bien Hoa), III

Corps; and E Flight (Binh Thuy), IV Corps. All these flights operated on the same basic plan: two aircraft orbited on airborne alert to cover areas of usual enemy activity while one backup aircraft on ground alert provided additional assistance as required. (Only E Flight in the Mekong Delta kept two gunships on ground alert.)[128]

In the northern part of South Vietnam (I Corps), A Flight gunships continued to provide close support of U.S. Marine Corps, Republic of Korea (ROK), and ARVN troops. Gunship action in the first phase of Operation Lien Ket I—a joint Marine Corps, ROK, and ARVN thrust sixteen miles southwest of Chu Lai—typified the support of multinational forces. Six AC–47s supported friendly troops in close contact with the enemy from dusk to dawn on February 19. The gunships fired 123,000 rounds during more than twelve hours over the embattled area.[129] It was just such missions that prompted Lt. Gen. Robert E. Cushman, Jr., USMC, commander of the III Marine Amphibious Force, to commend the 4th Air Commando Squadron on September 26:

> Please extend to the members of the "Spooky" crews that have served with us here in I Corps my best wishes and congratulations for a continuing outstanding performance of duty. Immediate response and enthusiastic and devastating support have become the trademarks of "Spooky" in I Corps. "Spooky" crews have earned the profound respect of all whom they have supported of free world armed forces and have accounted for over 200 enemy confirmed killed and 520 enemy probably killed. Their splendid display of professionalism and devotion to duty have been a significant contribution to the defeat of enemy forces in I Corps. Well done![130]

In early 1967 poor weather over the I Corps area masked the Viet Cong movement to positions closer to bases near the coastal cities and bases at Hue, Da Nang, and Chu Lai. This more southerly enemy activity caused abandonment of alert aircraft at Dong Ha near the Demilitarized Zone and generated more II Corps gunship missions. In addition, major ground sweeps against infiltration routes from Cambodia (Operation Sam Houston) called for many AC–47 sorties.[131]

Defense of forts and hamlets, however, remained the major gunship effort. On the night of June 27/28, Dragonships from Binh Thuy AB in the Delta region flew four sorties in defense of Tra Ech outpost in Phong Dinh Province. About a hundred Viet Cong were launching a heavy attack on the post with 82-mm mortars and 75-mm recoilless rifles. By the time the first Spooky arrived and fired into Viet Cong positions along canals adjacent to the outpost, the intense enemy fire had killed ten of the defenders and wounded two. When flares lighted the area, the Viet Cong ceased their attacks but resumed them the instant the flares flickered out. Another AC–47 was called in when flares of the first were used up. Three armed helicopters added their firepower as did fighters directed by the gunships. By the time the fight was over, the gunships had fired 29,500 rounds in helping to repulse the Viet Cong. The night's performance constituted a milestone—the 1,000th outpost successfully assisted by

Spooky crews.[132] A similar defense of Headquarters Quang Tin Province on the morning of September 6 drew praise from General Westmoreland, MACV commander, who offered his "heartiest congratulations to aircrews involved for this outstanding example of quick reaction and professional airmanship resulting in significant loss to the enemy."[133]

Earlier in 1967, high-level interest in the greater use of the gunships for base defense was aroused after the Viet Cong bombarded Da Nang AB and the adjoining Vietnamese village of Ap Do during the early morning hours of February 27. The shelling killed forty-seven persons and wounded forty-five others, including twelve and thirty U.S. servicemen respectively. Eleven U.S. aircraft were destroyed or damaged.[134] This was the first time the enemy had put into action his 140-mm rockets which gave him an effective range beyond the base's defense perimeter. The implications for base defense throughout South Vietnam were immediately obvious. Any airfield the enemy judged worthy of attack was now a potential target. He could fire from previously prepared sites and drastically cut his time in position during an attack. What's more, the vast firepower of the Russian-made 122-mm and 140-mm rockets could be devastating. These factors underscored an urgent need for more aircraft to bolster the static ground defenses of air bases.[135]

The Da Nang attack touched off a reassessment of the base defense system and a fresh look at the gunship role. The first reaction was to expand the alert orbit over Tuy Hoa and several other bases.[136] This proved largely an expedient since the Viet Cong timed their attacks while the AC-47s were on the far side of the orbit. What was really needed to help counter the expected upturn in enemy attacks was an AC-47 alert orbit over every base throughout the critical night hours. As one base security officer sized up the situation: "At the present time and in the foreseeable future the AC-47 is the best deterrent we have to attack by mortar, recoilless rifle, or rocket."[137]

Reacting to the Da Nang attack, Air Force headquarters asked the Commander in Chief, PACAF, on February 28 if he needed additional AC-47s for airbase security.[138] On March 8 the latter replied that more AC-47s were desirable but not if a "trade-off of other priority items would be required."[139] The Seventh Air Force pressed PACAF on March 20 for an increase in the 4th Air Commando Squadron's total AC-47 authorization from twenty-two to thirty-two along with 297 additional manpower spaces. In support of this request, Seventh Air Force cited the Da Nang attack, noting that the AC-47 had continually proved an effective weapon system in combating night attacks but that "the present force of twenty-two AC-47s is insufficient to provide all-night airborne alert over major U.S. military bases."[140] In fact, about one-half the bases could not be covered. Faced with more frequent and aggressive night attacks on South Vietnamese bases and military complexes, the Seventh Air Force believed the extra gunships essential. As an interim measure, it would divert four C-47s, equipped for psychological warfare, to nightly flare missions beginning March 23. An analysis of enemy attacks had shown the hours from 2200 to 0300 as most crucial. The AC–47s on hand would fly most sorties during these hours.[141] Intermittent flaredrops would be made around Bien Hoa Air Base with all-night flaring in a six- to nine-mile area surrounding Da Nang.[142]

Headquarters PACAF urged CINCPAC to approve the Seventh Air Force request without a trade-off.[143] In turn, CINCPAC sought Joint Chiefs' approval of the requirement but warned that manpower spaces were not available "to compensate for requirements submitted."[144] On April 13 CINCPACAF told the Air Force Chief of Staff that the base security situation· was critical and that the additional gunships were a priority matter.[145]

Two enemy attacks further highlighted the crucial condition of base defense—one on May 7 at Binh Thuy AB destroying four A–1 aircraft and two Vietnamese H–34 helicopters, another on May 12 at Bien Hoa destroying one F–100, one O–1, one Vietnamese A–1H, and some facilities. COMUSMACV and the Seventh Air Force therefore moved quickly to convert some C–47s obtained from the Vietnam Air Force's 417th Transport Squadron to gunships. Ten were to be converted by September 1 and another six by January 1, 1968, but supply shortages, primarily guns, plagued the conversion program. There was some hope that new MXU–470 guns for American AC–47s would arrive and free the older SUU–11 guns for the Vietnamese. The MACV commander went all out to spur the lagging operation, declaring that "the requirement for the tactical firepower capability of the AC–47 aircraft is immediate."[146] He also added his weight and solid backing to the request for additional gunships in a message to CINCPAC.[147] In the meantime, the Seventh Air Force informed COMUSMACV it was arming UH–1F helicopters for defense of jet air bases.[148]

The request for extra gunships hit Air Force headquarters and the Defense Department at a time when debate was under way to find a better aircraft as follow-on for the AC–47. Consequently, there was some hesitancy in approving an increase in AC–47s. Then too, the Air Staff advised CINCPACAF that even after the Secretary of Defense's approval, it might be six to eight months before the gunships could be in place. Alarmed, the PACAF commander replied that he saw the "six to eight month delay in receiving additional capability inconsonant with urgency of requirement" and urged the time be sharply reduced. He proposed "beginning modification" of the aircraft at once on the basis of advanced attrition. This would, his argument ran, point up the possibility of fast deployment of the additional AC–47s and might help get the request approved.[149] At the same time, PACAF directed that the Seventh Air Force survey its current resources to see if more gunship capability might be obtained in some way.

With base defense still a hot subject in Vietnam, MACV planned a seminar for June 10, 1967, to discuss it. In preparing for the seminar and conducting the PACAF-directed survey of current resources, the Seventh Air Force examined various aircraft as possible substitutes for gunships.[150] It evaluated but rejected the C–7A Caribou as inferior to the AC–47 in loiter time and armament capability.[151] In the eyes of Seventh Air Force officials the quickest way to beef up airbase defense was to expedite the VNAF C–47 conversion. To this end, a Southeast Asia Operational Requirement (SEAOR) was submitted to Air Force headquarters on May 28. It covered the modification of sixteen VNAF C–47s with SUU–11 guns then being removed from American AC–47s to make way for the new MXU–470 guns.[152]

On May 27 Air Force headquarters advised the PACAF commander that five "advanced attrition replacement AC–47s" would be rushed in response to urgent airbase defense requirements—delivery hopefully to begin about August 15. Simultaneously, the Air Staff asked TAC to see if it could spare PACAF some AC–47s, then receive replacements from among the five AC–47s due out of modification around August 15.[153] TAC replied that it could send PACAF two gunships without seriously harming its Southeast Asia training program.[154] Air Force headquarters therefore directed TAC to have the best available crews ferry the aircraft to PACAF as soon as possible. Near the end of June and before the two gunships left TAC, the Air Staff informed CINCPACAF that substitutions of equipment would insure delivery of the additional AC–47s within four months of the Secretary of Defense's approval of the AC–47 request, an approval still pending. The Air Staff further stipulated that upon such approval the five advanced attrition gunships would be applied against the ten additional AC–47s.[155] The PACAF commander approved the accelerated deployment of the five gunships. He turned down TAC's offer of the two gunships, noting that expenditure of funds and equipment for their transfer seemed unwarranted.[156]

While these steps were being taken to shore up airbase defenses and augment the gunship force, the enemy launched a second major attack on Da Nang. It came early on July 15—a seventeen minute barrage of 140-mm and 122-mm rockets that created havoc. Eight Air Force men were killed and 138 wounded. Eleven aircraft were destroyed, thirty-one damaged. Structural damage was slight except in the bomb-storage area. Five AC–47s supported Da Nang during the attack, dropping flares and raking the rocket-firing positions with 26,000 rounds.[157] Once again the base defense problem was spotlighted but not resolved.

On August 15, the Office of the Secretary of Defense revised guidelines for additional military deployments to Southeast Asia, authorizing an additional ten AC–47s for Southeast Asia effective October 1967. In line with this, the Air Force directed the 14th Air Commando Squadron (Fire Support) be activated in October 1967 with an authorization of sixteen AC–47s. It also cut the gunship authorization of the 4th Air Commando Squadron (Fire Support) from twenty-two to sixteen.[158] Thus the thirty-two authorized AC–47s were evenly split between the two gunship squadrons.

To fill the increased authorization and to meet attrition requirements, Air Force headquarters instructed AFLC to modify eight more AC–47s by December 1967.[159] Headquarters noted that the aircraft were available from command excess and should be programmed promptly into the contract facility for inspection and repair as necessary, camouflaged, and modified. On September 9, 1967, the Air Staff requested TAC and PACAF to coordinate deployment schedules, personnel requirements, and Southeast Asia base problems.[160]

Representatives of the Seventh Air Force and the 14th Air Commando Wing (the gunship parent unit) met on September 15, 1967, to plan operations for the larger gunship force. They produced a new plan for AC–47 deployment (Table 1). The operational concept called for a better contribution by gunships to airbase defense.[161] The Forward Operating Location (FOL) at Da Nang would be augmented and a new FOL added at Phan Rang. The special value of Da Nang stemmed from its nearness to an operationally active area. Phan Rang gave greater tactical dispersion and better coverage in that area.[162] The larger (five aircraft) flights at Da Nang and Binh Thuy would have the heavier firepower essential in the highland and delta regions. The two flights at Nha Trang on the central coast would form a supplementary pool for support either to the north or south.[163] The entire concept pivoted upon the dispersal of flexible and quick-reacting units of workable size.

The 14th Air Commando Squadron was to be activated on October 25, 1967, at Nha Trang AB and assigned to the 14th Air Commando Wing. Since the squadron would be organized on a one-officer-and-one airman basis, it would likely be December before all its aircraft and aircrews

TABLE 1 AC-47 DEPLOYMENT

Flight	Air Base Location	Aircraft	Aircrews
	4th Air Commando Squadron		
A	Da Nang (FOL)	5	7
B	Pleiku (FOL)	4	6
C	Phu Cat (FOL)	4	6
D	Nha Trang (MOB)	3	5
	14th Air Commando Squadron		
A	Nha Trang (MOB)	3	5
B	Phan Rang (FOL)	4	6
C	Bien Hoa (FOL)	4	6
D	Binh Thuy (FOL)	5	7

FOL. forward operating location; MOB— main operating base
Source: Staff Summary Sheet, 7th AF, AC 47 Realignment, September 16, 1967.

arrived to implement the new operational plan. In the interim the 4th Air Commando Squadron was to continue as before.[164] When the additional aircraft and aircrews arrived in the theater, they were first to go to the main operating base at Nha Trang then to the 14th ACSq's operating flights.[165]

Amid these preparations a modified C–130A—the prototype Gunship II—reached Nha Trang AB on September 21 to undergo Southeast Asia combat evaluation. This follow-on gunship carried four 20-mm Vulcan cannons, four 7.62-mm miniguns, sensors, and illumination devices.[166] It represented a major advance in gunship development, but its effectiveness could only be surmised at that time.[167] The Seventh Air Force, however, had already gone on record as recommending just this aircraft to replace the effective but aging AC–47. Still, the substitution of AC–130 gunships for AC–47s remained uncertain at this point.

Refinements to perfect the AC–47 went on. In January 1967, the Air Force received the first MXU–470/A minigun modules for the Spooky aircraft.[168] Features of the new gun, surpassing those of the SUU–11A, included: electric loading, a vertical drum holding five hundred more rounds, easier access for inflight maintenance, and a simplified boresight. The MXU–470/A's vertical design also took up less space. It was anticipated that mounting the guns closer together would leave the cargo door clear. Further, the MXU–470/A was expected to overcome a serious problem of the SUU–11A—the need to manually load and delink belted ammunition during combat which at times dented or damaged rounds that could jam the drum-feeder system.[169] Two of the new guns were mounted on each of three AC–47s from C Flight, 4th Air Commando Squadron. Unfortunately, the mounting proved unsatisfactory, so all MXU–470/A modules were withdrawn pending a review of installation instructions.[170] The difficulties were largely overcome a few months later except for spare parts. These became so critical during July–September 1967 that the firing rate was cut back from 6,000 to 3,000 rounds per minute to prolong barrel life and reduce feeder mechanism wear. Concerted action of units in South Vietnam and WRAMA eventually eased the gun problems.[171]

Other AC–47 modifications centered on increased safety of operations. In Southeast Asia a newly designed ceramic, armorplated flareholder was installed along with a 2½-gallon, 100-pounds per square inch, water fire extinguisher.[172] Meanwhile, in the United States the Air Force and Navy jointly developed and tested a four-tube, twenty-four-flare, semiautomatic flare launcher. This remotely-controlled launcher could be reloaded in flight and jettisoned automatically should a flare accidentally ignite inside the aircraft. The Air Force Logistics Command concentrated on an emergency smoke removal system for the AC–47. Experience had shown crew survival to depend on swift removal of toxic smoke resulting from an onboard flare ignition. Evaluation of smoke removal kits began in late 1967.[173] Lastly, flak curtains were hung behind gun positions to protect gunners from shrapnel flying off an operating weapon.[174]* All these developments aimed at more crew security.

As 1967 ended the U.S. Air Force could point to another highly productive year of gunship operations. The Spooky Count had soared to 1,596 outposts and hamlets successfully defended. Crews spoke proudly of not having an outpost overrun while a dragonship was overhead.[175] Ammunition expenditure, peaking in September at 4,733,633 rounds, testified to the intense activity of the AC–47s.[176] Operations expanded even more as stepped-up enemy attacks impelled military commanders to look to the gunships as a critical supplement to base defenses. A total of 3,650 enemy were credited as confirmed kills for the AC–47s with about an equal number categorized as probable. The 4th Air Commando Squadron lost three aircraft to enemy ground fire. A fourth disappeared while on normal orbit off the coast near Cam Ranh Bay. A fifth crashed on landing and was destroyed at Binh Thuy AB. All losses happened during the first half of the year.[177]

Significantly, the first major gunship increase began in 1967. The year saw a new gunship squadron added, ten more AC–47s authorized, and conversion of some Vietnamese C–47s to gunships started. Entering the picture for the first time was the follow-on aircraft for the AC–47. Debate in Washington had seemingly settled on the C–119 as the best available replacement for the AC–47. Nonetheless, the AC–130A (Gunship II) had arrived in South Vietnam for combat evaluation. The gunship force was not only expanding in Southeast Asia (a sign of its efficiency), it was also on the climb to greater sophistication.

As 1968 began, there was an air of optimism in South Vietnam and Washington, that the tide in the war had turned against the Viet Cong and the North Vietnamese. U.S. and South Vietnamese officials warmed at the thought of their vastly reinforced air, ground, and naval forces arrayed against a foe believed weakening. They singled out the enemy's loss of men, decline in control over the population, and failure to mount major offensives as proof that the allies were closing in on their objectives. This optimism was severely jolted during the early morning hours of January 30 as the North Vietnamese touched off their month-long Tet† offensive. Coincident with the shock came American concern over the enemy's encirclement and siege of six thousand U.S. Marines and a South Vietnamese Ranger battalion at Khe Sanh.[178]

---

*Six explosions, apparently due to hangfires or cookoffs, took place with injury to crewmen during July minigun operations.

† The Vietnamese New Year based on the first day of the lunar year. In 1968 it fell on January 30.

Before the Tet offensive, military commanders in South Vietnam had shared the pervading optimism but considered a large-scale enemy assault as highly possible. Gen. William W. Momyer, Commander, Seventh Air Force, and General Westmoreland both expressed such concern in January. Nevertheless, the period of Tet was a most important celebration, and the Saigon government left ARVN units (outside I Corps) at forty to fifty percent of their normal strength. Some units were on alert, many were not.[179] Consequently, the severe and widespread attacks rocked American and South Vietnamese troops. Heavy fighting hit Saigon. The old Vietnamese capital of Hue was overrun and largely destroyed in the ensuing battle. The enemy struck 36 of 45 provincial capitals, 64 of 242 district capitals, and 50 hamlets. His attacks on major airfields and other installations destroyed 53 aircraft and damaged 344.[180] One of the enemy's greatest offensives of the war, it inflicted immense damage. Its timing, strength, and psychological shock (particularly on the American public) overshadowed any impact on the Viet Cong and North Vietnamese strength.

The enemy's Tet offensive dictated an almost complete commitment of airpower. Spooky gunships were hard-pressed to keep up with demands on them. On several occasions AC–47s on airborne alert were able to instantly pinpoint rocket and mortar positions firing on friendly installations. For example, as the offensive began, the 4th Air Commando Squadron AC–47s and crews were sent from Nha Trang and Phu Cat to Da Nang to bolster security in that often hit area. On the night of March 3/4 the Viet Cong and North Vietnamese assaulted twelve separate locations in the Da Nang tactical area of operations but did not strike the air base. At the time, Spooky 11 and Spooky 12 were flying airborne combat air patrol over Da Nang and its helicopter satellite field, Marble Mountain. Minutes after the enemy attacked southwest of the main base, Spooky 11 engaged the site firing the rockets. Secondary explosions erupted. The next day, ground parties came upon unused rocket rounds indicating a premature end of the enemy attack.[181] The quick response of the gunships in striking enemy firing locations was credited with curtailing the attacks and reducing damage and losses.

The 14th Air Commando Squadron, under the command of Lt. Col. Charles A. Hodgson, became operational January 15. Almost at once its AC–47s were tested in the southern half of the country by the Tet offensive. During February, with only thirteen aircraft, the 14th averaged eleven missions and 168,000 rounds expended each night. In the first three months its gunships flew 170 missions in support of troops in contact, 491 in defense of villages, and six in defense of air bases. Gunship and maintenance crews had to exert an all-out effort to handle the expanded flying requirements.[182]

Two other operations underscored the advantages of the Spooky gunships in 1968. The night of March 1, Spooky 41 and Spooky 42 attacked a 700-ton munitions trawler at Bai Cay Bay, eleven miles north of the gunships' base at Nha Trang. The trawler was exchanging fire with

Major Battles—Tet 1968

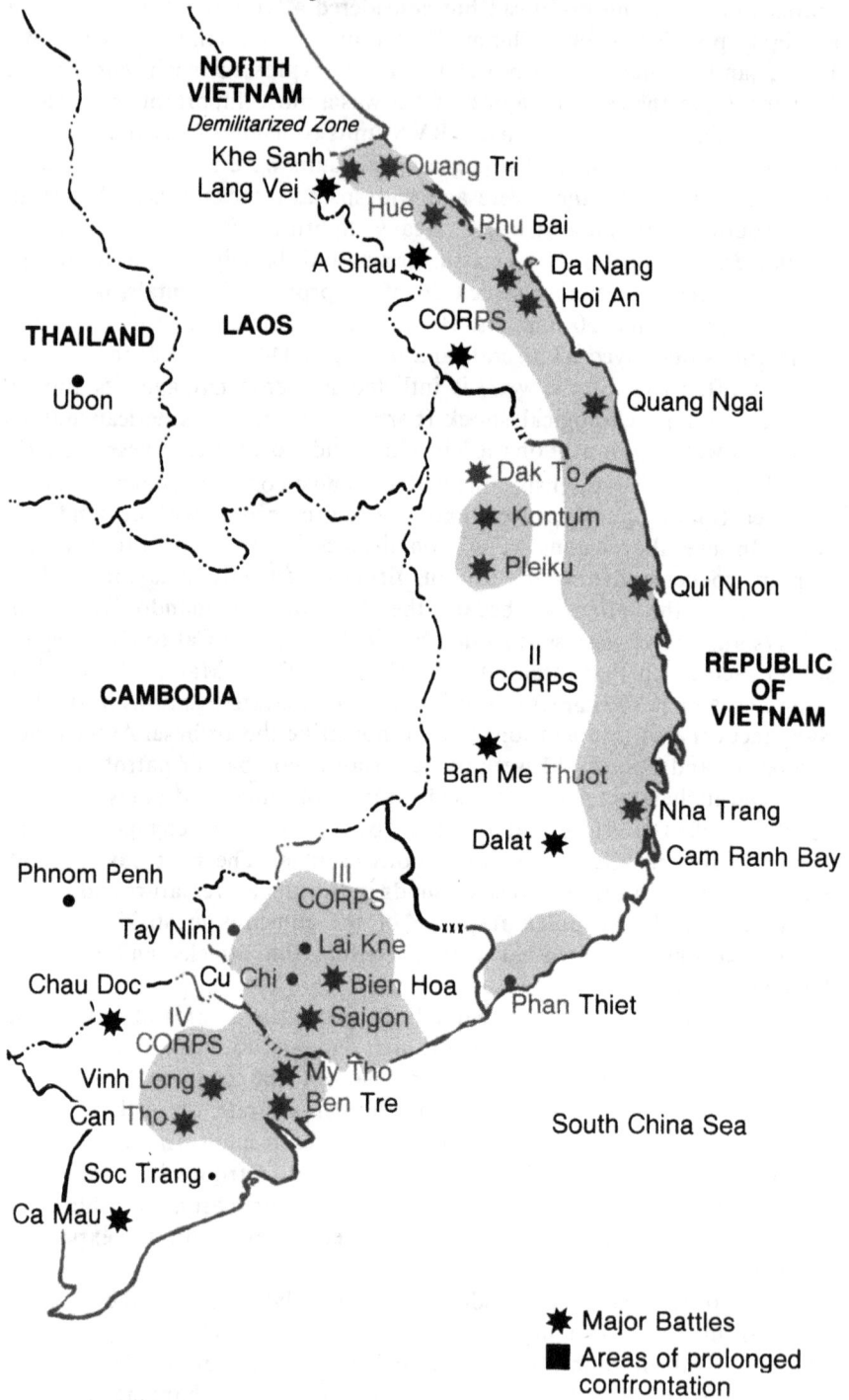

NORTH VIETNAM
Demilitarized Zone
Khe Sanh
Quang Tri
Lang Vei
Hue
Phu Bai
A Shau
Da Nang
Hoi An
I CORPS
Quang Ngai

THAILAND
Ubon

LAOS

Dak To
Kontum
Pleiku
Qui Nhon

II CORPS

CAMBODIA

REPUBLIC OF VIETNAM

Ban Me Thuot
Nha Trang
Dalat
Cam Ranh Bay

Phnom Penh
III CORPS
Tay Ninh
Lai Kne
Chau Doc
Cu Chi
Bien Hoa
Saigon
Phan Thiet
IV CORPS
Vinh Long
My Tho
Can Tho
Ben Tre
South China Sea
Soc Trang
Ca Mau

✹ Major Battles
■ Areas of prolonged confrontation

Location of Enemy Initiated Incidents
II Corps Tactical Zone
1969

I CTZ

Dak Pek

Ben Het

Bong Son

Dak To

BINH DINH

Phu My

KONTUM

Camp Radcliff

Phu Cat

Polei Kleng

Kontum

An Khe

Qui Nhon

Plei Mrong

Chu Pa Mountains

N

Pleiku

PLEIKU

Cheo Reo

Tuy Hoa

Plei Me

PHU BON

PHU YEN

Tieu Atar

KHANH HOA

Duc My

DARLAC

Ninh Hoa

Ban Me Thuot

Nha Trang

Duc Lap

Cam Ranh

TUYEN

NINH THUAN

Bu Prang

Dalat

QUANG DUC

Phan Rang

LAM DONG

BINH THUAN

Song Mao

Luong Son

III CTZ

Phan Thiet

61

U.S. and Vietnamese gunboats. In the words of Spooky 41's commander, Lt. Col. Richard C. Lothrop:

> We had been firing on the ship and it had run aground about twenty yards from the shore. It began burning. In a few minutes, the intensity of the fire had greatly increased. Then it just blew up. It was a spectacular explosion . . . A fireball went 1000 feet into the air. It was obviously a load of munitions.[183]

Lt. Col. Robert C. Dillon, commander of Spooky 42 (which relieved Spooky 41), reported:

> There was a large secondary explosion when we fired on the tree line just north of the beach area where the ship was grounded. Ten minutes later we were working over an area southwest of the burning ship when we caused another secondary explosion about 180 feet up the side of a hill.[184]

Together, Spooky 41 and Spooky 42 expended more than 38,000 rounds while on the scene from 0130 to 0700. They were credited with sinking one ship and destroying tons of enemy munitions.[185]

The second Spooky operation occurred in western Quang Duc Province. It was in defense of a compound at Duc Lap consisting of MACV subsector headquarters, Civilian Irregular Defense Group camp, and outposts. The Viet Cong and North Vietnamese opened up on the compound at 0105 on August 23. Firing of rockets and mortars was instantly followed by a sapper attack on key positions. U.S. Army helicopters arrived within thirty minutes of a call for air support. Two Spookies from Nha Trang and Pleiku joined the action fifteen minutes later. At once they illuminated the area and raked the defense perimeter with minigun fire. Enemy sappers cut through extensive wire emplacements and several fire fights broke out within the compound. Eight American advisors, six wounded, abandoned their burning bunker at 0700 to take up positions on the northeast defense perimeter. The gunships experienced heavy automatic fire from at least ten antiaircraft sites spotted around the embattled area. Maj. Daniel J. Rehm, pilot of Spooky 41, observed:

> When we arrived, the buildings in the compound were all afire and the men were grouped in a blockhouse below the burning operations center. I set up a quick orbit of the area and began firing on targets about 200 to 300 meters from the camp. Almost immediately we began receiving intense antiaircraft fire from four different points. I began with a long burst at a target from my mini-guns but when the tracers started to fly close to us, I moved to another altitude and began to "peck" with short bursts at the enemy locations.[186]

The enemy held to the attack in the teeth of an onslaught of gunships, tactical fighters, B–52s, and assorted Army aircraft. For the next several nights, at least one Spooky supplied flare illumination and firepower over Duc Lap. In 228 flying hours the gunships expended 761,044 rounds and 1,162 flares. During the first days of the assault as many as four AC–47s worked the area simultaneously. The heavy air traffic led to the designation of the first aircraft over the target (usually a gunship) as on-scene commander. His job was to assure safe altitude separation, target entry and departure, and maximum on-target fire of all aircraft. Most important, however, was that all this air effort saved another outpost. The AC–47s not only dealt the attackers savage blows but stiffened the confidence of the defenders—particularly at night. As the men at Duc Lap put it, Spooky truly became their "Guardian Angel."[187]

Excellence of gunship operations brought the Presidential Unit Citation in June 1968 to the 14th Air Commando Wing and thereby to the 4th Air Commando Squadron. The award covered the wing's operations in South Vietnam from March 8, 1966, to March 7, 1967.[188] On July 3 the 14th Air Commando Wing also passed the 100,000th mission mark in the Republic of Vietnam.[189] The gunships figured prominently in the attainment of both these milestones. Moreover, as the mission milestone was reached, the gunship squadrons celebrated their own successful defense of 2,284 allied outposts[190] and the Spooky Count continued to mount.

The nature of AC–47 operations deviated little during the year but there were some organizational changes. On May 1 the 14th Air Commando Squadron became the 3d Air Commando Squadron (Fire Support).[191] After a further redesignation on August 1 the wing and two squadrons became the 14th Special Operations Wing, 3d Special Operations Squadron, and 4th Special Operations Squadron.[192]

The need for closer relations with ground units became evident at midyear. The constant turnover of ground personnel prompted some Spooky crews to report that ground controllers did not know what a gunship was or what it could do. This gap in understanding impaired the quality of gunship ground support. Hence the 14th Special Operations Wing* and the gunship squadrons tried to brief Spooky's operational capabilities to members of the Direct Air Support Centers (DASCs) and air liaison officers in each of the four corps areas.[193] Some progress along this line had been made over the years since the gunships first appeared in Southeast Asia. For example, the U.S. Army's I Field Force Vietnam had written a regulation explaining the missions, characteristics, capabilities, limitations, rules of engagement, and operations of the gunships. It briefly covered what a ground commander needed to request and employ a gunship. In addition, an effort was made to keep the regulation up to date. Nevertheless, maintaining liaison with the Army on Spooky operational capability seemed a recurring problem.†

---

*On August 1, 1968, the "Air Commando" designation was changed to "Special Operations."

†To improve communications with ground troops, a pamphlet on "Gruntisms" (terminology and vocabulary used by ground troops) and Southeast Asia radio terminology was available.

Scenes of Duc Lap Special Forces Camp, August 1968, where USAF gunships beat off a 4,000-man enemy force.

Top: Duc Lap; below: Army Lt. W. L. Harp and USAF Capt. W. F. Arnold, a forward air control team that diverted an airstrike at the camp.

The Direct Air Support Center in each corps area formed the key link in gunship operations. Ground units requested Spooky support through the proper support center by giving a unit call sign along with a primary and alternate radio frequency (FM, UHF, VHF, or HF). The DASC relayed this information to a Spooky on airborne or ground alert. In light of the scarcity of gunships, it was understood they would be diverted only to assist troops in contact with the enemy. Once Spooky and the engaged unit were in contact, the ground controller marked the location of friendly elements and the enemy's position by fire arrow (or other pyrotechnic), strobe light, or flashlight. If possible, the ground controller also supplied information on probable enemy routes of approach and withdrawal, location of any friendly artillery fire, and the maximum arc of such fire above the terrain. Next the gunship dropped flares on order of the ground commanders. The rules of engagement forbade Spooky's firing on a target until contact with the ground commander was made directly or through forward air controllers. Furthermore, Spooky could not open fire without a forward air controller clearance unless the ground commander identified himself and reported an emergency. At times a "walk-in"* adjustment of fire would be coordinated between the ground controller and gunship crew.

In September 1968 an Air Force experiment coupled an AC-47 with a Marine helicopter gunship. Dubbed Night Hawk, this night hunter-killer operation had the helicopter use a night observation device (NOD) to locate enemy troop concentrations and mark the target area for Spooky's superior firepower. The first mission on September 16 obtained no results. The same was true of a later "well planned and well executed" mission.[194] Commanders considered the concept promising, but Night Hawk never became a standard operation. It did, however, bring to the fore the need for a night observation device in the AC-47 so it could detect and destroy targets without aid from other aircraft.[195]

Several AC-47 modifications were considered and tested during the year. The Special Air Warfare Center requested a semiautomatic flare launcher for its gunships, complete with bulletproof jettisonable flare-storage containers. The center added to this request the proposed installation of an emergency smoke-removal (eraser) system for six AC-47s.[196] Both these improvements were eventually to become standard on gunships. Additionally, to vary the use of C-47 aircraft, SAWC asked that some of the AC-47s' flare launchers be pallet-mounted for rapid installation and removal. Since August, Microtale sensor-monitoring receivers had been evaluated in Southeast Asia. The results turned out so well that the Seventh Air Force proposed in October that twenty-six AC-47s be so equipped. It maintained that with the growth of airdropped sensor fields, the gunship's sensor monitor refined target detection in enemy base areas, along trails,

---

*A step-by-step adjustment of fire by the forward air controller until the gunship had zeroed in on the target.

and around friendly bases. The Seventh Air Force accordingly recommended the portable receiver be used in all gunship aircraft.[197]

The year 1968 had commenced with frenzied response to the enemy's Tet offensive. It closed with the AC-47s showing steady solid performance in a variety of missions. Perhaps only a few people realized that 1968 was to be the peak year of Air Force AC-47 operations and strength. Signs of decline came into view—the equipping of the Vietnamese Air Force with Spookies and the planned arrival of the more advanced AC-119s.

The year 1969 would mark the final year of Air Force Spooky operations in the Southeast Asian war. Both the 3d and 4th Special Operations Squadrons would be inactivated and their aircraft turned over to the Vietnamese Air Force and Royal Laotian Air Force. The return of the Spookies to Laotian operations after an absence of more than three years would leave in Thailand at year's end only a trace of the once-strong AC-47 force. While most attention fell on unit inactivation and the return to Laotian operations, Spooky would fly the usual missions in South Vietnam almost up to the year's close.

The dragonships went back to Laos, because that portion of the Southeast Asian war took a sudden turn for the worse. The conflict there had seesawed since 1962. Each dry season (roughly from mid-September to mid-May) the North Vietnamese and Pathet Lao* would move from bases in northeast Laos toward the Plain of Jars. Every wet season the Royal Laotian forces and those under the Meo† General Vang Pao would strike back as the enemy met with supply problems. In December 1967 the enemy set about making the roads more serviceable in bad weather and stockpiling supplies. This let him push farther into central Laos, where he ensconced himself as poor weather arrived. From January 1 to May 15, 1969, an enemy offensive had wrested thirty-four major operational or support (Lima Site)‡ bases from pro-government forces in the northern (Barrel Roll) area of Laos.[198] The rapid loss of Lima Sites and splintering of government forces brought on a crisis by March.

The 1969 crisis siphoned aircraft from Commando Hunt** operations: C-130 Blind Bat flareships, AC-130 Spectre gunships, and at times C-123 Candlestick flareships. This diversion grew until it hurt Commando Hunt

---

*A Laotian communist military force or person.

†Meo—An aboriginal people of China inhabiting southwest China and the northern parts of Laos, Thailand, and Vietnam.

‡Lima Site—An aircraft landing site (dirt strip) used as a resupply point.

**Commando Hunt I, III, V, and VII were air interdiction campaigns directed against the flow of supplies from North Vietnam to Viet Cong and North Vietnamese forces in South Vietnam and Cambodia. These campaigns in southern Laos (Steel Tiger area of operations) bore numerical designations that changed with the semiannual monsoonal shift. The northeast-monsoon, or dry-season campaigns, took place in 1968/1969, 1969/1970, 1970/1971, and 1971/1972. They covered roughly the period from October through April.

Laos

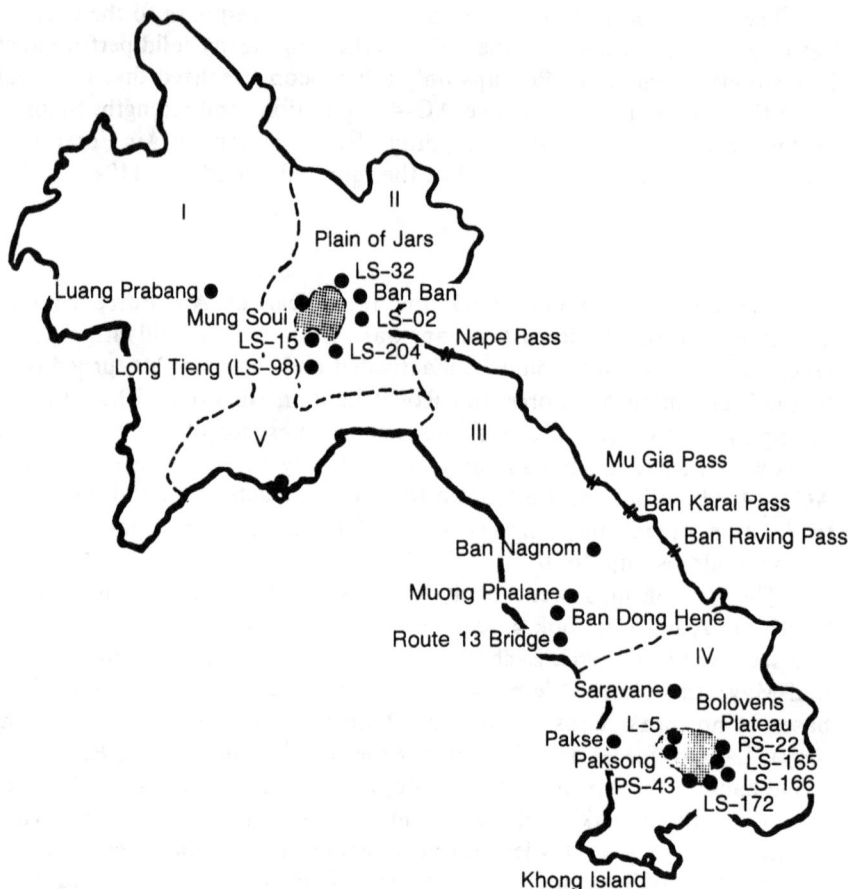

operations. To fill the gap temporarily, the Seventh Air Force decided to shift some AC–47s to Thailand to help meet flaredrop/fire support requests from commanders in Laos.[199]

Col. William H. Ginn, Jr., Deputy Commander for Operations, 14th Special Operations Wing, flew to Laos to visit General Vang Pao to explain how the Thai-based Spooky gunships could best be used. He found the Meo leader hard-pressed by North Vietnamese attacks in Military Region II, the enemy apparently intending to oust Meo and Laotian units from the area north of the Plain of Jars. Colonel Ginn projected an aura of professional toughness in his meeting with Vang Pao as he sought to bolster Meo morale and convince his hosts that "we knew our business and that we were good at it." He provided the general with strobe lights for better marking of Meo positions and briefed Vang Pao on gunship capabilities. The colonel assured the general that he "had lost his last Lima Site."[200] The

Meo chief responded enthusiastically, and Colonel Ginn departed believing he had not only given Vang Pao more combat effectiveness but also a tremendous morale boost.

The Seventh Air Force in coordination with the Thirteenth Air Force ordered the Spooky gunships to Udorn RTAFB for support of Lima Site defense in the Barrel Roll area. Two AC-47s and twenty-three personnel from the 4th Special Operations Squadron (SOSq) went to Udorn on March 12 followed by an additional two AC-47s and twenty-eight personnel three days later.[201] Blue Chip (the out-country control agency at Headquarters, Seventh Air Force) would direct Spooky operations over Laos. The orders would be relayed through Alleycat, the nighttime orbiting airborne battlefield command and control center controlling the Spookies.[202] One AC-47 would be on night airborne alert backed up by another on ground alert.

Quickly the AC-47s moved into action. On the night of March 15, 1969, a ground forward air guide, called Swamprat, directed a Spooky and two A-1 aircraft against enemy troops attacking a friendly outpost. One ground unit reported: "Fire from the 'Spooky' was extremely accurate and following the attack, friendly troops reported seeing enemy troops carrying their wounded to high ground northeast of the target area." The outpost stayed in friendly hands.[203]

During March 19-20, Spooky put withering fire in enemy troops assaulting a friendly outpost. The site commander saw 175 to 200 enemy dead and wounded being carried from the battlefield. He attributed most of these casualties to AC-47 miniguns. On March 20 a forward air controller in the Bouam Long area reported an enemy withdrawal from an 82-mm mortar position in the wake of accurate Spooky fire.[204] Such actions did double duty. They broke up enemy attacks and at the same time lifted the morale of the besieged men. As in South Vietnam, the gunships were at their best against concentrations of troops breaking into the open in attacks on outposts.

Profuse praise poured in for gunship deeds in Laos. In May the American Air Attache in Vientiane, the Laotian capital, congratulated the Seventh Air Force for the "outstanding support" supplied by the Udorn Spooky detachment. He wrote: "The concentrated firepower provided by AC-47s of this detachment has been a major factor in site defense and air to ground support for tactical operations in northern Laos."[205] Site commanders expressed similar sentiments.[206] After commitments of the Spookies in March, no Lima Site fell, thus making good Colonel Ginn's promise to General Vang Pao. Indeed, the general recaptured some Lima Sites previously lost.

Recommendations that the AC-47s be left at Udorn grew out of their success in the Barrel Roll area of Laos.[207] Moreover, North Vietnamese strength in Laos had risen by four to five battalions. As of May 5, 1969, about nine battalions threatened nine hundred friendly troops defending Lima Sites 32 and 50.[208] In July CINCPACAF agreed that gunship operations might have to continue from Udorn but he suggested to the Seventh Air Force a possible permanent deployment of AC–119G gunships instead of the Spookies.[209] Meantime, the onset of the southwest-monsoon rain so limited air activity that two Udorn-based AC–47s were sent back to Vietnamese bases on June 9.[210]

Spooky successes in Laos also gave impetus to a program for converting Royal Laotian Air Force (RLAF) C–47s to gunships. Originally, four were to be modified. A series of events, however, caused abandonment of the conversion. The transfer of eight Vietnamese C–47s to the Laotians was arranged instead. The first five Vietnamese Air Force aircraft were turned over on July 5 and the last one on October 2, 1969. By September 30, 1969, five of these aircraft had been modified into gunships.[211] This equipping of the Royal Laotian Air Force with gunships was assisted by transfer of the 3d Special Operation Squadron's AC–47s to the Vietnamese Air Force.[212]

The significant downturn in Air Force Spooky strength marked the mounting stress on Vietnamization of the war, a highly publicized national policy embraced by the Nixon administration. The arrival of the follow-on AC–119G gunships began the one-for-one tradeoff that was to make the AC–47 surplus to Air Force needs. On June 26, 1969, all Spookies of D Flight, 3d Special Operations Squadron, were flown from Binh Thuy to Nha Trang, where their ceremonial transfer to the Vietnamese Air Force took place on June 30.[213] The 3d SOSq flew its last mission on August 7 and was inactivated on September 1, 1969.[214] This left the 4th SOSq the sole surviving Air Force Spooky unit and it was scheduled for inactivation on December 15, 1969.[215] The end of American Spooky operations was definitely in sight.

As the 3d Special Operations Squadron left the scene, the 4th SOSq had to reshuffle its AC–47 forces. It closed out its forward operating location at Phu Cat and took over the former 3d SOSq forward operating location at Bien Hoa. Squadron deployment then stood:[216]

Air Base Location	Aircraft	Missions Per Night
Da Nang (FOL)	4	3
Pleiku (FOL)	2	1
Nha Trang (MOB)	4	1
Bien Hoa (FOL)	3	2
Udorn (FOL)	2	2

The 4th Special Operations Squadron's return to control of AC–47 flights in the III and IV Corps areas of South Vietnam harked back to its 1965 operations in the war theater. Seemingly the 4th had come full circle after nearly four years of war.

Spooky deployment after the inactivation of the 3d SOSq was rather short-lived. The change of bases planned in the Nha Trang Proposal* and the anticipated arrival in late 1969 of the AC-119Ks would bring additional realignment in gunship force locations. However, the October 15, 1969, relocation of the 4th SOSq's flight and squadron headquarters from Nha Trang to Phan Rang was the sole major move involving AC-47s.[217] Before this shift, a Bien Hoa Spooky fell to enemy ground fire on September 1 and two others suffered damage from mortar fire at Pleiku. This forced a reduction of the 4th's missions to six airborne and one ground alert in September.[218]

As the Spookies gradually reduced operations, they could proudly look back over the year at a fattened statistical record. The AC-47s had averaged twenty sorties each night throughout the Republic of Vietnam. Flight A of the 4th SOSq, based at Da Nang, hit a new daily high on February 27 when it fired 219,800 rounds in defense of friendly forces.[219] During the first six months of 1969, the two Spooky squadrons were credited with 1,473 enemy killed.[220] The boast of having successfully defended more than 3,000 outposts, villages, and hamlets was often heard. The intense pride in this record stood out strongly in 14th Special Operations Wing's vigorous opposition to a Seventh Air Force suggestion that the call signs of the AC-47 and AC-119 be changed regularly.[†] In light of the gunship's reputation, the Wing reported, the call sign Spooky "identified the aircraft and its capabilities and is used frequently as the method for requesting the required support."[221] For the moment that argument won out.

With respect to Spooky's renown, a fitting event occurred on the night of March 2, 1969. Col. Conrad S. Allman, commander of the 14th Special Operations Wing, climbed into a 3d SOSq AC-47 to mark the Wing's 150,000th combat mission. This milestone total surpassed that of any other Air Force combat unit in Vietnam and the gunships had contributed a major portion of it. Two days later the 14th Wing was awarded the Vietnamese Cross of Gallantry with Palm—the first U.S. Air Force unit so honored by the Vietnamese government. In the course of the recognition, attention was called to such engagements as Dak To, A Shau, and Duc Lap where the Spookies had played important roles.[222]

An act of heroism on the night of February 24, 1969, epitomized the valor of Spooky crews. A 3d SOSq AC-47 (Spooky 71) was on combat air patrol in the Saigon area. Nearly 4½ hours passed before Maj. Ken Carpenter, aircraft commander, received word of enemy activity in the vicinity of Bien Hoa. As Spooky 71 turned to meet the enemy, the pilot and copilot spotted muzzle flashes on the southern and eastern perimeters of Long Binh Army Base. With hot activity below they moved into attack orbit

---

*The proposal to return Nha Trang Air Base to the Vietnamese was approved by CINCPACAF and CSAF between Jan 15-18, 1969, by COMUSMACV Feb 6, by CINCPAC Feb 19, and by JCS Feb 26.

† Seventh Air Force believed the continued use of the call sign Spooky alerted the enemy to the nature of the mission and allowed him to prepare defensive countermeasures.

and fired about 3,000 rounds. After the second pass, they were directed to give the ground troops more flare illumination about two miles south of Long Binh and to remain over the area. In the cargo compartment, Spooky 71's loadmaster, A1C John L. Levitow from Connecticut, was busily setting ejection and ignition controls on the MK–24, two-million candlepower, magnesium flares. He carefully handed the flares to one of the gunners, Sgt. Ellis C. Owen, who hooked them into the lanyard. The sound of mortar fire rose above the engine noise. A turn of the aircraft indicated the pilot was fixing on a new target. Then came the sudden shock of a blast, a white flash, showers of flying metal, and the sinking sensation of the aircraft veering sharply right and down. Crewmembers in the rear of the aircraft were thrown violently about and injured. Unknown at the time, a North Vietnamese Army 82-mm mortar shell had hit Spooky 71's right wing.[223]

At the moment of the blast, Sergeant Owen had one finger through the safety pin ring preparatory to dropping a flare. Knocked from his hand, the armed flare rolled on the floor. The crew knew it took but twenty seconds for the flare to ignite. They also knew the consequences of an ignited flare on board—the 4,000 degree Fahrenheit burn and the incapacitating toxic smoke. In that instant of crisis, A1C Levitow, severely injured with shrapnel on his right side, was dragging himself to the open cargo door to pull away one of his injured comrades. Suddenly he saw the armed flare for the first time. It was rolling between number one minigun and a jumble of spilled ammunition and storage cans. Filled with terror at the sight of the smoking flare, Levitow knew he had to get it out at once or all would be lost. Moving in pain and with great difficulty in the pitching gunship, he finally reached the flare. He grasped it and crawled slowly but determinedly to the open door. At last he pushed the flare out—it ignited almost instantly. Major Carpenter regained control of the aircraft and managed to get it and the injured crew back to Bien Hoa AB. Later he said, "It is my belief that this story could not have been told by any other member of my crew had Levitow failed to perform his heroic action." But the story was told and A1C John L. Levitow received America's highest military award, the Medal of Honor.[224]

The flight of Spooky 71 and A1C Levitow's brave actions were, in a sense, a fitting climax for all the many missions of AC–47 crews over a span of four years. Numerous crewmembers had responded courageously to emergencies and the enemy effort to knock them from the skies. Now the gunship missions had almost become routine.

In late October 1969 the 4th Special Operations Squadron Spookies engaged in their final major operation in South Vietnam. North Vietnamese regulars and Viet Cong had attacked between Bu Prang and Duc Lap on the II Corps border with Cambodia. Evidently the enemy wanted to push new supply routes into the interior of II Corps. In the ensuing thirty days the AC–47s flew two missions nightly. Frequently they landed, restocked ammunition and flares, then returned to the attack. The gunships fired more than 400,000 rounds and dropped more than 8,000 flares in support of ground units. Heavy ground fire, however, compelled adoption of modified combat techniques. The AC-47s maintained complete blackout over targets where they received intense ground fire, desynchronized the engines to hinder ground fire that keyed on engine noise, and moved off target for safer and faster reloading of the miniguns.[225]

As in past years, AC-47 operations had their difficulties in 1969. A serious shortage of 7.62-mm tracer ammunition developed in late May. Immediate steps were taken to conserve tracer rounds and thereby avoid having solely ball ammunition left for the miniguns. Units were ordered to use only ball ammunition in daytime training missions and to restrict the rounds expended for pilot upgrading. Expenditure of rounds on interdiction targets was held to 6,000 unless the firing touched off a secondary explosion or ground fire. By July the tracer shortages had tapered off.[226] In October and November all C-47s were scheduled for fuel-cell explosive-suppressant modifications which put more work on a burdened maintenance section.[227]

Problems arose in the manning of certain crew positions, mainly enlisted ones. Early in the year a shortage of gunners hampered the 4th SOSq's operational readiness. AC-47 loadmasters were also in short supply.[228] By the end of March, however, assignees began to catch up with projected inputs and shortages eased. High personnel turnover (nothing new to a gunship squadron or any other Southeast Asian unit) required continuous and aggressive in-country training programs. Moreover, a higher percentage of newly assigned personnel were recently flying-school graduates. This placed more stress on training, standardization, and checkout of aircrew members than ever before. It also dictated care in balancing the crew experience level at all forward operating locations.[229]

Force changes further hindered gunship operations. Arrival of the AC-119s and the phaseout of the AC-47s added, deleted, and moved gunship forces. Under the Nha Trang Proposal, the 14th Special Operations Wing and other units left Nha Trang and that base was returned to the Vietnamese. More force reshuffling was planned when the AC-119Ks arrived in Vietnam.[230] All this activity aggravated the normal difficulties in communication between many operating locations.

The upcoming inactivation of the 4th SOSq and phaseout of Air Force AC-47 operations forced a further review of AC-47 missions flown over Laos from Udorn RTAFB. Since it would probably take the Royal Laotian Air Force more than six months to attain an AC-47 capability,[231] proposals were made to support Lima Sites in the Barrel Roll area with AC-119Gs in lieu of AC-47s. On August 12, the Seventh Air Force directed two AC-47s at Udorn be replaced by two AC-119Gs effective September 9. This exchange included the idea of using the AC-119G to fly armed interdiction over the Ho Chi Minh Trail and also act as a forward air controller. While arranging the exchange, the 14th SOWg pointed out that the AC-119G offered no particular advantage over the AC-47 in Lima Site defense, troops-in-contact support or armed reconnaissance (considering its limited sensor capability). In fact, over the rugged Laotian terrain the AC–47 might possess a better recovery advantage in an emergency than the AC–119G. Covey* FAC reports and debriefings of AC–119G crews following FAC missions also raised questions as to the AC–119G's suitability in a forward air controller role.[232] The AC–119K was likewise considered as a substitute for the AC–47 but rejected at this time because Udorn could not properly support this aircraft's auxiliary jet engines.[233] These arguments, plus the strong support from the U.S. Ambassador to Thailand for continued AC–47 operations from Udorn, led to cancellation of the exchange order on August 23.[234] It was later decided to assign three AC–47s and five gunship aircrews to the 432d Tactical Reconnaissance Wing at Udorn. These AC–47s would fly missions until the Laotians were ready to handle them.[235]

On November 30, Lt. Col. Adam W. Swigler, Jr., commander of the 4th Special Operations Squadron, boarded Spooky 41 and took off on a very routine yet momentous mission. When he landed at Phan Rang AB at 0710, December 1, 1969, the last mission of the squadron had been flown. Fifteen days later the 4th Special Operations Squadron was inactivated and its AC–47s redistributed under the Military Assistance Program (MAP) as follows: 432d Tactical Reconnaissance Wing at Udorn, three; Vietnamese Air Force, three; and Royal Laotian Air Force, eight.[236]

Since November 1965, the 4th Special Operations Squadron had pioneered in the deployment and tactical development of the gunship. It had flown a broad spectrum of missions over varied terrain, covering all of South Vietnam and parts of Laos. At one time or another it provided fire support during many major battles of the war. Over four years of operations the Spookies successfully defended 3,926 hamlets, outposts, or forts. The unit fired 97 million rounds and was credited with killing 5,300 enemy soldiers. It dropped nearly 270,000 flares as it sought to strip away the cover of darkness from the enemy. Thus the 4th Special Operations Squadron left the war with an enviable record.

As the curtain closed on 1969, so ended the role of the Air Force's AC–47s in the Southeast Asian war. For four years Spooky had met a critical need beyond all expectations. It early earned a reputation as a nighttime defender and never lost it. Whether it was convoy, special forces camp, isolated Vietnamese hamlet, airbase troops engaging the enemy, or medical evacuation team, Spooky's stream of minigun fire dealt attackers deadly blows and lifted defenders' spirits. Spooky could loiter over and illuminate an area then strike with pinpoint precision, proving the predictions of its originators that it was well-suited for counterinsurgency

---

*The call sign of the O–2 and OV–10 FAC aircraft of the 20th Tactical Air Support Squadron operating in North Vietnam and Laos.

situations. The Spooky Count and the airmen's boast that no outpost or village was ever lost while under gunship protection reflected Spooky's great contribution to the war. The gunship's full impact on Viet Cong and North Vietnamese strategy is hard to pin down. It is clear that from 1965 on Spooky countered the enemy's previous advantage of picking out friendly positions to strike and overrun at night. It forged key links in a security chain that protected the pacification effort and strengthened friendly control over the South Vietnam countryside. Most important, it was just this pacification aspect of guerrilla warfare that counterinsurgency experts claimed would spell final success or failure.

While pointing to the importance of the first gunship effort, one should not lose sight of its limitations. The AC–47 was an aging aircraft to say the least. Its design did not afford the best view of a target, and the miniguns proved ineffective against troops not in the open. Spooky's firing orbit had to be at a fairly low altitude, which put it in range of enemy small arms fire. Its limited power and slow rate of climb magnified operational problems over mountainous areas. Lack of sensors made it a marginal performer on night armed reconnaissance.[237]

What's more, the AC–47's initial commitment over the Ho Chi Minh Trail in 1966 was questioned after a combination of rugged terrain and heavy antiaircraft fire laid bare Spooky's vulnerability. The successful return of the AC–47 gunships to Laotian operations in 1969 failed to silence critics of the aircraft's survivability, since Spooky was defending Lima Sites in a slightly defended environment similar to that in South Vietnam. Also, in spite of Spooky successes in airbase defense, some consideration was given to alternative aircraft. On April 7, 1969, PACAF submitted requirements for a helicopter to replace Spooky. PACAF believed a helicopter more flexible, faster-reacting, and capable of operating within base perimeters.[238] Age, design, and armament clearly circumscribed the AC–47's role.

The end of Air Force C–47 operations did not mean that Spooky was being retired to storage or put out to pasture. Despite the aircraft's lengthening years, its simplicity of operation, versatility, and legendary dependability* made it an almost ideal weapon system for transfer to indigenous air forces. Consequently, AC–47 operations went on under new banners. A total of 53 AC–47s had been built at a cost of about $6.7 million so a considerable number of them would be around for some time.[239] As the gunship pioneer, the AC–47 was the progenitor of gunship operations by allied air forces and a second generation of improved Air Force gunships as well.

---

*It was remarkable this 25- to 26-year old aircraft had so few maintenance problems. Its operational readiness stayed high over the years. Quality maintenance, a critical factor in Southeast Asia, was made more difficult to attain by a high personnel turnover and a manning level of ninety percent at times.

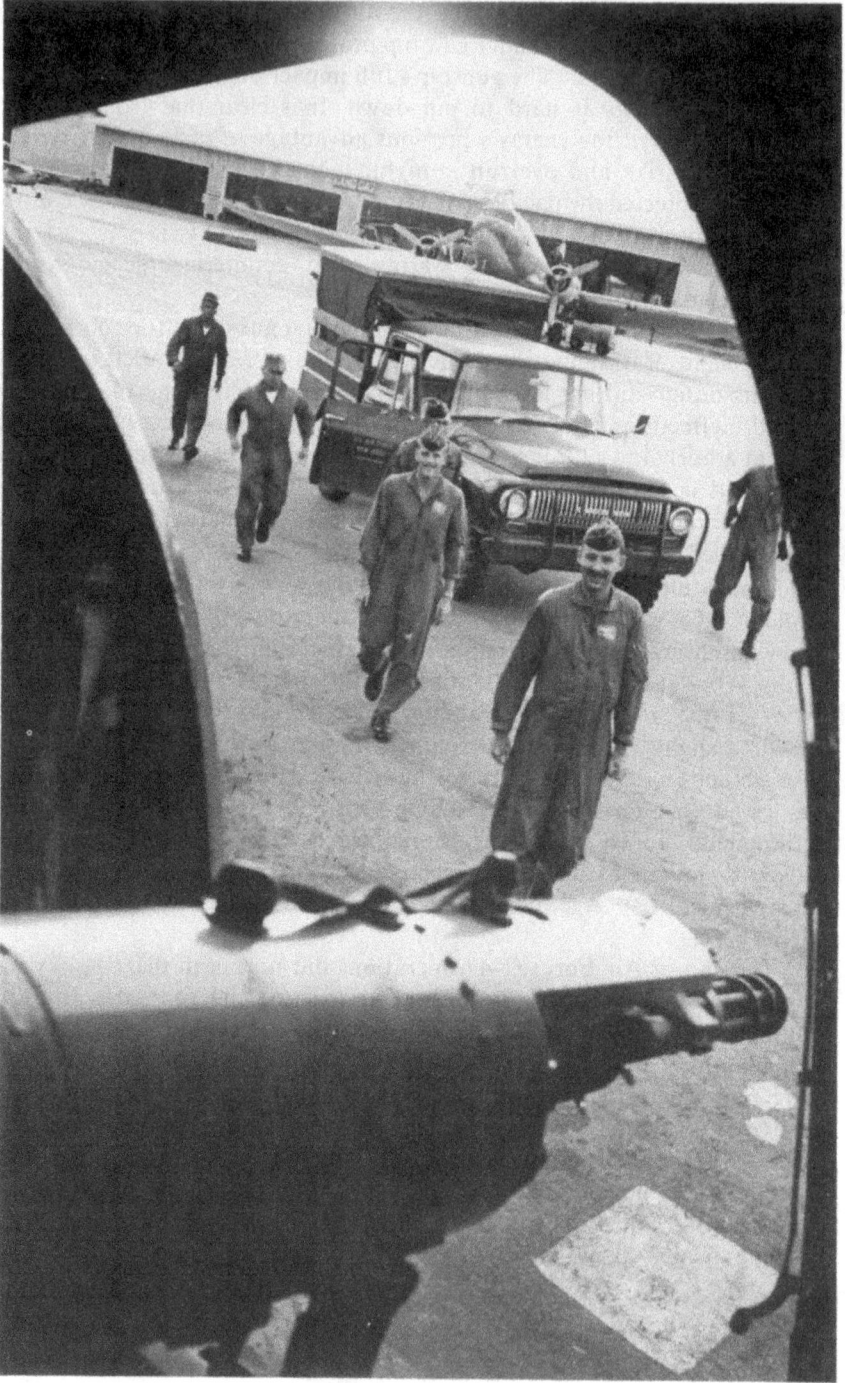

An AC–47 crew approaches its Dragonship prior to a dusk takeoff.

III. Gunship II (AC–130)

The imaginative and resourceful men who spurred on the first gunship's development foresaw the weapon system's immense potential for growth, refinement, and improvement. Captain Simons suggested various missions a more sophisticated gunship might perform. As early as 1963 he mentioned the possible inclusion of infrared and laser-beam equipment to enhance night target acquisition. Captain Terry noted, as the AC–47's first combat test and evaluation got under way, that his thoughts turned to using bigger and better aircraft that could accommodate the more advanced sensory components and heavier armament.

The ideas of these men picked up support. The initial test unit's evaluation report ended with a recommendation that an aircraft of greater payload be considered for future gunships. In February 1965 the Air Force Systems Command urged planning for a better transport than the C–47 for the gunship role. Thus, from the beginning, ideas and recommendations abounded for gunship development.

Various AC–47 shortcomings were apparent despite its combat successes and reliability. An old aircraft of limited cargo space, its low wing prevented a full view of the target and posed problems in minigun placement. Its top speed was a relatively slow 200 knots and its takeoff weight restricted ammunition and flare loads. A follow-on gunship had to overcome some of these disadvantages and permit equipment changes or additions that would strengthen the weapon system.

Most attention focused on a higher-performance aircraft, although some thought was given to a smaller side-firing airplane. One such proposal, Operation Little Brother, stemmed from June 1966 discussions of a Limited War Study Group and a Systems Command task force. Talk dwelt on a prototype aircraft that could provide close support of counterinsurgency ground forces with an accuracy "equal to or better than Army organic ground-based fire support." On June 21, 1966, Captain Terry and Capt. James Wolverton briefed the study group on side-firing operations. On July 1, the group proposed a twin-engine aircraft of 2,000-pound payload and high-wing design. The Cessna Super Sky Master Model 337 was initially deemed appropriate. The projected aircraft's armament would be a semirecoilless, 40- to 42-mm gun capable of firing 500 rounds per minute. The MXU–470/A Minigun Module was proposed after studying availability, cost, weight, recoil, and reliability. A pilot and gunner would crew the aircraft which could operate from unimproved landing and takeoff areas. The plane would be equipped with an automatic pilot and instruments for visual flight rules day and night operations. It

LITTLE BROTHER CONCEPT

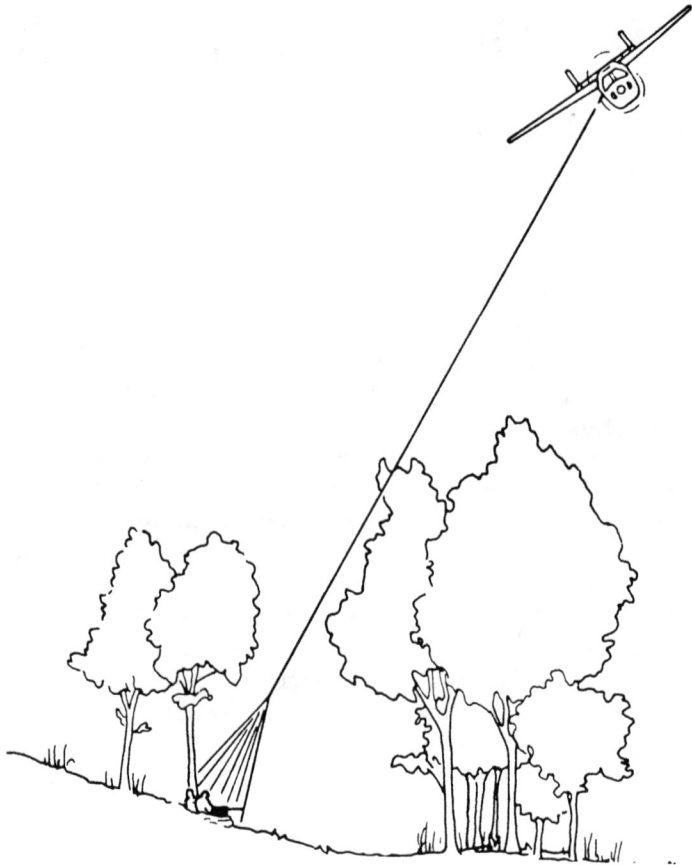

would cruise at speeds between 100 and 190 mph and fly ten hours without refueling. A fire-control system would afford the pilot/gunner the best firing position for greatest accuracy.[1]

The development of a fire-control system was assigned to the Air Force Avionics Laboratory (AFAL). Wing Commander Thomas C. Pinkerton, a Royal Air Force officer with the avionics laboratory, largely designed the critical system and it was then fabricated in the Air Force shops. For flight tests AFAL leased an aircraft from Cessna Aircraft Corporation and ASD's shops modified it. After several successful flight tests, the fire-control system's potential was so apparent that work on a suitable system for a bigger aircraft like the C–130 began before Little Brother ended. The improved and more reliable AC–130 fire-control system owed a lot to the Little Brother tests.[2]

BASIC GUNSHIP WEAPON SYSTEM

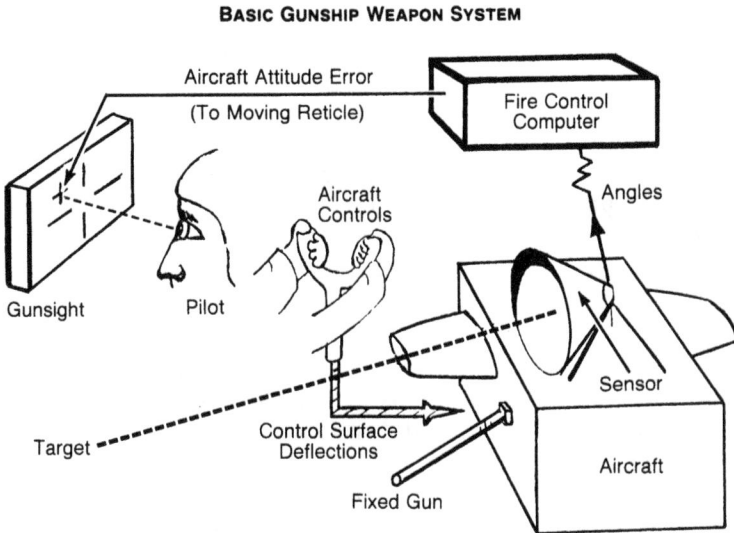

The Air Force pursued the Little Brother project for a few months during the latter half of 1966. The project died from the shortage of available funds and resource demands of other projects, including the development of heavier gunships to replace the AC–47.

Developments regarding the Air Force's night attack capability dovetailed with its desire to improve the gunship. Deeper U.S. involvement in the Southeast Asian conflict put problems of night air operations in stark relief. The Viet Cong were obviously attacking and moving supplies during darkness to exploit the Air Force's inability to strike effectively twenty-four hours a day. Putting it simply—the Air Force had to see a target to hit it. Furthermore, the rugged terrain and dense foliage in many parts of Southeast Asia offered day-and-night cover for insurgent base camps and truck parks. The Air Force faced the fact it had no around-the-clock capability and launched an all-out effort to get one. This in turn was to shape gunship improvements.

In 1964 and 1965 the Military Aircraft Panel of the President's Science Advisory Committee turned its attention to night operations. The panel reviewed and recommended expansion of the Army's night vision program. On May 18, 1965, it urged Dr. Donald F. Hornig, Special Assistant to the President on Science and Technology, to push night vision developments to aircraft, suggesting the technical status of current projects justified a crash program. On June 3, Dr. Hornig conveyed the panel's recommendations to Dr. Harold Brown, Director of Defense Research and Engineering (DDR&E), Office of the Secretary of Defense. He pointed to the need for "early experimental assessments" and giving night capability "to our units in Vietnam as rapidly and on as large a scale as practicable." Dr. Brown replied on June 18 that, in line with the panel's recommendations, high-priority

79

programs had been "designed to assure the utility of the devices in helicopter and slow- and high-speed fixed-wing aircraft."[3]

In early December President Lyndon B. Johnson expressed interest in the night vision program and asked Deputy Secretary of Defense Cyrus R. Vance about it. Secretary Vance informed the President that helicopter-mounted systems were to be tested in Vietnam in March 1966 and A–1E-mounted systems in August 1966. A transport aircraft reconnaissance-strike system, primarily designed for interdiction missions, would be evaluated in Vietnam during January 1967. President Johnson likewise questioned Dr. Hornig about the subject. The science adviser's response of January 3, 1966, stressed the importance of the problem, noted the program's limited funding, and voiced the opinion that faster progress could be made.[4]

This White House interest spawned several conferences attended by: Dr. Vincent V. McRae, Technical Assistant to the President's Advisor on Science and Technology; Dr. Richard S. Garwin, member of the President's Science Advisory Committee; Gen. Bernard A. Schriever, Commander, Air Force Systems Command; and Lt. Gen. James Ferguson, Air Force Deputy Chief of Staff for Research and Development. These meetings and others involving the Office of Defense Research and Engineering set the stage for an extensive Air Force effort to attain a night strike reconnaissance capability. The high-priority program that took shape was labeled Operation Shed Light.[5]

As the first step in Operation Shed Light, Air Force headquarters designated a team on February 7, 1966, to "clarify the capability as well as limitations of the night attack problem." On March 5 the team ended its deliberations and made twenty-nine specific recommendations for insuring the best around-the-clock capability. It identified the main development needs as: (1) a self-contained night attack capability in the low-threat environment for targets of opportunity on lines of communication, (2) a battlefield illumination airborne system (BIAS) to perform real-time reconnaissance for Army field units and serve as hunter-illuminator for strike aircraft carrying out close air support, (3) a night hunter for high-threat environment, and (4) enhancement of ground and airborne forward air controller capabilities. The team also set development requirements in the fields of navigation, illumination, target marking and sensors for target detection and acquisition. After review of the team's findings, the Air Staff commenced an Air Force-wide program on March 18, 1966, to achieve a creditable, tactical, night attack capability without delay. It informed the major commands of Operation Shed Light the same day. Central supervision of the program was vested in the Deputy Chief of Staff, Research and Development, who asked other Air Staff agencies concerned and all major commands to organize offices for coordinating Operation Shed Light matters.[6]

On March 23 Air Force headquarters instructed the Air Force Systems Command to prepare a plan showing time phases and cost of the

BASIC C–130A TRANSPORT—GENERAL ARRANGEMENT

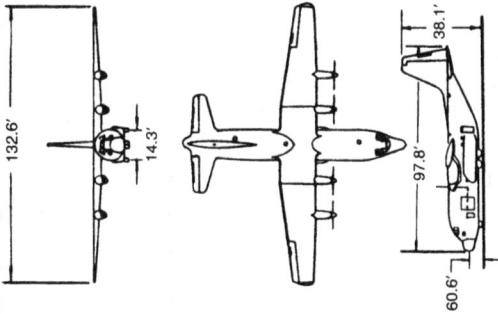

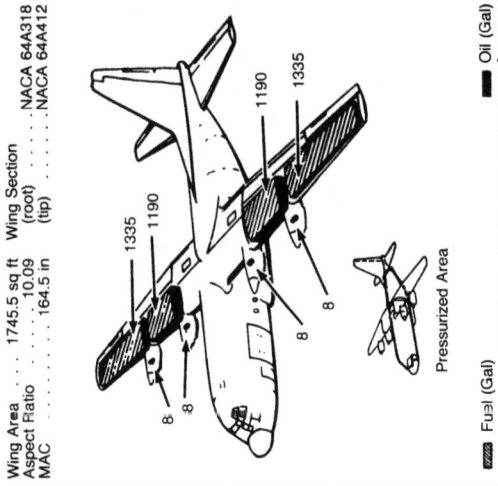

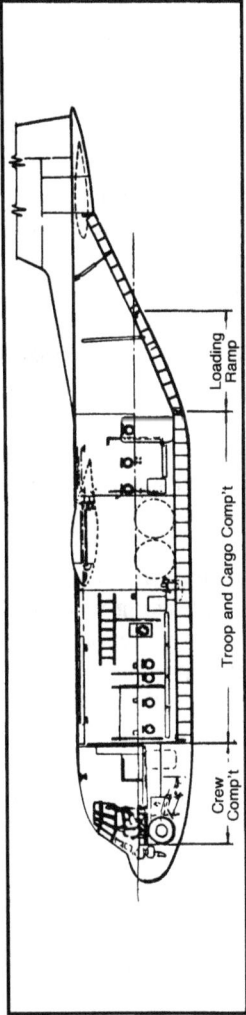

Wing Area . . . . . 1745.5 sq ft
Aspect Ratio 10.09
MAC . . . . . 164.5 in

Wing Section
(root) . . . . . . NACA 64A318
(tip) . . . . . . NACA 64A412

1335
1190
1190
1335

8
8
8
8

Pressurized Area

▨ Fuel (Gal)   ■ Oil (Gal)

132.6'
14.3'
38.1'
97.8'
60.6'

Loading
Ramp

Troop and Cargo Comp't

Crew
Comp't

twenty-nine recommendations. The Limited War Office at the Aeronautical Systems Division did the spadework on the plan and became the focal point for planning work on the twenty-nine items. From the various in-house discussions, proper integration of sensors and weapons emerged as the key to improved night capability. The completed AFSC Program Package Plan was coordinated with the Army and Navy to foster better sharing of developments among the military services. The Air Staff reviewed the plan on June 9 and on July 15 the Air Force Chief of Staff told AFSC to implement it.[7]

Project Gunboat emerged as one of the proposals under Operation Shed Light.[8] It was viewed as an extension of the AC–47 side-firing system. It would, however, realize vastly increased operational effectiveness by putting heavier and more accurate firepower in a bigger aircraft. By adding guns of different caliber and a larger ammunition load, firing could continue longer and with improved fire patterns. An image intensifier—obtained from the Army's night-vision development—would team with the fire-control system to pick up targets in the dark. A radar beacon, direction finder homer reception, and loran D could, when available, bolster night and bad-weather operations. Stronger armor plate would protect the crew and the inverted fuel tanks would retard fire. The Gunboat aircraft would have about the same mission as the AC–47: close support of hamlets, special forces camps, and installations. But in addition, the new gunship with 20-mm guns and sensor equipment could far better interdict targets, even fleeting ones.[9]

In July 1966 the Director of Development, Deputy Chief of Staff, Research and Development, USAF, took charge of Project Gunboat. The first planning meeting was held on September 2 at Wright-Patterson AFB with representatives of the Air Force Systems Command and the Aeronautical Systems Division. Project objectives were discussed and configuration of the prototype aircraft considered. Next, ASD quickly surveyed various laboratories and companies for necessary equipment and rushed into development of components not on hand. The Air Force Armament Laboratory started an armament effectiveness study on use of high-caliber weapons. While ASD laid the groundwork for the prototype test program, Air Force headquarters analyzed mission requirements.[10] On November 16 Project Gunboat personnel tentatively picked the C–130 as the prototype, the same aircraft selected for the BIAS-Hunter project. Armament would consist of 7.62-mm miniguns, 20-mm guns, and maybe .50-caliber machineguns. Funding for the Gunboat prototype was quickly obtained.[11]

The Air Staff directed AFSC in January 1967 to configure a C–130 under Project Gunboat, an in-house effort expected to take six months. Planned tests were to determine if it was desirable to use the 20-mm cannon at altitudes of six to ten thousand feet, how well the starlight image intensifier optical viewer and fire-control system worked in pinpointing targets at night, and the best mix of 7.62-mm and 20-mm guns.[12]

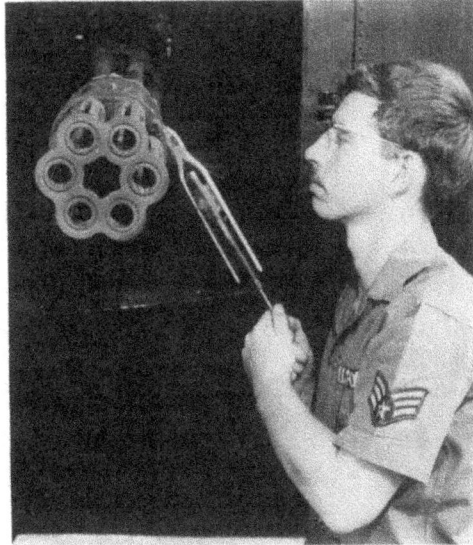

Right: Sgt. Bob C. Rayburn, weapons mechanic, 16th Special Operations Squadron, adjusts a 20-mm gun on an AC-130; below: Close-up of the multi-barrel muzzle.

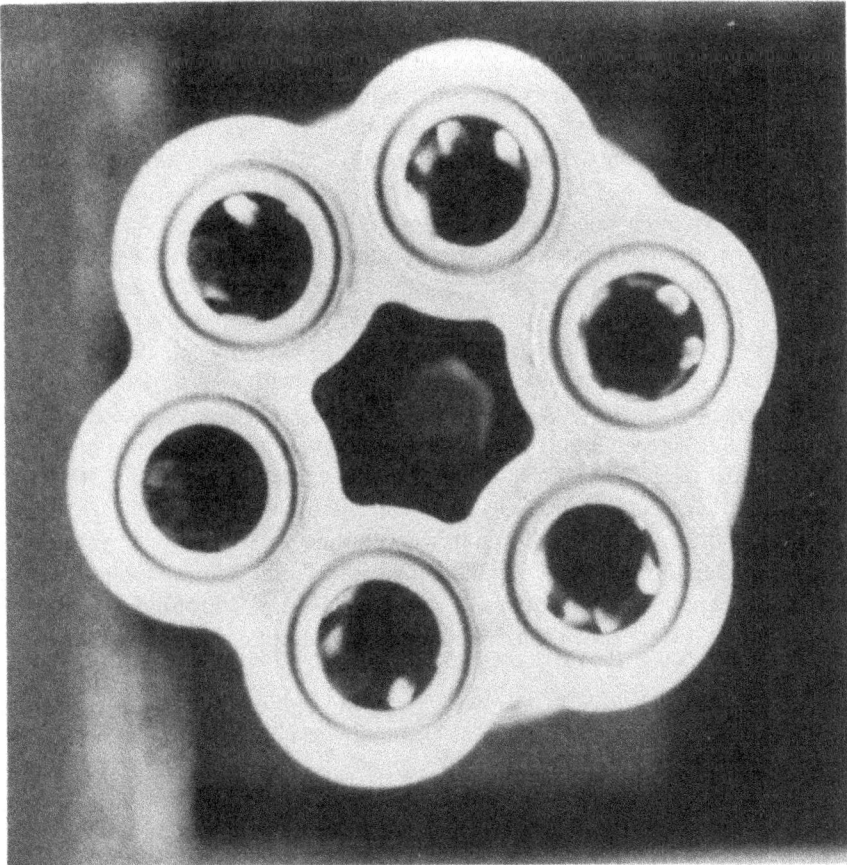

The first AC-130A gunship at Wright-Patterson AFB, Ohio.

Choice of C-130A serial number 54-1626[13] as the Gunboat aircraft on February 26, 1967, marked a momentous milestone, but there was no great rejoicing. The aircraft had been in three major accidents before being assigned to the project. At one time number "626" had been nicknamed "sick-two-six."[14] Nevertheless, the Aeronautical Systems Division commenced modification of the aircraft on April 1, 1967, at Wright-Patterson AFB.[15]

Benefits from selection of the four-engine, high-wing, Lockheed-built Hercules transport became apparent at once. A chief advantage lay in the substantial increase in compartment space and load capacity over the C-47, making room for more equipment. Four 7.62-mm miniguns and four 20-mm M-61 Vulcan cannons (able to fire 2,500 rounds of high-explosive incendiary shells per minute) were installed. Sensor equipment included a night observation device,* side-looking radar, and forward-looking radar. A computerized fire-control system linked guns and sensors. This was a giant step toward giving the gunship crew a target acquisition system that could aim and strike precisely—even at night. Also added were: a Bell optical sight; a steerable illuminator containing two twenty-kilowatt xenon arc lamps giving off visible, infrared, or ultraviolet light; a semiautomatic flare dispenser; armor plating; inert fuel tanks; doppler radar for navigation; direction-finding homing instruments; and an FM radio transceiver.[16]

As modifications progressed, the Air Force decided to substitute Gunship II for the more nautical Gunboat designation.[17] Gunship II was

---

*The night observation device (also called Starlight scope) intensified images through use of ambient (surrounding) moonlight or starlight. This telescope-like instrument had a limited capability to detect personnel, vehicular, and riverboat traffic. The Air Force tested the night observation device in its aircraft, putting one in an AC-47 in Southeast Asia.

AC-130A GUNSHIP II SPECIAL EQUIPMENT ARRANGEMENT

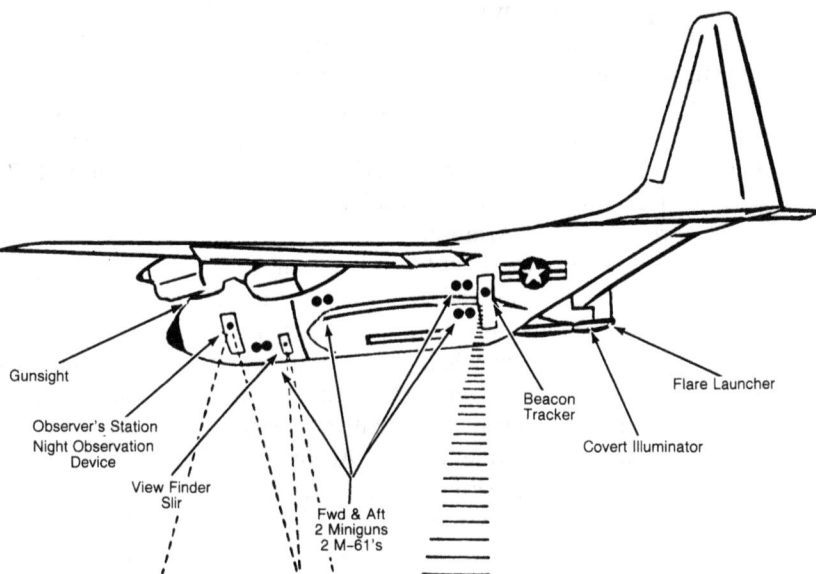

Gunsight

Observer's Station
Night Observation
Device

View Finder
Slir

Fwd & Aft
2 Miniguns
2 M-61's

Beacon
Tracker

Covert Illuminator

Flare Launcher

more in keeping with a follow-on gunship to the AC-47 and also denoted the second-generation nature of the C-130 prototype.

Modifications were completed on the Gunship II prototype, and it entered the flight-test phase on June 6, 1967.[18] It was flown to Eglin AFB for checkout of sensors, fire-control system and armament. Initial flight tests (June 12–23) demonstrated the successful integration of the night observation device, fire-control system, and gunsight. The pilot aimed, fired, and hit the target without ever seeing it with the naked eye.[19] Next the aircraft went through a "cut and try" cycle that included tests and modifications.[20] After about one month of testing at Eglin, another forty-five days were spent at Wright-Patterson AFB putting in more equipment. Eventually three major sensors for locating and identifying targets were installed: a night observation device, a side-looking radar, and a forward-looking infrared system— all mounted on the left side of the aircraft. A major improvement, the FLIR enabled the Gunship II to detect the heat from vehicles after they turned off their lights or drove under the jungle canopy. The fire-control system integrated inputs from the three sensors and provided position and attitude information to the pilot. This allowed him to place the aircraft in a search or attack orbit. Signals from the fire-control system drove a pipper (bead) in the pilot's gunsight. When the fixed reticle (system of lines) in the gunsight was aligned with the pipper, the pilot had completed aiming and was ready to fire.[21]

In a final series of tests at Eglin, Gunship II scored high on a number of covert search and attack missions. The night observation device and other sensors searched a designated area on the range to detect, identify, and track targets. The aircraft then made firing passes utilizing the battlefield illumination airborne system. It also proved its ability to detect targets at night on the water range. The weapon firing was devastating and accurate, hitting the target twenty-nine times of thirty firing passes.[22] Based on these results, the prototype was certified ready for September deployment to Southeast Asia for combat evaluation.[23]

The flying tests likewise helped establish basic crew requirements for the AC-130. These positions were identified as: Aircraft Commander, Pilot, Fire Direction Officer, Navigator, Navigator/Sensor Operator (NOD), Navigator/Sensor Operator (IR and Radar), Flight Engineer, Loadmaster, Master Armorer/Scanner, Armorer/7.62-mm, Armorer/20-mm.[24]

At first, the new experimental subsystems in Gunship II required crewmen who were scientists and engineers in the various technical areas. The Air Force Systems Command development team had these skills and thus made up half the crew when the aircraft was tested and deployed. (The rest of the crew came from TAC.) An outstanding example was Lt. Col. James R. Krause, master navigator, former Air Force Avionics Laboratory engineer, and one of the Aeronautical Systems Division's leading infrared experts. He showed what the infrared system could really do in the hands of an operator with skill and know-how. Moreover, he instilled confidence in the future crewmembers who would operate the sensor. Majors Terry and Wolverton similarly carried their expertise into crew positions. A remarkable group of men, they flew thousands of hours in tests and combat-evaluation missions, often working on their equipment by day and flying combat at night. They formulated tactics and procedures for using the systems and instructed follow-on crews.[25] Perhaps even more significant, these intensely dedicated men formed a nucleus around which future development effort would flourish.

The AFSC-TAC crew flew the prototype Gunship II to South Vietnam for a sixty- to ninety-day combat evaluation, arriving on September 21, 1967.[26] The evaluation task force, commanded by Maj. Jack L. Kalow and based at Nha Trang AB, divided the combat test into three phases. The first was devoted to close air support missions from airborne alert in the Delta region—IV Corps Tactical Zone (CTZ)—around Binh Thuy. (This traced the pattern of the AC-47's combat evaluation wherein the first flights were over areas posing the least terrain or enemy-defense problems.) The second phase tried the Gunship II weapon system against enemy lines of communication in Tiger Hound. The third phase involved armed reconnaissance and ground support missions in the highlands of II Corps CTZ.[27] The first evaluation sortie was flown on September 24, the last on December 1.[28] The phased test program ended on December 8, 1967.[29]

The Air Force invited the U.S. Army to participate in the test and evaluation to insure a realistic program. From the outset they were partners and contributed people and equipment to the test.[30] After combat missions involving its troops, Army test personnel reported Gunship II operations in support of ground combat units were "significantly better than

FIRE CONTROL SYSTEM

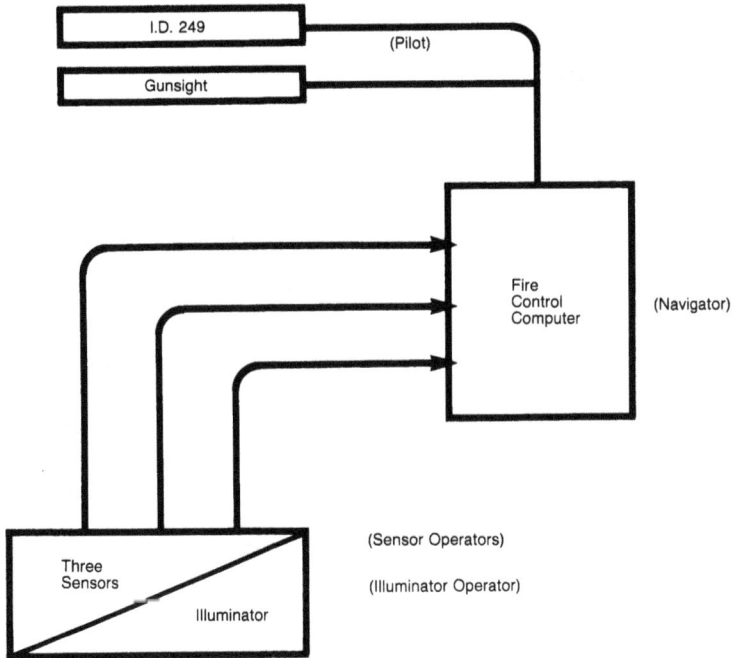

```
┌────────────────────┐
│      I.D. 249      │
└────────────────────┘
            (Pilot)
┌────────────────────┐
│     Gunsight       │
└────────────────────┘

                    ┌──────────────┐
                    │  Fire        │
                    │  Control     │   (Navigator)
                    │  Computer    │
                    └──────────────┘

                    (Sensor Operators)

┌────────────────────┐   (Illuminator Operator)
│  Three             │
│  Sensors           │
│          Illuminator│
└────────────────────┘
```

OPTICAL GUNSIGHT

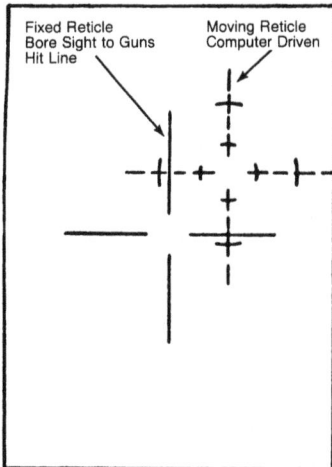

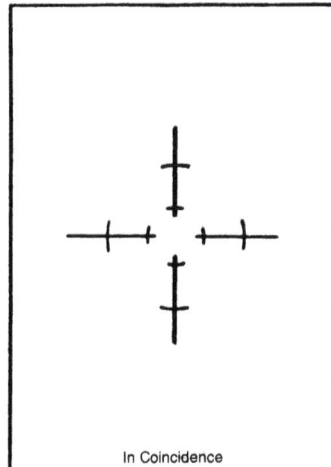

Fixed Reticle
Bore Sight to Guns
Hit Line

Moving Reticle
Computer Driven

In Coincidence

87

BASIC FIRING GEOMETRY (NO WIND—NO OFFSET)

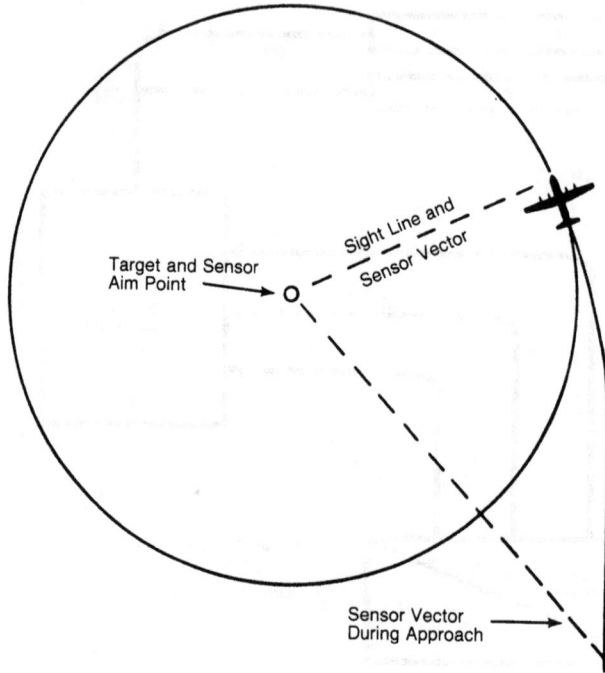

Sight Line and Sensor Vector

Target and Sensor Aim Point

Sensor Vector During Approach

Firing Order (Wind Corrected—No Offset)

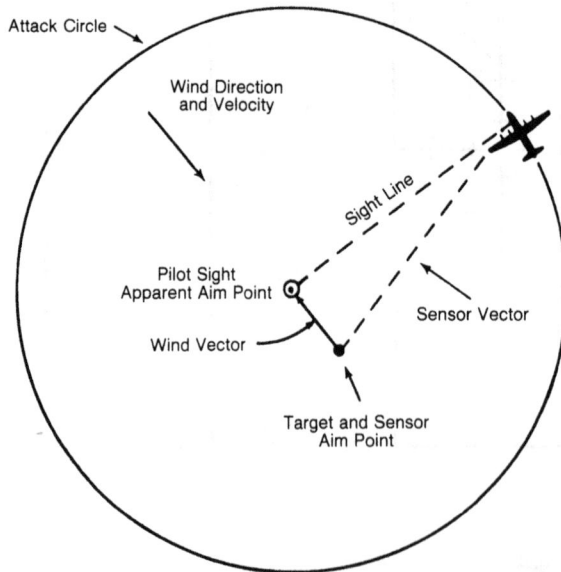

Attack Circle

Wind Direction and Velocity

Sight Line

Pilot Sight Apparent Aim Point

Sensor Vector

Wind Vector

Target and Sensor Aim Point

that of other comparable existing gunships."[31] They expected even more improvement "by increased reliability of equipment and further development and refinement of operational techniques and procedures." The Army evaluators stopped short of an unqualified endorsement, however, pending "receipt and review of the Air Force proposal for further development, production, deployment and employment."[32]

The prototype Gunship II test results were most favorable,[33] particularly as to interdiction. During September to December, the AC–130 sighted ninety-four trucks and destroyed thirty-eight.[34] Major Terry was piloting the prototype on an armed reconnaissance mission in November when a large convoy of enemy vehicles was detected. He repeatedly attacked, destroying or damaging eight vehicles. (Later he received the Distinguished Flying Cross for his performance on this mission).[35] Maj. Gen. William G. Moore, Air Force Deputy Chief of Staff, Research and Development, praised the new system, stating that "the C–130 Gunship II test bed aircraft had unprecedented success in identifying and destroying enemy lines of communication both in South Vietnam and Laos." In doing so it had "far exceeded fighter type kill ratios on enemy trucks and other equipment."[36] In fact, the interdiction strikes went so well that the prototype almost skipped the close-support part of the evaluation.[37] During the entire evaluation period, Gunship II fired 87,720 rounds of 20 mm and 222,800 rounds of 7.62-mm ammunition and dropped 310 flares.[38] By the end of 1967, the Southeast Asia evaluation showed the prototype "a three-fold improvement over its predecessor, the AC–47."[39]

During the tests, the prototype's main system components were used for both close support and armed reconnaissance of enemy supply lines. Only the APS–42 navigational radar failed to measure up—a serious shortcoming over rugged terrain.[40] At a Wright-Patterson AFB conference on December 11–12, 1967, this item was discussed, along with about two hundred engineering changes proposed for Gunship II. The meeting failed to reach a firm decision on a radar change but the conferees did decide to add radar homing and warning equipment to the prototype for better defense.[41]

Gunship II's strenuous testing, which involved at least one and sometimes two or three missions a day, generated maintenance problems with the "breadboard"* equipment. Whereupon, General Momyer decided to return the prototype to the United States for a general refurbishing. When he so informed General Westmoreland, the MACV commander was reluctant to let the aircraft go for an estimated seven-month reworking. He asked General Momyer to look into "all alternatives which might accomplish the modifications and still get some use out of it before the end of the Northeast Monsoon." General Momyer then directed only a minimum overhaul of Gunship II so that it could be back in the theater by the first

---

*A term for equipment put together for test purposes, often on rather crude mountings, to detect trouble spots before final engineering design.

half of February.[42] This required an all-out effort to refurbish sensors and other equipment. Nevertheless, the job was done and the prototype returned to Southeast Asia on February 12, 1968.[43]

Almost at once the Seventh Air Force committed the prototype to working the Ho Chi Minh Trail in Laos.[44] The aircraft was based at Ubon RTAFB in eastern Thailand, a strategic staging point for missions over the southern Laotian panhandle.[45] After several fire-control harmonization flights, the AC-130A began flying combat on February 27. On the third sortie it destroyed nine trucks and two storage areas.[46]

Gunship II flew combat in Southeast Asia from February to November 1968. The prototype sighted 1,000 trucks, destroying 228 and damaging 133. It attacked 481 trucks with no visible results. The aircraft destroyed 9 and damaged 8 of 32 sampans or boats sighted.[47] These figures kindled enthusiasm in commanders and officials about the gunship's operations. It appeared that at last an effective weapon system was available for night strikes on the supply trails.

The prototype compiled most of this interdiction record during its relatively short time in Laotian operations. In June 1968 the 14th Air Commando Wing recommended that Gunship II be returned to South Vietnam. It pointed to the deteriorating weather over Laos, the drop in truck traffic, and the mounting threat of antiaircraft fire in many Trail areas. With the monsoon change the prototype's truck-kill rate had fallen from nine trucks per night to one.[48] The 14th suggested the aircraft operate from Da Nang and thus remain close to Laos, so it could still be diverted there for lucrative truck targets. It was also pointed out that the prototype could perform test and evaluation projects in South Vietnam before the AC-119s arrived. This would give crews experience in close air support.[49]

On June 14 General Momyer ordered the prototype transferred to Tan Son Nhut AB near Saigon for about sixty days.[50] The next day representatives from Seventh Air Force headquarters, 834th Air Division, 14th Air Commando Wing, and the prototype crew met to discuss Gunship II's in-country use.[51] This group believed the gunship could, if necessary, help meet an expected third phase of the enemy's big Tet offensive in the III and IV CTZs and combat the rocket threat in the Saigon area.[52]

Gunship II flew all sorts of missions in South Vietnam. Twenty-eight of 151 missions (246 sorties) supported troops in contact with the enemy and accounted for 240 enemy killed.[53] Missions ranged almost the length of South Vietnam and several special ones went as far north as the Demilitarized Zone in search of suspected enemy helicopters. Even while supporting troops, the prototype continued to interdict sampan and truck traffic on the rivers, canals, and roads.[54]

Besieged with equipment malfunctions, the Gunship II prototype flew its last mission on November 18, 1968. It was then ferried back to Wright-Patterson AFB, arriving on November 26, 1968.[55] Subsystem problems had reached "such proportions as to critically limit operational capability" of the

Top: Armament on an AC–130 gunship at Nha Trang AB, 1967; below: The first AC–130A gunship, with camouflage.

prototype in Southeast Asia. An ineffective infrared system and failures in other equipment had dimmed chances of the aircraft's success in the forthcoming interdiction campaign. The 14th Air Commando Wing and the Seventh Air Force recommended the prototype be exchanged for a production model AC–130 as soon as possible.[56]

After the prototype wound up combat operations, the Air Force examined its cost effectiveness. Development costs totaled $724,237, including $166,312 for the refurbishment. Spares and services ran another $357,399. Flying costs were estimated at $552,784, figuring 1,484 hours at $326 an hour plus the salaries of crewmembers. A twenty-month depreciation cost of $539,500 was tacked on despite the aircraft's having already passed its eight-year depreciation period. Ammunition costs ($1,469,606) constituted a sizable chunk of the overall expenditures. The flares cost $99,300. Amounts for flares, ammunition, depreciation, development, and flying pushed the overall cost of the prototype's development and operation to $3,742,826. Dividing this total amount by the results of the missions would give an estimate of Gunship II's cost effectiveness. To find a yardstick for operational results, the number of trucks destroyed or damaged, boats destroyed or damaged, secondary fires and explosions recorded, gunsites destroyed, and every five enemy killed were each considered a major event. A total of 749 major events was arrived at which brought the cost per event to less than $5,000.[57] This computation proved the Gunship II prototype to be one of the most cost effective close support and interdiction systems in the U.S. Air Force inventory.

During the early phase of the prototype's combat evaluation, weekly reports were so promising that the Air Staff proposed to Dr. Harold Brown, then Secretary of the Air Force, that seven JC–130A aircraft be modified into gunships. Eleven JC–130As used for telemetry acquisition on the Eastern Test Range (ETR) had recently become available for other missions. On September 27–28, 1967, twelve generals from Air Force headquarters, TAC, PACAF, and the Seventh Air Force reviewed the Shed Light program. These officers proposed four of the JC–130As be modified for a near real-time reconnaissance intelligence function (BIAS-Hunter) and the other seven be configured like the Gunship II prototype.[58] When he eventually reviewed the proposal, Secretary Brown approved the four BIAS-Hunter aircraft but cut the number of JC–130As for Gunship II modification to two. He desired "that the number of additional Gunship II type aircraft be limited to a test quantity that can be covered within the allocated R&D and modification funds."[59] The Secretary was not sure how well the gunship's sensor systems would work. He also questioned the need to add another costly gunship type to the AC–47 and the AC–119, his choice for the follow-on gunship.

Secretary Brown's selection of the C–119G to replace the AC–47 disappointed gunship proponents and most Pacific air commanders. It had come about, however, after much debate and serious study.

As early as May 1967, General McConnell, Air Force Chief of Staff, had informed CINCPACAF and TAC of AFSC's work on the C–130 gunship test-bed and of a "separate project under way to determine a follow-on aircraft for the AC–47." The Air Staff made clear the C–130 and C–123 were not being seriously considered for the role because they were needed for airlift. An ongoing study was already comparing the C–121, C–119G/K, C–54, C–118, P–2E, and C–97. The study group sought an aircraft of greater payload, longer loiter time, and better survivability than the AC–47, capable of carrying the new sensor equipment under development. The Air Staff Board set May 12, 1967, for review of the follow-on aircraft.[60] From the study and review came a recommendation to the Secretary of the Air Force that the C–119K be the substitute for the AC–47.

Important factors entered into the C–119K selection. Developers of the AC–47 had recognized that a high-wing design was most desirable for a side-firing gunship. Such design afforded a clear line-of-sight along the length of the fuselage for both firing and use of sensors. This point alone tended to eliminate the C–121, C–54, C–118, and C–97. Also the availability of the aircraft had to be considered due to the need for early deployment to Southeast Asia. A ready source of C–119s was to be found in Air Force Reserve units. The power-limited payload of the more plentiful C–119Gs, however, could not accommodate the sensor and other equipment planned for the gunship. This serious problem could be somewhat overcome by turning to the C–119K which had two additional J–85 jet engines. Modification of the C–119Gs into the C–119K configuration seemed feasible from the standpoint of funds, time, and resources. For these reasons the Air Staff Board recommended the C–119K as the best follow-on gunship aircraft.

Secretary Brown considered several factors in acting on this recommendation. In January 1967 he had talked with people in Southeast Asia about the need for greater payload, longer loiter, and better survivability of the AC–47 replacement. Hence he knew the requirements as well as the preference of commanders for the C–130. Dr. Brown believed, however, that once modified into gunships the C–130s would most likely remain so. This would therefore adversely affect critical airlift resources.[61] On June 8 he approved selection of the C–119 but directed that the C–119G be modified as the immediate AC–47 successor. He further agreed the jet pod-equipped C–119K could be modified later should an increased payload seem necessary. In effect, the Secretary adopted a wait-and-see policy on weight demands and sensor equipment pending outcome of the AC–130 prototype tests. If the tests proved out, the C–119K could be used to accommodate the new target acquisition systems.[62] In the wake of this decision, Air Force headquarters sponsored a conference on June 22 for representatives of TAC, AFLC, and WRAMA to figure how best to execute the C–119 program. At this time the Office of the Secretary of Defense was reviewing the PACAF request for ten more AC–47s for base defense and weighing the possibility of filling it with AC–119Gs.[63]

Choice of the C-119G as the AC-47 replacement aroused considerable resistance in the field. General Momyer, Seventh Air Force commander, strongly opposed the selection in a June 30 message to General Ryan, CINCPACAF. He argued that "maintenance and logistics problems alone attendant to the introduction of yet another obsolete system into the theater weighs heavily against the C-119." The General felt that "employment of the C-119 aircraft in the gunship role would be mere substitution, and possibly regression rather than an advance." He recommended use of the C-130 because of its "four-engine survivability, a relatively low time airframe, greater speed, altitude, and loiter time, and growth potential." He pointed to the economical use of the AC-130 prototype design and its important advantages. General Momyer said that impact on the airlift mission from selection of the AC-130 would be "slight and that the base defense, hamlet and outpost protection" warranted this inroad into the airlift fleet.[64] General Ryan supported these views, for they echoed his earlier expressed preference for the C-130.[65] TAC also backed use of the C-130.[66]

Amid the swirl of controversy over a follow-on gunship, the Secretary of the Air Force's authorization on November 7, 1967, for modification of two JC-130As was warmly welcomed. The two conversions were viewed as an opening wedge which would yield extra data to support a decision for an expanded AC-130 gunship force, a foot-in-the-door so to speak. Meantime, ASD gathered cost and schedule data for Gunship II aircraft. On December 1, 1967, $200,000 was authorized to procure long-leadtime equipment for the first production AC-130.[67]

The interim report of the Gunship II prototype's combat test and evaluation[68] opened the way to approach Secretary Brown on modifying the remaining five JC-130As. In forwarding the evaluation, General McConnell said "this report responds to our desires for test results, and I consider it justifies the conversion of the remaining five (5) C-130A aircraft made available for the Shed Light program from ETR resources."[69] He added in a handwritten memo: "I have gone into this subject in considerable detail, both in the study and in conversation with the users in SVN [South Vietnam]. In my opinion Gunship II is the most effective 'breakthru' we have experienced in tactical aviation. I believe we should exploit it as far as we reasonably can."[70] The Air Force chief, while arguing for more Gunship IIs, felt for the present the C-119G/K program should go on "as a matter of correlative priority." In the meanwhile, the Air Staff would probe deeper into Gunship II's impact on the gunship force.[71]

On December 20, 1967, the Air Force secretary broke new ground when he authorized modification of the five remaining JC-130As.[72] First, the secretary noted that the AC-130 was a new weapon system which would "go a long way toward providing an improved night/all weather interdiction capability in an air environment of low-to-moderate risk." As such, it represented a "clear distinction between the more localized support and protective role of the AC-47 and the predominantly search-and-destroy concept envisioned for the AC-130." At the same time the AC-47s—until replaced by AC-119s—would have to provide both local base defense, and hamlet defense and supporting fire for the Army. Consequently, to firm up the AC-119s exact configuration and its modification and deployment schedule without delay, Dr. Brown asked the Air Staff for AC-119G and AC-119K modification and deployment options by January 5.[73] Clearly the Secretary was not abandoning the AC-119 selection. His approval of eight Gunship II aircraft (including one prototype) and breakout of mission categories spelled the start of a mixed gunship force. This marked a major departure from what had been the main consideration—merely the replacement of the AC-47.

The Seventh Air Force reacted strongly to the idea of a mixed gunship force. It was not convinced the concept was valid. In fact, it maintained that day/night all-weather operations entailing either interdiction or firepower in support of ground forces required the same gunship capability. The Seventh Air Force considered the AC-130 the right aircraft for the gunship force. Its speed permitted more rapid reaction, greater area coverage, and minimum exposure to hostile fire. Besides, it possessed the load capacity for improved sensors, heavier firepower, and armor plating. The command further argued that use of three different aircraft would be weighted with disadvantages.[74]

The Seventh Air Force had already reinforced its stated preference for an AC-130 gunship force. On November 18, 1967, it had informed PACAF that thirty-two Gunship IIs were required as replacements for the AC-47 on a one-for-one basis during fiscal years 1969 and 1970.[75] Then, on December 14, the Commander in Chief, Pacific Command recommended that PACAF give this program full support and prompt action.[76] The next day PACAF asked the Seventh Air Force to submit a concept of operation for the proposed Gunship II force to cover such matters as deployment, unit of assignment, personnel requirements, support concept, and possible trade-offs to keep personnel within the country manpower ceiling.[77] On December 31, 1967, the Seventh Air Force outlined the organization, basing (eight AC-130s in Thailand and the rest in South Vietnam), and personnel and support requirements. It figured that the AC-130s would require 1,402 additional personnel over the AC-47s and suggested the increase might fit within the ceiling if Blind Bat aircraft and some similar missions were terminated.[78]

General Ryan, CINCPACAF, pondered the Seventh Air Force's objections to the mixed gunship force, its counterproposals for an all AC-130 force, and the final report on the prototype's combat test and evaluation. On February 12, 1968, he strongly set forth his views on the future Southeast Asia gunship force in a message to the Air Force Chief of Staff:

> Recent highly successful combat evaluation Gunship II favors AC-130 as logical replacement for AC-47. AC-130 possesses needed capabilities as follows:
>
> Speed (rapid reaction, area coverage, minimum exposure).

> Sensors (locate enemy and friendly positions, deliver accurate firepower).
>
> Increased payload (essential to carry increased firepower, sensors, armor).
>
> Further advantages of C-130 are superior performance/flexibility, worldwide maintenance/supply support, contemporary navigation systems, established pilot training, schools and post-hostility airframe reconversion potential . . . . Gunship II C-130s should not be considered at expense of current and projected airlift assets. New production C-130 aircraft appears warranted in view recent mortar attacks on forward installations. Requirement for 32 AC-130 gunship force . . . considered urgent as it provides most effective reaction capability against attack on installations.
>
> Recommend reconsideration C-130 as follow-on gunship for AC-47 on one-for-one basis.[79]

These recommendations, timed as they were, reflected once more a hope that Air Force Secretary Brown might reconsider his selection of the C-119 as follow-on for the AC-47. Pacific commanders seized upon the Gunship II prototype's success to urge further review of the AC-130's merits.

Despite the arguments emanating from the Pacific, planning for a mixed gunship force continued. As requested by Secretary Brown when he approved the five additional AC-130s, the Air Staff furnished by January 5, 1968, a study of operational, basing, and organizational concepts. It recommended a Southeast Asia gunship contingent of six AC-130s, thirty-two AC-47s, and thirty-two AC-119s. The two squadrons of AC-119s would now augment rather than replace the AC-47s. The AC-119s and AC-47s would perform day and night missions of hamlet defense, close air support, convoy escort, and fire support for ground forces. Six orbit points were visualized in South Vietnam from which the AC-119s/AC-47s could respond to targets within a radius of 100 nautical miles from the orbit point. The AC-119s would be on orbit station during all hours of darkness and at other times when needed. The AC-119s and AC-47s would operate from bases at Nha Trang, Da Nang, Phu Cat, Pleiku, Phan Rang, Bien Hoa, and Binh Thuy. The existing tactical air control system would exercise command control. As the AC-119s became operational, the AC-47s would gradually turn over all missions except local base defense. Existing organizational or operating location arrangements would not change.[80]

In addition, a new squadron of AC-130s would be organized and based at Ubon with some of its aircraft possibly detached to Nakhon Phanom, Thailand. As their main mission, the six AC-130s would interdict enemy resupply routes in Laos around the clock, utilizing the Gunship II's night and all-weather sensor equipment and heavier armament. The first operational AC-130 was projected for June 1968, the seventh for October 1968. The first AC-119 was not expected to be on hand before December 1968 due to component procurement leadtimes. The Air Staff took note of the July 1, 1968, date set by the Secretary of Defense for deployment of at least six AC-119Gs to Southeast Asia. They believed, however, that AC-119Gs modified by that time would differ little from the AC-47 configuration. Consequently, they recommended to the secretary that the resources be applied toward the AC–119K configuration.[81]

The Air Staff plan for the mixed gunship force was adopted in the main and became the keystone for later actions. The major exception was the Air Force desire to push for AC–119K instead of AC–119G aircraft. On February 8, 1968, the Air Force secretary sought OSD's approval of a thirty-two AC–119G/K gunship force. Deputy Secretary of Defense Paul H. Nitze granted the request on February 24. However, when the deployment adjustment request was submitted for the AC–119s, Secretary Nitze asked for an "analysis on the continued need for the AC–47 force."[82] This seemed to again inject some uncertainty regarding the composition of the final gunship force.

In early February TAC proposed all eight AC–130As be sent to Southeast Asia in lieu of keeping two in the United States for crew training. TAC said that the small number of replacement crews could not fully utilize two training aircraft.[83] PACAF agreed on February 20, 1968, and suggested the first production AC–130A be held for crew training then deployed when training was over. PACAF reiterated its eagerness to have as many AC–130As as possible at the start of the northeast monsoon season.[84] After weighing the two major command proposals, Air Force headquarters ordered all AC–130As sent to Southeast Asia.* This would boost the planned gunship force for the theater to seventy-two aircraft (thirty-two AC–47s, thirty-two AC–119G/Ks, and eight AC–130As).

The Viet Cong and North Vietnamese Tet offensive in early 1968 and gunship successes in the war helped trigger studies of an even larger gunship force. In late March Secretary Brown wanted the Air Staff to see if the current and programmed gunship force could be tripled as soon as possible. The secretary requested a report by March 29, 1968, covering identification and selection of available aircraft, aircraft configurations, delivery schedules, support requirements, costs, manning and training requirements, and force recommendations. The Air Staff was to assume the program would have top national priority.[85]

The hurried request to examine a greatly expanded gunship force prompted study of three alternatives. In each, the Air Force secretary set guidelines on aircraft type, aircraft configuration, and the force ceiling. The Air Staff was to determine the most cost-effective mixed gunship arrangement. It recommended a mix of forty-four AC–47s, twenty-six AC–119Gs, fifty-two AC–119Ks, and thirty-two AC–130As as most desirable, and one of eighteen AC–130As, twenty-six AC–119Gs, twenty-six AC–119Ks, and fourteen AC–97(X) turboprop aircraft as least desirable.[86]

---

*With all AC–130As in Southeast Asia, controversy flared over training future crew replacements. TAC proposed that future crewmembers be C–130A-qualified, given ground training on sensors in the United States then brought to combat readiness in Southeast Asia. Major Kalow, Gunship II Task Force commander, sharply disagreed: "The idea of training missions in theater should never even be considered" because of the heavily committed aircraft and scarcity of practice areas and ammunition in Southeast Asia.

Consideration of the C–97 as a gunship stemmed in part from AFLC's preliminary evaluation of the aircraft, modified with either J–47 jet pods or turboprop engines.[87] The C–97 had the size and it was available. On the other hand, its higher maintenance and support costs, need of a longer runway for takeoffs, higher acquisition costs, manning implications, and the time required for modification made it less attractive as a gunship than the AC–130A or AC–119K.[88]

Secretary Brown evaluated the pros and cons of the proposals and on April 12, 1968, decided to limit any program to 110 gunships. Within this force ceiling the secretary asked the Air Staff to: modify current AC–119G and AC–119Ks into a single-type aircraft employing two 7.62-mm miniguns and one 20-mm gun; develop and modify forty AC–97 gunships with J–47 jet pods; and add no more than ten AC–130s (eighteen total).[89] In response, the Air Staff recommended twenty-six AC–119Gs, fifty-two AC–119Ks, and thirty-two AC–130As as most cost-effective. In light of the limitation of eighteen AC–130As, the next most cost-effective would be eighteen AC–130s, twenty-six AC–119Gs, fifty-two AC–119Ks, and fourteen AC–97(X) turboprop aircraft. Air Staff analysis disclosed that any amendment of existing AC–119G/AC–119K contracts would cost $7,630,000 and delay deployment four months. The Air Staff did not recommend J–47 jet engines for the AC–97 since they added 10,000 pounds to the basic aircraft's weight and operated poorly at planned operating altitudes.[90]

On April 29, 1968, Dr. Brown announced he was approving a force of fifty-five AC–47s, twenty-six AC–119Gs, twenty-six AC–119Ks, and eighteen AC–130As. His decision changed no aircraft type but did expand the gunship force to 125 aircraft, including ten more AC–130As.[91]

Approval of a 125-gunship force took the Seventh Air Force aback. It deemed the 72 gunships previously programmed ample for Southeast Asia needs and argued against a bigger force. In the Seventh Air Force's view, the forthcoming improved truck-killing munitions would augment the truck-busting capability of fighter and attack aircraft. Hence, only eight to twelve AC–130s would be needed for the out-country interdiction effort.[92] In-country, larger forces would touch off agonizing trade-offs to stay within manpower ceilings. The AC–119 gunships had been "well down on the 7AF Priorities List" until pressures from the Joint Chiefs of Staff and Air Force Chief of Staff forced them to the top at the "expense of many requirements considered more urgent by 7AF."[93] Finding room for further gunship expansion would be truly difficult.

Arguments over the proposed mixed gunship force again pushed to the fore and entered into the protest over a larger force. The Seventh Air Force pointed out that only AC–130s had a reasonable chance to survive the enemy defenses protecting southbound truck traffic in the Steel Tiger and Tiger Hound areas of Laos. Seventh further said the C–119G and C–97 aircraft were unsuitable. The C–119G would apparently lack the firepower, sensors, and single-engine performance for mountainous regions. The C–97 fell short in maneuverability, climb performance, maintenance, logistics, and in support requirements. The Seventh Air Force again suggested that the AC-47 be replaced one-for-one by the AC-130 or, as a second preference, one-for-one by the AC-119K. The latter trade-off would at least lift gunship capability. The higher performance AC-130 or AC-119K would pare response time and strengthen support coverage.[94]

The Seventh Air Force's views were noted but other more immediate factors shaped the gunship force. Secretary Brown held to the use of the AC-119G, primarily because he believed it would most quickly fill Southeast Asia requirements. Use of the C-97 as a gunship was only tentatively discussed due to its deficiencies previously highlighted. OSD dashed any hope for more AC-130As when on July 15, 1968, it rejected the planned ten additional ones.[95]

Ironically, the turndown of ten additional AC-130As came just as an increase in Gunship II aircraft appeared justified by cost-effectiveness data beginning to circulate among Secretary Brown's staff. The AC-130 had flown few interdiction-type missions by the end of 1967. Its superiority nevertheless showed up in comparison with other 1967 leading truck-killers:[96]

1967 Armed Reconnaissance	Sorties	Vehicles D/D†	Sorties per Vehicle D/D	Cost Per Vehicle D/D
All U.S. Aircraft	13,846	2,160	6.4	$ 55,700
F-105	2,836	262	10.8	$118,000
A-26	1,156	1,281	0.9	$ 5,900
Gunship II (Test Results in Laos Oct–Nov 1967)	9	51	0.2	$ 5,100

† Destroyed or Damaged.

The Air Force bolstered its arguments for a bigger Gunship II force and promptly sent them to the new Secretary of Defense, Clark M. Clifford, but to no avail. The OSD systems analysis office advised Mr. Clifford to defer the decision on modifying an additional ten AC-130As "pending further review of SEA experience."[97] In a program change decision of November 27, 1968, the deputy defense secretary ruled against the AC-130A augmentation. He argued that the Air Force "had not provided satisfactory justification for further increase in the size of this force."[98] For the time being, no change would occur in the total number of AC-130As.[99]

The next major move affecting the mixed force planning came from Southeast Asia. By mid-1968 the Seventh Air Force commander and CINCPACAF had resolved to trade off AC-47s on a one-for-one basis for the AC-119G/Ks.[100] Gen. Creighton W. Abrams, Jr., MACV commander, agreed to this plan,[101] but the Air Force Chief of Staff took the position that "all possibilities should be exhausted before AC-47/AC-119 one-for-one trade-off is considered."[102] Interestingly, a situation had unfolded where Air Force headquarters was planning a larger gunship force than the Pacific commanders wanted. This conflict of views continued until later in 1968 when the Air Force Advisory Group in South Vietnam recommended equipping a Vietnamese unit with Spooky gunships. This opened a way for the Air Force to keep some AC-47s active in the war, yet drop one gunship type from the Air Force inventory.

What had begun as a search for an aircraft to replace the AC-47 evolved into a mixed force—a family of gunships. Soon the gunship would become multinational, as several U.S. allies in Southeast Asia adopted it. Spirited debate had accompanied the mixed gunship force development and altered its course from time to time. Dynamic change would continue to yield more and better gunships, but the greater emphasis was on the AC-130 aircraft due to its richer growth potential.

Amid discussion of the gunship force, the Air Force tried to hurry modification of seven JC-130A aircraft into Gunship IIs. A modification program directive, dated December 14, 1967, authorized conversion of two JC-130As into gunships.[103] Secretary Brown approved a February 13, 1968, amendment to this directive which upped the number to seven JC-130As at a total cost of $19,366,475.[104] Under a letter contract, Ling-Temco-Vought Electrosystems (LTVE), Greenville, Texas, proceeded with the work in December 1967. Delivery of the first gunship was set for June 1968, the seventh by October 1968. The prototype Gunship II had performed so well in Southeast Asia that it served as a guide for production of the seven gunships.[105]

The Air Force took a close look at modification program management. The mixed gunship force meant two concurrent aircraft modification programs, one for the AC-130, the other for the AC-119. Air Force headquarters split responsibility for gunship program management, designating AFSC program manager for the AC-130s and AFLC for the AC-119s.[106] The matter of coordination bothered the Air Staff, however, since the two managers would be competing for such subsystems as sensors, guns, and illuminators. Hence, the Chief of Staff instructed AFSC and AFLC on January 6, 1968, to set up a joint project office for coordinating action on priority programs.[107] AFLC questioned the need for the office, pointing out that normal contacts with AFSC on the programs gave ample opportunity to negotiate and resolve priorities and allocation of critical items.[108] The Chief of Staff accepted this view and the management remained at first divided.

In late January 1968 at Greenville, Texas, representatives from LTVE, TAC, AFLC, WRAMA, and ASD reviewed the Gunship II program and defined responsibilities of the various parties. It was agreed that LTVE would provide special support including aerospace ground equipment, spares, contractor field support, and depot maintenance. LTVE's support would also extend to training units at Lockbourne AFB, Ohio, and to the detachment at Ubon RTAFB, Thailand. The Air Force Logistics Command would furnish common support through usual supply channels. The command also warned that the program's urgency would require certain deviations from normal procedures, mainly related to the limited testing.[109]

Gunship II's more sophisticated equipment, some of it relatively new to the Air Force, generated difficult support problems. These had begun with the prototype AC-130A.[110] With AFLC agreement, Aeronautical Systems Division had contracted with LTVE for equipment support of systems peculiar to the prototype. On February 12, 1968, ASD announced that an LTVE field team would oversee supply and maintenance of all Gunship II peculiar items. A sixteen-man team was to be in place in SEA on August 1, 1968, to care for: the fire-control system (computer, gunsight, and safety display unit), the forward-looking infrared equipment, the airborne illuminator-xenon lights, the night optical device, the beacon tracking radar set, the Mk-24 flare dispenser system, and the UHF homing and ranging system.[111]

This provision for contractor support contained seeds of controversy that surfaced on April 23-24, 1968, during a joint AC-130A and AC-119G/K gunship logistic support conference at WRAMA. The Air Staff questioned the efficiency of such support and expressed concern about balancing support for both the AC-130 and AC-119 programs. CINCPACAF backed the Air Staff position and stated its concern regarding the impact on the AC-119 program.[112] On the other hand, AFLC and ASD pointed out the lack of "organic depot level maintenance" capability and time delays associated with "separate contracts to various vendors." They insisted that contract maintenance and field service offered the only feasible solution to the high-priority AC-130 modifications.[113] WRAMA argued that "the significant reason for using the contractor to fully support this program is the fact that for this initial operational deployment we will be supporting the program from the contractor's production line and from the contractor's vendors."[114]

The conferees did not agree on the plan for logistic support so considerable message traffic followed to hammer one out. The initial logistic support concept was revised May 24, 1968, in line with Air Force headquarters instructions and an ASD-proposed compromise. The revision signified a shift from total contractor support for one year to basically Air Force support but with a large role for the contractor.[115] By July 1968 a Gunship II materiel support plan had firmed up major responsibilities. ASD would continue as the modification program manager with responsibility for "engineering, prototype, configuration, testing and modification of the end item." WRAMA or AFLC would be the AC-130 system manager. As prime contractor, LTVE was to modify the aircraft, manage a supply system of peculiar components, and operate a repair depot when necessary. Air Training Command would train the crews and test their ability to operate Gunship II's equipment. Finally, TAC and PACAF would be the using commands.[116]

To further review support progress and problems, twenty-four representatives from seven organizations gathered at the LTVE plant on August 19-23, 1968. Attention centered on preparing technical publications and identifying, requisitioning, and shipping of all necessary spare parts

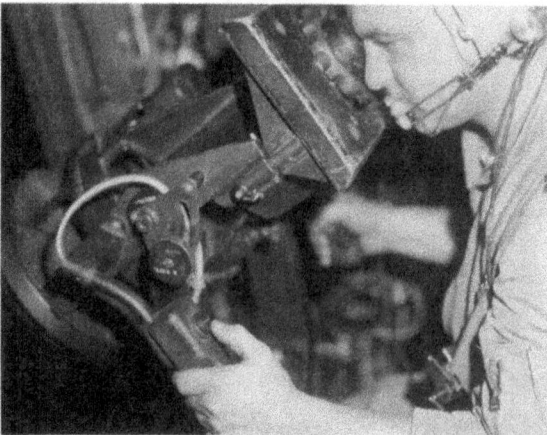

Top: View of guns in an AC-130A gunship; center: AC-130 of the 16th Special Operations Squadron in Thailand; bottom: Capt. Gilbert L. Camburn, 16th SOS, at the controls of a night observation device.

and aerospace ground equipment. The status of the logistic support was increasingly critical because the first two AC-130s were already in use for crew training. The conference estimated that one hundred percent of the initial spares would be identified and procured by September 1, 1968. Completion date for the final technical orders was expected on November 1, 1968. Eventual success of the whole rush project, as with many others, would hinge on the vast and coordinated logistic effort.[117]

The Aeronautical Systems Division struggled through most of 1968 to keep the AC-130 modification program on schedule. The Seventh Air Force, PACAF, and TAC pressed for early deployment of the Gunship II aircraft to Southeast Asia. They wanted the AC-130s at the start of the northeast monsoon season when Laotian roads and trails were sufficiently dried out for the enemy to push through most of his supplies.[118] It seemed, however, a number of difficulties conspired to defeat attainment of this goal. Original proposals to prospective contractors said the Gunship II prototype would be on hand as a guide for modifications. Nevertheless, after winning the contract in December 1967, Ling-Temco-Vought Electrosystems had scant access to the prototype before its return to Southeast Asia in February 1968. Moreover, LTVE failed to use the time effectively and delays occurred as the Air Force sought to clarify its requirements with drawings and in meetings. All this boosted costs.[119] An Air Force decision in February 1968 posed a second complication. It specified that the first two contractor-modified aircraft be used for combat crew training, enabling the other five AC-130s to arrive in Southeast Asia with trained crews. This meant a later Southeast Asia arrival date for the first two aircraft.[120]

The situation grew more complex, when it was realized that the first two AC-130s would have slightly different equipment than the other five. This resulted from changes made after the first two modifications had been approved.[121] On March 5, 1968, for example, Air Force headquarters amended the modification program directive to install terrain-avoidance and terrain-following radar at an additional cost of $2,553,225 (new total modification cost: $21,919,700).[122] In addition, the last five aircraft would have an improved forward-looking infrared system. While all seven AC-130s were to receive this new equipment, the first two AC-130s would require a later retrofit. This caused TAC to question use of the first two aircraft for combat crew training, seeing that it would send crews to Southeast Asia unfamiliar with the new electronics equipment. Although TAC and AFLC debated the problem, the program proceeded as first planned.[123]

The Air Force contended with another difficulty—slippage in delivery schedules for the first two AC-130s that in turn delayed crew training. At first the training cadre had hoped the two aircraft would be on hand in June 1968.[124] Near the end of June, however, ASD told TAC and AFSC that contractor flight tests had "revealed airframe, sensor, and integration problems." The best estimate for delivery of the first AC-130 was now mid-July.[125] The slippage forced adjustment in class schedules and personnel suffered inconvenient delays. In April 1968 TAC had informed PACAF that the 4413th Combat Crew Training Squadron at Lockbourne AFB would fill AC–130 crew requirements with three crews each in September, October, and November 1968.[126] This had to be adjusted, and in August the Pacific Air Forces deployment schedule was revised as follows:

	Number of Crews	Number of Aircraft
Oct 1968	3	3
Nov 1968	3	1
Jan 1969	2	0
Feb 1969	1	1

The two AC–130s used for training, and their crews, would be sent to Southeast Asia as soon as retrofitting was completed.[127]

As July 1968 moved to a close, Pacific Air Forces became alarmed about the slippage in AC–130 modifications and again stressed the urgent need for the aircraft by the northeast monsoon season. The Seventh Air Force, equally concerned, underscored the importance of the upcoming Project Commando Hunt, an "intensive interdiction truck killing campaign."[128] It urged that the contractor be pressed to deliver the last two AC–130s in November 1968 rather than in January 1969. ASD and the contractor came up with the following schedule:[129]

Aircraft Number	Placed for Modification	Estimate of[130] Original Completion	Contract Schedule	Returned to Air Force
1	21 Dec 1967	Jun 1968	9 Aug 1968	6 Aug 1968
2	9 Jan 1968	Jun 1968	12 Aug 1968	8 Aug 1968
3	26 Jan 1968	Jul 1968	4 Oct 1968	10 Oct 1968
4	6 Feb 1968	Aug 1968	6 Sep 1968	22 Oct 1968
5	18 Mar 1968	Aug 1968	15 Sep 1968	29 Oct 1968
6	1 Apr 1968	Sep 1968	1 Oct 1968	7 Nov 1968
7	15 Apr 1968	Oct 1968	15 Oct 1968	9 Dec 1968

Just about the time the first AC–130As off the Ling-Temco-Vought production line were sent to Southeast Asia, the prototype aircraft was on its way back to the United States. In view of the logistic problems in supporting the AC–130As, one-of-a-kind equipment, the Air Force decided to modify the prototype accordingly. How to do this was open to question, however, because of a dispute with LTVE over the cost of modifying this eighth Gunship II. Moreover, the Air Force was not entirely satisfied with LTVE's performance.[131] During December 1968 and January 1969 ASD therefore considered contracting for the modification with another company or doing the job itself. If neither of these options seemed feasible, ASD might recommend the prototype's modification be canceled. On January 23, 1969, Maj. Gen. Harry E. Goldsworthy, ASD commander, proposed the work be done in ASD shops and the Air Staff agreed. In February, ASD's Gunship II Project Branch sent the necessary work orders and contractor's production drawings to the shops so fabrication of parts could begin. The

Gunship II prototype was in place at Wright-Patterson AFB on May 10 for the conversion. Its delivery to PACAF was projected for October 1, 1969.[132]

Before the end of 1968, four AC-130 gunships were in Thailand flying combat. However, despite vigorous efforts of support personnel, equipment malfunctions plagued operations almost from the start. On December 20, 1968, the Seventh Air Force reported three major and fifty-seven other discrepancies to AFSC and AFLC. An AFSC maintenance assistance team, headed by Brig. Gen. Guy M. Townsend, arrived at Ubon on January 17, 1969, and at once explored the problems and assisted in their correction. Texas Instruments, subcontractor for the infrared set, rushed a technical representative to Ubon to keep the units operating.[133] By December 31, 1968, seven sets had been built and conditionally accepted. (The first two were later deemed unsatisfactory and returned to Texas Instruments for reworking.)[134] LTVE personnel analyzed and repaired the radar air conditioning. Use of technical orders and test equipment (which had been on hand but overlooked) resolved the doppler radar difficulties. In spite of these equipment troubles, Gunship II sorties over Laos had risen considerably by year's end.[135]

The effort to rush development and logistic support arrangements had not removed serious problems and delays. The high-priority modification program fell behind the desired schedule. Only half the planned Gunship IIs were in Southeast Asia by the spring of 1969. Production of critical subsystems accounted for most of the delays but some reflected changing Air Force requirements. Too little time for a complete systems approach led to a lack of trained personnel, particularly on new subsystems.[136] Initially, the Air Force Logistics Command was slow to identify and stock sufficient spare parts, publications, and supporting ground-equipment.[137] Costs climbed to $47 million due mainly to expanded spare requirements. Shortage of Class V modification funds further slowed procurement of spare and support items.[138] Nevertheless, while falling short of its goals, the development support effort did get AC-130s into combat during the northeast monsoon season.

Certain organizational steps had been taken in preparation for the arrival of the Gunship IIs. At first there were differences of opinion concerning command and control of the Ubon-based AC-130s. The 14th Air Commando Wing, which supervised the prototype, proposed in July 1968 that it continue to command the AC-130s, stressing the idea of a single manager for the gunships.[139] The Seventh Air Force replied that on January 5, 1968, it had recommended to PACAF just such an arrangement. The Air Force Chief of Staff and PACAF, however, decided to activate a new AC-130 unit, the 16th Air Commando Squadron, under command of the 8th Tactical Fighter Wing at Ubon. They rebutted the Seventh Air Force plan with these points: (1) The 16th ACSq by being colocated with its parent

Operational Control of Air Units in SEA

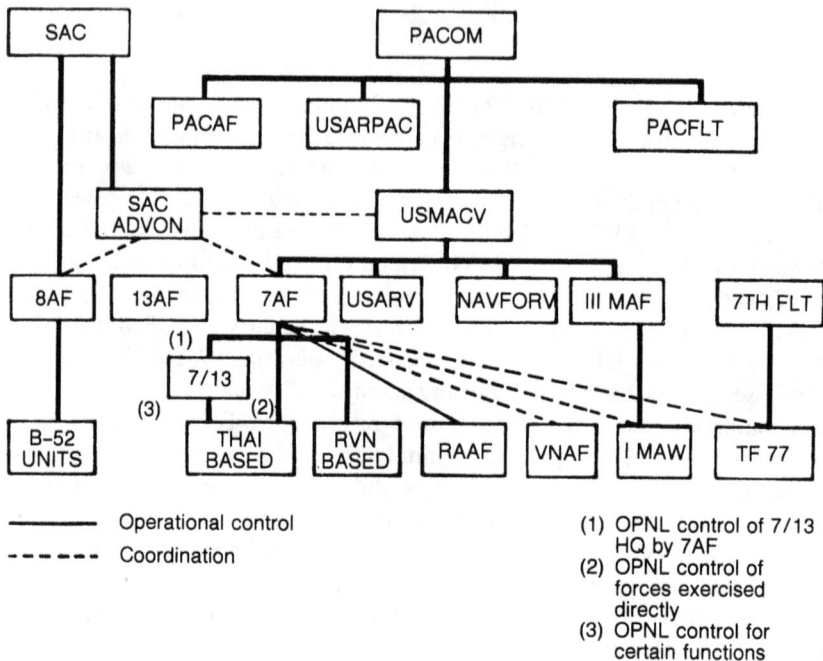

```
   SAC                      PACOM

        PACAF    USARPAC              PACFLT

   SAC  ADVON  - - - - - -  USMACV

   8AF   13AF    7AF   USARV  NAVFORV  III MAF    7TH FLT

              (1)
              7/13
   (3)        (2)
   B-52       THAI    RVN
   UNITS      BASED   BASED   RAAF  VNAF  I MAW   TF 77
```

—————— Operational control

- - - - - - Coordination

(1) OPNL control of 7/13 HQ by 7AF
(2) OPNL control of forces exercised directly
(3) OPNL control for certain functions

wing could maintain a "close and more responsive logistics relationship" with the Ubon support base, (2) the Royal Thai government had continually showed reluctance to have Thailand-based units assigned to a headquarters outside the country, and (3) the Seventh Air Force would still exercise operational control over the AC–130s, permitting great flexibility for missions in South Vietnam and Laos.[140] The 16th Air Commando Squadron was set for activation on August 1, 1968.[141] This date began to slip, however, because of the need to obtain approval of the higher manpower ceiling from the Royal Thai government.[142] It was October 31, 1968, when the 16th Special Operations Squadron* came into being with only one aircraft, the prototype.[143] This marked the first time a gunship unit was organized outside the jurisdiction of the 14th Special Operations Wing and highlighted the role planned for the AC–130s—out-country interdiction.

The 16th Special Operations Squadron's mission was "to provide firepower offensively and defensively in support of USAF combat support activities and other U.S. sponsored activities in SEA. The 16th Special Operations Squadron may deploy to and maintain continuous alert posture at operating locations [OLs] and designated bases in its area of responsibility."[144] Seventh Air Force Operations Order 543–69 spelled out

---

*The "Air Commando" designation became "Special Operations" on August 1, 1968.

priorities for airborne firepower support that supplemented this broad mission statement:[145]

Priority	Type of Mission
1	Night interdiction and armed reconnaissance to destroy wheeled and tracked vehicular traffic on roads and sampans on waterways.
2	Night interdiction of targets that have been bombed and then hit with fire-suppression missions.
3	Close fire support of U.S. and friendly military installations including forts, outposts, and strategic towns and cities.
4	Search and Rescue support.
5	Offset firing in support of troops in contact by use of aircraft radar and ground beacons.
6	Daylight armed escort of road and offshore convoys.
7	Harassment and interdiction.

Clearly, Priority 1 missions were designed to capitalize on the AC–130's new sophisticated sensors, heavier armament, and greater slant range capabilities.

Upon arrival, the AC–130s quickly adapted to various missions. In December 1968 they were diverted from interdiction sorties to support defenders of a fortified post on the southeast corner of Ban Thateng, Laos. This position in central-southern Laos commanded one of the major north-south supply routes and was under constant threat of being overrun.[146] For four nights the AC–130s supplied illumination and firepower helping to thwart the attacks. They used 16,200 rounds of 20-mm and 16,500 rounds of 7.62-mm ammunition to break the town's siege. The gunship strikes touched off a large fire and a great explosion and during the first two nights killed an estimated 240 of the enemy.[147] These AC–130 defensive-type missions recalled those of Spooky.

Although AC–130s might be diverted to save Laotian hamlets, their primary commitment was night interdiction. Since 1964 American aircraft had flown interdiction strikes in Southeast Asia. As the conflict persisted, the interdiction aspect took on fresh importance and absorbed more of the available resources on both sides. Through January 1968 the ordnance delivered by the gunships during interdiction strikes equaled half the total ordnance expended in the Korean War.[148] The tempo of the conflict beat faster, and by 1968 the North Vietnamese and Viet Cong required a heavier flow of supplies to South Vietnam. The need stemmed from the more intense fighting (1968 Tet offensive) following the enemy's introduction of bigger and more conventional forces. At the same time, the United States and South Vietnam were determined to choke off as much of the supply flow as possible and render the enemy forces ineffective.

The supplies reached communist forces in South Vietnam by (1) infiltration through the demilitarized zone, (2) via coastal vessels through the Cambodian port of Sihanoukville then on northward and eastward, and (3) southward over the maze of roads in the Laotian panhandle. It was the latter route that carried the greatest supply tonnage and number of troops.

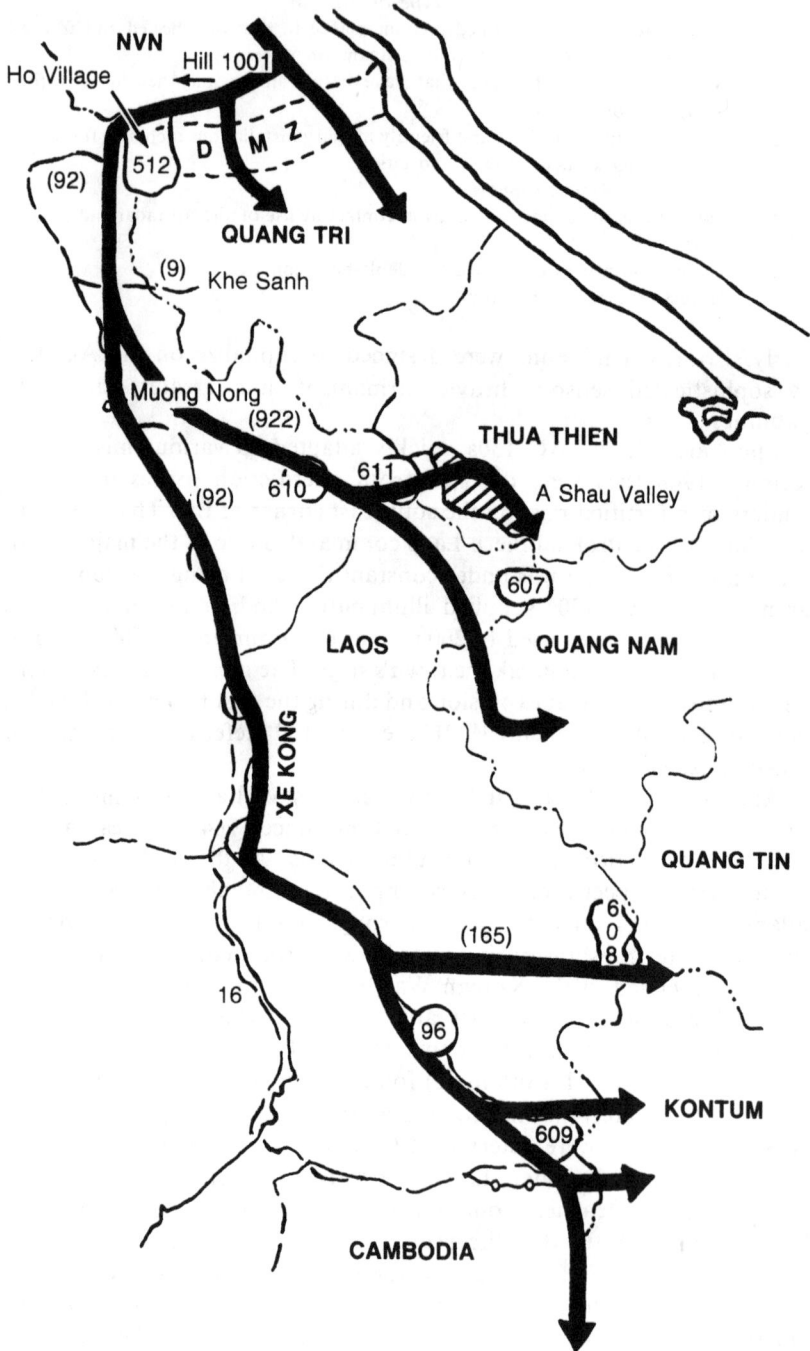

**Infiltration Corridors
1967**

Commando Hunt Main Target Areas

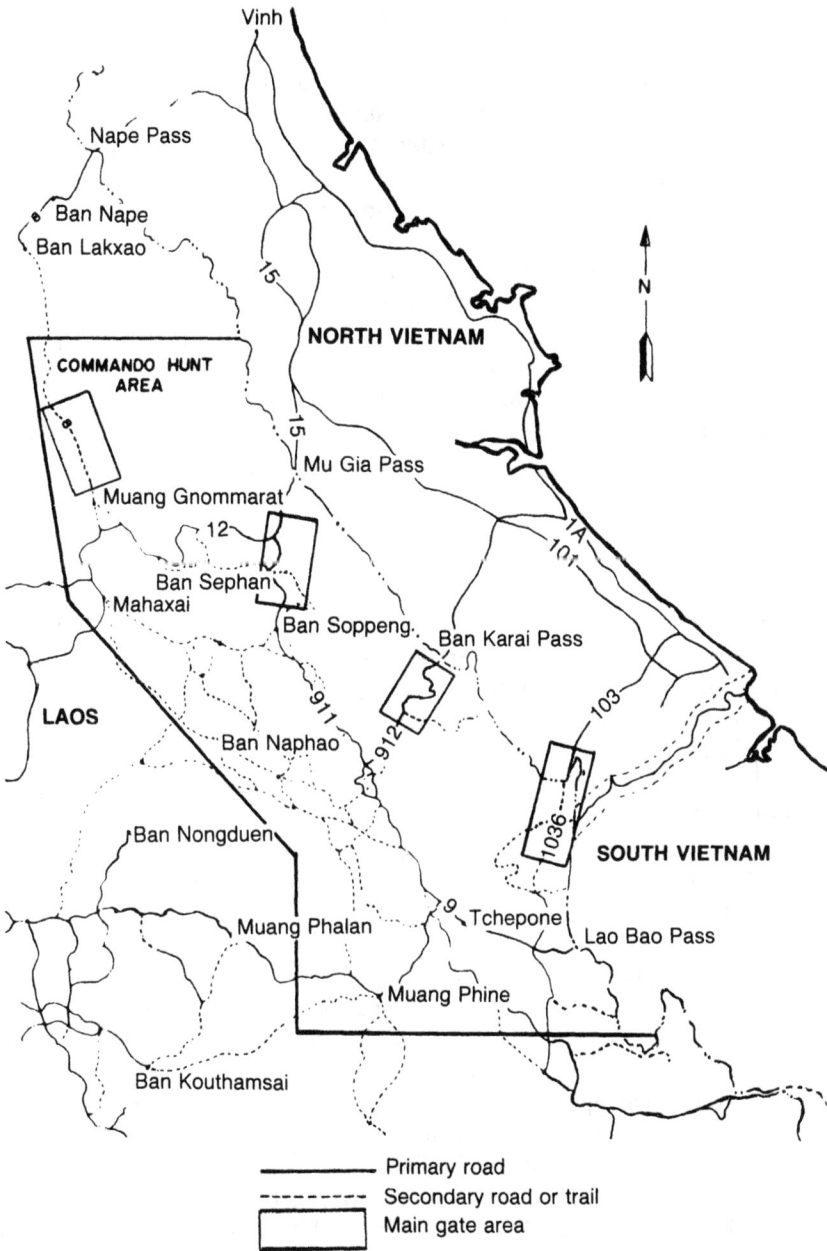

Primary road
Secondary road or trail
Main gate area

Consequently, it received the greatest interdiction effort, particularly from the Air Force and its gunships.

Interdicting the Ho Chi Minh Trail was a difficult task. By the beginning of 1969, this extensive road and trail network (for movement of materiel by truck or on bicycles or the backs of porters) threaded through steep mountainous terrain frequently covered by jungle canopy. In caves of the limestone karsts, the enemy stored supplies and occasionally concealed antiaircraft guns.[149] Wherever possible, he also transported cargo by river. Numerous road crews labored diligently to repair roads and construct quick detours and alternate routes. Most roadwork and movement of supplies took place at night under the cover of darkness. Peak traffic hours would be shifted if air attacks seemed concentrated at certain times. Antiaircraft guns defended particularly vulnerable Trail points, a protection that continually expanded with more and better weapons. In short, interdicting this rugged region of approximately 1,700 square miles, used by a firmly determined enemy, presented a most formidable challenge.

As with most air operations, weather proved pivotal in the interdiction effort. The Southeast Asian monsoon seasons generated cyclic periods of bad and good weather. This in turn forced relatively sharp peaks and deep valleys of air activity. The warm moist air shifted inland from the seas during the southwest monsoon, striking and flowing over the Annam Cordillera to produce cloudy, rainy weather. Hence from about May to November air operations over Laotian trails faced very rough going, and enemy truck traffic declined over the nearly impassable roads. With the northeast monsoon (November to May) came comparatively good dry weather over Laos as the airflow came from the colder, less humid land mass to the north.[150] Since this weather favored air operations and vehicular movement, it was dubbed the "hunting season." These rhythmic weather periods shaped AC–130 operations and the aircraft's ongoing development as a weapon system. Equipment changes and modifications were keyed to the southwest monsoon so that the aircraft could be in combat at the time of greatest need.

By the fall of 1968, interdiction of enemy supply routes had evolved into a complex many-faceted operation. Covert roadwatch teams, mostly indigenous, spotted trucks and determined main traffic routes. Other Trail intelligence flowed from intensive aerial reconnaissance, forward air controller observations, and captured North Vietnamese. Two geographically defined operational areas, Barrel Roll in the north and Steel Tiger in the southern panhandle, had been designated for organizational convenience. Chief interest lay in Steel Tiger with its important routes running south from two major mountain passes on the North Vietnamese border—Mu Gia and Ban Karai. Within Steel Tiger several past programs such as Tiger Hound and Cricket had sought better ways for target generation, strike control, and damage assessment.[151] A wide range of aircraft types, B–52s to A–1s, flew over trails and passes to locate and impede traffic. The Air Force tried new tactics such as hunter-killer teams and new equipment in an unending search for better results. Planning, coordinating, and managing the entire interdiction operation taxed the most skillful leadership.

In spite of improved interdiction effectiveness, the enemy still supplied his units in South Vietnam to the dismay of allied military and government leaders. Most disturbing in early 1968 was evidence of a truck-kill plateau. An analysis of 1967 truck detections and truck attrition showed sightings of trucks in Laos during 1967 up 165 percent over 1966, yet truck kills stayed roughly the same. One report commented: "The fact remains we are seeing far more trucks in Laos than we are able to destroy."[152]

A number of reasons accounted for the enemy's success in getting his supplies through. First, North Vietnamese ability to reconstruct roads at night and in adverse weather always offset much of the interdiction effort.[153] Ironically, years of bombing some good interdiction points had changed them into easily repairable gravel piles. Second, the enemy had astutely capitalized on Air Force deficiencies in night and all-weather operations both in the realm of detecting targets and destroying those of a fleeting nature such as trucks.[154] Third, despite a major push to gain more intelligence, Air Force traffic analysis was incomplete and insufficient. It lacked information on road capacities, length of time to transit areas, extent of roads and trails, and the number of available trucks. Fourth, the Air Force had not yet found the right aircraft or aircraft team combining target detection, tracking, and destruction capabilities.* Fifth, the interdiction effort was fragmented and without an overall strategy. Sixth, the Air Force concentrated its interdiction very close to the utilization area. This contrasted with the preferred concept of striking deep at supplies close to their source and at troops in training and staging bases.[155] Without improvement in most of these areas, there was doubt the Air Force could significantly impair the enemy's logistic support.

New developments made the Air Force far more optimistic about interdicting the Ho Chi Minh Trail when the 1968–69 hunting season opened. The greater quantity of new equipment from the Shed Light program gave promise of trimming the enemy's nighttime advantage. A case in point was the night observation device (starlight scope) tested in 1966 and introduced in early 1967. The scope's impact was reflected in a comparison made by the PACAF Directorate of Tactical Evaluation of the period November 30–December 2, 1966, (before the scope's introduction) with a three-day period in 1967 following its extensive use:[156]

---

*A debate over jet versus propeller aircraft was typical of the problem. The Joint Chiefs of Staff told CINCPAC in December 1967 that a Joint Chiefs' study had shown "Propeller aircraft are approximately 9 times as effective as jet aircraft per sortie in destroying trucks and water craft in Laos." [Msg JCS to CINCPAC, subj: The Use of Propeller and Jet Aircraft In Laos, 201740Z Dec 67.] Commanders of jet units argued that speed was essential for survivability in many areas. The message admitted that "loss rates for propeller aircraft operating in Laos are approximately 4 times greater than the comparable loss rates for jet aircraft."

Trucks sighted	1966	1967
Visually	20	30
Night observation device	—	597
Destroyed	8	83

The Air Force had installed low-light-level television (LLLTV) in two A–1s and two B–57s during 1968. Test programs for this night sensor development were under way in Southeast Asia under the nickname Tropic Moon. The use of airborne-deployed sensor fields (labeled Igloo White) tied via relay aircraft to the infiltration surveillance center at Nakhon Phanom, Thailand, was expected to improve traffic analysis. Task Force Alpha (a wing-level unit) would control this all-weather, around-the-clock surveillance network of seismic and acoustic sensors. In addition, a completely integrated interdiction effort for the Laotian panhandle (code name "Commando Hunt"*) had been developed.[157]

Furthermore, President Johnson had ordered a halt to the bombing of most of North Vietnam on November 1, 1968, allowing more attention and resources to be concentrated on the interdiction campaign.† New specialized munitions for suppressing antiaircraft guns and killing trucks were available. Finally, Gunship II's potent combination of sensors, illuminator, fire-control system, and heavier armament could be employed. Secretary Brown pinned his hope for a "good interdiction campaign" on the better traffic analysis, new equipment, and improved tactics. Noting that one or more of these factors was lacking in the past, the Secretary considered use of AC–130 gunships one of the important positive changes.[158]

Air Force Commando Hunt strategy in 1968–69 called for a flexible allocation of forces against priority-listed targets. First priority was assigned interdiction points, specific road segments difficult to detour or which, when blocked, would divert traffic into predictable areas. These were carefully selected from aerial photography, forward air controller observations, and Igloo White sensor information.[159] They were attacked with precision bombing followed by use of delayed-action-fused bombs, air-delivered landmines or area-denial munitions. The strikes took place in late afternoon making it harder for repair crews to reopen the roads before nightfall. As darkness came, the AC–130s and strike aircraft, supported by flak-suppression flights and flareships, attacked vehicles backed up or attempting alternate routes. The second target priority went to truck parks and supply caches, the third to moving trucks, and the last to antiaircraft

---

*Air interdiction campaigns directed against the flow of supplies from North Vietnam to Viet Cong and North Vietnam forces in South Vietnam and Cambodia; these campaigns in southern Laos (Steel Tiger area of operations) bore numerical designtions that changed with the semi-annual monsoonal shift; the three northeast monsoon, or dry-season campaigns, took place in 1968/1969, 1969/1970, and 1970/1971, and covered the period from October through April.

†The bombing halt had a negative side. It permitted the North Vietnamese to move supplies unhindered up to the Annam mountain range along the Laotian border. Soon after the bombing halt, large convoys of uncamouflaged trucks, traveling bumper to bumper, were reported heading for the Laotian border in daylight.

artillery.[160] Coordinated use of aircraft* against these target categories created an integrated interdiction effort in depth. It substantially slowed the enemy's transit of Laos and afforded more opportunities for up to five hundred sorties a day to destroy his trucks and supplies.[161]

Reports of more than 14,000 trucks moving through Laos in April 1968 imparted a sense of urgency to the interdiction effort. This unprecedented traffic flow was placed against the knowledge that the enemy had successfully moved some 10,000 tons of supplies to prepare for the 1968 Tet offensive. Moreover, the bombing halt would now free thousands more trucks from support requirements north of the 19th parallel. It was becoming obvious that the "insatiable logistic demands of heavy mortars, modern rocket weapons, and a complete family of light infantry automatic weapons" widened the enemy's dependence on truck transportation. It seemed highly possible that a surge of truck traffic would be in the offing for support of a "third general offensive."[162]

As a key element of the overall interdiction strategy, the AC-130s were used at once in armed reconnaissance of roads. The first flights kept to the less heavily defended southern portion of Steel Tiger while crews got to know the area and control procedures. As proficiency progressed, missions shifted northward.[163]

On familiarization sorties the AC-130 combat crews first mastered the command and control system and the theater rules of engagement. The command structure consisted of dual channels. An administrative channel ran from the Thirteenth Air Force through the 8th Tactical Fighter Wing to the 16th Special Operations Squadron at Ubon, Thailand. An operational channel, for mission assignments or fragging, flowed from the Seventh Air Force through 8th Tactical Fighter Wing to the 16th Special Operations Squadron. The Seventh Air Force tactical air control center exercised battlefield direction through the airborne command and control center, with sensor inputs from Task Force Alpha and finally with on-the-spot assistance from forward air controllers.[164] Restraints on airstrikes in Laos supplemented this control arrangement. Attacks were forbidden near specified villages, and use of certain types of ordnance was tightly controlled. The U.S. Ambassador in Vientiane, Laos, had to approve plans for air operations in some parts of Laos so not to disturb the delicate relationships with the neutral Royal Laotian government.[165]

At first, forward air controllers in O-2 aircraft helped keep the gunships within restrictions and control requirements while operating over Laos. This practice, however, proved impractical for the entire Gunship II program. In February 1969 AC-130 pilots were required to qualify as forward air controllers by attending the forward air controller school at Ubon. Both pilots on an AC-130 crew were to be trained. But when one had completed school, the crew was designated FAC-qualified. As an interim measure, Seventh Air

---

*Aircraft types used were the B-52, B-57, F-4, F-105, F-100, Navy A-4, A-6, A-7, A-26, A-1, AC-130, and AC-123.

Out-Country Tactical Operations

Force directed that a forward air controller be an additional crewmember.[166] Eventually, the Gunship II would provide FAC assistance for other strike aircraft in Laos.[167]

No two Gunship II sorties were exactly alike, but a pattern of operations did develop. A typical sequence unfolded on a significant* December 30, 1968, mission:

> Ubon ground crews readied aircraft 1629 for the evening's flight. They put aboard Mk-24 and Mk-6 flares and 6,000 rounds of 20-mm ammunition. Meantime the crew studied the night's armed reconnaissance mission. The aircraft lifted off before dusk (at 1705) and while still over Ubon a checkout of equipment commenced. Operators aligned and prepared for operation the night observation device and other sensors. Gunners loaded and checked the weapons. Within 10 minutes the gunship was "crossing the fence" (the Mekong River separating Thailand and Laos) and making radio contact with Moonbeam, the ABCCC operating over southern Laos. Using current intelligence information the ABCCC assigned the AC-130 to a specific operating area whereupon the gunship's

---

*The mission had historical importance for it marked the official beginning of preplanned fighter escorts for AC-130s.

navigator assumed a key role as he plotted coordinates. The Gunship II's radio call sign was Spectre 01.*

Spectre 01 reported "on station" at 1720. For the next 55 minutes it practiced intercepts with F-4 flights in case their help was needed to suppress AA fire. At 1815 gunship sensor operators probed infiltration route 922 working a 15-mile road segment until 2035. At 1840 four eastbound "movers" were detected. (Normally one sensor was used to maintain a fix while another searched.) The sensor inputs fed the fire-control computer and the information reflected in the pilot's gunsight as he turned into a left orbit at 4,500 feet AGL [above ground level]. Selecting the lead truck to stall traffic, the pilot pushed the trigger button as the movable and fixed target reticles superimposed in his gunsight. The 1,000 rounds of 20-mm fired in a 4-minute attack damaged 1 truck.

At 1855 Spectre 01 detected target 2—1 mover—and in a 2-minute attack orbit fired another 1,000 rounds of 20-mm damaging 1 truck. Farther down the road the gunship discovered three stationary trucks and a suspected truck park. While marking the area with flares Spectre 01 met with 37-mm AA fire. From 1902 to 1925 the pilot squeezed off 1,000 more rounds of 20-mm on both the suspected truck park and the 37-mm site. An explosion and fire told of the AA emplacement's destruction.

Two more stationary trucks became target 4. Spectre 01 attacked from 2002 to 2006 and damaged both of them. Two F-4 flights—call signs Schlitz and Combine—worked on AA sites together with Spectre strikes and claimed two sites destroyed. From 2021 to 2026, Spectre 01 once more fired 1,000 20-mm rounds upon return to the scene of the suspected truck park of target 3. No visual results were obtained of this final attack. Spectre 01 left the target area at 2035 after an elapsed time of 3 hours and 15 minutes with 6,000 rounds of 20-mm ammunition and 15 Mk-6 flares expended. The night's work totaled four trucks damaged, one 37-mm antiaircraft site destroyed, and one 37-mm AA site silenced. Spectre 01 recrossed the fence and touched down at Ubon at 2115. Total mission time stood at four hours and ten minutes.[168]

Such a mission illustrated the growing effectiveness of AC-130s in the interdiction effort, which quickly compiled an unusual record. In January 1969, with but four aircraft and relatively inexperienced crews, they accounted for twenty-eight percent of the truck kills (Table 2).[169] As the months passed, their role took on even more significance. In April 1969 the 16th Special Operations Squadron flew just 3.7 percent of the sorties but accounted for more than forty-four percent of the trucks destroyed or damaged in Laos.[170]

An example of a new flawless Gunship II mission occurred on April 7, 1969, when aircraft 627, equipped with a fully operational FLIR, attained a one hundred percent kill ratio:

The AC-130, labeled Schlitz for the night mission, took off at 1905 and the crew went through the usual prestrike checks of sensor equipment, pilot's gunsight, and fire-control system. (A central traffic circle in downtown Ubon, easily seen by sensor operators and the pilot, was used for the checks.) Equipment in order, the gunship flew to the fragged area of routes 23 and 917 in central Laos. In the face of light antiaircraft fire the aircraft sighted, attacked, and destroyed two vehicles within the first thirty minutes.

The ABCCC next diverted Schlitz to interdict vehicles spotted on one of the most heavily defended areas of Laos—route 911, just south of Mu

---

* Spectre became the common name of all AC-130s just as Spooky did for all AC-47s.

TABLE 2. GUNSHIP II RECORD
(First Quarter 1969)

	Jan	Feb	Mar	Total
Missions fragged	65	81	99	245
Missions flown	63	73	89	225
Air aborts	3	7	4	14
Ground aborts	2	3	11	16
Trucks sighted	542	618	693	1,853
Trucks destroyed	105	210	292	607
Trucks damaged	115	138	98	351
Trucks (results not observed)	140	181	226	547
Boats sighted	1	22	0	23
Boats destroyed	1	10	0	11
Helicopters sighted	0	0	4	4
Helicopters destroyed	0	0	0	0
Troops-in-contact	8	2	3	13
Secondary fires	126	421	630	1,177
Secondary explosions	182	514	805	1,501
20-mm ammunition expended	237,436	376,652	312,147	926,235
7.62-mm ammunition expended	31,221	344,621	324,594	700,436

Source: Maj. Richard F. Kott, *The Role of USAF Gunships in SEASIA* (HQ PACAF, Project CHECO, August 30, 1969).

Gia Pass. The route segment pushed northwest to southeast through rolling jungle country with karsts soaring 2,000 feet above the road its entire length. Many rivers and creeks bisected the route slowing traffic. Utilizing the NOD and FLIR, the gunship crew sighted twenty three trucks. All were struck, the twenty seven secondary explosions and twelve secondary fires destroyed twenty three trucks. Even more remarkable the job was done amid an estimated 900-round barrage of 37-mm fire. Schlitz' work for the night totaled twenty five vehicles detected and twenty five destroyed.[171]

Not all missions matched the excellence of the April 7 Schlitz sortie. One week later, fire-control system trouble beset aircraft 627 (call sign Carter). Only two of fifteen trucks sighted could be destroyed, due to unreliable roll-in guidance and erratic gun patterns. Moreover, about halfway through the mission, Carter's NOD operator detected a convoy of southbound vehicles on route 911. The ABCCC turned down the gunship's request to strike because other aircraft were working in the area. It approved Carter's second request, but by then the trucks had vanished into the jungle. The night's mission ended with two vehicles destroyed of thirty-seven spotted.[172]

The 16th Special Operations Squadron and the gunships scored a notable first on a May 8 mission. At 0140 the NOD operator of aircraft 629 (call sign Bennet) detected a blurred, gray object moving across the jungle canopy at less than 1,000 feet above the terrain. He reported sighting a possible helicopter. The navigator quickly plotted the position and called Moonbeam (the ABCCC) for firing clearance. While awaiting

**Airborne Battlefield Command and
Control Center
Night Orbit Locations**

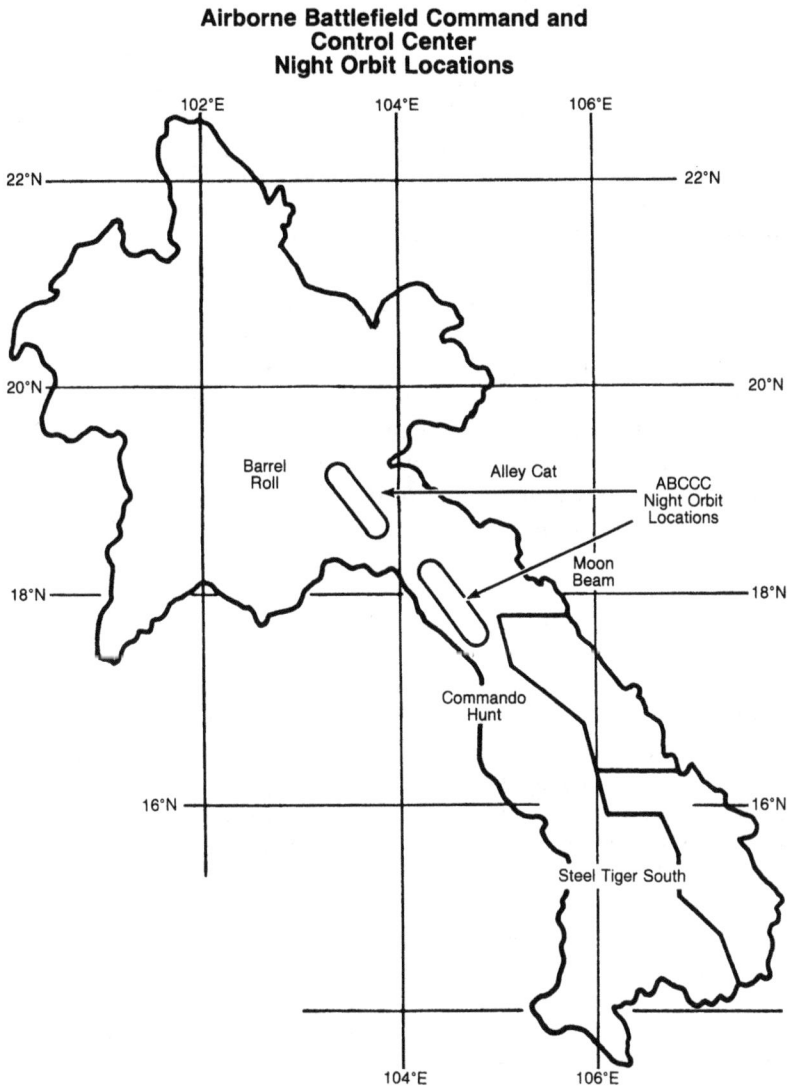

strike approval the gunship tracked the helicopter to a landing in a rectangular clearing. The NOD operator could make out several trails in the area. The FLIR operator, despite degraded equipment, was able to track the helicopter during one small segment of the firing orbit. After twenty minutes, Bennet received permission to fire and began attack passes. Several 20-mm cannon bursts struck the clearing's perimeter and set off many small secondary explosions. The NOD operator reported seeing five rounds hit home and small explosions come from the helicopter. Several gunship crews had reported suspected helicopter sightings before. Bennet was the first gunship to claim destruction of one.[173]

From the very first commitment of AC-130s to Southeast Asia, there was considerable concern about their vulnerability in operations over Laos. During its development the Air Force had tried to strengthen Gunship II's survivability by adding some 7,000 pounds of armor in the lower fuselage to protect the crew and vital components. It had also put polyurethane in the fuel cells (tanks) to make them explosion-proof.[174] Other survival advantages were expected from (1) the AC-130A's higher operational altitude made possible by greater-performance engines and 20-mm guns, (2) the aircraft's capability to fly on two engines at normal combat weight, and (3) the planned night and poor weather operations.[175]

The enemy's buildup of antiaircraft guns in Laos countered these efforts for gunship survivability. By June 1968 the prototype AC-130A had taken enemy fire on fifty-six of fifty-seven sorties—sighting an average of sixty rounds.[176] The North Vietnamese welcomed the November 1968 bombing halt and redeployed many antiaircraft guns to Laos just as the production AC-130s were about to arrive in Southeast Asia. When the Spectres began flying over the Trail, the Ubon-based AC-130 squadron reported quite simply: "Where there are trucks there are very many 37-mm positions." Before November 1, 1968, the enemy had an estimated two hundred guns of all calibers in Laos. From that date to May 1970 the number of guns in Laos (some of large caliber) jumped 400 percent.[177] The 37-mm fire (by far the most common) grew so intense and more accurate that some major roads were no longer deemed permissive for the gunship. Air Force headquarters' concern over gunship vulnerability deepened in June 1968 upon studying the AC-130A prototype's reports. Subsequently the Air Staff asked for more information on the extent of battle damage, so that it could further monitor the survivability aspect of gunship operations.[178]

Gunship crews adjusted their tactics to counter enemy defensive measures, and at times simply waited for targets to move out of a heavily defended area or called for fighter strikes to destroy antiaircraft batteries.[179]

Questions arose concerning the advantages that moonlight might offer to enemy gunners, so from February 1 to May 31, 1969, the 16th Special Operations Squadron studied the effects of lunar illumination on combat operations. It found no correlation between the "phase of the moon and the amount of antiaircraft artillery as some of the AAA reactions have occurred during periods of less than a half moon." The study of data suggested to the investigators that the enemy was increasing traffic when the moon was less than half full—possibly to reduce detection by the night observer device and employing more antiaircraft fire to cover the peak traffic times.[180]

Crewmembers assisted the pilot by scanning for antiaircraft firing flashes and calling out evasive actions for him to take to avoid the fire. The most effective response to enemy defenses in Laos, however, was the development of fighter-escort tactics. When the AC-130 prototype met with

Military Region III, Laos (Routes 911/912)

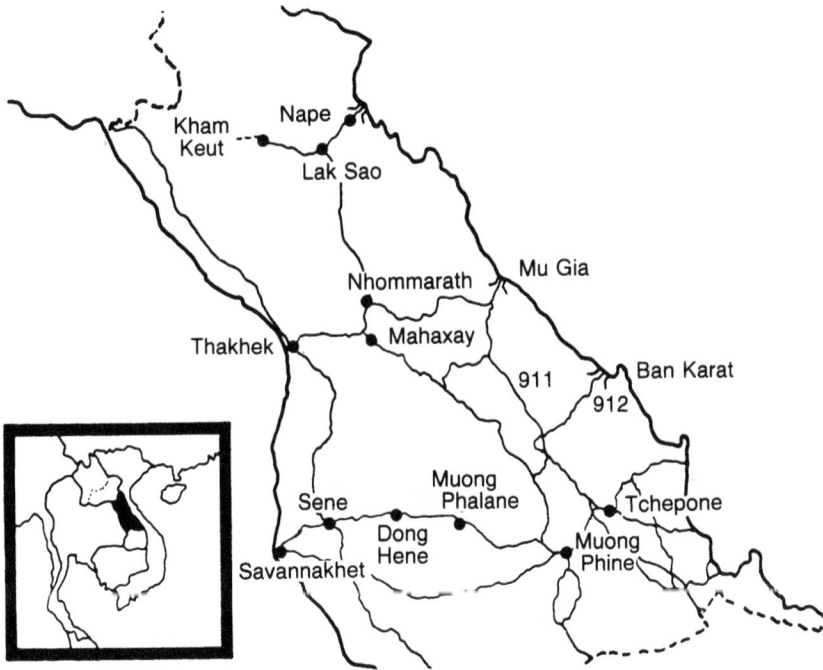

more intense antiaircraft fire, it had called for flak-suppression by fighter-bomber aircraft. The requests were made in a random fashion and little planning had occurred. The solution to the problems of penetration of heavily defended areas surrounding lucrative targets seemed to lie in the gunship/fighter team approach. A December 10, 1968, study by the Seventh Air Force Directorate of Tactical Analysis concluded that F–4s and AC–130s could kill more trucks by operating together rather than separately.[181] Twenty days later the 8th Tactical Fighter Wing's 497th Tactical Fighter Squadron, the "only night attack squadron in the Air Force," ushered in a new mission—armed escort and flak-suppression for Spectre aircraft. On the gunship/fighter team's first night, F–4Ds of Schlitz and Combine flights destroyed or silenced two 37-mm sites that were firing at Spectre 01.[182]

The difference in airspeed between the gunship and the escorts and the latter's mid-mission refueling needs—normally from a tanker over Thailand*—required changes in tactics.[183] At the target the gunship and the escorts flew differing attack orbits. When an enemy gun opened up on Spectre, the gunship coordinated with the Phantoms by radio to grant clearance for attacks and to assure aircraft separation. This was vital as the

---

*Referred to as the "Spectre Shuttle."

AA Weapon Threat

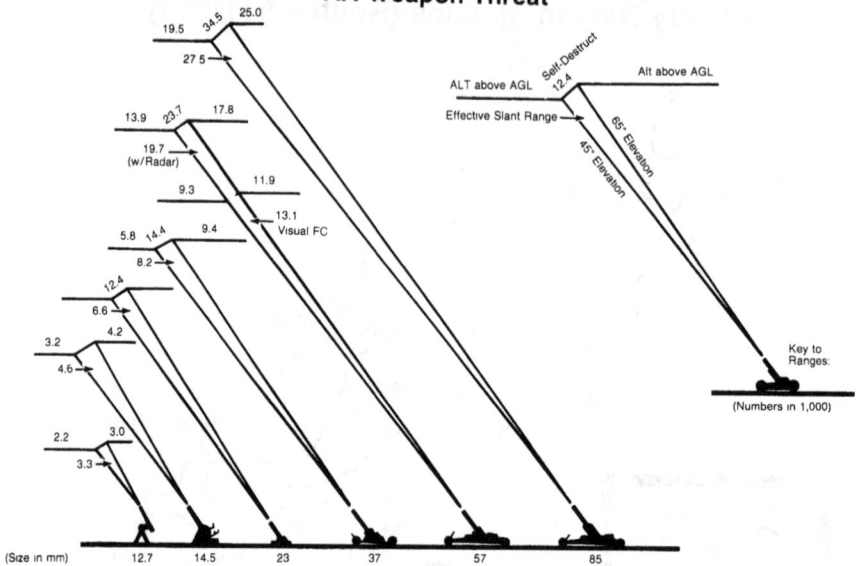

F-4's firing pass—dropping a single cluster bomb unit (CBU) or bomb—carried it twice through Spectre's orbiting altitude. Consequently, the escort had to know the gunship's position at all times. This became far harder when the escort and gunship were on the same side of the orbit, since the F-4 pilot could not easily see the shielded rotating beacon.

At times the hostile guns fired only occasionally and the Spectre could act as a forward air controller. It dropped logs (ground flares to create reference points) to mark the enemy gun emplacements and cleared the Phantoms for attack.[184]

These tactics were gradually refined and the AC-130/F-4 team proved to be a potent gun-killer as well as truck-killer. Maj. Gen. Robert L. Petit, Seventh/Thirteenth Air Force deputy commander, thought it evident: "The enemy pays a hell of a price to go after a Spectre."[185] The success of the AC-130/F-4 teams enabled interdiction strategists to continue the great truck-killing capabilities of Gunship II throughout the Laotian panhandle. The following fighter bomb damage assessment was recorded during the first four months of 1969:

	11 Jan–28 Feb	March	April
37-mm guns destroyed	19	26	18
37-mm guns silenced	23	16	20
Secondary explosions	166	393	367
Large fires	287	482	383
Road fires	2	1	0
Trucks destroyed	10	4	12

The gunship/fighter tactical combination had to bridge the unit esprit de corps gulf that tends to divide combat airmen. Expressions of disagreement now and then surfaced through the usual good-natured banter between Spectre and Phantom crewmembers. Some of the fighter pilots believed that the escort role was a misuse of their aircraft's strike capabilities. On the other hand, some of the gunship crewmembers resented what they thought was a lack of recognition for their contribution. And some in each camp resisted the change of tactics and only accepted the team concept gradually. Ultimately, a majority of the crewmembers recognized the arrangement's mutual advantages and generated new ideas for their units' combined operations.[186]

In the Laotian interdiction battle, the shrewd and determined North Vietnamese often turned the apparent advantage of gunship/fighter task forces into a tenuous, or at best a fleeting edge. The enemy employed various deceptions and stratagems, one of which was the shifting of gun emplacements. The North Vietnamese had improved their defense by use of 57-mm and larger weapons, and the possible incorporation of gun-laying radar. The effective slant range of the 57-mm was 13,100 feet with optical sighting; the range increased to 19,700 feet with radar assistance.[187] The enemy used missiles with limited success, but the threat of improved ground-to-air missile fire existed.[188] Improvements in enemy defenses were a serious menace to the AC-130 operations in view of the plane's predictable attack maneuver and modest airspeed.

One way to restrict the effect of enemy defensive advances was to upgrade the gunship's systems. In February 1968 the Tactical Air Warfare Center at Eglin AFB recommended an electronic countermeasure capability for the AC-130s to combat antiaircraft radar.[189] The experts also concentrated early attention on methods of overcoming the operating altitude limitations of gunship weapons, including one obvious solution—the installation of larger-caliber guns.[190]

Concern about AC-130 vulnerability increased when a 37-mm round hit a Spectre on March 3, 1969, and intensified with the loss of the first AC-130 on May 24.[191] The following account is taken from the battle damage report:

> Aircraft 1629 reached its Laotian target at 1935 local time and was joined by a fighter escort. Spectre made a firing pass 5 minutes later at a moving truck. It then flew to a road intersection and began a 120° turn to reconnoiter the new route. As the turn was completed, illuminator operator SSgt. Jack W. Troglen reported antiaircraft fire at 6 o'clock and accurate. Ten 37-mm rounds were seen—four on each side, one striking the gunship's tail section, and one hitting an undetermined spot on the fuselage.[192]

> The wounded Spectre turned westward toward home base. Its utility hydraulic system was out followed by the booster hydraulic system a few seconds later—leaving the aircraft temporarily out of control. The aircraft commander and copilot brought the gunship out of a nearly uncontrollable climb by bracing the control column to full forward position and by bringing all crewmembers to the flight deck.

> Further aircraft checks disclosed Sergeant Troglen wounded and dying and the rudder, elevator trim, and autopilot inoperative. The gunship was nursed back toward Ubon by use of aileron trim and engine power. Near the base the aircraft commander ordered non-essential crewmembers to bail out. Left aboard were pilot/aircraft commander Lt. Col. William Schwehm and copilot Maj. Gerald H. Piehl (to control the

The AC-130 Spectre Shuttle

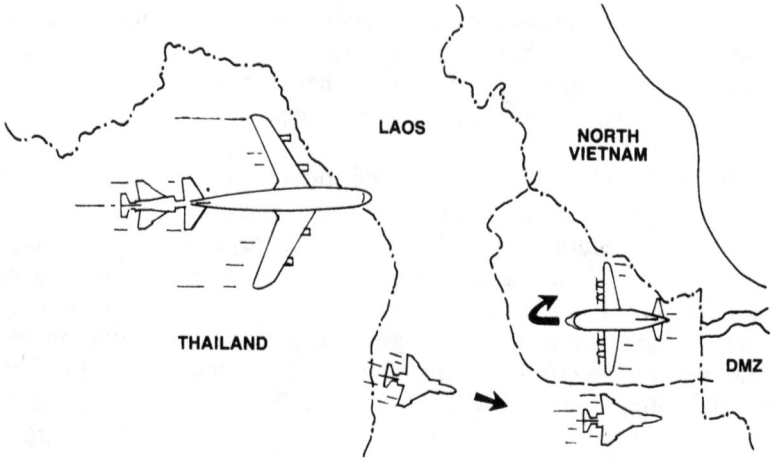

LAOS

NORTH VIETNAM

THAILAND

DMZ

F-4 Escort Tactics

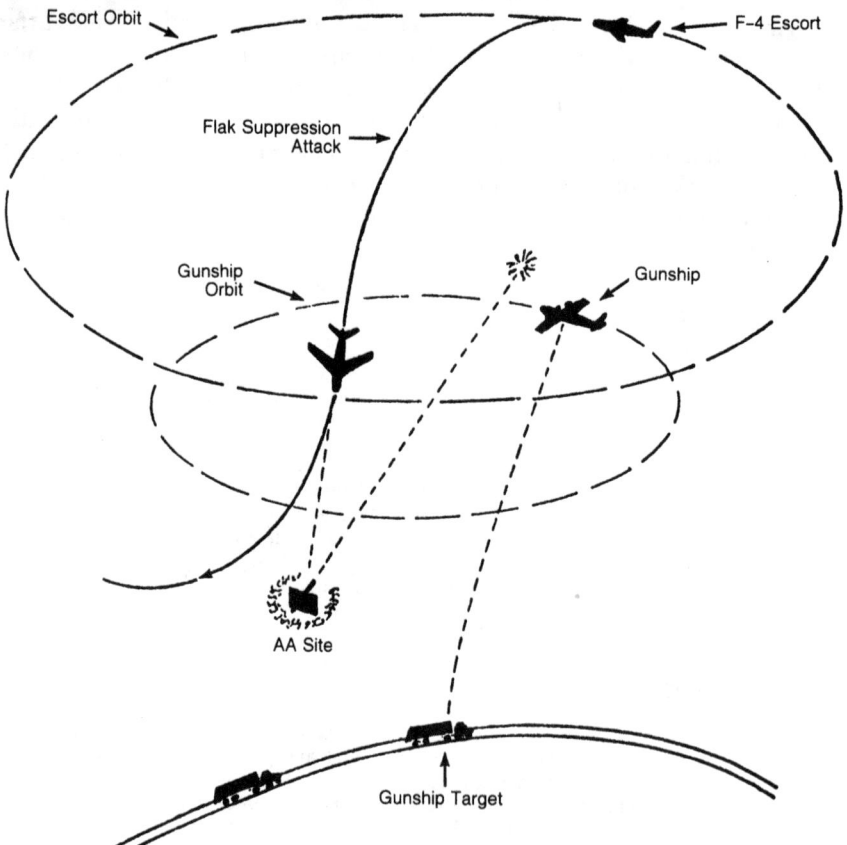

Escort Orbit

F-4 Escort

Flak Suppression Attack

Gunship Orbit

Gunship

AA Site

Gunship Target

aircraft), flight engineer SSgt. Cecil F. Taylor (to manually lower the gear), and a navigator sensor operator who wanted to stay.[193]

As Colonel Schwehm slightly reduced power the aircraft's nose dropped hard on the runway. The gunship bounced and hit heavily on the landing gear. An attempt to reverse engines was futile. Some 2,000 feet down the runway the gunship veered to the right, despite application of more power to number 3 and 4 engines (nose-wheel steering was inoperative). The right wing was sheared off. The gunship burst into flames as the pilot, copilot, and navigator sensor operator safely evacuated. The body of Sergeant Troglen and that of flight engineer Taylor were lost in the billowing flames and explosions of burning ammunition. All crewmembers who had bailed out were rescued.[194]

The loss of one AC-130 jolted the small Gunship II force. In a single stroke it had reduced operational aircraft by twenty-five percent.[195] Fortunately, the three remaining AC-130s (other than the prototype) arrived from the United States about the same time as the first gunship loss.[196] The 16th Special Operations Squadron thus had six AC-130s available for the closing months of the 1968-69 northeast monsoon season.

As bad weather moved in over the Trail network, the interdiction hunting season drew to a close. The Air Force carefully evaluated the performance of the Spectre gunships in Commando Hunt. Results of the primary mission—destruction of trucks—continued to be impressive for the second quarter of 1969.[197]

				Total
	Apr	*May*	*Jun*	*1st & 2d Qtr*
Trucks sighted	963	985	140	3,941
Trucks destroyed	493	427	46	1,573
Trucks damaged	100	120	21	592
Trucks (results not observed)	356	247	45	1,195

The Seventh Air Force pointed with satisfaction to the high percentage of total truck kills versus the gunship's share of the sorties:

> The contribution of the AC-130 gunships to the air interdiction campaign in Laos has been truly magnificent. During the period from January through April, the Spectre accounted for over twenty-nine percent of the total destroyed and damaged trucks in Laos while flying less than four percent of the total sorties used to attack moving vehicles.[198]

This gunship success against trucks hampered support of enemy forces in South Vietnam and southern Laos. The Seventh Air Force judged it a factor in "limiting the magnitude of the North Vietnamese army's northeast monsoon offensive."[199] The American embassy in Laos shared this satisfaction in the AC-130's performance. It cabled the State Department that use of Spectre gunships was an "unqualified success" and urged that "additional C-130s be configured as gunships ASAP [as soon as possible]."[200]

On June 9, 1969, Gen. George S. Brown, who succeeded General Momyer in August 1968 as Seventh Air Force commander, commended the 8th Tactical Fighter Wing on progress made in the first Commando Hunt effort. He noted that truck kills in April and May had reached new highs forcing the enemy "to replenish his entire truck inventory at frequent intervals." In summing up, General Brown stated that: "Our actions combined to slow the movement of materiel and forced the enemy to consume enroute an increasing amount of the supplies intended for stockpile or delivery to RVN. So effective were our efforts that of each five tons of supplies the enemy started southward through Laos, only one entered the Republic of Vietnam."*[201]

As the Air Force pushed Commando Hunt interdiction operations in Steel Tiger, military developments in northeastern Laos (Barrel Roll) forced it to consider using AC–130s there. An enemy dry-season offensive had strongly pressured General Vang Pao and his Meo army and threatened Air Force radar and air navigation sites. At the close of November 1968, the Joint Planning and Targets Conference requested the Seventh Air Force to supplement AC–47 Spooky operations in Barrel Roll with Spectre gunships. The Seventh Air Force alerted the 8th Tactical Fighter Wing in January 1969 that Spectre crews should get to know northeast Laotian terrain and Barrel Roll operational procedures.[202] By March 1969 the North Vietnamese and Pathet Lao had largely shifted to night attacks. Maj. Gen. Louis T. Seith, the Seventh/Thirteenth Air Force deputy commander, therefore recommended AC–130 diversions to aid Lima Site defenders and attack truck traffic moving in the Plain of Jars area.[203] Air commanders were also aware of the morale and psychological boost the gunship would impart to friendly forces under night attack and its deterrent effect on the attackers.

An operation typical of Spectre's Barrel Roll activity occurred on June 25–28, 1969, when AC–130s were diverted to assist Lima Site 108, a neutralist Laotian camp at Muong Soui, forty-seven miles east-southeast of Luang Prabang. From mortar and rocket positions on hills surrounding the friendly forces, the North Vietnamese and Pathet Lao began bombardment the night of June 25. The friendly forces ground controller, "City Hall," called for the gunship to direct fire on enemy positions. Some sixteen secondary explosions were recorded as the AC–130 helped suppress enemy assaults during nearly 2½ hours in orbit over the area. On

---

*While General Brown was commending this interdiction record, some analysts, critics, and skeptics of the Air Force's interdiction role were not so sure. They pointed to the complementary need for in-country ground operations to destroy or capture supplies of the enemy and force him to consume more. It was argued that the enemy's monthly supply to South Vietnam was just about enough to meet his minimal requirements for "normal" operations in the I and II Corps areas. Hence, the one-fifth going through Laos to South Vietnam was sufficient to replace supplies the enemy expended in combat or lost to U.S. and allied forces. On the other hand, it was estimated that a steady flow of 3,600 tons per day could flow from the southern end of the enemy system if not interdicted during dry-season air operations. This tonnage would far exceed enemy needs to resupply his troops in South Vietnam and stockpile for large operations.

subsequent nights the Spectres answered requests to aid the embattled camp. Several times ground forces called for attacks on tanks, but bad weather prevented acquisition of such targets. On the fourth night poor weather stopped gunship attacks altogether. Only several large fires in the friendly camp itself could be seen as the position was overrun.[204]

Even in Barrel Roll the AC–130s made important truck kills. The enemy had to step up logistic support of his offensives so truck traffic and road improvements rose dramatically. The Spectres found choice targets and thus opened up a second major area of Gunship II operations. From this point on, the Air Force would exploit the AC–130 as a truck-killer in Barrel Roll as well as Steel Tiger. What actually started out as a diversion turned into an additional commitment.

While Gunship II operations progressed in Southeast Asia, plans were made to send a TAC AC–130 to the other side of the world to participate in a NATO exercise in Europe. On January 19, 1969, the AC–130A sustained damage during a landing accident at Goose Bay, Labrador, following an in-flight emergency. Due to the limited number of AC–130s and the pressing Southeast Asia training requirements, no replacement aircraft was provided. This constituted the only attempt to demonstrate AC–130 fire-power in a European environment.

The faith of the promoters and developers of Gunship II was well rewarded by the Southeast Asia combat reports. If anything, the AC–130, with its sensors, fire-control system, and better armament, had proved more effective than hoped. Its reputation as the number one truck-killer in Southeast Asia had been steadily enhanced as the interdiction effort intensified. As a self-contained night attack aircraft, combining the capabilities of target search, acquisition, tracking, and destruction, it had no equal. Even its vulnerability had, in low- and medium-threat areas, been at least momentarily overcome by the gunship/fighter team. But despite these solid achievements, the weapon system did not remain static in a prolonged and everchanging war. Gunship II was but one phase in the side-firing weapon system's dynamic evolution.

IV. Advanced AC-130 Gunships

The year 1969 marked a turning point of American involvement in the Southeast Asian war. During the summer, President Richard M. Nixon made the first notable reduction of U.S. military strength in South Vietnam. He embarked on a long-range course to strengthen indigenous forces and at the same time withdraw U.S. troops. This momentous change of policy affected the role of U.S. air power the least. As before, air power pressured enemy supply lines and aided ground units in defensive and offensive operations. As the air war continued, the high hopes for the AC-130 gunships fueled efforts to make them less vulnerable and more effective. The end result was a force of advanced AC-130s. Paradoxically, as overall U.S. strategy called for disengagement, gunship operations increased and the AC-130 grew into an ever more sophisticated and deadly weapon system.

As previously indicated, gunship development had been a continuing interest right from the side-firing aircraft's beginning. Various messages, for example, were sent from the Seventh Air Force, and Pacific Air Forces in turn, identifying needed improvements in gunship aircraft. One field request in June 1968 called for an all-weather capability, an improved fire-control system and larger-caliber guns (such as the 25-mm).[1] Air Force Systems Command believed it possible to furnish these capabilities, the AFSC commander having already suggested approaches to them to the chief of staff on April 6, 1968. AFSC pointed out one difficulty, however— the lack of specific, documented, operational demands from Southeast Asia. AFSC urged that these be submitted.[2] Air Force headquarters backed AFSC on its call for more precise field requirements but cautioned that "procurement of new and/or improved items for gunship aircraft will be at the expense of other research, development, test, and evaluation, and modified programs also identified as vital to Southeast Asia operations."[3] This concern with and progress on gunship improvements did not diminish in Southeast Asia or the United States. Nevertheless, it took unusual anxiety about gunship operations to trigger a package improvement plan.

After returning from a Far East visit during May 1969, Secretary of the Air Force Robert C. Seamans, Jr. expressed concern about the AC-130's vulnerability to enemy fire despite the protection of Phantom escorts. An intelligence analysis of the enemy's response to gunship attacks focused more attention on the problem and induced a study of methods to make the AC-130 less vulnerable. In July 1969 James A. Reamer, the Directorate of Technology's Deputy for Tactical Warfare, brought together a group that had worked with the AC-130 program before. Major Terry, chief of the AC-130 Gunship Program Office, Lieutenant Colonel Krause, and Major

Wolverton, all key men in the first AC-130 gunship deployment, joined Reamer in "vigorous" discussions on how to meet the expanding threat to the gunship. After intensive study the group developed a new gunship proposal, later known as Surprise Package.[4]

The group's "Package" called for a gunship with greater standoff range to improve its capacity for survival and better night-targeting equipment. It recommended, for example, two 20-mm Gatling guns and two 40-mm Bofors antiaircraft type guns to replace the standard AC-130A armament of four 20-mm guns and four 7.62-mm miniguns. Also recommended were low-light-level television and improved infrared equipment to complement the added firepower and enhance night vision and detection capability. The fire-control system's analog computer would be replaced by a digital computer with greater capacity and flexibility to assimilate the better sensor inputs. Crews in the Surprise Package-equipped AC-130s would be able to pinpoint tactical targets for conventional strike forces by use of a two-kilowatt (kw) illuminator and a Pave Way I laser designator. An inertial navigation system would store in its memory the location of targets to be struck later by the gunship or fighters. Several of these Surprise Package components were available, but others were just emerging from the development phase.[5]

A plan within the group's proposal would take the previously approved eighth AC-130A, then being modified in ASD shops, and convert it to this new configuration.[6] Originally, the recycled prototype gunship had been picked as the eighth AC-130A. When the prototype returned from Southeast Asia, however, its airframe was carefully inspected at Wright-Patterson AFB and judged to be below combat-duty standards. Moreover, the rebuilding price tag would exceed that of converting another C-130A.[7] A different C-130A, therefore, was provided for conversion to the eighth gunship. It was this aircraft that was now proposed for the Surprise Package modification.

On July 18, 1969, ASD presented the Surprise Package concept, drafted by Reamer and team, to General Ferguson, the AFSC commander. Accompanying it was a recommendation that the aircraft be modified in ASD shops on a high-priority basis, with the projected starting date of August 1, 1969. General Ferguson supported the plan, and the Surprise Package program made the rounds in rapid succession to the Air Staff, PACAF, and the Seventh Air Force.[8] Serious opposition to the proposal developed in the Air Staff. CINCPACAF wanted the aircraft available not later than November 15, 1969, the capability to restore it to a standard configuration in-theater if tests were not successful, and AFSC support for the specialized subsystems at Ubon RTAFB.[9] General Brown, Seventh Air Force commander, endorsed the project on August 12, 1969, provided these provisions could be met.[10]

General Ryan told General Ferguson on September 2, 1969, to go ahead with the proposed Surprise Package program. "Your engineers are to be commended for evolving an inventive and unique proposal to

Surprise Package Configuration

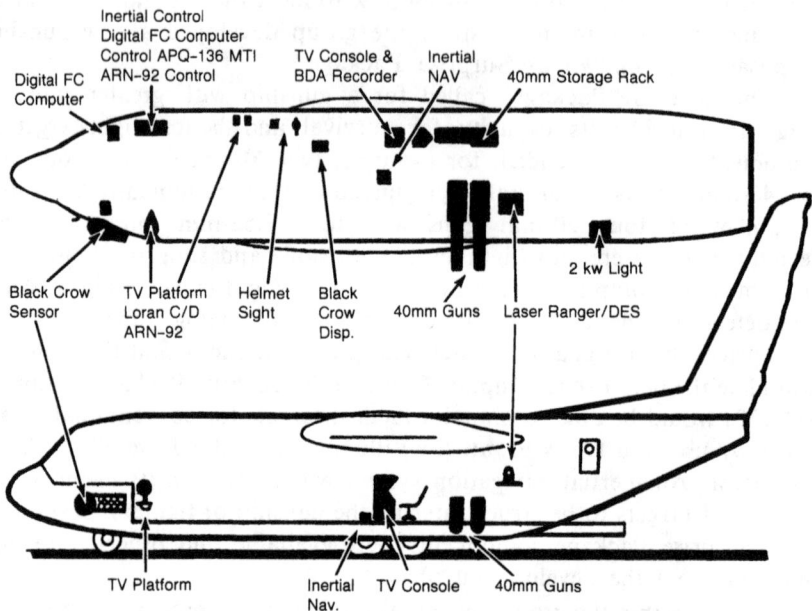

Inertial Control
Digital FC Computer
Control APQ–136 MTI   TV Console &   Inertial
Digital FC   ARN–92 Control   BDA Recorder   NAV   40mm Storage Rack
Computer

Black Crow   TV Platform   Helmet   Black   2 kw Light
Sensor   Loran C/D   Sight   Crow   40mm Guns   Laser Ranger/DES
ARN–92   Disp.

TV Platform   Inertial   TV Console   40mm Guns
Nav.

counter a potentially serious threat to our gunship operations," he said. The Air Force chief rejected any thought that the gunship, either in a primary or secondary role, might counter antiaircraft sites. Nevertheless, he agreed with the idea of bolstering its survivability with the 40-mm standoff range. General Ryan made certain stipulations to his approval of Surprise Package. The projected deployment of the eighth AC–130 could not be delayed beyond mid-November. Provisions could be made for the specialized subsystems but only the new guns and the digital fire-control system were to be mandatory. Beyond these items, the present AC–130 equipment would be used to meet the deployment date. Authorized funds for the project were pegged at $1.5 million.[11]

The time limit imposed by the chief of staff was a stiffer challenge than the ASD group had expected. The Surprise Package developers literally worked day and night to modify the aircraft. Each day new problems exacted the utmost in managerial skill and technical ingenuity. Harmonization of sensors, computers, and the fire-control system, basically Major Wolverton's job, demanded daily coordination with various subcontractors on the development of components. Colonel Krause, the expert on infrared systems, set about integrating the infrared equipment, the display systems, and low-light-level television. Simultaneously, Major Terry issued daily instructions to installation design engineers and to the ASD shops preparing the aircraft for the subsystems. The small task force was totally immersed in solving installation or fabrication problems.[12]

Surprise Package aircraft.

Use of the 40-mm Bofors gun from the Navy typified the problems faced by the team. These guns had never been fired downward, so a new gun mount needed to be designed, fabricated, and evaluated. During the first ground-firing tests at Eglin AFB, firing overpressure produced cracks on the underside of the aircraft's left wing. It took more analysis and tests to show that the cracks would not occur in actual flight.[13] This consumed valuable time, and time was at a premium.

By October 27, 1969, the Surprise Package aircraft stood ready for systems testing at Eglin. The test flights (Oct 28–Nov 15, 1969) were delayed due to bad weather and some slow equipment deliveries. Nevertheless, they sufficiently proved the technical integrity of the gunship's systems. On November 15 General Ferguson recommended to General Ryan that the aircraft be deployed. Orders received two days later directed that the aircraft proceed to Southeast Asia for combat evaluation.[14] The ASD group had met the deployment goal. Subsequently, Major Terry received the Dr. Harold Brown Award for 1969 because his professional leadership, skill, and energy played so important a part in making the deployment possible.[15]

The Surprise Package gunship (labeled Coronet Surprise by TAC) left for Southeast Asia on November 25, 1969.[16] An engine change at Guam[17] put off the gunship's arrival at Ubon RTAFB until December 5.[18] Maj. R. C. Binderim of TAC commanded the main Coronet Surprise task force which reached Ubon on November 27. The force included Major Terry and consisted of aircrew personnel from TAC and PACAF and technical personnel and engineering specialists from ASD and contractors. Tactical Air Command Operations Plan 132, October 17, 1969, guided the combat evaluation.[19] On December 12, just seven days after the aircraft touched down at Ubon, the TAC/AFSC task force flew its maiden operational mission against North Vietnamese truck traffic.[20]

The early Surprise Package sorties went far better than hoped. From December 12–19 the gunship flew six missions that were in effect equipment tests left over from the short evaluation period at Eglin. Still the aircraft destroyed eleven and damaged nine of twenty-four trucks sighted. Attacking three antiaircraft sites, it destroyed one and caused two explosions. From December 19-30 the gunship destroyed nineteen and damaged eight of thirty trucks detected. It also attacked fourteen storage areas, touching off six explosions and seven fires. The gunship compiled this record in spite of equipment problems that were annoying and at times crippling.[21] The final combat evaluation mission was flown on January 18, 1970.

The evaluation team described the performance of the Surprise Package weapon system as "very satisfactory" during the thirty-eight-day combat test. The gunship spotted 313 trucks destroying 178, damaging 63, and logging 37 "results not observed" while flying 86.8 percent (33 total sorties) of the missions scheduled. The enemy responded to these missions with an estimated 3,475 rounds, most of it 23-mm and 37-mm antiaircraft fire.[22]

Although the combat evaluation ended on January 18, 1970, the Seventh Air Force continued Surprise Package missions over the Ho Chi Minh Trail. Engineering adjustments strengthened certain areas of the aircraft's performance.[23] As Commando Hunt III closed at the end of April, Surprise Package had accounted for 604 trucks destroyed and 218 damaged.[24] A comparative study of trucks destroyed/damaged produced evidence that Surprise Package was far more deadly than other gunships and tactical fighters.[25] Moreover, the improved Spectre weapons system was nearly twice as effective as the standard AC-130's.[26] Seventh Air Force declared it the "single most successful truck killer in SEA [Southeast Asia] during Commando Hunt III."[27]

Several missions flown during January 1970 graphically illustrated how potent and versatile the Surprise Package gunship (sometimes called Super Chicken) was in its interdiction role.

The Case of the Vanishing Bridge

Sensor transmission had indicated that the North Vietnamese were bypassing a main Laotian road and escaping airpower harassment. A target study of the area turned up a new road carved through dense jungle parallel to the main line of communication but no bridge spanning a major river the enemy had to cross. The Seventh Air Force fragged Surprise Package and escorts into the area on 5 separate nights. Each time the gunship detected a bridge over the river at any of four points. During daylight the bridge could not be found. The enemy evidently put it in place at his choosing, sent 30 or more trucks across, then hid the span from FAC reconnaissance by day. Surprise Package attacked and destroyed trucks on the bridge and marked the target for destruction by escort fighters.

The Case of the Interdicted Pipeline

Task Force Alpha had obtained photographs and approximate routing of an enemy pipeline with pumping stations in Laos through intelligence sources. Alpha passed this information to Surprise Package crewmembers on January 7, 1970. Sent into the area two days later, Surprise Package put 40-mm fire on two pumping stations and the pipeline causing intense petroleum fires. An escort F–4 placed 500-pound bombs on a pumping station. The soaring flames spread over an area the size of a city block. The same mission destroyed sixteen trucks. Returning on January 10, Surprise Package and F–4 escorts destroyed thirty trucks apparently awaiting fuel. Two large gasoline-tanker vehicles appeared during the attack and succumbed to 40-mm fire. Similarly, the Surprise Package/F–4 team claimed destruction or damage of twenty-five more vehicles the next night.

The Case of the Amphitheater

Day forward air controller pilots nicknamed a karst area covered by heavy jungle the "amphitheater." A study of strip photographs had singled out the area as a potential storage point or truck park, so the Seventh Air Force sent a task force to reconnoiter. The force consisted of Surprise Package, three F–4 fighter escorts, one loran-equipped F–4, and six additional fighter-bombers allocated by the Airborne Battlefield Command and Control Center. On January 7, 1970, Surprise Package discovered and destroyed four trucks near the amphitheater then found the area a hotbed of activity with supplies, trucks, and defending antiaircraft artillery.

After special sensors had detected a radar site colocated with a 57-mm gun, television and infrared sensors verified the presence of vans. The 57-mm gave its position away by firing at the aircraft, and airstrikes on various loran-targeted sites left many secondary fires and explosions. Surprise Package moved north of the position, locating and destroying twelve vehicles. As low fuel forced task force elements to return to base, the target locations were relayed to ABCCC and Task Force Alpha. At daybreak an F–4 Wolf* forward air controller led an 8th Tactical Fighter Wing F–4 flight, equipped with laser-guided bombs, to the amphitheater. The attacks destroyed the radar vans—just fifty meters from the given coordinates.[28]

Surprise Package shattered all 16th Special Operations Squadron records on February 14, 1970, by destroying forty-three trucks and damaging two in a single mission. Successes like this enabled the unit to claim its 5,000th truck destroyed or damaged on February 21, 1970.[29]

Surprise Package's outstanding combat results were achieved chiefly as the result of new and better equipment. Many components had been borrowed from other projects or the other services. Low-light-level television

---

*Wolf was the call sign of the 8th Tactical Fighter Wing's F–4 forward air controller at Ubon RTAFB.

Top: Night observation device; left: Capts. Charles Mayo, Claude Bolton, and Clarence Johnson discuss 40-mm guns on an AC–130 prior to an attack on the Ho Chi Minh Trail.

Top: TSgt. George S. Byrd, 16th SOS, loads a 40-mm gun on an AC–130 for an attack on the Ho Chi Minh Trail; bottom: Key sensors on Surprise Package.

came from Project Tropic Moon, and the 40-mm Bofors gun and the Black Crow sensor system from the Navy. Other equipment had been developed in response to operational needs and past AC–130 problems. Not all subsystems worked as expected without troubles, but the new equipment served simultaneously to make the gunship weapon system unique and a veritable testbed, or flying laboratory, for proving new hardware. It also was a further illustration of what skillful improvisation could do.

Low-light-level television, a major sensor addition to Surprise Package along with Black Crow, was mounted in the left-side crew entrance door just behind the crew compartment. The installation consisted of two cameras, one with a wide field of view for the area search and one with a narrow field for precise target tracking. The LLLTV could view targets in light levels varying from bright sunlight to nighttime. It could detect trucks at night from a considerable distance. After early troubles with short tube life and sluggish tracking tendencies were overcome, the television set became a very important gunship sensor.[30]

An air-to-ground moving target indicator processor supplemented Black Crow, the infrared sensor, and the low-light television. The radar could detect moving targets from several miles away and signaled the detection with an alert signal. Evaluators rated the moving target indicator "outstanding" during the combat test.[31]

As early as May 2, 1969, a standard AC–130 aircraft had arrived at Ubon equipped with extensively improved forward-looking infrared. Gunship personnel were quite impressed with the improvements and pressed for the installation of the infrared equipment in the other AC–130s.[32] Acting as gunship spokesman, the 8th Tactical Fighter Wing told the Thirteenth Air Force on June 1, 1969, that the improved infrared design had a superior picture presentation and was easier to maintain.[33] The wing argued that since the infrared was becoming the most important truck-detection system, it was imperative the advanced equipment be on all the AC–130s. The arguments were productive and gradually the advanced forward-looking infrared set became a part of the standard AC–130A systems.

A chief goal of Surprise Package equipment was to reduce the gunship's vulnerability and increase its survivability. Surprise Package operated at higher altitudes due to the greater ranges afforded by its systems and the greater precision of its navigational components. Consequently, certain enemy antiaircraft guns were unable to reach the squadron's AC–130s and other guns were less effective. The higher operating altitudes also made it more difficult for enemy gunners to track a gunship either by sight or engine noise.[34] The recorded comparisons made during Commando Hunt III (winter, 1969) provided evidence for reduced vulnerability:[35]

	Direct Hits	Shrapnel Hits	Losses
AC–130A	6	1	1
Surprise Package	0	2	0

Surprise Package also received a laser target designator during combat evaluation. The new device improved the aircrew's ability to pinpoint antiaircraft guns and to work more effectively with the F-4 escort aircraft to destroy them. The gunship's loran equipment also complemented the laser designator.

Further equipment changes developed from renewed interest in solving an old damage assessment problem—the validation of truck kills. As the recorded number of trucks mounted, especially those destroyed by AC-130 strikes, skepticism of the claims had arisen. In December 1967, for example, General Westmoreland, COMUSMACV, had questioned the validity of the truck-kill rate. He noted the figures were above anything recorded the previous year and seemed very high. He further asked what hard evidence the Air Force had to confirm the truck kills. In response to these queries, General Momyer, Seventh Air Force commander, ordered a reexamination of the rules for recording trucks destroyed and damaged.[36] This triggered fresh emphasis on accurate reporting and a search for some device to document strikes.

To better assess strike results, Detachment 2 of the 14th Air Commando Wing conducted a firing test on a moving vehicle and stationary containers at a Ubon range on March 31, 1968. From information gathered, detachment personnel believed that the gunship attacks destroyed or damaged a good many trucks and targets reported in the "no visible results" category.[37] Gunship crews believed their scoring procedures were conservative. In counts of "destroyed," "damaged," or "no visible results" under March 1968 bomb damage criteria, a vehicle or storage area hit and exploding was "damaged," a vehicle taking a direct hit from Surprise Package 40-mm fire was "destroyed" regardless of secondary explosions or fires, hits in the vicinity of a vehicle or with the target obscured were counted "no visible results." The night observation device operator, the television operator (on Surprise Package only), and/or the infrared operator had to observe that 40-mm/20-mm ordnance was impacting and detonating on target. The higher slant ranges of Surprise Package operations required two sensor operators to confirm claims of "destroyed."[38]

The review of reporting procedures was not likely to convince skeptics of gunship bomb damage assessment (BDA), so the search went on for a mechanical means of validating claims. The Seventh Air Force first tried using RF-4C reconnaissance aircraft to photograph the area of Spectre night strikes early the next morning. The RF-4C had trouble pinpointing the previous night's kills because of the Spectre's imprecise navigational equipment, the poor-quality maps of many Laotian areas, and the small sensor look-angle of RF-4C photo equipment. Reconnaissance tactics were modified by lowering altitude, scanning the crooked Laotian roads visually, and filming short road segments. In this manner the reconnaissance missions found nineteen trucks in ten days, May 15-25, 1969, although weather hampered the missions.[39] Even with reconnaissance improvements the Spectre crews remained convinced they were destroying more trucks than the RF–4Cs could locate. At one point, cartoons and jokes circulated in the 16th Special Operations Squadron about the "Great Laotian Truck Eater" that mysteriously gobbled up the night's truck-kills so reconnaissance aircraft could not find them.[40]

Two things prompted the Seventh Air Force's next step to improve bomb damage assessment—the high-level interest in identifying the best truck-killers and a concern of many (especially gunship personnel) to make BDA claims credible. Hence, in early 1969, the Seventh Air Force directed the 432d Tactical Reconnaissance Wing at Udorn RTAFB to obtain BDA of Spectre strikes by night photoreconnaissance.[41] When Spectre strikes set secondary fires, reconnaissance crews acquired the target visually and ran a night pinpoint. Spectre crews, however, disliked these tactics which required them to suspend their attacks for six minutes after a fire was noted to let reconnaissance aircraft make a photo pass.[42] This BDA method photographed more truck-kills but it was not considered satisfactory. The problem of telling a damaged truck from an able one remained.[43] There were also difficulties with film quality. The major disadvantages of using more aircraft to support Spectre and the added complexity of operations were obvious.

On January 7, 1969, PACAF agreed to place a bomb damage recorder on board the AC–130A and AC–119K. A kinescope-type recorder was recommended that could fix on film sensor inputs, chiefly infrared imagery.[44] An AFSC assistance team agreed that some means had to be found for recording gunship strikes. It likewise recognized that reconnaissance photo problems reinforced the need for better navigational equipment in gunships.[45]

While a BDA recorder was under development, Seventh Air Force decided to film damage assessment with onboard cameras. Brig. Gen. Robert J. Holbury, the Seventh's Director of Combat Operations, emphasized to the 8th Tactical Fighter Wing on May 18, 1969, the urgent need for photos to document Spectre truck-kills. He proposed to produce them by filming burning targets through the AC–130's night observation device and by the closest coordination between AC–130 and RF–4C aircraft.[46] A photographer from the 600th Photo Squadron at Tan Son Nhut AB was put aboard the AC–130s; he tried filming with a 16-mm motion-picture camera on the observation device eyepiece. However, this approach was eventually abandoned because the night observation device could not be held steady enough on the target without the device's operator sighting it. Several methods were tried, but the best results came from a camera mounted on a second night device.[47] The extra devices, borrowed from Security Police stock, were positioned forward of the left paratroop door and behind the 20-mm guns.[48] The night device was then boresighted with the weapons. A video-recorder camera was mounted in the fixed night observation device, with recording and playback equipment

Firing Geometry (Offset and Wind Corrected)

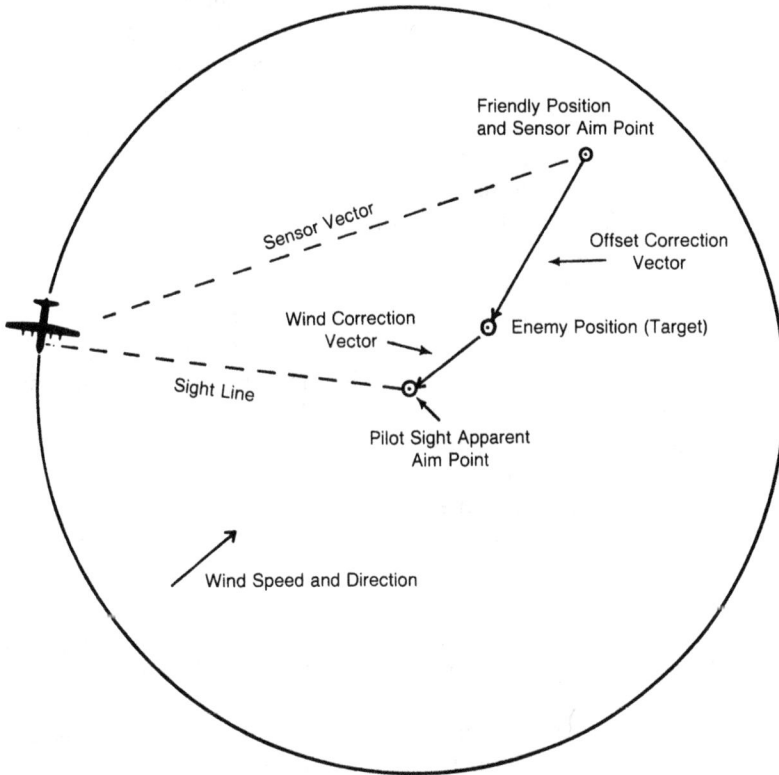

Friendly Position
and Sensor Aim Point

Sensor Vector

Offset Correction
Vector

Wind Correction
Vector

Enemy Position (Target)

Sight Line

Pilot Sight Apparent
Aim Point

Wind Speed and Direction

being located in the cargo compartment booth.[49] Step by step a satisfactory damage assessment recorder was evolving.

The assessment equipment developed for the special requirements of Surprise Package represented a further advancement. This Westel-built equipment joined a video-audio recorder with the infrared sensor instead of the night observation device.[50] The Westel came close to giving the desired documentation of gunship strikes. Refinements eventually enabled it to obtain video/audio tapes of high resolution from several sensors. A complete film validation of the gunship's strikes thus became possible. The Seventh Air Force accepted the Westel used on Surprise Package as the "final satisfactory solution," in March 1970.[51]

The standard AC-130A computerized fire-control system fell far short of Surprise Package's vastly improved one. Its weakness was primarily an inconsistency in the directional data developed by the system; the erratic nature of the error made manual corrections difficult. The system's directional errors had a crucial impact on the use of offset targeting procedures. Ultimately the Seventh Air Force decided to suspend offset firing operations and reported the decision to PACAF in August 1969.[52]

In the summer of 1969 Aeronautical Systems Division personnel spent a great deal of time on the fire-control system malfunctions. They went over the gunship carefully to discover and resolve the problems. Officers from the Air Force Academy's Department of Astronautics and Computer Science offered valuable assistance. Lt. Col. Bradford W. Parkinson and Maj. Richard E. Willes, for example, helped troubleshoot and solve system deficiencies.[53] The men finally found that the installation of a dual-axis gyro and a complete-solution computer would free the system of errors.[54] The Tactical Air Command verified the new equipment's accuracy and Air Force headquarters approved modification of the AC–130 and AC–119G/K fire-control systems on August 30, 1969.[55]

The loran navigation set proved so accurate and reliable on the Surprise Package aircraft that the Air Force ordered it installed in all AC–130As on a quick-reaction basis. The order reflected the understanding that precise navigation was an absolute "must" for armed reconnaissance missions in Laos. As added advantages, loran provided target coordinates for later strikes by loran-equipped F–4D fighter bombers, accurately pinpointed radar sites, and assured strict adherence to rules of engagement. It served in addition as a cross-check for Surprise Package's inertial navigation/targeting subsystem, which generated accurate attitude and velocity inputs to the digital fire-control system computer and kept minimum positional error over the entire flight. The loran set's cross-checking function was particularly valuable in light of the computer's sensitivity to variations in the aircraft electrical power, the changes that caused the system to be unreliable in storing targets and in generating synthetic azimuth.[56]

Electrical troubles had hindered total integration of new equipment during Surprise Package's combat evaluation Erratic electrical power from engine generators caused erroneous computations, uncertain target storage, accidental memory "wipes," incorrect azimuth, and wander of sensor input angles. Additionally, platforms for pointing the low-light-level television, laser designator, and two-kw illuminator were poorly designed for the precision required, especially when it came to compensation for the aircraft's movement. An Air Force Academy laboratory later reworked and improved the platforms, and toward the end of Commando Hunt III, the new television platform sustained smoother and more accurate/responsive tracking than before. Another problem was caused by the failure to have the Black Crow sensor tied into the fire-control system. Furthermore, cannibalization could only partially overcome the problems with LLLTV tubes.[57] As the months rolled by, concern mounted over possible structural fatigue from the 40-mm gun's recoil, which loosened locking bolts and the aircraft cargo floor. Intratheater construction of a new floor support solved the gun-mount problem. Nonetheless, an Air Force Academy team in an effort to guard against future troubles installed instruments in Surprise Package to measure recoil effect on the mount and basic structure.[58] Despite the various problems, eight special subsystems had

TABLE 3. CONFIGURATION COMPARISON:
AC–130A GUNSHIP AND SURPRISE PACKAGE

AC–130A	Surprise Package
Armament	
4 M 61 20-mm cannons 4 GAU 2B/A 7.62-mm miniguns	2 M–1 40-mm guns 2 M–61 20-mm cannons
Airborne Illumination System	
40-kw illuminator flare launcher (LAU-74/A)	2-kw illuminator
Sensors	
forward-looking infrared (AN AAD 4) night observation device radar set (AN APQ-133)	forward-looking infrared (AN/AAD-4) low-light-level television radar set (AN/APQ-133) helmet sight Black Crow moving target indicator
Fire Control System	
AWG 13 analog computer fire-control display optical gunsight ID 48 steering indicator sensor and light angle display	digital fire-control computer fire-control display optical gunsight ID–48 steering indicator sensor and light angle display inertial navigation targeting system
Other Equipment	
	laser target designator

Source: Tech rprt TAC OPlan 132, Final Report Combat Introduction/Evaluation (Coronet Surprise), Aug 1970, pp 1-2.

shown "acceptable reliability" and "effective operation."[59] Table 3 shows the basic AC–130A and Surprise Package components.

The equipment additions did not significantly alter the normal gunship tactics except for certain changes in attack distances. The gunship fleet, including Surprise Package, continued to employ basic interdiction methods. The various sensors were used to detect targets, such as trucks, in the assigned area. Once targets were detected, firing began with the assistance of the forward-looking infrared sensor, the low-light-level television, or the night observation device.

The new equipment caused a change in the composition of Surprise Package's crew and their stations. TAC had previously pointed to the requirement for an electronic warfare officer when certain sensors were installed on the AC–130; there had also been recommendations to increase the number of weapons mechanics or gunners from three to five. The latter crew addition was based on the requirement for a right-side antiaircraft scanner and for the need to maintain, reload and clear ejected brass at separate gun stations.[60] By the same token, Southeast Asian operations accented a need for more weapons mechanics to cover ordnance loading for premission and turnaround (rapid reloading for another sortie) times. At Ubon RTAFB neither the maintenance munitions squadron servicing the gunship nor the 16th Special Operations Squadron thought it had enough mechanics to handle this job.[61]

PACAF requested Headquarters USAF to increase weapons mechanic spaces on AC–130 crews from three to five on June 4, 1970. The command also asked for an electronic warfare officer on July 6. Meanwhile, the AC–130 Gunship Program Office believed that Surprise Package should have still another navigator to monitor the sensor inputs and assist the aircraft commander in firing operations.[62] With the increase of more sophisticated equipment, the pilot became overburdened with firing data while flying the aircraft. The new position—called "mission commander" and later "fire-control officer"—became part of Surprise Package's crew when the gunship began combat operations. Surprise Package then set the standard for other upgraded AC–130s with its fourteen-man crew: pilot, copilot, flight engineer, fire-control officer, table navigator, LLLTV operator, FLIR operator, electronic warfare officer, illuminator operator, and five gunners. The AC–130A compartment booth at about midfuselage was revamped to house the Black Crow, FLIR operator, LLLTV operator, and fire-control officer.

Because of its many crew and equipment changes, Surprise Package was a big jump forward in gunship development. Just as the AC–130 surpassed the AC–47, so Surprise Package displayed great superiority over the standard AC–130A. Thus the weapon system dynamically grew, evolving in effectiveness and complexity.

Being pioneers, the AC–130A prototype and Surprise Package were test-bed aircraft and experienced similar combat-evaluation troubles. Surprise Package's performance fell off with time despite remarkable in-theater support from ASD, Air Force Academy, and contractor personnel. Like the AC–130A prototype, Surprise Package's new systems and their breadboard installation (often on rather crude mountings for testing) brought on numerous maintenance headaches. In March 1970 Secretary of the Air Force Seamans asked why weekly summaries of truck-kills/sorties in Southeast Asia reflected greater improvement of AC–119K and AC–130A performance relative to Surprise Package.[63] The Air Staff gave as a reason a decrease in truck traffic in Surprise Package's area of operations along with some technical and maintenance problems in the aircraft and equipment.[64]

A later recommendation was made that Surprise Package be configured to a standard AC–130 because it was difficult and expensive to

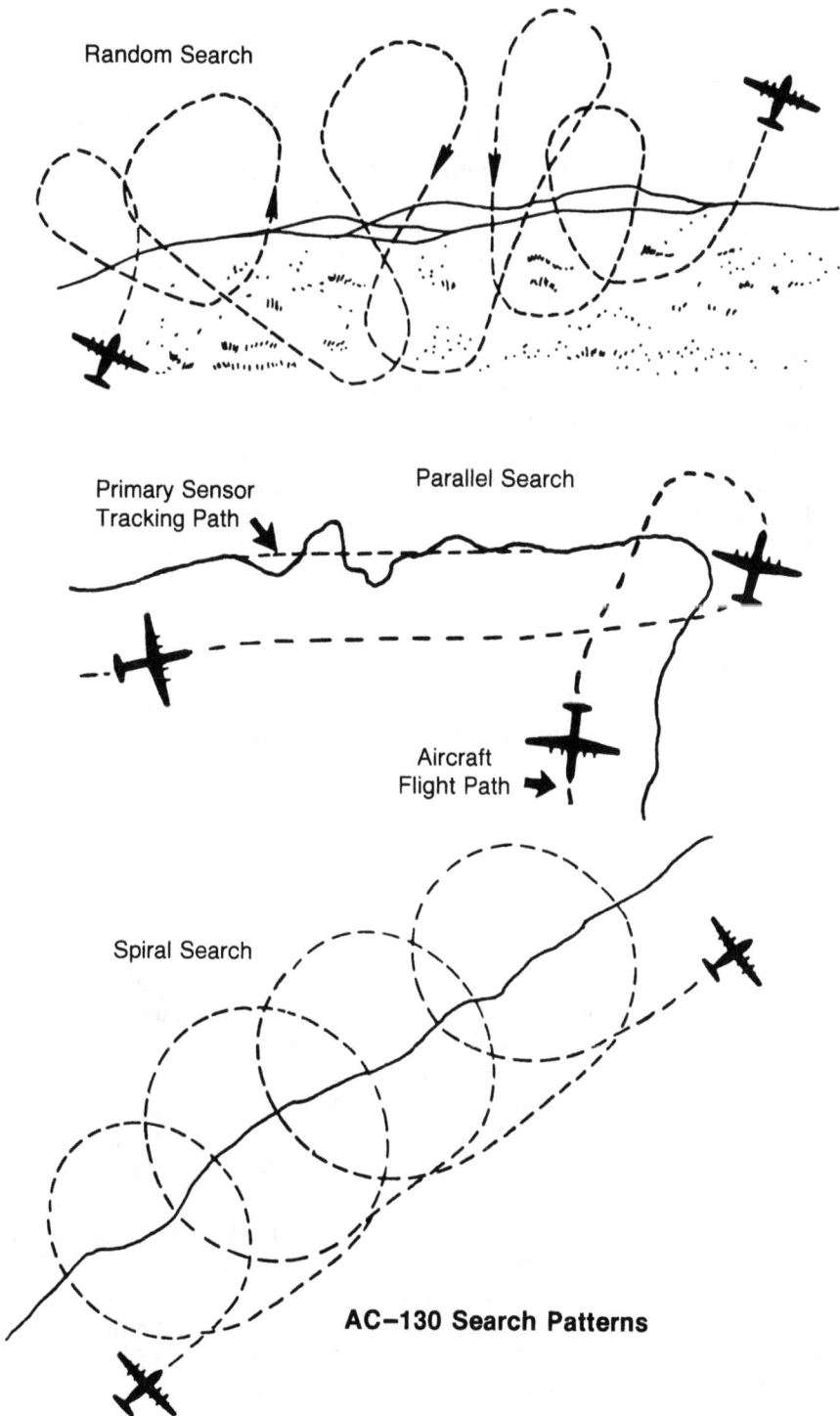

Random Search

Primary Sensor
Tracking Path

Parallel Search

Aircraft
Flight Path

Spiral Search

AC–130 Search Patterns

maintain,[65] but this was swiftly rejected by the Seventh Air Force. On May 1, 1970, ASD proposed spending $3.4 million to refurbish the aircraft and return it to Southeast Asia for the 1970–71 dry season.[66] The Seventh Air Force agreed on May 6, 1970.[67] PACAF on May 20,[68] and Air Force headquarters ordered the return of Surprise Package.[69] The aircraft arrived at Wright-Patterson AFB on June 4 and immediately underwent refitting in ASD shops for return to combat in the fall. Surprise Package had ably demonstrated the advantages of the advanced Gunship II and quickly generated requests for more such aircraft.

Surprise Package's performance in the Southeast Asian war exacerbated long-standing, high-level debate on gunship limitations and the size and nature of the gunship force. Secretary of the Air Force Seamans visited Southeast Asia from January 10–21, 1970, and one of his chief aims was to look at the gunship program, Surprise Package operations in particular.[70] The secretary arrived at Ubon RTAFB on January 18, the day combat evaluation ended.[71] He was so impressed with the advanced gunship's effectiveness that he called Under Secretary of the Air Force John L. McLucas in Washington, saying he believed all Spectre aircraft should be modified to the Surprise Package configuration.[72] McLucas passed this information to the Air Staff.[73]

In his January 23, 1970, trip report to the Secretary of Defense, Dr. Seamans said he had directed the Air Staff to modernize the other AC–130s with "those portions of the Surprise Package equipment that can be installed in the field during the current dry season."[74] At about this time, General Brown, Seventh Air Force commander, asked for faster action on Surprise Package modification of other AC–130As then in combat. He also sought support in getting AC–130Es to replace aging AC–130As.[75] These proposals for updating all Gunship IIs more clearly focused opposing views on the gunship force evolution. On one side, TAC, Air Force headquarters and the Joint Chiefs of Staff urged restrained expansion and improvement. On the other, the Secretaries of the Air Force and Defense wanted greater force development.

When the Air Force Systems Command proposed Surprise Package, Tactical Air Command had accepted the need for a better gunship, but had reservations about how far the Air Force should pursue the weapons system. TAC concluded that the AC–130 had reached its operational limits when it required F–4 protection from enemy fire.[76] Although satisfied with Surprise Package's combat debut, TAC still considered AC–130 gunships suitable only for special warfare forces in low-order conflicts and lightly defended areas. Discussion of converting additional C–130 aircraft to gunships and modifying more with the Surprise Package configuration caused further TAC opposition. The command did not want more C–130s diverted from the airlift role, arguing that the 1971 budget did not provide for new C–130s and pointing out that the tactical airlift force was declining through attrition. Consequently, TAC was opposed to conversion of the C–130E aircraft unless a "new buy" of the aircraft was approved. Objecting to another "panic program" on gunships, TAC strongly suggested that the Air Staff clarify the future of the AC-130—a weapon system it regarded as survivable only if the enemy chose not to use all his weapons.[77]

In contrast, the Secretary of Defense adopted a far more favorable stance toward gunship growth due in part to the influence of the President's Science Advisory Committee. Dr. Lee A. DuBridge, the committee chief and science adviser to President Nixon, stressed to Secretary of Defense Melvin R. Laird the "problems of getting more effective weapons into the Vietnam theater." Dr. DuBridge criticized the "severe delays" in applying new weaponry and cited gunships as a chief case in point. The science adviser said gunship development had not been fully exploited despite the system's proven potency as a truck-killer in Laos. DuBridge made the following argument to Secretary Laird:

> It was clear from the initial tests of the AC-130 gunship, which demonstrated kills of about five trucks/sortie, that the 18 AC-130 and 26 119K gunships should possess a potential truck killing capacity of 100 to 200 trucks/night if a sortie rate of one per day could be maintained. Comparing this with the infiltration rate of around 200 trucks/day entering Laos in 1968 from North Vietnam, and an estimated truck inventory in Laos of about 1,300 trucks, and the kill rate of 20-30 trucks/day otherwise being achieved, we see that the gunship could have made a truly significant impact on the infiltration of supplies. To be sure they would encounter antiaircraft fire, and a massive suppression effort would be needed. However, as an interim program it might well have been highly successful. It was surely worth the gamble at the price tag involved. The fact that the Department of Defense was haggling about cost effectiveness studies, delaying authorization from the total buy, etc., with a program of such imagination and potential for helping the war effort, supported by the Executive Office of the President and the Secretary of the Air Force, gives eloquent support to the contention that changes in the system are vital.[78]

Dr. DuBridge's keen interest in the gunship program stimulated a closer look at Air Force plans. Secretary Laird wanted answers to the following questions: How many gunships were now in Southeast Asia? How many were programmed to be there? What thought had been given to greater use of gunships as opposed to other means of attack?[79] Replying the same day, the Air Force secretary said there were presently forty-five Air Force gunships in the theater (forty-three gunships plus two AC-123K Black Spot aircraft). By the end of 1969, the completely deployed force would total seven AC-130s, eighteen AC-119Ks, eighteen AC-119Gs, and two AC-123Ks.

Almost simultaneously, General Ryan, then Air Force vice chief of staff, reported to the Air Force secretary that the time was not right for expanding the AC-130 gunship fleet. The vice chief indicated no actions were under way to procure additional gunships and gave these main reasons: (1) more gunships would mean deeper, unacceptable cuts into critical airlift assets; (2) recent deployment of sixteen AC-119Ks, two AC-123Ks, and three AC-130s to Southeast Asia represented a three-hundred percent rise in truck-killing resources; (3) the vulnerability of gunships dictated their use in lightly defended areas; (4) the enemy was rapidly reinforcing his antiaircraft defense; (5) fund limitations and proposed budget cuts made modification costs prohibitive in view of the gunship's limited operations, and (6) a better use of limited funds would obtain an improved and advanced self-contained night attack system with greater survivability.[80] General Ryan reiterated some of these points to the Air Force Systems Command and declared that the "additional gunships and Black Spot aircraft currently planned for deployment in the October–December time frame should be adequate to meet existing requirements."[81]

Secretary Laird responded to the Air Force on August 5, 1969, asking for further analysis of gunship possibilities and Air Force plans based on the analysis. The Air Force secretary wrote to Mr. Laird about the aircraft's advantages and disadvantages, incorporating many of General Ryan's points. Secretary Seamans recommended continued deployment of gunships, spending funds to advance a self-contained night attack system, and evaluation of the B–57G, whose deployment was imminent. Dr. Seamans did not recommend more gunships. Instead, he concluded that "while the gunships have proved to be effective truck killers, we believe that we have responded as well as the tight budget will allow in providing gunships to SEAsia."[82] The Air Force secretary clearly was supporting the views of Air Force military chiefs at this stage of the discussion.

The Joint Chiefs of Staff also agreed with the Air Force position that the gunship force was adequate for Southeast Asian operations. In reply to Secretary Laird's query of December 27, 1969, on gunship requirements, the chiefs pointed to the sizable increase in gunships for Laotian operations since the 1969 northeast monsoon season and said that the current number of gunships appeared sufficient. They believed that the Vietnamese and Laotian Air Forces could neither operate nor maintain more gunships than they now had. The Joint Chiefs recommended tying gunship requirements to overall theater needs and not to separate ones for Laos and South Vietnam. The Military Assistance Command could assure satisfactory gunship support through flexible allocation of gunship sorties.[83]

Deputy Secretary of Defense David Packard entered the gunship force discussion decisively in December 1969. After participating in a live-firing AC–130A flight at Lockbourne AFB range, the deputy secretary wrote Secretary Seamans that the gunship was an "impressive weapon" and that "its enviable record in SEA is easily understood." Mr. Packard favored "at least a vestigial capability" for the future to carry out tactical night detection and attack missions. He also thought the aircraft might be suitable for the Military Assistance Program. He asked the Air Force to "formulate an R&D program for improved GUNSHIPS and that a minimal number be included in . . . plans for the decade 1970–1980."[84] This significant directive clearly opened up a future for gunships beyond the Southeast Asian war. Coming as it did from top defense department leadership, it formed the cornerstone for further gunship development.

AC-130E Gunship

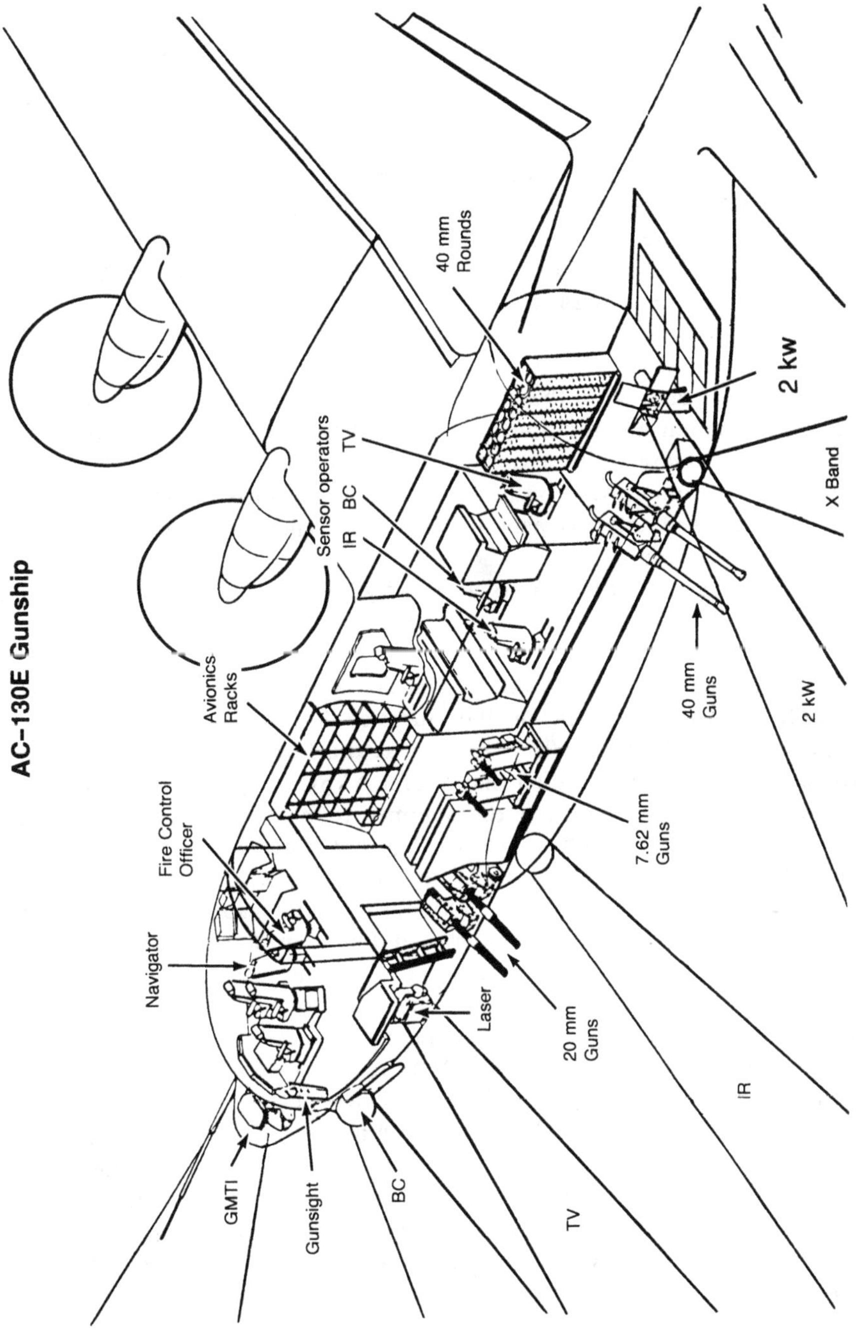
Avionics Racks
Fire Control Officer
Navigator
Sensor operators
IR
BC
TV
40 mm Rounds
2 kW
X Band
40 mm Guns
2 kW
7.62 mm Guns
20 mm Guns
Laser
IR
TV
BC
Gunsight
GMTI

After his January 1970 trip to Southeast Asia, Secretary of the Air Force Seamans replied to Deputy Secretary of Defense Packard: "I share your keen interest in gunship capabilities and have carefully monitored and encouraged our current programs since becoming Secretary of the Air Force to assure that we continue to make progress in this important field." Secretary Seamans then described his investigation of AC–130 effectiveness in the combat theater and dwelt upon Surprise Package's impressive record. He said he had already taken three actions: directed that the other AC–130s be modified into the Surprise Package configuration, started the Air Staff examining requirements for additional improved AC–130s with possible use of the C–130E, and continued prototyping of other gunship-equipment improvements. The latter took in foliage attenuation tests of a ground beacon to be used with the side-looking beacon-tracking radar, 20-mm depleted-uranium ammunition, and Pave Auger, a project for advanced development of lasers with sensory systems. Seamans declared the Air Force intended "to support vigorously a wide range of efforts to help assure the maintenance and improvement of the effectiveness of gunship weapon systems in the future."[85]

On January 21, 1970, Aeronautical Systems Division briefed the Air Staff on the cost of modifying all AC–130As to the Surprise Package configuration as desired by the Secretary of the Air Force. The next day Air Force headquarters directed AFSC and AFLC to modify five Gunship II aircraft, incorporating six of the Surprise Package subsystems at an approved cost of $1,570,000.[86] Known as the Limited Surprise Package Update Program,[87] it specified that a joint AFSC/AFLC team modify the AC–130s in the field during the summer to have them ready for the forthcoming 1970–71 hunting season. The Air Force later considered this impractical and moved the work to the United States. A key factor in the shift was the need of the five AC–130As for a general inspection (IRAN)—it had been at least two years since they had undergone a periodic overhaul.[88]

The AC–130A update program approved, the secretary and Air Staff turned to a far more controversial issue—the proposed use of C–130Es as gunships. Still vigorously resisting the idea unless more C–130Es were procured from Lockheed, General Momyer, TAC commander, told the vice chief of staff on February 24, 1970: "I reiterate that I oppose diversion of urgently needed airlift C–130Es to the gunship role."[89] In contrast, the concern of the Seventh Air Force and other gunship proponents centered on the older AC–130A airframes. They deemed it far more economical to put the sophisticated and expensive subsystems on an airframe that would last into the 1980s. Secretary Seamans, aware of the impact on the tactical airlift force of using E-model aircraft asked the Air Staff to examine alternatives to the use of these airframes.[90]

The Air Staff requested PACAF to furnish more definite Seventh Air Force requirements.[91] PACAF replied that either the C–130B or C–130E would represent the desired improvement. The command pointed to the increase in gross-weight capability over the AC-130A—10,000 pounds for the C-130B and 30,000 pounds for the C-130E. This could stretch mission time one and two hours respectively. Additional armor could also be provided. The more reliable B and E models had experienced fewer maintenance and support problems. Furthermore, the present AC-130As were fifteen-years-old or more and still being flown at maximum sortie rates. PACAF accordingly recommended that the modernization program begin by adding two new AC-130s by the end of 1971. The other AC-130s would be phased in with at least six in place by December 1972. PACAF envisioned a final force of nine AC-130Es.[92]

The Air Staff and Air Force secretary weighed PACAF's statement of new gunship requirements and on March 12, 1970, considered options of five, nine, and twelve AC-130 aircraft. Secretary Seamans tentatively approved securing the aircraft in this priority: (1) new production of C-130Es, (2) use of C-130Bs modified to C-130E gross-weight capability, and (3) C-130Es from airlift assets. Time had ruled out adequate staffing of the options, so the secretary directed that this be done with a study of costs and a further review of the desired gunship force structure.[93]

A series of meetings ensued during the latter part of March and the first of April involving the Force Structure Panel, Program Review Committee, Air Staff Board, and Air Force Council.[94] Among the problems studied were the expected cutoff of C-130E production in 1971 and TAC's objections. On March 18, 1970, Headquarters USAF asked ASD for facts on a conversion program of two or six C-130Es.[95] ASD's Gunship Program Office, which favored using C-130Es, supplied the data. Both AFSC and AFLC had given the Air Staff, on January 2, 1970, their "unqualified recommendation" that the C-130E model be used for a semipermanent or permanent force. After much discussion, the Air Force chief of staff approved, on April 28, 1970, the modification of two inventory C-130Es to the Surprise Package configuration.[96] He directed WRAMA to modify the two prototypes at an estimated cost of $17.3 million[97] and have them in Southeast Asia for combat by October–December 1971.[98] As an interim solution to the improved/expanded gunship-force issue, this would meet the PACAF 1971 requirement and form the nucleus of the 1970–1980 gunship force. It would also buy more time for evaluating the AC-130E and fixing on the number of AC-130Es to be built. When the chief of staff's decision went to the field for action on May 7, 1970,[99] the AC-130E modification program was nicknamed Pave Spectre.

On May 1, 1970, presidential science adviser DuBridge recommended to Air Force Secretary Seamans that the number of Surprise Package gunships be upped to twenty. He believed such a program of less vulnerable gunships could only be carried out with the wholehearted support of top government and Department of Defense officials, since it posed difficult budget problems and force-structure questions for a wide range of conflicts. Dr. DuBridge called attention to some past disappointing decisions: withdrawal of the AC–26 (one of the better truck-killers), and the acquisition of just seven AC–130s when at one point in 1967 the Secretary of the Air Force had approved as many as twenty.[100]

Replying to Dr. DuBridge for the Air Staff on May 11, Maj. Gen. Joseph J. Kruzel, Deputy Director of Operations, stated that the small number of Surprise Package gunships stemmed from a desire to conserve critical airlift aircraft. Nevertheless, all AC–130As were to be modified to the more effective Surprise Package configuration by December 1970 and two AC–130Es added by November 1971. Beyond these actions, General Kruzel said, "further expansion of the AC–130 gunship force is not now planned, pending combat evaluation of the two prototypes."[101] The Air Staff's reply could have cited several complementary Air Force actions expected to solidly strengthen night interdiction capability. In addition to the upgrading of the six AC–130As, the actions included the introduction of OV–10 aircraft as night air controllers, F–4 laser seekers, an additional loran-equipped F–4 squadron, loran-targeting for gunships, and employment of B–57Gs.[102]

Secretary Seamans was briefed on the status of the gunship programs on May 14, 1970. A delay of two to four months in the AC–130E prototype modification (Pave Spectre) due to insufficient Aeronautical Systems Division personnel was mentioned as a possibility. However, Dr. Seamans emphatically rejected the possible delay and called for broadening the base of experience in the division in order to maintain the schedule.[103] Under Secretary McLucas, who was also present at the briefing, questioned the procurement of only two AC–130Es. Gen. John C. Meyer, Vice Chief of Staff, explained that the two aircraft could serve as prototypes for follow-on procurement and a decision on that action could occur after further Air Staff study. It was decided that the gunship programs would be reviewed quarterly, and the secretary would himself decide in January 1971 whether more AC–130Es would be built.[104] The Air Staff knew well Tactical Air Command's reservations concerning the AC–130E program. On June 17, 1970, it asked the command for "comments and recommendations" by September 1, 1970, "regarding the post-SEAsia gunship concept of operation, force level and combat crew/maintenance support training requirements."[105]

On May 20, 1970, Defense Secretary Laird refocused attention from the postwar force to AC–130 gunships for the Southeast Asian war. He asked the chairman of the Joint Chiefs for a new interdiction strategy and specifically stressed the successes of the gunships with a relatively small percentage of total sorties. Secretary Laird suggested "that more concentration on gunship sorties, coupled perhaps with judicious choke-point strikes by B–52s or TAC air equipped with modern ordnance could produce major increases in interdiction results or free the less productive air resources for other purposes."[106]

In May also the Seventh Air Force reported results of the Commando Hunt III (1969–70) interdiction campaign. It reached the following

TABLE 4 EFFECTIVENESS OF COMMANDO HUNT III AIRCRAFT

Aircraft	Trucks Destroyed or Damaged	Sorties Attacking Trucks	Trucks Destroyed or Damaged per Sortie
AC-130 Surprise Package	822	112	7.34
AC-130 Other	2,562	591	4.34
AC-123	440	141	3.12
AC-119	987	435	2.27
A-6	977	1,486	.66
A-1	1,271	2,332	.55
A-7	959	3,147	.30
F-4	1,576	6,310	.25
A-4	245	1,223	.20
Total	9,839	15,777	.62

Source: Rprt, 7th AF, Commando Hunt III, May 1970; hist, MACV, I, annex A, VI-95, VI 96.

conclusions after analyzing the effectiveness of various aircraft against enemy supply trucks:

1. A majority of the aircraft showed significant increase in effectiveness in attacks against trucks.

2. Jet fighter and attack aircraft destroyed or damaged 3,900 trucks, thirty-nine percent of the total.

3. Gunships were the most effective truck-killers, obtaining forty-eight percent of the trucks destroyed or damaged while flying only eight percent of the sorties.

4. Gunships required two to three escort sorties for each attack sortie they flew, reflecting a team effort.

5. The AC-130 Surprise Package was the most effective individual aircraft in destroying or damaging trucks.[107]

These conclusions and the more precise data in Table 4 furnished extra "ammunition" to gunship adherents.[108]

Adm. Thomas H. Moorer, chairman of the Joint Chiefs of Staff, defended current interdiction programs in a June 10 reply to Secretary Laird. He declared that the new munitions and systems being added and the modification of all AC-130s would yield still more interdiction strength. Nevertheless, he prescribed caution, observing that "enthusiasm [for the gunship] must be tempered with an awareness of its vulnerability to enemy defenses." Two of the limited AC-130 fleet had been lost in the past thirteen months and gunships were "precluded, even with fighter escort, from operation along certain defended LOCs."[109]

In the meanwhile the President's Science Advisory Committee discussed ways to improve the Laotian interdiction effort. The committee outlined several conclusions to Deputy Defense Secretary Packard and invited him to attend sessions on the subject in mid-June. The group continued to stress the effectiveness of gunships as one of the main issues— forty-eight percent of all trucks destroyed or damaged while flying only eight percent of the total attack sorties, the Surprise Package being even more deadly. In contrast, the F–4s flew thirty-nine percent of the sorties but eliminated sixteen percent of the trucks. The committee reasoned that it would be wise to buy more Surprise Package aircraft and fewer F–4s. After sitting in the committee, Secretary Packard telephoned Dr. McLucas, the Air Force under secretary, for more information on the Air Force gunship program. When informed of the prototype AC–130E Pave Spectre, Mr. Packard wanted to reduce the projected eighteen-month development time. He asked McLucas to examine the current use of C–130 resources and to let him know what could be done to significantly increase the number of gunships by the end of the year.[110]

The Air Staff argued against the committee's position with these principal points: (1) no clear presidential guidance exists on retention of U.S. air' support after overall U.S. military withdrawal, thus the uncertainty as to future interdiction campaigns; (2) Surprise Package is peculiarly suited for a Southeast Asian-type war, but the postwar force faces difficult budget choices and must be tailored in light of other type conflicts; (3) there must be a balanced force of gunships and F–4s inasmuch as the aircraft complement each other; and (4) the Air Force is developing and documenting support for a Surprise Package program.[111]

Caught in the debate crossfire, Under Secretary McLucas contended that the Air Staff planned too conservatively for future gunship use. He said the Air Force would most likely be in Southeast Asia for some time and the demand for air power would probably intensify with the withdrawal of ground forces. He considered the gunship record and its cost effectiveness in truck-killing beyond dispute. Furthermore, the Air Force needed airplanes with effective guns in planning for the future. Dr. McLucas spoke of the detrimental decline in this capability from the Korean to the Vietnam war. He discounted the great objections on gunship vulnerability and claimed that at about $5 million per gunship he didn't "see how we can go wrong in converting a dozen or so."[112]

The Air Staff buckled down to planning the larger gunship force desired by Deputy Defense Secretary Packard for December 1970. A briefing of Air Force Under Secretary McLucas on June 18 presented the Air Staff position on Surprise Package production and laser-guided bombs. After the briefing, the group reviewed Pave Spectre and AC–130A updating, then discussed proposals for additional gunships. One suggestion considered would modify three to four AC–130As by January 1971 at $6 to $7 million per aircraft (excluding airframe cost) by resorting to a sole-source contract with Ling-Temco-Vought at Greenville, Tex. Even then, the Systems Division and Warner-Robins Materiel personnel would need unlimited authority and a virtually open purse to expedite the program. The

Top: MSgt. Garfield Jackson, Jr., 16th SOS, prepares a marker flare; bottom: Secretary Seamans briefed on AC–130s in Southeast Asia.

discussion turned to other possible limitations such as the need for night observation device yokes, scarcity of management talent, computer and gun availability, and the uncertainty of Ling-Temco's work force. Next Dr. McLucas addressed Air Staff concern over the Air Force's future role in the Southeast Asia war. He pointed out that Dr. Henry A. Kissinger, the President's Assistant for National Security Affairs, had acknowledged the need for more positive guidance for the longer view. Meanwhile, he said, Mr. Packard looked to the gunships to replace in some degree the decrease in tactical air sorties.[113] More detailed briefings and discussions followed: General Meyer, on June 22; Secretary Seamans, June 23; and General Ryan, June 29. From these meetings emerged a plan for modifying six additional C–130As with a ninety-day contract option to modify three more. Subsystems for the latter aircraft would be procured during the contract-option period.[114]

As these Air Force headquarters discussions went on, various opinions on additional AC–130 gunships percolated in the lower commands. Maj. Gen. Abe J. Beck, WRAMA commander, thought it unwise to use more C–130A airframes for Southeast Asia gunship requirements. He saw definite advantages in adopting the AC–130E—bigger payload, three more hours of loiter time, longer ferry range, better reliability, and a newer state-of-the-art airframe. General Beck felt that problems of mixing A and E models would be offset by gaining a more permanent force and by investing much valuable equipment in a better airframe.[115] Earlier, General Momyer had complained of the gunship program being "a series of ad hoc actions" and argued that whatever the number and type of C–130s finally selected they should be the same. Only this would obtain "economy of training, supply support, and standardization of tactical employment."[116] These views spotlighted the many complex ramifications involved in what on the surface seemed a relatively simple decision.

On July 2, 1970, the Secretary of the Air Force presented to Mr. Packard the proposal for increasing AC–130A gunships. Secretary Seamans said the January 1971 deployment goal would exact a three-shift, seven-day-a-week production schedule from Ling-Temco-Vought Electrosystems. The cost would run about $45.3 million for six aircraft, $52 million for nine. The AC–130As would be fitted with Surprise Package 40-mm guns, special equipment, and sensors. However, the tight delivery schedule ruled out installation of the digital fire-control computer and inertial navigation system. Program funding would have to come from the Special Activities portion of 1970 Air Force missile procurement and research, development, test and evaluation appropriations. Dr. Seamans cautioned that the planned delivery date demanded all-out effort and support. He additionally outlined the new AC–130A program to the deputy defense secretary and said it would move the Air Force "well down the road toward a more survivable self-contained night attack aircraft."[117]

Deputy Secretary Packard verbally approved the Air Force plans for acquiring the additional AC–130As that would eventually double the Gunship II force. Air Force Secretary Seamans notified Mr. Packard on July 10, 1970, that procurement was under way and three contractors in addition to Ling-Temco-Vought were being considered, all with C–130 experience: Lockheed, Fairchild-Hiller, and Hayes International Corporation. Secretary Seamans referred to a "learning curve associated with producing an acceptable Gunship weapon system" and considered Ling-Temco-Vought "further ahead of this learning curve than any other contractor." This firm had taken eleven months to modify the first AC–130A, but only four months to complete the last aircraft, which also included a complete inspection and repair procedure concentrated on the airframe. Dr. Seamans remarked that he was arranging for briefings for concerned congressional committees to advise them of Air Force plans to reprogram funds for the modification and to release funds for purchase of "long-lead" subsystem items.[118] Mr. Packard formally approved the program on July 11.

The Air Force chief of staff informed interested field commanders on July 14, 1970, that he had approved a new modification of six additional C–130A aircraft to an upgraded configuration. The program's approved cost, including some equipment for three optional gunships, totaled $46,659,000. The modification included: flare launcher, forty-kw illuminator, moving target radar indicator, damage assessment system, laser target designator, Southeast Asia communications package, low-light-level television, fire-control system, a two-axis gyro, two 7.62-mm, two 20-mm, and two 40-mm guns, electronic countermeasures gear, sensor-light angle display system, loran, survivability package (foam in fuel tanks, armor), two-kw illuminator, beacon-tracking radar, ac/dc distribution modification, sensor operator console, mission commander console, and forward-looking infrared.[119]

Having received orders to begin the modification program, the Aeronautical Systems Division held a conference on the project at Wright-Patterson AFB on July 22–25, 1970. Representatives from interested commands worldwide met to design a coordinated plan for acquiring and logistically supporting the aircraft and to review their tasks. The high precedence Department of Defense rating required a deployment schedule of three AC–130As to Southeast Asia by January 1, 1971, and three by February 1, 1971. The representatives at the conference concluded that with modest construction and rehabilitation Ubon RTAFB facilities could accommodate the six additional aircraft. They did not expect equipment procurement to present any serious problem.[120]

A second conference of commands and agency representatives organized a preliminary plan for the project's total training effort and plans for other AC–130 gunship training programs.[121] After a good deal of discussion, the conference reached the decision that aircrew training should be conducted at Lockbourne AFB, Ohio. TAC would conduct the flying

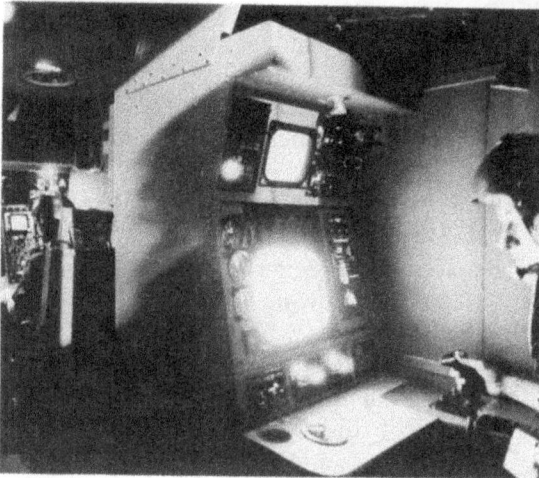

Top: View of 40-mm cannon inside an AC–130; left: an operator at the controls of an infrared console aboard a 16th SOS AC–130; bottom: AC–130 with advanced modifications.

training with two AC–130s and two AC–119Ks;. Air Training Command and Tactical Air Command would provide the ground training. The conferees forecast a future need to assign three AC–130s to TAC for aircrew training to support a twelve-gunship force in Southeast Asia.[122]

Counting the AC–130A modification, the Air Force had five advanced gunship programs under way in the summer of 1970:

Program	Approved Funds (in millions)
AC–130A update	$ 4.3
Surprise Package Second Season*	3.4
SEAOR improvements†	5.4
AC–130A	46.7
AC–130E	17.3
Total	$77.1

*Surprise Package Second Season was the term sometimes applied to the Surprise Package refurbishment.

†SEAOR improvements included a damage assessment subsystem, Black Crow, and the laser target designator.

The Air Force geared this array of gunship activity to: (1) producing a vastly more potent gunship force for the 1970–71 Laotian "hunting season," and (2) forming a core for the gunship force beyond the Southeast Asian war.[123]

Pleased with the Air Force's planned increase in gunship capabilities, Deputy Defense Secretary Packard wrote the chairman of the Joint Chiefs and the service secretaries on July 11, 1970. He singled out this "aggressive program" as an example of what was needed to bolster the interdiction effort in the 1970–71 campaign. Mr. Packard urged departure "from normal operating procedures and customs wherever significant benefits" could be derived in strengthening interdiction. He recommended that the Air Force consider greater use of AC–119Ks in Laos, employ additional F–4 aircraft, maintain adequate supplies of truck-killing ordnance, reduce B–52 sorties because of truck-park dispersal, and commit more aircraft at night and in bad weather in an effort to cut daylight aircraft losses.[124]

On July 23, 1970, Secretary of Defense Laird drew Dr. Kissinger's attention to plans for doubling the AC–130 gunship fleet. He told the presidential assistant he was recommending lower sortie rates in light of the growing number of AC–130s, development of better ordnance, lower combat levels in South Vietnam, and U.S. ability to meet new airpower requirements.[125]

General Ryan replied to Mr. Packard's interdiction recommendations on July 29; he stated that it was virtually impossible to put more AC–119Ks over Laos. Two of the aircraft had been lost and some were needed in the United States for replacement crew training. In addition, the antiaircraft threat had forced gunship operations to higher altitudes, requiring the Seventh Air Force to submit suggested solutions to this new combat-required operational capability. He noted that testing of Pave Sword aircraft was continuing as were constant efforts to enhance ordnance, counter the threat of enemy antiaircraft fire, and improve truck-killing capability by such actions as updating AC–130s. General Ryan also observed that B–52 sorties could be decreased if more leeway were allowed in diverting airborne B–52s to other targets.[126]

Admiral Moorer emphasized some of the same points in defending current interdiction practices to Secretary Laird. He believed the most improvement in interdiction would come from better air munitions.[127]

The work on advanced gunship programs continued amid discussions and plans for the 1970–1971 dry-season interdiction campaign. The Air Force contracted with Ling-Temco-Vought on July 23, 1970, for the integration of subsystems in the six AC–130As. Four days later the Aeronautical Systems Division completed surveys of Fairchild-Hiller and Hayes International as possible second sources for the optional three AC–130As, and sent the results to Air Force headquarters for a final decision.[128]

The five unmodified AC–130As (dubbed "Plain Janes") began leaving Ubon RTAFB, Thailand, in May 1970 for the United States for limited Surprise Package modification. The Air Force at this point authorized a change in plans. The Deputy for Limited War at the Systems Division had been at work on Black Crow, lasers for target designation, and bomb damage assessment equipment as part of Shed Light development programs (the overall Air Force program to improve night attack/interdiction capability). Headquarters, 8th Tactical Fighter Wing and PACAF were so impressed with Surprise Package results from these systems that they urged all Gunship IIs be so equipped. Air Force headquarters approved on June 2, 1970, the installation of the three subsystems.[129]

During the period from June 6 through November 1970, the five AC–130s received bomb damage assessment equipment* at approximately one-month intervals along with the previously authorized 40-mm guns, moving target indicator, and two-kw illuminator. Hayes International installed the equipment in conjunction with the "inspection-and-repair-as-necessary" program.[130] Lockheed Air Service of Ontario, California, placed Black Crow sensors in four AC–130As before their final trans-Pacific movement. Hayes fitted the fifth aircraft with Black Crow sensors as part of IRAN work. Although installation of the laser target designator was delayed by the competing requirements of another program, it was ultimately provided at Ubon.[131]

Plans were developed by TAC, PACAF, and Systems Division representatives to test the refurbished Surprise Package aircraft. A group met at Wright-Patterson AFB on August 4, 1970, to design tactics for a gunship to designate targets for both fighter-bombers and Strategic Air Command

---

*The equipment consisted of a videotape recorder, a videotape playback, and an electron-beam recorder which converted videotape to 16-mm sound film. The system could record inputs from either the forward-looking infrared or the television set.

**Combat Sierra Offset Bombing
(AC-130/B-52)**

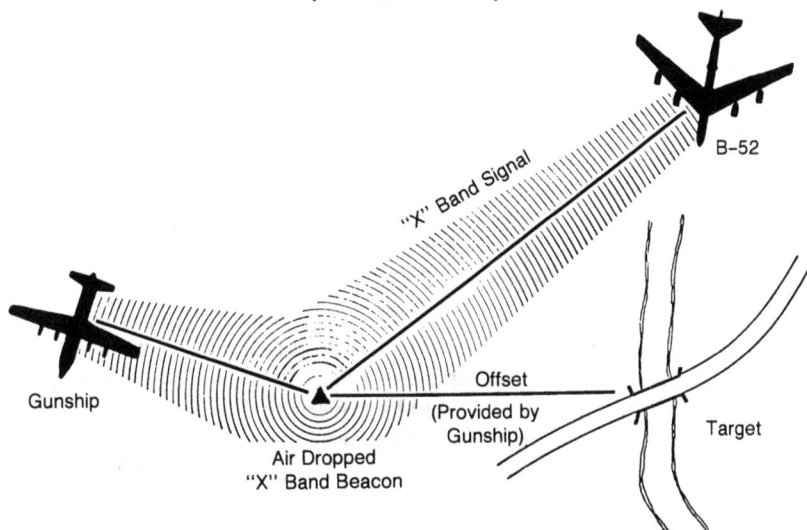

B-52s. SAC and the Air Staff agreed on the value of a Southeast Asia evaluation of the concept and the latter informed TAC and PACAF in January 1971. However, during a planning conference at Air Force headquarters on February 8, Tactical Air Command representatives opposed the tests on the grounds of "non-availability of excess AC-130 sorties and lack of suitable targets for the B-52s." PACAF and the Seventh Air Force also added objections and the Air Staff decided to cancel the project on March 10, 1971.[132]

Testing of new tactics by Surprise Package aircraft did take place at Eglin AFB. The gunship flew fifteen test missions between September 8-28, 1970. The AC-130A and a loran-equipped F-4 collaborated to place laser-guided bombs on the target.[133]

In addition to the tactical tests, Surprise Package continued its role as a flying laboratory. An Air Force Academy group of officers, for example, installed a number of strain gauges and accelerometers with associated recorders to detect the aircraft's stresses and strains during firing passes.[134]

Actively interested in the gunship programs, Air Force Secretary Seamans visited the Ling-Temco-Vought plant at Greenville, Texas, on September 15, 1970. He checked the corporation's progress in carrying through its $7.2 million AC-130E modification.[135] During the evening he visited Eglin AFB and flew on a Surprise Package test flight.[136] The visits were but one indication of high-level concern in seeing advanced gunship development completed on time.

A decision on procurement of three optional AC-130A aircraft became necessary at the end of September. Deferring the acquisition of the aircraft would mean revised schedules and increased cost.[137] On October 1 Secretary Seamans informed Deputy Defense Secretary Packard that the Air Force would buy the additional aircraft. It would use them in the 1970-71 interdiction campaign as attrition replacements, and in support of replacement aircrew training. Amendment of Ling-Temco's contract added the three aircraft with delivery scheduled from February 1–March 1, 1971.[138] The changes increased total funding to just under $80 million for the entire advanced gunship program.

The new modification projects slowed the preceding gunship program. At first, the Gunship Program Office hoped to build the two AC-130E prototypes at the Systems Division, but the consequent disruption of flight tests and personnel shortages ruled out the idea. The Air Staff therefore instructed WRAMA to take over the task with shop personnel who normally handled C-130 IRAN work. The differing structure and electrical systems of the C-130A and the C-130E required extra engineering effort to integrate gunship systems into the E model.[139] Although work began as soon as authorized, the AC-130As overriding precedence delayed installation of some AC-130E subsystems by at least a month. One contract procured those subsystems identical in A and E models and some engineering effort applied to both projects. Nonetheless, the notable differences in other areas canceled out these advantages.[140] Even so, doing the work in house rather than by contractor trimmed C-130E modification costs $2.5 million.[141]

The first C-130E arrived at Warner-Robins Air Materiel Area on October 6, 1970,[142] the second on January 6, 1971.[143] The modification entailed very close coordination and teamwork between Systems Division engineers and Air Materiel Area personnel. The engineers sifted data from other advanced gunship projects to see what could be adapted to the C-130E airframe. Considerable new engineering effort sought to enhance the aircraft's survivability by relocating hydraulic tubing and reservoirs and by improving the emergency exit for crewmembers located near the right scanner's position.[144] Colonel Parkinson led a group of Air Force Academy specialists who assisted in the major task of improving the fire-control system. The A-7D fighter's fire-control system was eventually selected. The entire project took on unusual significance for both WRAMA and ASD. It soon broadened to include six more AC-130Es and become one of the largest aircraft modification programs ever conducted in house by AFLC.[145] Despite AC-130As higher priority for equipment procurement and engineering imposed delays, the two prototypes nevertheless met their completion schedule of June 15, 1971, and July 15, 1971, respectively.[146]

Improvement of 20-mm and 40-mm ammunition moved in step with the two AC-130 programs. In search of a better 20-mm round, the Air Force on October 20, 1970, approved acquisition of improved high-density 20-mm rounds. In addition, improved 40-mm ammunition enlarged the incendiary pattern by fitting a standard round with a Misch-metal liner, a highly pyrophoric metal resembling cigarette lighter flint developed by the Naval Weapons Laboratory. Airborne tests at Eglin on October 27 disclosed that near-misses by Misch-metal rounds set trucks on fire while regular 40-mm rounds did not.[147] In December the Air Force sent 1,000 of the improved rounds to Ubon for combat evaluation and, pending the results, it ordered 400,000 40-mm rounds modified.[148] An 8th Tactical Fighter Wing combat test on January 21, 1971, revealed that Misch-metal rounds kindled four to five times more secondary fires and explosions than the standard 40-mm; the rounds also marked targets better. During the complete combat evaluation between January 21 and February 10, 1971, it took sixteen Misch-metal rounds to destroy one truck compared to fifty-one regular 40-mm. However, some debate arose concerning the conditions of the test and whether an accurate comparison had in fact been achieved. During April 1971, shell-extraction problems temporarily halted use of the improved round. Air Force Armament Laboratory tests completed in September found the standard 40-mm round better for inflicting fragment damage and leaks in petroleum cargo but the Misch-metal round most effective for touching off fires.[149]

During early fall 1970, AC-130A gunship modification was winding up in the United States and the planes were returning to Southeast Asia. Surprise Package flew its first combat sortie of the 1970-71 interdiction campaign on October 25, 1970, sixteen days ahead of schedule.[150] The AC-130A updated aircraft began arriving at Ubon in October and readying for combat,[151] they entered the war theater on November 17, forty-five days before the planned time.[152]

As this "new" gunship fleet conducted combat operations against the enemy's network of trails and roads, disappointment grew over the results. In November the gunships destroyed or damaged only 37 of the 202 trucks attacked—a poor eighteen percent record. The Seventh Air Force commander was concerned over this less-than-expected effectiveness.[153] He and the PACAF commander backed the 8th Tactical Fighter Wing's urgent request for an ASD assistance team to find out the reasons. Colonel Terry (a stalwart of the gunship program since 1964) headed the team of seven other "gunship experts" that got to Ubon on December 1, 1970.[154] Colonel Terry undertook combat missions at once to discover the difficulty. Very quickly the team established that the deficiencies stemmed largely from technical procedures and a relatively low level of aircrew experience. The results changed dramatically between December 1-22 as Terry and his group showed how it should be done. Of 532 trucks attacked, 361 (sixty-eight percent) were destroyed or damaged.*[155]

---

*Maj. Edward J. Bauman, one observer, said Terry's leadership charisma was very significant. Like a "White Knight on a white horse," he swept aside complaints, focused on the equipment and reestablished general confidence. Squadron personnel respected Terry as he seemingly could hit the target with the gunship at any angle and had great insight into the functioning of the various subsystems. Major Bauman also suggested that high winds during the start of the hunting season may have contributed to some of the disappointing gunship results. [Intvw, author with Maj. Edward J. Bauman, Dept. of Astronautics & Computer Sci, USAFA, May 5, 1971.]

Standard 40-mm Round Effect

Misch-metal 40-mm Round Effect

The AC-130 gunship fleet's expansion and improvement increased pressure on the replacement crew training program. Already problems had arisen because of the all-out emphasis on operations. Every available gunship was committed during the dry hunting season with most gunship updating and refurbishing deferred to the wet off-season. The crew-manning curve reflected this pattern. The one-year duty tour in Southeast Asia often brought an influx of green or inexperienced crews to Ubon just before the hunting season commenced and operational demands soared. These crews needed more checkout time in the aircraft to become familiar with the new and more sophisticated equipment frequently installed during the off-season. Moreover, to free AC-130s for combat, flight training sorties at Lockbourne AFB were conducted at times in the AC-119K. For approximately eighteen months, AC-130A aircrews flew five orientation missions in an AC-119K before entering combat in the AC-130A. Surprise Package greatly widened the disparity between the AC-130 and AC-119K, seriously weakening the effectiveness of such training.[156] When the AC-130A Plain Janes returned to the United States for IRAN and modification, it stopped the training and upgrading of incoming crews (the "New Guys") at Ubon for about a month. The first two Plain Janes finishing IRAN and two instructor crews went to Lockbourne.[157] They assisted the 415th CCT Squadron in training crews and better preparing other replacements headed for Southeast Asia. These training problems contributed to the decision to procure the three optional updated aircraft which later joined the crew-training program at Lockbourne.[158]

As 1970 closed, General Ryan reported to Air Force Secretary Seamans: "All primary objectives of the . . . program have been exceeded or met and the critical phases of the Gunship Acquisition Program for this interdiction campaign have been completed."[159] Considering the complexity, speed, and size of the AC-130 expansion and improvement program, the Air Force had compiled a remarkable record. It had updated five basic AC-130A gunships with 40-mm guns, improved sensors, and a new computer. Back in time for the 1970-71 dry season, these gunships came close to Surprise Package as truck-killers. In October Surprise Package had been refurbished and redeployed for combat. And six of the newly developed AC-130As arrived in Thailand "significantly ahead of schedule" to fly combat sorties.[160]

Gunship	Scheduled SEA Arrival Date	Date Deployed	Actual SEA Arrival Date	Days Early
1	1 Jan 71	10 Nov 70	17 Nov 70	45
2	1 Jan 71	18 Nov 70	1 Dec 70	31
3	1 Jan 71	24 Nov 70	1 Dec 70	31
4	1 Feb 71	12 Dec 70	21 Dec 70	42
5	1 Feb 71	20 Dec 70	4 Jan 71	28
6	1 Feb 71	31 Dec 70	16 Jan 71	16*

*Delayed by bad weather at Adak Island in the Aleutians.

Three additional AC–130As were being procured to shore up crew training. The AC–130A force available for the 1970–71 interdiction effort (Commando Hunt V) had not only been vastly improved but doubled in strength as well. Furthermore, Secretary Seamans told the Secretary of Defense: "it appears on initial review that the program will stay within, if not under, the budgeted amount."[161] Indeed—at a time headlined with serious cost overruns for many weapon-system developments—some eyebrows arched in disbelief as the Gunship II program office announced on August 27, 1970, the turnback of $625,704 in surplus fiscal year 1969 funds.[162] On January 21, 1971, the gunship program director declared he was returning $5 million of the funds (then totaling $52 million) allocated by the Air Force for the newly developed program.[163]

Good reasons underlay this management feat. In the first place, there had been "excellent support by all Air Force agencies and contractors involved."[164] Much debate accompanied and affected the gunship program's course but once a decision was made, strong support followed. Central to this were the personal contacts nurtured at all command levels by the comparatively small gunship program staff at ASD. Lt. Col. Charles R. Gentzel and Lt. Col. Charles F. Spicka* were among the chief gunship advocates at Air Force headquarters. They expedited and strengthened the program, speaking persuasively at times of important decisions. Key organizations—such as ASD's Deputy for Tactical Warfare, Deputy for Engineering, and AF Avionics Laboratory; the Shed Light Office at Air Force headquarters; the Air Force Academy; and WRAMA—interacted smoothly and efficiently.[165] Especially important was the backing of high-ranking government officials from the White House down through the defense department.

In spite of the keen top-level interest, ASD's Gunship Program Office had wide management latitude in the funds and systems area. The Gunship Program director could use letter contracts† and go to single-source contracts.‡ Even more important, a small, dedicated group of officers and civilians expertly managed the program. The group's character held the key to management success. Terry, Krause, Wolverton, Hubbard,** and Pinkerton had shared the early development of the side-firing system and it gave them strong personal identification with its progress. Highly motivated and goal-conscious, they felt this was *their* weapon system and its ultimate fate hinged on *their* actions. An officer who had observed and worked with the group said this was "management by objective rather than by control."[166]

---

*Known as "Gunship Charlie" for his aggressive sponsorship of gunship development.

†A letter contract is a written preliminary instrument to get work under way immediately. It is later confirmed by a formal contract.

‡A single-source contract is awarded to a single firm without competitive bidding or under circumstances that dictate the contract be given to a single firm.

** Maj. Lawrence R. Hubbard, Deputy Program Director for Subsystems, managed crucial subsystem programs.

By the same token, this balanced group of engineers, managers, and combat-capable* men could develop, then try out their systems. Knowing firsthand what the systems could do in combat buoyed their confidence in the gunship. This in turn reinforced their courage to defend its role and sell its advantages. Furthermore, the team's broad spectrum of experience and continuity permitted it to quickly spot unreliable equipment, unrealistic support, and unsubstantiated costs. Its flexible pragmatic approach rested not on a dogmatic desire to prove the worth of the theoretical views, but on a desire to see if a system worked and discard it if it didn't. Always alert to improvising with equipment and systems at hand, the group could concentrate on high-payoff improvements. Terry's leadership and implicit trust in his subordinates accounted for part of this flexibility. In recognition of these qualities, the Gunship Program Office of ASD received the Air Force Organizational Excellence Award on January 28, 1972. At the Pentagon ceremony, Secretary Seamans cited the management team for outstanding initiative, leadership, and professional ability.[167]

The makeup of the gunship management team and the constant prototyping and experimenting for gunship improvement dovetailed with Deputy Defense Secretary Packard's ideas on weapon-system management. "I told the Services to select people with the right background and education for management, give them appropriate training, give them recognition, and leave them on the job long enough to get something done," Mr. Packard told members of the Armed Forces Management Association on August 20, 1970. Certainly the gunship team came close to this prescribed model and produced timely results. Packard scored the drawnout development in the Air Force's "formal system" and noted that gunship management got more gunships in six months by working outside it.[168] Moreover, advanced gunship development typified Deputy Secretary Packard's so-called "fly before buy" concept. The AC-130A prototype and then Surprise Package turned out to be test-beds leading to future production models. Admittedly, the gunship program was characterized more by improvising on older known airframes than by developing an entirely new, sophisticated, and complex weapon system. Yet this improvisation helped point a course for research and development in other areas.

The payoff of the big AC-130 gunship development program in 1970 came during Commando Hunt V—the 1970 dry season interdiction campaign. Doubling the AC-130A force and stepping up the commitment of AC-119Ks reflected the determination of U.S. military planners to choke off as much enemy logistic effort as possible.† Under the Nixon policy of Vietnamization and gradual U.S. withdrawal, air interdiction

---

*Terry, for instance, had flown 56 AC-47 and 140 AC-130 combat missions from February 1968 through January 1970.

†The force increased but the Joint Chiefs of Staff imposed in August 1970 the first sortie ceiling on fixed-wing gunships—1,000 sorties per month.

assumed a critical role. It had to prevent disruptive enemy offensive actions and to buy valuable time for the overall policy to succeed. Yet North Vietnamese determination to put supplies through the gauntlet had certainly not diminished. Backed by a steady and unrestricted flow of provisions and trucks from the Soviet Union and China, the communists marshaled their resources and ingenuity for the annual logistic surge south. This time the battle promised to be more intense, and crucial, than ever before.

Several new elements changed the 1970–71 interdiction picture. A leadership more hostile to the North Vietnamese communists replaced the Cambodian government of Prince Norodom Sihanouk in March 1970. This prevented North Vietnamese use of the port of Sihanoukville and the so-called Sihanouk Trail supply line from the port northeastward. Forced to expand their Ho Chi Minh Trail operation, the North Vietnamese supplemented it by floating barrels down streams and by pipelines. Enemy antiaircraft defenses also grew in strength and improved in quality. Surface-to-air emplacements gradually moved southward and westward more seriously threatening air operations. In January 1971 the South Vietnamese army launched a ground offensive (Lam Son 719) into the Laotian panhandle to cut the enemy's logistical umbilical cord. The operation was but briefly disruptive.

Commando Hunt V commenced on October 10, 1970; it consisted of variations on the basic pattern of other dry-season interdiction campaigns. The Air Force allocated intensive sorties against four "interdiction boxes" on the main routes and passes from North Vietnam into Laos. B–52 bombing missions and jet fighter strikes centered on the heavily defended interdiction boxes, seeking to set up chokepoints or to channel the traffic. Gunships, B–57G jet bombers, and other tactical aircraft attacked trucks slipping through to the south.[169] The Igloo White sensor system had been refined, so now gunships and other aircraft could be assigned more efficiently against trucks moving along certain road sections. These many elements—combined with forward air controllers, control aircraft, tankers, photo-reconnaissance, and search and rescue aircraft—yielded a complex yet more flexible team effort. It was a major attempt at interdiction in depth against an increasingly hydra-like logistic network.

The Russian-built ZIL 157 truck emerged as the chief gunship target of the massive interdiction effort. Dependable, with six-wheel drive, it could convey five tons at forty mph over Laotian routes. The driver inflated or deflated the tires, while in motion, to suit the changing road surface. One estimate put the enemy truck inventory at 2,400,* seventy-two percent of which were in-commission at all times in the Steel Tiger area. An average of 450 trucks operated nightly. A series of short hauls and many transfers marked most truck movements; each driver knew his assigned road segment thoroughly.[170] As truck traffic mounted, the North Vietnamese

---

*A figure later to prove ridiculously conservative.

**POL Pipeline Activity,
ROUTE PACKAGE 1
May 1971**

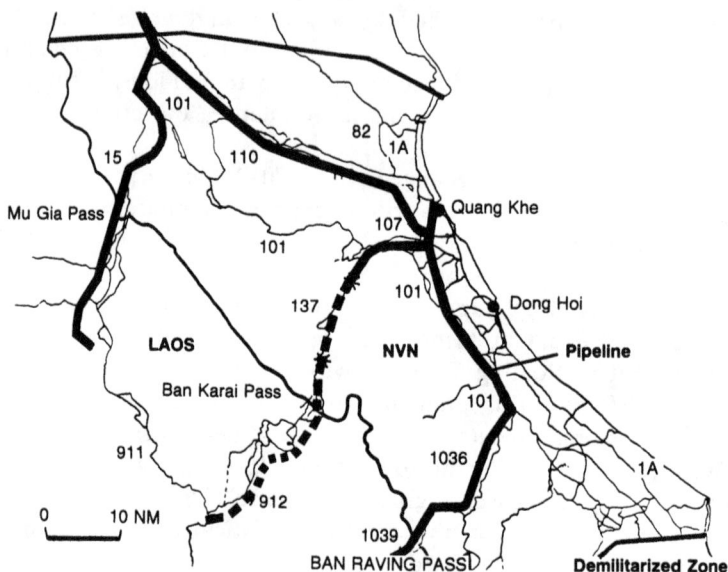

faced a serious shortage of fuel—hence their fresh stress on floating barrels down streams and extending pipelines.

The dry-season interdiction campaign got off to a slow start. Air Force Secretary Seamans reported to Defense Secretary Laird on November 19, 1970: "The combination of bad weather and the current strategy seemed to have produced four straight weeks in which no trucks were counted as having transited key interdiction points."[171] As the weeks passed, however, the enemy truck traffic picked up dramatically, and AC–130s compiled new records in truck-kills. On January 14, 1971, an AC–130 crew set a new squadron mark—fifty-eight trucks destroyed and seven damaged on a single mission.[172] By March the Spectres were averaging thirteen trucks destroyed per sortie. Results for the first quarter of 1971 were:[173]

	Trucks Attacked	Trucks Destroyed	Trucks Damaged	Percent Trucks Destroyed/Damaged
January	1,998	1,253	343	80
February	3,088	2,083	529	85
March	4,515	3,240	787	89

Despite an upturn in sorties, total trucks destroyed and damaged in April dipped to 3,687 and to 1,063 in May. With the beginning of the wet season in June sorties decreased to fifty-seven, trucks destroyed and damaged to 118.[174] Nevertheless, during Commando Hunt V (November 1, 1970–June 30, 1971) the AC–130s amassed a total 13,809 trucks destroyed and

Strike Efforts Against Output Routes
Laotian Panhandle—May 1971

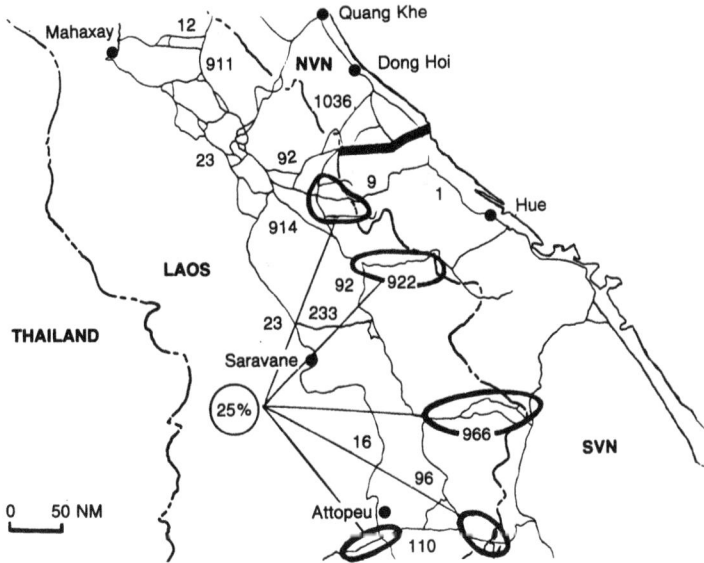

damaged—a three-fold rise over a like 1969–70 period.[175] In the peak month of March, Spectres scored 70 percent of all truck-kills in the Steel Tiger area.[176]

The truck-killing record of escort fighter aircraft improved as well, due largely to new laser-guided bomb development. The first successful team test of Pave Sword (the laser-seeker pod) in actual combat occurred on February 3, 1971. F–4 Phantoms escorting Spectre 12 destroyed a 37-mm gun with a laser-guided bomb. Sixteen days later the F–4s demolished two more trucks with the laser-directed bombs.[177]

Other interdiction indicators matched the impressive gunship/fighter-escort results and statistics. The percentage of trucks destroyed and damaged of those attacked soared from 44.2 percent in 1970 to 72.4 percent in 1971—convincing evidence of improved effectiveness.[178] The crucial figure, however, was the amount of supplies that actually reached South Vietnam. The Air Force estimated that in March 1971—the peak month of enemy effort—14,560 short tons of supplies entered the Laotian panhandle and 2,088 arrived in South Vietnam.[179] The Secretary of the Air Force presented information charts to a press conference on December 6, 1971, which favorably compared results of the last three interdiction campaigns.[180]

There were other statistics, however, which dampened this encouraging assessment. The number of trucks had increased: 8,000 were spotted from the air in each of the first four months of 1971.[181] An estimated 400 new trucks a month arrived from Russia and other communist countries.

167

Command and Control of Interdiction Task Force

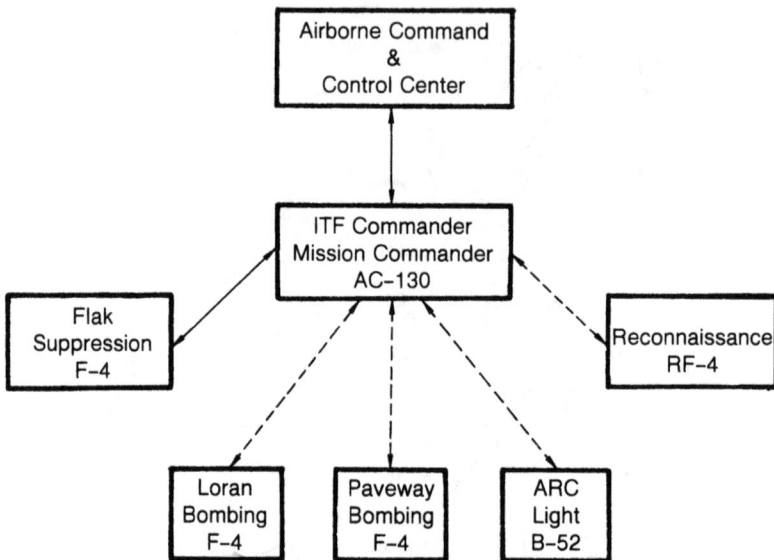

```
                    ┌─────────────────────┐
                    │  Airborne Command   │
                    │          &          │
                    │   Control Center    │
                    └─────────────────────┘
                               ▲
                               │
                    ┌─────────────────────┐
                    │   ITF Commander     │
                    │  Mission Commander  │
                    │      AC–130         │
                    └─────────────────────┘
   ┌──────────┐                                    ┌──────────────┐
   │   Flak   │                                    │Reconnaissance│
   │Suppression│                                   │    RF–4      │
   │   F–4    │                                    └──────────────┘
   └──────────┘
      ┌──────────┐    ┌──────────┐    ┌──────────┐
      │  Loran   │    │ Paveway  │    │   ARC    │
      │ Bombing  │    │ Bombing  │    │  Light   │
      │   F–4    │    │   F–4    │    │   B–52   │
      └──────────┘    └──────────┘    └──────────┘
```

Although more and more trucks were destroyed or disabled, replacements sent by allies of the North Vietnamese were offsetting the American interdiction effort. One pilot observed: "North Vietnam must be one huge truck park."[182] In addition, the enemy's ability to repair and enlarge his road network had not diminished. Furthermore, successful interdiction of the North Vietnamese pipeline and of their increased waterway shipments had not been achieved. Some supplies were shipped through to South Vietnam, others were stockpiled along the way.* These facts undercut any feelings of complete success.

The truck-kill count by AC–130 and AC–119K crews was so high that its accuracy was once again thrown into question. During an April 7, 1971, briefing of Lt. Gen. Donald V. Bennett, Director of the Defense Intelligence Agency, concern arose over possible false impressions gained from gunship bomb damage films. The Defense Intelligence director did not doubt the gunship figures but, in light of their estimates of enemy truck totals, some top-level officials in Washington did. The Air Staff relayed the doubts about the credibility of truck-kills to USAF commanders in Southeast Asia with a result reflected in this comment:

---

*Most Air Force leaders realized that the flow of supplies couldn't be completely cut off. General LeMay, for example, said all supplies had not been intercepted in the Korean War or in the World War II interdiction camaign in Italy. He fingered the added difficulty in the Southeast Asia war: "You can't stop a trickle of supplies that somebody can throw on their back or a bicycle and wiggle through a jungle." [Intvw, Dr. Thomas G. Belden, Chief Historian, USAF, with Gen. Curtis E. LeMay, retired, March 29, 1972.]

Estimated Supply "Input" vs. "Output"
Laos Panhandle
November–June

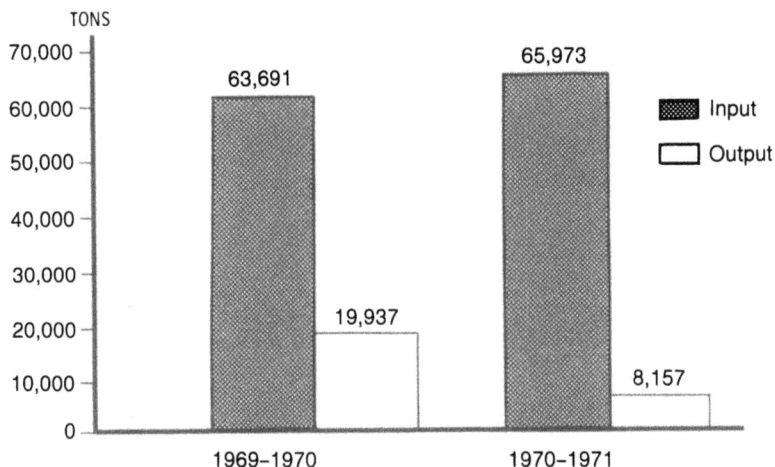

TONS

	1969–1970	1970–1971
Input	63,691	65,973
Output	19,937	8,157

Input

Output

AC-130 BDA is the hottest thing in the theater this moment. Seventh Air Force is really concerned about the validity of the BDA reported by the AC-130 gunships in their truck killing operation. They stated all aircraft BDA for this hunting season indicates over 20,000 trucks destroyed or damaged to date, and if intelligence figures are correct, North Vietnam should be out of rolling stock. The trucks continue to roll however.[183]

The Seventh Air Force commander convened a conference on April 28, 1971, to examine gunship truck claims. The conferees concluded that gunship crews were making honest, accurate reports. The Seventh Air Force nonetheless adjusted the criteria on May 1, 1971. It now required a secondary explosion or a sustained fire for a truck to be listed as destroyed. Direct hits counted as damaged only. The 40-mm near-miss, previously accepted for a damaged-truck listing, was dropped. The tightened BDA criteria rested in part on the realization that bags of rice on a truck might absorb most of a 40-mm blast. A special test of Spectre gunship munitions took place on May 12, 1971, at Bien Hoa AB as part of a continuing study of truck-kill assessment. Test results supported the revised BDA criteria. The BDA revision reduced the proportion of trucks claimed as destroyed but changed overall statistical effectiveness very little.[184]

Questioning of gunship claims was joined by criticism of the emphasis on truck-kill statistics. Several intelligence analysts argued for more attention to through-put of supplies rather than the number of trucks destroyed or damaged.[185] It proved far harder, however, to assess through-put than results of the attacks. The challenging of the statistics nevertheless revealed one thing: regardless of more sophisticated gunship bomb

169

Lam Son 719 Support

30 January–31 March 1971

damage assessment and some outstanding film records, there were those who discounted the claims and the overall interdiction effectiveness as well.

The interdiction effort in the Laotian panhandle held the spotlight, but the Seventh Air Force also sent AC–130s and AC–119Ks to strike targets in northern Laos (Barrel Roll) and in Cambodia. Gunship attacks on supply lines leading to both fronts resembled those in the Steel Tiger area. The gunships destroyed 800 trucks in Barrel Roll during the first six months of 1971.[186] Additional sorties supported hard-pressed Laotian and Cambodian ground forces in both countries. More than 1,100 gunship sorties were flown in Cambodia during the first half of 1971.[187]

A major ground-support effort developed when the South Vietnamese army launched its offensive against the Ho Chi Minh Trail in the area between Khe Sanh and Tchepone. Operation Lam Son 719 continued from January 30 to March 24, 1971. The AC-130s and AC-119Ks flew 239 sorties in support of the operation, one-fourth of them in the critical last five days when the South Vietnamese were withdrawn.[188] In thirty-nine attacks the gunships destroyed twenty-four enemy tanks.[189] The AC-130 share of the total was fourteen PT-76 light tanks in twenty-eight attacks.[190]

Like the Spookies in South Vietnam, the Spectres hovered constantly over threatened posts in the Lam Son 719 operation. One AC-130, for example, remained over an ARVN position at Objective 31 for three consecutive nights.[191] Its intensive fire inflicted heavy losses on the enemy. Several times the North Vietnamese troops tried to get in close to the ARVN perimeter to counteract the gunship attacks, requiring calls in some cases for Spectre fire on the post's trenches.[192] An American observer described how this gunship night support at Objective 31 prevented serious friendly losses:

> In between gunships, three to four minutes, the enemy would be up and into the wire. The gunship would then shoot them back from the wire and do this until the next gunship came up. It continued all night. There is no doubt in my mind that Hill 31 would have been overrun that first day or at least that first night, if it had not been for TAC air and gunships.[193]

Extensive attack operations with few losses was one gratifying result of the AC-130 role in Commando Hunt V and throughout Southeast Asia. On April 22, 1970, the enemy had downed a second AC-130A over the trail.* Despite growth of enemy defenses and a rise in sorties, however, no more gunships were lost in the 1970–71 campaign. The Commando Hunt V evaluation reported: "The AC-130 and AC-119 gunships experienced the largest number of AAA reactions per sortie flown, although a small fraction of these sorties were hit and no aircraft were lost."[194] This singular record for the "vulnerable gunships" stemmed largely from antiaircraft suppression by fighter escorts, higher operating altitudes, careful tactics, and aircraft armor.

The Commando Hunt V no-loss record did not lessen concern for AC-130 gunship survivability. Concern in fact soared when the enemy suddenly fired two surface-to-air-missiles (SAMs) at Spectres in March 1971 and two more in April.† The Seventh Air Force rushed through a request to equip all AC-130s with electronic countermeasures (ECM) to defend against SAMs, and PACAF validated it and tagged it priority one.[195]

Meantime, the Air Force reached other AC-130 gunship development decisions. During the quarterly gunship review for the Air Force secretary on January 20, 1971, General Meyer, Air Force vice chief of staff, said a decision was needed soon on additional AC-130Es.[196] A minute examination of the AC-130E program followed. On February 19, the Air Staff asked AFSC and AFLC for data on the possible addition of an

---

*One crewmember was recovered but ten were listed as missing in action.
† Figures vary on the exact number of "confirmed" SAM firings.

AC–130E squadron of twelve aircraft. Of special concern were the cost and the scheduling of such an expansion and the impact at ASD and WRAMA on existing programs. An ASD–WRAMA coordinated program was presented on February 21.[197]

Five days later the Air Staff recommended: (1) six instead of twelve AC–130Es be acquired for the 1971–72 interdiction campaign, and (2) the five Plain Jane AC–130As be sent back to the United States during the summer interdiction lull for a full updated modification. The second part of this proposal was motivated by a desire to standardize the AC–130A configuration and thereby ease logistic and maintenance problems. General Ryan and Secretary Seamans approved the entire recommendation and set up the following program and deadlines:

1. Eleven latest AC–130As in Southeast Asia by October 1, 1971 (including the five Plain Janes to undergo further modification).
2. Surprise Package IRAN and refurbishment (including standardized configuration) and return to Southeast Asia by October 1, 1971.
3. Six AC–130E Spectres in Southeast Asia by January 1, 1972.
4. Two AC–130E prototypes to remain in the United States for crew training.
5. Procurement of twelve sets of gunship subsystems (looking to eventual modification of a total of twelve AC–130Es).[198]

This decision went to the field on March 23, 1971.[199] Cost of the modification program was set at $56.2 million ($33.9 million for modifying in-service aircraft, $14.9 million for spare equipment, $7.4 million for spare equipment support and for operation and maintenance labor). This required reprogramming approval by Congress.[200] A budget squeeze to accommodate cost overruns in other areas dictated the decision to cut six AC–130Es from the proposed squadron of twelve.

Secretary of Defense Laird reported to President Nixon on March 10, 1971, that "immediate action to purchase an additional six AC–130 fixed-wing gunships" was underway to comply with the chief executive's desire for greater gunship capability in Southeast Asia. At the same time, twenty-seven more Cobra helicopter gunships were being sent to South Vietnam. Laird stressed that he was impressed with the gunship's truck-killing effectiveness, but nevertheless believed it important to "maintain a balanced posture for our assets in Southeast Asia." The environment ranged from permissive to extremely hostile, and high-performance aircraft were needed to fly escort in case of the latter.[201] Even with the increase in gunships, Mr. Laird said there were still those who would be convinced that the increase was not large enough.

The chief of staff's decision to return the five updated "Plain Jane" AC–130As for latest modification ran counter to PACAF's and Seventh Air Force's desires. The commands wanted to keep the maximum number of AC–130 gunships in Southeast Asia until the wet season. In order to have all AC–130As back in the war zone by fall, two had to be sent to the

United States in May and one in June. On March 3 the Seventh Air Force asked that the three training AC–130As be sent to Southeast Asia as replacements.[202] General Ryan decided to send only two.[203] The return of the five Plain Janes then began, and modification work progressed during the summer at Ling-Temco-Vought.

The summer of 1971 was another cycle in the continual struggle to keep AC–130 gunships one step ahead of enemy defenses. The six AC–130E aircraft undergoing modification would have a digital fire-control computer that would continuously solve the fire-control problem, permitting faster target acquisition. The aircraft's higher gross weight limit would permit greater fuel capacity, longer operating time, and a larger ammunition load. The Air Force also selected electronic countermeasures equipment which would strengthen the AC–130E's defenses against enemy missiles.[204] In addition it agreed to a modification contract for 1,000 Mk–24 flare canisters loaded with chaff to counter the anticipated SAM threat.*[205]

The ceaseless concern with gunship survivability and potency turned ASD attention to the U.S. Army's 105-mm howitzer as a possible AC–130 weapon. On an aircraft this gun's 5.6 pounds of high-explosive (compared with the 40-mm gun's 0.6 pounds) could multiply the chances of target destruction. The gun's shell would leave a valuable ground-mark for fighter escorts and its longer range would enable the gunship to fly higher.[206] The Air Force Academy team's careful stress analysis on Surprise Package indicated that the larger gun could be used safely.[207] Next came quietly conducted ground and airborne feasibility tests during August–September 1971. Briefed on test results, the chief of staff gave the go-ahead on November 18 to ongoing development leading to combat evaluation.[208] The project was named Pave Aegis. An ASD conference in early December prepared the development program. Plans prescribed installation of the 105-mm cannon in place of the aft 40-mm gun and the APQ–150 beacon-tracking radar. AC–130E armament would then consist of: one 40-mm gun, two 20-mm, and the 105-mm. ASD expected no trouble nor need for special modification in integrating the heavy gun with the fire-control computer and other gunship subsystems.[209]

The Pave Aegis program and preparations for the 1971–1972 interdiction campaign (Commando Hunt VII) seemed to encapsulate the advanced AC–130 gunship's history. In the first place, it typified the ongoing evolving weapon-system development that had now stretched more than five years. It

---

*Gunship tactics against SAMs evolved. The Black Crow operator, illuminator operator, and the scanner would try to detect a SAM launch. If detected, the illuminator operator would observe the missile until impact was imminent then call for the pilot to dive. This maneuver had the drawback of increasing the antiaircraft threat. [Cole, *Fixed Wing Gunships in SEA*, p. 45.]

AC–130E Pave Aegis

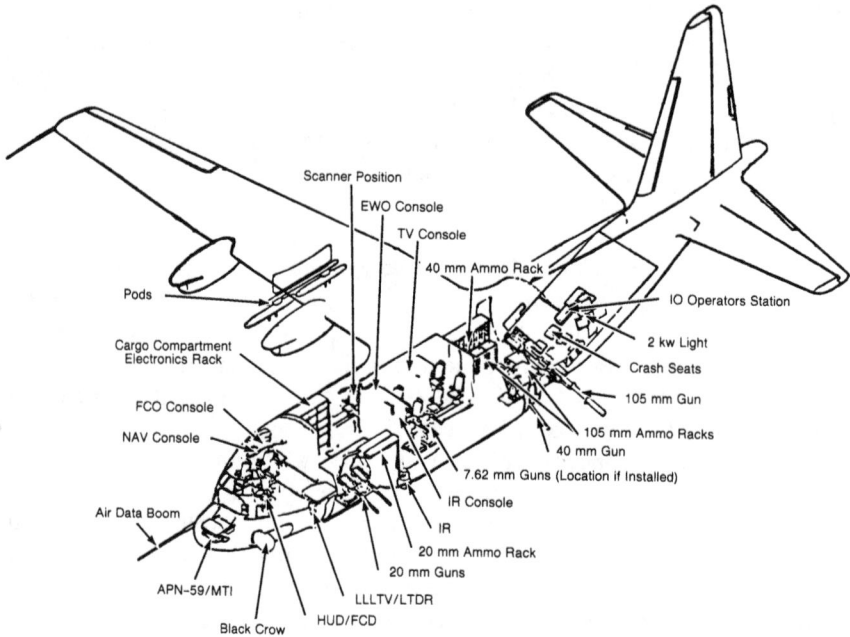

also reflected the innovative and imaginative minds of the gunship-development team. They were ever alert for new ways to bolster the gunship's effectiveness and enhance its chances for survival. There was a concerted effort to keep ahead of the enemy's defenses and not always respond after the fact.

Second, the 1971 summer gunship improvement and expansion program attested to unfailing confidence in the gunship's worth. The Air Force leadership and others knew all enemy supplies could not be interdicted. The AC–130 gunships nevertheless stood out as the most economical and most productive weapon system for destroying enemy vehicular traffic. Task force operations clustering around the AC–130 spotlighted the gunship's limitations but at the same time its importance. The extra force of six AC–130Es was one more attempt to capitalize on the weapon system's proven capabilities.

Third, the Air Force gunships progressed in a cyclic pattern of summer refurbishment/development after winter combat. Confidence in the management team's ability to finish the required modification in a few months paralleled the trust placed in gunship operations. Thus the actions involving AC–130 gunships in 1971 exemplified a larger train of events packed with more meaning than was certainly apparent at the time.

By 1971 the AC–130 gunship had grown into a weapon system far removed from the 1967 prototype. As noted, this change contained some unique aspects of management, research, and development, and combat operations. After much controversy, success in these areas had been crowned with plans to retain a small gunship force within the Air Force's post-Southeast Asian war structure. While this did not convert all skeptics of the gunship's vulnerability, it did carve a more substantial niche for the gunship as one of the Air Force's valued combat aircraft.

Pre-flight check of Pave Aegis.

V. Gunship III (AC–119G/K)

A visitor to one of the offices associated with AC–119 gunship operations might find conspicuously posted a small business card:

> When Uninvited Guests Drop In Call for "The Shadow."
>
> We provide: Lighting for all occasions
> Beaucoup 7.62
> Mortar Suppression
>
> We defend: Special Forces Camps
> Air Bases
> Outposts
> Troops in Contact
>
> Who knows what evil lurks below the jungle canopy?
> The Shadow knows!

This card summarizes in brief the operations of the AC–119G Shadow in the Southeast Asian war in late 1968. Add "Beaucoup 20-mm," "Interdiction Services," and change the name to "Stinger," then one can also fairly state the activity of the AC–119K (Stinger). These two models of the old C–119 Flying Boxcar transport were the chief replacements for the AC–47s and the most numerous of Air Force gunships. "Gunship III" in chronology, they represented a distinct chapter of the total gunship story.

In 1967 the search for a follow-on aircraft to the AC–47 Spooky had narrowed down to the C–119 and C–130. The Air Force deemed these high-wing aircraft best suited as gunships. Commanders in the Pacific favored the advantages of the larger four-engine C–130. Nonetheless, urgent Southeast Asia gunship requirements, the definite need of C–130s for airlift, and the availability of C–119G airframes tilted the scale to the C–119. The Air Staff wanted the jet-assisted C–119K, but in June 1967 Air Force Secretary Brown chose the AC–119G (with a later option on the AC–119K) as the AC–47's immediate successor. His decision sparked considerable controversy, but the program of converting C–119Gs into gunships began in earnest.

Soon after Secretary Brown's decision, Air Force headquarters instructed AFLC to submit a cost and feasibility study on the modification of thirty-four and forty-six C–119Gs. The directive also called for similar data on conversion of C–119Ks.*[1] The Air Staff planned to deploy twelve

---

*Items specified for the AC–119G included: standard Southeast Asia communications equipment; four GAU-2B/A (7.62-mm) guns; 50,000 rounds of ammunition for day operations (35,000 rounds and sixty flares for night); inert fuel tanks; gunsight; jettisonable

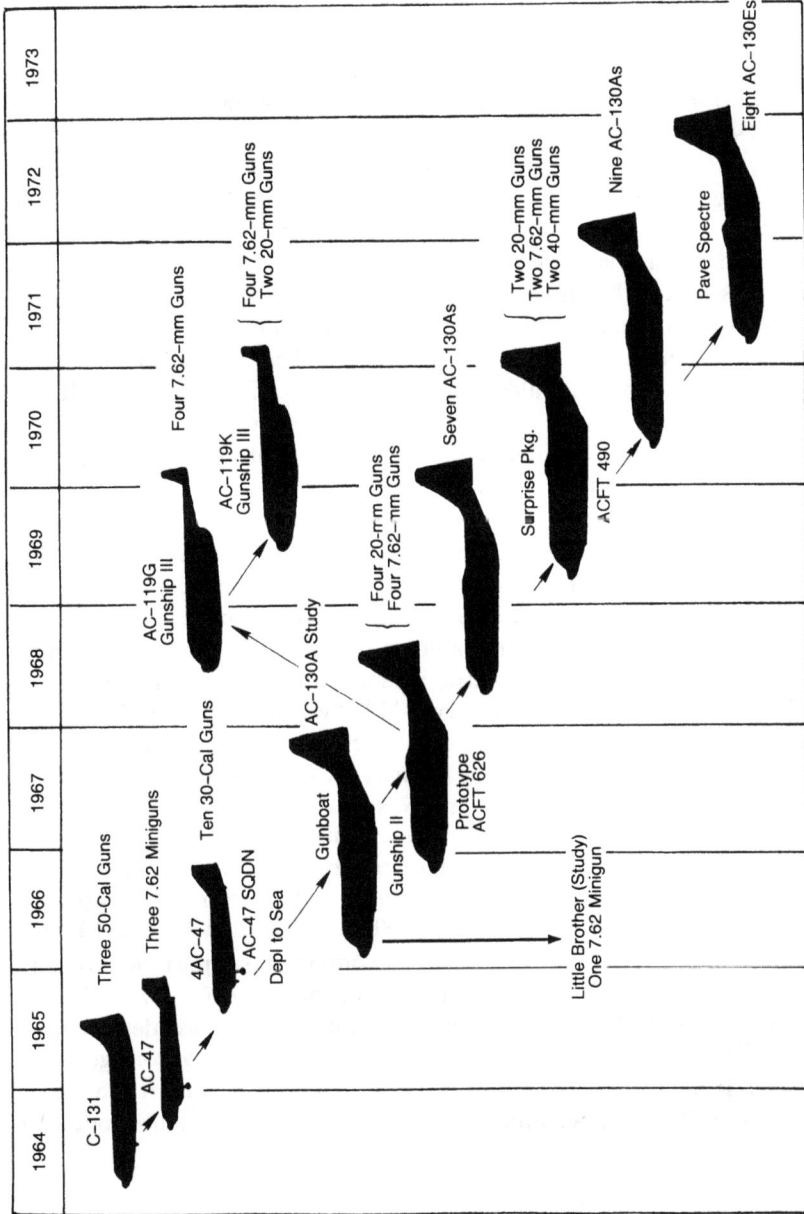

GUNSHIP EVOLUTION

1964	1965	1966	1967	1968	1969	1970	1971	1972	1973

C-131

AC-47

Three 50-Cal Guns

Three 7.62 Miniguns

4AC-47

Ten 30-Cal Guns

AC-47 SQDN

Depl to Sea

Gunboat

Gunship II

Prototype
ACFT 626

AC-130A Study

Little Brother (Study)
One 7.62 Minigun

AC-119G
Gunship III

AC-119K
Gunship III

Four 7.62-mm Guns

Four 7.62-mm Guns
Two 20-mm Guns

Four 20-mm Guns
Four 7.62-mm Guns

Seven AC-130As

Surprise Pkg.

ACFT 490

Two 20-mm Guns
Two 7.62-mm Guns
Two 40-mm Guns

Nine AC-130As

Pave Spectre

Eight AC-130Es

AC–119Gs to Southeast Asia in or shortly after October 1967.[2] So on July 20, Dr. Brown asked Secretary of Defense McNamara to allow transfer of forty-six Air Force Reserve C–119Gs to the active force.[3] Mr. McNamara tentatively agreed on August 10 but requested more facts for a detailed review.[4]

Though approved in June 1967, the AC–119 gunship program progressed at a snail's pace. Modification scheduling slipped due to a major funding problem, Mr. McNamara's hesitant approval to release C–119 airframes, and changes in plans for equipment.[5] All hope for an early AC–119 deployment rapidly vanished. While needed decisions were pending, however, action got under way on an AC–119G prototype. On October 20, 1967, Air Force headquarters directed installation of equipment in the prototype.[6]

As agreed by the Air Force Logistics Command and the Air Force Systems Command, the prototype modification and test could be done either by contract or "in house" at a depot. The two commands decided on a contract with Fairchild-Hiller. The Air Staff designated WRAMA as program manager and Systems Division to supply engineering support. It set a March 15, 1968, delivery date for the prototype, and fixed the total cost at $200,500 (later revised upward).[7]

Further review of the AC–119 program took place toward the close of 1967. By dint of favorable reports from Southeast Asia on the AC–130 prototype, the Air Force secretary decided on a mixed AC–130/AC–119 force. The Air Staff follow-up study on this proposal, required by Dr. Brown and submitted on January 26, 1968, recommended thirty-two AC–119s, backed up by extra training/attrition aircraft. In the mixed gunship force concept the AC–119 "would specialize in in-country day/night tasks associated with hamlet defense, fire support for ground forces, close air support, and convoy escort."[8] The projected thirty-two AC–119s would be organized in two squadrons of the 14th Air Commando Wing and operated from six bases suitably spaced thoughout South Vietnam. The AC–119s could take up continuous orbit stations during the hours of darkness at about a 100-mile radius from such bases as Nha Trang, Da Nang, Phu Cat, Pleiku, Phan Rang, Bien Hoa, and Binh Thuy. Seventh Air Force would exercise command support and operational control. The AC–119s would of course assume the AC–47s' role in South Vietnam as the Spookies shifted more and more to base defense missions.

The Air Staff study also addressed the AC–119 configuration and costs. It highlighted the problems in holding down aircraft gross weight to insure a 200 foot-per-minute, single-engine rate of climb under hot-day

---

(footnote continued from previous page)
flare launcher and sixty flares; and ceramic armor protection for six-eight crew members and critical components. Conversions of the C-119K would add these items: an improved fire-control system, four 20-mm guns, 1,500 rounds of 20-mm ammunition (35,000 rounds of 7.62-mm and sixty flares), night observation device, infrared capability, doppler radar, and an illumination system.

conditions.* The desired configuration clearly implied that the AC-119K with its jet pods, twenty-five percent more loading capacity, and significantly greater single-engine performance, would be an improvement over the G model. The study said that the deployment schedule would be about the same whether the G or K model was selected—gun procurement possibly being critical. The K model would afford the best configuration, the G model would cut costs.[9]

	AC-119G (millions of $)	AC-119K (millions of $)
1 prototype aircraft	.5	2.0
Unit cost (production aircraft)	.3	1.3
51 aircraft	16.2	68.7
Spares and support†	1.8	16.6
Total program cost	18.8	88.6

---

†Includes equipment and technical data for the AC-119G equipment and engines for the AC-119K.

If the Air Staff entertained hopes of persuading Secretary of the Air Force Brown to turn to the AC-119K, they succeeded only in part. The secretary reviewed the mixed gunship force data then let the chief of staff know, on February 2, 1968, he was approving one squadron (sixteen aircraft) of AC-119Gs and one squadron (sixteen aircraft) of AC-119Ks. A total fifty-two C-119s would be modified (twenty-six of each model) to take care of losses and crew training. Dr. Brown believed at least six AC-119Gs with crews should be in Southeast Asia by July, four AC-119Ks with crews by November. He agreed that Phase I training be conducted at Clinton County AFB, Ohio, and Phase II at England AFB, La. The secretary went beyond the Air Staff proposal and suggested the AC-119G include a better illuminator and a night observation device along with the associated fire-control system. Dr. Brown thought that this equipment's weight could be handled by cutting back on flare storage and by removing the beacon-tracking radar. "The important element," he said, "is that we provide a substantially improved gunship as augmentation to the AC-47 force—at an early date and at reasonable cost." An option could be taken later—if needed—to upgrade more AC-119Gs to AC-119Ks. For the present, however, the AC-119K offered "very little more in the way of capability" yet cost far more than the AC-119G. In fact, the AC-119K program surpassed "the AC-119G program cost by a factor of almost five."[10]

On February 8 Secretary Brown asked Secretary McNamara to approve the AC-119G/K force of thirty-two gunships for Southeast Asia and modification of a total fifty-two aircraft. Dr. Brown said: "I see a clear distinction between the more localized support and protective role of the AC-119 aircraft and the predominantly search-and-destroy concept envisioned for the AC-130." He planned to "proceed with the AC-119G in the interim, while working at full speed on the AC-119K as well."

---

*Hot-day conditions were 100° Fahrenheit, 80 percent dewpoint, and 400-foot-pressure altitude, the worst climate conditions in which the aircraft could safely conduct operations.

Approval of this force would lift the total to seventy combat-unit gunships—thirty-two AC–119G/Ks, thirty-two AC–47s, and six AC–130s (a total of seventy-two was attained by adding two more AC–130s). The enemy's 1968 Tet offensive had injected a note of urgency in the Air Force secretary's request.[11]

During the secretary of defense's review of the AC–119G/K force, the Air Staff on February 10, 1968, assigned AFLC management to the AC–119 program and directed an all-out effort. The first AC–119Gs were due in Southeast Asia by July 1968, AC–119Ks by November 1968. Inasmuch as the program funding was already assured, AFLC could go ahead with procuring long-leadtime items. The Air Staff harbored misgivings over possible competition between the AC–130 and AC–119G/K programs for sensor, gun and illuminator subsystems. It cautioned AFLC and AFSC that the aims of both programs had to be met.[12]

The Air Force Logistics Command picked WRAMA as project manager for the AC-119 modifications on February 10 and the latter created a program office the same day. Maj. Gen. Francis C. Gideon, WRAMA commander, quickly selected Col. John M. Christenson as overall manager and formed a special engineering team within the WRAMA Service Engineering Division to expedite the work.[13] WRAMA perused the proposed program and advised AFLC a higher priority for the project "compatible with or greater than that assigned the C–130" would be needed if schedule deadlines were to be met. It further proposed that the C–119s undergo IRAN concurrently with the reconfiguration and that some equipment be removed from other aircraft to overcome delays foreseen with new procurement.[14]

WRAMA believed Fairchild-Hiller, manufacturer of the C–119, could best accomplish the modification program.[15] The firm had completed engineering work on the AC–119G prototype in early February which lent further weight toward its selection.[16] On February 17, 1968, WRAMA awarded a letter contract to the company for modification and IRAN of fifty-one C–119s (the prototype was separate). Fairchild-Hiller's Aircraft Service Division at St. Augustine, Fla., would do the bulk of the work. Cost estimates for the project (including IRAN, spares, and aerospace ground equipment) totaled about $81 million.*[17]

On February 21 the Air Staff designated the AC–119G/K project "Combat Hornet."[18] It also told AFLC and AFSC the high precedence rating of AC–130 components now applied to certain equipment items of the AC–119G prototype and the first six follow-on aircraft. These were: NODs, FLIRs, DPN–34 radars, 20-kw illuminators, SPR–3 radars, associated fire-control system computers, as well as 7.62-mm and 20-mm

---

*Air Force Modification Requirement 1932 (FS–2151/C–119K), March 20, 1968, formally directed conversion of twenty-six C–119G aircraft to AC–119K gunships. These aircraft would have two additional J–85GE–17 jet engines at an approximate cost of $110,000 per airframe. The Air Force chose the J–85 engine for its 5,700 pounds of thrust at an additional weight of 1,500 pounds and because it was already in use on the C–123K which eased its logistic support.

Top: Crew chief Sgt. James R. Alvis, attaches the "Shadow" sign on 71st SOS equipment; left: Mr. Harold Henderson of Fairchild Systems and Lt. Col. William E. Long, CO, 71st SOS, Phan Rang AB.

guns. The Air Force kept tight rein on these high ratings and used them solely to meet aircraft delivery schedules. Other Combat Hornet items were procured under the previously assigned precedence rating.[19]

WRAMA suggested to AFLC that the C-119s be obtained from one or two units of the Continental Air Command (CONAC) rather than securing a few aircraft from several units. The one or two units could then give up aerospace ground equipment and spare parts along with the aircraft and thereby expedite the eventual AC-119 deployment to Southeast Asia.[20]

On February 24 Deputy Secretary of Defense Paul H. Nitze approved Secretary Brown's mixed gunship force plans, including the thirty-two AC-119 gunships for Southeast Asia. He stipulated that the actual AC-119 deployment be funneled through the deployment adjustment request system* and contain an analysis on the continued need for the AC-47 force.[21]

The Commander in Chief, Pacific Command, sent the Joint Chiefs of Staff a request for the mixed gunship force on March 3, 1968. The proposal would add 1,161 personnel in South Vietnam for supporting 32 AC-119s, 387 in Thailand for eight AC-130s, and twenty in Okinawa for maintaining AC-119s and AC-130s.[22]

At about this time, the President announced a new ceiling on SEA increases, based on MACV recommendations. Known as Program 6 and disclosed by the Joint Chiefs of Staff on April 6, it lifted the South Vietnam ceiling by 24,500 to a total of 549,500. It did not provide for the 1,161 spaces CINCPAC asked for to support the AC-119s, however.[23] The Joint Chiefs held off seeking a further rise in the ceiling because of the timing of CINCPAC's request with respect to the new ceiling approval. Instead, the Joint Chiefs asked CINCPAC to rework the AC-119 requirement to fit Program 6 manpower limits.[24] These limits quickened the study of ways to squeeze more gunships into South Vietnam[25] for at stake now was a possible trade-off with another desired program. Discussions on the matter continued for some months.

Amid AFLC modifications actions and high-level force decisions, TAC planned AC-119 crew training. It had tailored a fairly complete training program by the middle of February. Continental Air Command—responsible for releasing the Reserve C-119s—would also conduct simulator, field, and Phase I training through the 302d Tactical Airlift Wing at Clinton County AFB.[26] CONAC evaluated base facilities on February 6-7 and reported that it could handle the planned training.[27] It set a March 20, 1968, starting date for Phase I training which was essentially crew checkout. The Air Training Command (ATC) and TAC would administer peculiar equipment and sensor training and all Phase II flight training. TAC activated the 4413th CCT Squadron (under SAWC) to begin Phase II training on March 1 at Lockbourne AFB.[28]

---

*This request enabled OSD to monitor force changes with regard to theater manpower ceilings.

The Air Force secretary's queries on tripling the number of gunships triggered a flurry of activity in late March 1968 (see Chapter III). Several force options furnished the secretary by the Air Staff impacted little on final AC-119 plans. The AC-119G/K program of fifty-two gunships remained firm.[29]

Slippage in the procurement of several items (other than sensors and guns) loomed in April 1968. To keep gunships and gas turbines on schedule, Headquarters USAF extended the high precedence rating to them. During the first three weeks of May, it likewise put electronic components worth $1.3 million on priority lists, pushing up total program costs. To curb repeated requests for high precedence ratings and rising expenditures, Air Force headquarters told AFLC it would turn down any further appeals for special coverage. Forced to relent, on July 3, it granted a high precedence authorization to cover illuminator, image-intensifier tubes, and control switches, when it seemed that slippage of these items would retard the overall program. Air Force headquarters later reviewed procurement actions and discovered a number of high-priority contracts for AC-119 items being funded from production allotments in place of research and development money. It accordingly cracked down harder on the more costly high-priority procurement.[30]

Trouble beset procurement of guns for the AC-119G as modification got under way. At first it was thought 7.62-mm guns from the AC-47s could be switched to the AC-119Gs. The AC-119 fleet expanded beyond mere AC-47 replacement, however, and new sources had to be found. A search uncovered sufficient SUU-11 gun pods for ten AC-119Gs and the VNAF installation. In addition, the Seventh Air Force had another operated by the VNAF. The AC-119 program's higher precedence halted the VNAF installation. In addition, the Seventh Air Force had another sixteen gun pods inoperative due to parts. PACAF cautioned against using these pods and urged instead that AFLC speed up procurement of MXU-470A modules.[31] WRAMA originally intended to use the thirty-nine SUU-11 pods earmarked for the VNAF but in the middle of March 1968 arranged with the Army for enough guns to satisfy the program's monthly requirements.[32] On March 18 WRAMA notified PACAF it no longer needed the SUU-11 gun pods in Southeast Asia.[33] In May WRAMA awarded the General Electric Company a $1.3 million letter contract for new 7.62-mm gun modules that would in time meet gunship needs.[34]

Difficulties with Fairchild-Hiller on certain items surfaced at the outset of the modification program, the smoke-evacuation system being a chief case in point. Survival of aircraft and crew was at stake if a magnesium flare ignited. The fire would fill the plane with blinding, choking smoke, impairing vision and movement. The Air Force specified that to be safe a smoke-removal system had to clear the smoke in ten seconds. Since the AC-47 had such a system, Fairchild-Hiller was expected to have little trouble with an AC-119 design. Notwithstanding, on April 19, 1968, the Air Force notified the company it was dissatisfied

AC–119G Fuselage Arrangement

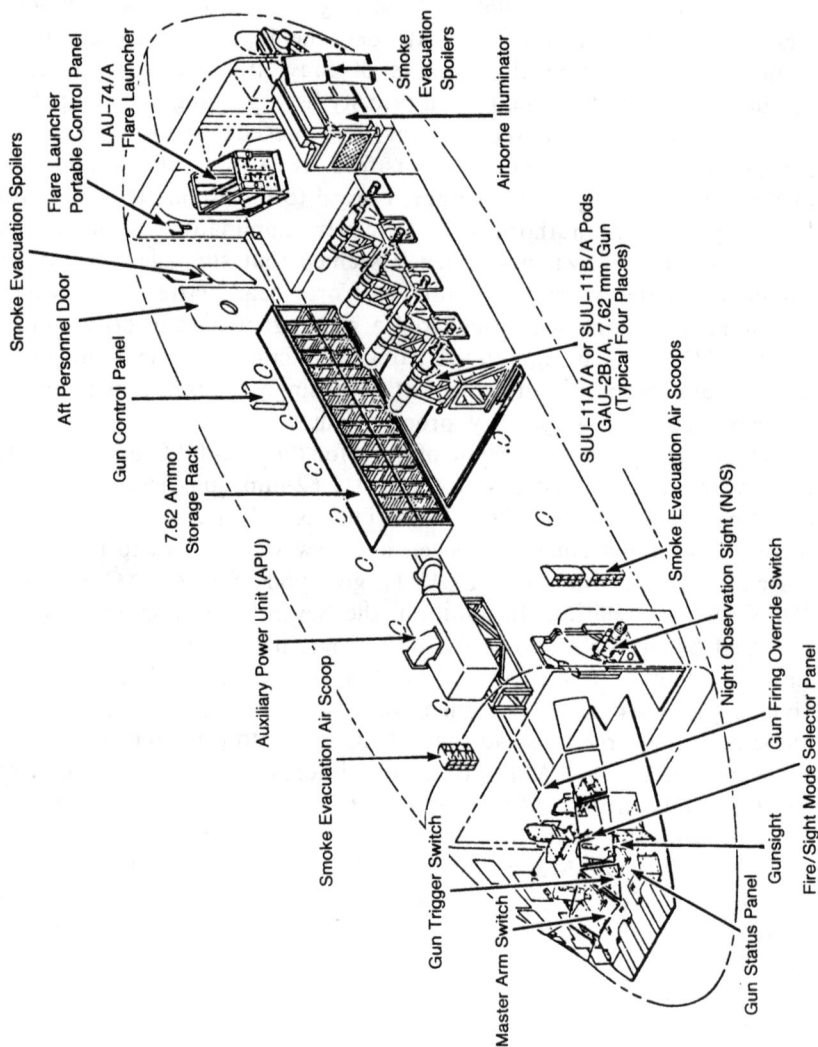

Smoke Evacuation Spoilers

Flare Launcher Portable Control Panel

LAU–74/A Flare Launcher

Smoke Evacuation Spoilers

Airborne Illuminator

Aft Personnel Door

Gun Control Panel

7.62 Ammo Storage Rack

SUU–11A/A or SUU–11B/A Pods GAU–2B/A, 7.62 mm Gun (Typical Four Places)

Smoke Evacuation Air Scoops

Auxiliary Power Unit (APU)

Night Observation Sight (NOS)

Smoke Evacuation Air Scoop

Gun Firing Override Switch

Gun Trigger Switch

Gunsight

Fire/Sight Mode Selector Panel

Master Arm Switch

Gun Status Panel

with their system's potential deficiencies and the contractor's attitude toward fulfilling requirements. Tests supported WRAMA's position and the contractor made adjustments, largely in the location of the air-inlet scoops. Successful tests of the smoke-evacuation system at Eglin AFB on June 26 ended months of strained relations between the Air Force and Fairchild-Hiller over the matter.[35]

WRAMA hosted logistic support conferences from time to time as the C-119 modifications made headway. An April 23-25, 1968, meeting on AC-130/AC-119 support was one of the most meaningful. The representatives* discussed ways to ease problems and coordinate aircraft delivery actions. They hammered out a revised production schedule specifying delivery of twenty-six AC-119Gs from May 21 through October 22, 1968, and the AC-119Ks from October 14 to March 31, 1969. The monthly forecast was:

	1968								1969		
	May	Jun	Jul	Aug	Sep	Oct	Nov	Dec	Jan	Feb	Mar
AC-119G	2	3	8	4	5	4					
AC-119K						1	2	4	6	6	7

The conferees confirmed the distribution of eighteen AC-119Gs to PACAF and eight to TAC with a like division of the AC-119Ks. They agreed that deployment deadlines would tightly limit testing of the AC-119s in the United States. As for logistic support, the representatives believed it would take up to a year for the Air Force to assemble an inventory of necessary spares. Up to that time, contractor support would supply peculiar items and aerospace ground equipment for the AC-119 program.[36]

Fairchild-Hiller delivered the first AC-119G gunship to the Air Force on May 21, 1968.[37] TAC received it on June 9 and instantly began limited flight-testing side by side with instructor-cadre upgrading. By June 15 two instructor pilots drawn from AC-47 instructor crews had trained four new instructor pilots. The achievement owed much to TAC's borrowing two CONAC C-119Gs to accelerate its training program.[38] With this limited instructor upgrading, the 4413th CCT Squadron accepted its first training class for Southeast Asian duty on July 3.[39]

Tactical Air Command's Special Operations Forces conducted the AC-119G test and evaluation at Eglin AFB. It included testing of the fire-control system, night observation device, illumination systems, smoke-removal system, flare launcher, and overall aircraft performance. The twenty-five test sorties flown during June 9-30 took more than fifty-three flying hours. Equipment problems and delays developed. For example, a modified computer didn't arrive until June 21 and its erratic operation

---

*Representatives were from Headquarters USAF, AFLC, PACAF, TAC, CONAC, ATC, ASD, WRAMA, Oklahoma City Materiel Area, Ogden Air Materiel Area, San Antonio Air Materiel Area, 1st ACWg, 4413th CCTSq, SAWC, General Electric, and Fairchild-Hiller.

prompted test personnel to term the offset performance of the fire-control system unsatisfactory. Even more serious was the aircraft's failure to reach Air Force profile standards.*[40] The AC-119G had to sustain a 200-foot-per-minute rate of climb with one engine feathered during hot-day conditions at a gross weight of 62,000 pounds. Minimum loiter time was specified as four hours out of total sortie time of five hours and forty minutes.

Test personnel saw that the AC-119G's combat configuration would go over the 62,000 weight, forcing a cutback in fuel load and in turn loiter time.[41] On June 21 WRAMA proposed reducing the single-engine rate-of-climb requirement to 100 feet-per-minute, but this was turned down[42] and tests on the Southeast Asia mission profile capabilities continued. The final test report recommended that AFLC conduct a weight-reduction program.[43] On July 1 TAC informed Air Force headquarters that tests confirmed "weight, performance, and capability problems exist in the AC-119G."[44] On July 11 Gen. Gabriel P. Disosway, TAC commander, reported to General McConnell, Air Force chief of staff, on a meeting he had on the subject with commanders† and other key Air Force officers. General Disosway said: "We are in agreement that the AC-119G as presently configured will not provide the desired SEA combat capability. We strongly recommend the deployment be delayed until the deficiencies are corrected."[45]

Air Force headquarters directed a conference be convened at Warner-Robins AFB "to discuss alternatives for improving the aircraft performance in order to meet mission requirements."[46] For the conference, Air Force headquarters asked: (1) WRAMA to identify nonessential items for removal to reduce the AC-119G's weight,‡ (2) PACAF and Seventh Air Force to review mission requirements and recommend removal of specific equipment items and/or reduction of the 200-foot-per-minute rate-of-climb standard, and (3) TAC to brief results of the AC-119G's Category III test and suggest any improvements.[47] The disappointing AC-119G test results and this call for a weight-reduction conference shattered optimism about meeting the deployment goals.[48]

---

*The Seventh Air Force typical day/night mission profile went like this: start engines, lift off, and climb to 3,000 feet; cruise five minutes to orbit start; loiter four hours at 130 knots; climb to 5,000 feet; forty mile dash at 180 knots to target area; one hour in attack mode, including descent to 3,500 feet, expend ammunition and flares; climb to 5,000 feet and cruise sixty miles to home base; land with 1,000 pounds of fuel reserve. [Ltr, Col. William S. Underwood, 7th AF Dir/Programs, to DCS/Plans, Seventh Air Force, Subj: AC-119G Performance Improvement Conference, Aug 13, 1968.]

†Gen. George S. Brown who assumed command of the Seventh Air Force on August 7, 1968; Gen. James Ferguson, Commander, Air Force Systems Command; Gen. Jack G. Merrell, Commander, Air Force Logistics Commands; and Gen. Joseph J. Nazzaro, Commander in Chief, Pacific Air Forces.

‡The AC-119G's weight problem had arisen because many components being installed proved heavier than expected. Also, PACAF had drawn up the mission profile after modifications had begun and performance standards were more stringent than the engineers anticipated.

On July 26, 1968, WRAMA hosted the two-day AC-119 weight-reduction and performance-improvement conference at the Fairchild-Hiller plant, St. Augustine, Fla., rather than at Warner-Robins AFB. In attendance were representatives from Headquarters USAF, PACAF, TAC, AFLC, Seventh Air Force, and the contractor. The conferees determined the G model's total weight when ready for takeoff was 66,282 pounds—3,350 pounds excess.[49] In the course of lengthy discussions, more than thirty items were listed for removal, weighing a total of 3,277 pounds.[50] Nearly 1,500 pounds of such equipment would be removed in Southeast Asia. Removing the rest of the excess weight would be up to Fairchild-Hiller or WRAMA.[51]

The conferees believed that PACAF and the Seventh Air Force needed to adopt the weight-reduction recommendation and at the same time relax the single-engine climb-rate standard from 200 to 100 feet-per-minute. (They emphasized that 100 feet-per-minute was standard for the AC-47.) The only alternative would be to strip an additional 3,500 pounds from the AC-119. This would of necessity be peculiar equipment such as sensors and guns, thereby degrading gunship capabilities.[52] Air Force headquarters pondered these recommendations then let PACAF know that the Southeast Asia mission profile could be met by adopting the conference's initial weight-reduction recommendation together with lowering the single-engine rate-of-climb standard of 100 feet-per-minute. Air Force headquarters stressed that the lower standard of performance afforded "adequate operational safety." Moreover, the AC-119 would be given a pilot-operated jettisonable flare launcher, weighing about 1,100 pounds with flares. Jettisoning the launcher in an emergency would boost the single-engine rate-of-climb to around 150 feet-per-minute.*[53]

On August 15, 1968, PACAF replied that it would lower the rate-of-climb criterion to 100 feet-per-minute. It urged "comprehensive flight testing before deployment" after the gunship's weight had been reduced. The command conveyed concern over armorplate removal, thinking it would make the gunship unsatisfactory for day missions.[54]

The Air Force looked for the best way to accomplish the weight-reduction program, expecting it to require some 350 manhours. On August 24, WRAMA suggested the aircraft be cycled through the contractor's St. Augustine plant rather than having contract/depot field teams attempt the job. WRAMA assumed weight-reduction engineering could be completed by September 20, engineering for other deficiencies by September 27. It forecast the first aircraft entering recycling on November 1 with a flow time of fifteen days for each aircraft. The estimated cost of the program

---

*An experienced C-119 pilot said survival in an emergency at 100 foot-per-minute rate-of-climb on one engine demanded perfect crew performance. A minute was a long time to a pilot trying to reach an altitude not much higher than good-sized trees. [Intvw, author with Col. Joe T. Pound, Asst for Res Affairs (AFR), Dir Aerosp Prgms, June 27, 1972 (Colonel Pound commanded the 930th Tactical Airlift Group (TAGp), CONAC, when it was mobilized to form the 71st SOSq).]

was $664,000.[55] The Air Staff accepted the plan, and Fairchild-Hiller reworked the AC-119G aircraft.

The slow resolution of the theater headroom problem softened the jolt of the weight-reduction program to the SEA deployment schedule. For almost six months after Deputy Defense Secretary Nitze's approval of the AC-119s in February 1968, work had focused on fitting the force under the headroom ceiling by trade-offs in other areas. One way had always been to replace AC-47s with AC-119s. On July 13, 1968, however, Air Force headquarters urged CINCPACAF to "exhaust all other possibilities" before considering this action.[56] Other courses had proven most difficult as General Momyer, Seventh Air Force commander, commented: "We have no room for maneuver on these directed programs. MACV is confronted with deficits they consider of more importance than these service interest programs." General Momyer saw the answer in taking AC-119s on a one-for-one trade with the AC-47s. Even then, this would require 337 more spaces which Momyer "agreed to dig . . . out of my hide." He reported to Gen. Bruce K. Holloway, Air Force vice chief of staff, that General Abrams, MACV commander, favored this one-for-one trade and was receptive to a message to CINCPAC and the Joint Chiefs of Staff along these lines. General Momyer restated his concern with the "operational deficiencies" of the AC-119 which he felt made it "less desirable than the AC-47 in many respects." He cautioned that if at all possible "we not go for a complete replacement of the thirty-two AC-47s."[57]

During the AC-119's modification, the Seventh Air Force had doubted the gunship's capabilities, especially that of the G model. On July 20 it predicted trouble, noting the AC-119G was "not suited for night operations over heavily canopied jungles or rugged mountainous terrain where targets are not easily identified." The Seventh also scored the AC-119G as inflexible because it had but one sensor, the night observation device.[58] In mid-1968 the Seventh Air Force ad hoc Program Review Committee (cost-review panel) addressed the question: "Should the AC-119 Gunship force programmed for introduction into the theater be deferred as a cost-savings measure?" The panel reported that the AC-119G was so "underpowered with a full fuel load and ordnance that on station time will be sacrificed for ordnance capability or vice versa." It likewise criticized the 7.62-mm minigun's "hitting power." The gun's top slant-range effectiveness of 5,500 feet would be potent against personnel but do scant damage to buildings, bunkers, or trenches. The cost-reduction panel viewed the AC-119K in a more favorable light due to that gunship's auxiliary jet engines and 20-mm guns. Despite anxiety over the AC-119's anticipated performance, the panel rejected a deferment of the two AC-119 squadron deployment.[59] Air Force headquarters tried to reassure the Seventh Air Force regarding the AC-119G. "The Air Staff," it advised, "is well aware of these deficiencies in its current configuration and its shortcomings as a combat aircraft. We are endeavoring to assure correction of these deficiencies that are correctable."[60]

At one time hope had existed that all AC-119Gs could be configured into AC-119Ks, thus ridding the G model of deficiencies that disturbed commanders in Southeast Asia. After study the Air Staff gave up the idea because: (1) converting twenty-six AC-119Gs into Ks would slip AC-119G deployment four or five months; and (2) expanding AC-119Ks beyond one squadron would demand more J-85 jet engines, seriously hurting the C-123K modification and maybe other programs. In short, configuring all AC-119s to the K model was clearly advantageous, but the Air Staff didn't think it practical to do in a fairly short time.[61]

With the approach of autumn, the several-times-delayed deployment of the AC-119s came closer to reality. On October 11, 1968, the Air Force officially accepted the last of the twenty-six AC-119Gs as it ended modification. On the other hand, only the first aircraft had gone through all test phases and begun its weight-reduction at Fairchild-Hiller's St. Augustine plant.[62]

Production delays stretched the time for readying support equipment and refining supply procedures. On September 20, 1968, the Air Force contracted logistic support from Fairchild-Hiller. The agreement called for the company to keep men around the clock at main support bases in Southeast Asia. Initially, they would perform "depot overhaul and depot supply" services for contractor-furnished equipment and modified government-furnished parts. Various civilian specialists would remain in Southeast Asia for six months. AFLC used normal budget channels to fund the contract.[63]

As weight-trimming of the AC-119s moved forward, the support equipment was collected and shipped to combat-theater locations. In October 1968 the stock level of various support items ranged from seventy-seven percent for ground equipment to ninety-two percent for common spare parts. Equipment peculiar to the AC-119G was to be delivered from December 1968 to June 1969 by Fairchild-Hiller. WRAMA dispatched a nine-man rapid area supply support team to Southeast Asia on November 8 to smooth out the receipt, identification, and storage of spare parts and support items.[64]

The late arrival of the AC-119Gs in South Vietnam also allowed extra time for completion of the base support facilities. At Tan Son Nhut AB, for example, the programmed revetment area and operations/maintenance facility slipped months beyond completion dates in the Seventh Air Force program.[65] Back in May 1968, the 14th Air Commando Wing had alerted Seventh Air Force headquarters that Red Horse (engineering/construction units) resources were "not sufficient to accomplish assigned Combat

Hornet projects within required time frames."[66] The Gunship III deployment slippage undoubtedly eliminated some severe crowding problems that loomed with the original mid-1968 goal.[67]

Composition of the AC-119G unit added one more complication. To keep abreast of the Gunship III timetable, the Air Force had decided in early 1968 to take both C-119G aircraft and personnel from the Air Force Reserve.*[68] On May 13, 1968, the 930th Tactical Airlift Group (CONAC), a C-119 Reserve unit based at Bakalar AFB, Ind., was called up for twenty-four months active service with the Tactical Air Command.[69] The 930th's 71st Tactical Airlift Squadron was redesignated the 71st Special Operations Squadron and TAC beefed it up with 930th Group resources, including more than 300 of the 383 personnel mobilized. During June 1-15, 1968, TAC moved the 71st Squadron from Bakalar to Lockbourne AFB, where its personnel formed the bulk of the first AC-119G training classes. Most of the 71st's men were experienced and qualified in C-119 crew and support positions, so the training stressed equipment and procedures peculiar to the gunship. The C-119Gs of the 71st Special Operations Squadron were gradually sent to St. Augustine for modification or to other units as replacements for their commitment to the modification program. The Air Staff ordered men from various Air Force sources to fully man the 71st Special Operations Squadron,[70] which was scheduled to depart for Southeast Asia on July 27, 1968.[71] Delays in the departure ensued however.

With the 71st Special Operations Squadron composed of many reservists ordered to active duty, concern grew over the future release of this force to inactive duty. On September 4, 1968, as the 71st Squadron awaited deployment to Southeast Asia, TAC hosted a conference on the matter. A proposal emerged calling for these actions: (1) deploy the 71st SOSq with the AC-119Gs between November 1968 and January 1969 (based on aircraft availability), (2) exchange AC-119Gs for Southeast Asia AC-47s one-for-one, (3) gear training of AC-119K personnel to aircraft deliveries and deploy in the fourth quarter of fiscal year 1969, (4) return the 71st SOSq to the United States in the fourth quarter of fiscal 1969 in a one-for-one trade of AC-119Ks for AC-119Gs, and (5) inactivate the 71st SOSq in the fourth quarter of fiscal 1969. The conferees expected that the AC-119Ks could begin deployment and commence the trade with the AC-119Gs as follows: three in April 1969, seven in May, and eight in June. (This would equip a squadron of sixteen AC-119Ks and allow two AC-119Ks for attrition.)[72]

In its initial review of the TAC conference proposal, Air Force headquarters noted that with AC-119K crew training beginning in October 1968, the April 1969 deployment would impose some personal hardships. It also cautioned that the trade-off for AC-47s—with their possible transfer to Vietnamese, Thai, or Laotian air forces—might have to exceed

---

*The C 119 had been out of the regular Air Force inventory since 1956.

one-for-one, to tuck the increased AC-119 squadron personnel under the theater manpower ceiling.[73] The Air Staff received more favorably the conference's suggestion that the Reserve personnel be demobilized in the fourth quarter of fiscal year 1969. It oriented planning toward this goal.

Adoption of the foregoing proposal would have shaped a gunship posture in South Vietnam of one sixteen-aircraft AC-47 squadron and one sixteen-aircraft AC-119K squadron. General Brown, Seventh Air Force commander, thought this unsatisfactory and reiterated that AC-119Gs and AC-119Ks should be deployed as additive forces—one squadron of AC-119Gs and one of AC-119Ks as originally approved. Seventh Air Force plans rested on a four-gunship-squadron concept and the general resisted any basic alteration of them.[74] As for the headroom problem, he felt that the proposed move of the Airborne Battlefield Command and Control Center to Thailand and new personnel accounting procedures might offer possible spaces.[75]

General Nazzaro, Commander in Chief, Pacific Air Forces, chose the middle ground on the deployment/headroom issue. He notified General McConnell, Chief of Staff, on September 25, 1968, that the enemy's stepped-up infiltration and attacks on populated areas and military installations proved the need for two AC-119 squadrons. Nevertheless, by reason of manpower ceilings and possible disruptive effects of a short-term AC-119G deployment, CINCPACAF recommended: (1) retention of two AC-47 squadrons, (2) holding the 71st Special Operations Squadron in the United States, and (3) earliest possible deployment of the one AC-119K squadron. He figured that a complete AC-119K squadron would need 662 manpower spaces. These could be covered by 454 spaces made available from the move of the ABCCC from Da Nang, South Vietnam, to Udorn, Thailand, and more than 300 spaces by other actions. General Nazzaro judged the alternatives entailing AC-47 trade-offs least desirable. Even so, he outlined how more AC-47s could be turned over to South Vietnam, Laos, or Thailand should such trade-offs be required.[76]

Debate over the headroom spaces and the AC-119 deployment extended into November. Air Force headquarters dismissed the idea of inactivating the 71st SOSq, with its replacement by AC-119Ks. It likewise rejected PACAF's recommendation for holding the AC-119G squadron in the United States. The search quickened for ways to shoehorn Gunship III manpower within the Vietnam headroom ceiling. In October the Air Staff approved 301 spaces for AC-119G/AC-47 trade-off actions. When these spaces were combined with those gained from accounting adjustments and the contemplated move of the ABCCC to Thailand, enough headroom would exist for deployment of one AC-119 squadron. Even then, the trade-off awaited CINCPAC and MACV approval and there was a question on the counting of transients in personnel strength figures. As of October 10, 1968, the Seventh Air Force was razor-close to its ceiling, just 82 under (including the transients), and leaving no room for an AC-119 unit.[77] The

662 spaces wanted for the AC-119K squadron presented yet another headache but one less time-pressing. All the same, PACAF reported by November it would allow deployment of three AC-119Gs in November, seven in December, and eight in January.[78] These aircraft would be additions to the AC-47s in Southeast Asia.

Deputy Defense Secretary Nitze approved on November 27, 1968, the deployment to South Vietnam of the 71st Special Operations Squadron (the AC-119G unit). He coupled the approval to a request for re-study of the need for the AC-47s. Deputy Secretary Nitze asserted: "I am not convinced we need to retain the two AC-47 squadrons in the U.S. force in South Vietnam." He proposed consideration of these points: "(1) the requirement for additional gunships as opposed to deletion of the AC-47s, (2) the acceleration of the turnover of AC-47s to RVNAF, and (3) retention of the four gunship squadrons and withdrawal of two tactical fighter squadrons." Mr. Nitze wanted this analysis ahead of any deployment request for the second AC-119 squadron.[79]

The approval by Deputy Secretary Nitze roughly coincided with the completion of the 71st Special Operations Squadron's training. The reservists, augmented by active duty members, had progressed through the 4413th Combat Crew Training Squadron's program at Lockbourne AFB and were considered ready for the combat-theater commitment in November. Most of these men had crewed the C-119 Flying Boxcar but they now shifted from paradrops to side-firing passes. The instruction climaxed with day- and night-firing on the range at Camp Atterbury, Ind.[80] The combat crews* had been hampered and delayed in their training by such problems as inoperable fire-control-system computers in the first four aircraft[81] but were now prepared to ferry the AC-119Gs to South Vietnam and start theater familiarization.[82]

A WRAMA conference of November 4, 1968, went into the ferrying of the AC-119Gs to South Vietnam. The conferees agreed to remove four guns (960 pounds) and their mounts (328 pounds) and to install a 500-gallon rubberized tank for extra fuel load. The aircraft would fly in pairs from St. Augustine to Nha Trang via: McClellan AFB, Calif.; McChord AFB, Wash.; Elmendorf AFB, Alaska; Adak; Midway; Wake; Kadena AB, Okinawa; and Clark AB, Philippines. The guns and mounts would be shipped to Nha Trang so as to arrive at the same time as the aircraft.[83]

Later in November, the Seventh Air Force questioned 14th Special Operations Wing plans for employing AC-119Gs in armed reconnaissance and interdiction roles. It told the Wing that General Brown desired Phase I of the AC-119G combat evaluation to center on a comparison of AC-119G and AC-47 capabilities in the AC-47's current role. The specified priorities were:

---

*Each crew comprised two pilots, two navigators (one a night observation device operator), one flight engineer, two gunners, and one loadmaster.

Priority	Mission
1	Close fire support of friendly troops in contact with the enemy.
2	Close fire support of U.S. and friendly military installations including forts and outposts.
3	Close fire support of strategic hamlets, villages, and district towns.
4	Preplanned armed reconnaissance and interdiction of hostile areas and infiltration routes.
5	Search and rescue support.
6	Night armed escort for road and close offshore convoys.
7	Illumination for night fighter strikes.
8	Harassment and interdiction.

Seventh Air Force said that the evaluation of armed reconnaissance and interdiction should be deferred until the later phases of the combat test.[84]

The advance elements of the 71st Special Operations Squadron were in place at Nha Trang by mid-December 1968.[85] The first two AC-119Gs left Lockbourne AFB on December 5 and touched down at Nha Trang on December 27, a total of four AC-119Gs arriving there by the end of the month. TAC and PACAF maintenance personnel set to work at once. They reinstalled and adjusted the miniguns, removed the special ferry fuel tanks, and in general got the aircraft operationally ready. This proved a stiffer job than expected. The first AC-119G arrived with a broken gunsight, hard nosewheel steering, poorly functioning hydraulic system, inoperative spark advance on one engine, and a faulty illuminating device.[86]

Seventh Air Force plans called for the 71st Special Operations Squadron to furnish air support mainly in the southern portion of the Republic of Vietnam. The AC-119K unit (designated the 18th Special Operations Squadron) would be assigned to the northern portion. Nha Trang, headquarters of the present 14th Special Operations Wing, would serve as the main support base for the 71st Special Operations Squadron as well as the location for five AC-119Gs. Forward operating locations were to be established at Phan Rang AB (six planes) and at Tan Son Nhut AB (five planes).[87] The first AC-119Gs would fly combat missions out of Nha Trang.

The AC-119G Shadow* began operational sorties and its combat evaluation. From January 5 to March 8, 1969 (date of the last evaluation combat sortie), the evaluation team analyzed the Shadow gunship's performance in: combat air patrol for base and hamlet defense, interdiction, armed reconnaissance, forward air control, and close air support missions. The evaluation report revealed that the weapon system performed all missions satisfactorily except forward air controlling. The aircraft was rather slow, hard to maneuver, and vulnerable to enemy fire—

---

*Initially, the call sign "Creep" had been authorized for the AC-119G. A howl of indignation arose from the 71st SOSq over this selection and a change of the call sign to Shadow was requested, to be effective December 1, 1968. [Msg, 14th CSGp to 7th AF, subj: 14th SOW Aircraft Call Sign, Oct 21, 1968.]

hence not well-suited to the forward air control role.* Four of the five main subsystems—the night observation device, side-firing guns, semiautomatic flare launcher, and fire-control system—demonstrated "acceptable reliability and effective operation." The illuminator worked well until maintenance problems made it unreliable. As expected, the AC-119G had decided limitations: its gross weight usually held mission flying time to not more than six hours. The miniguns were of limited value against vehicular traffic. Lack of an all-weather capability crippled its operation in fog and haze. All the evaluation missions took place in undefended or lightly defended areas. The evaluators recommended the aircraft not be used in a high-threat environment.[88]

Throughout the combat evaluation, the bulk of the targets (371 of 589) turned up during harrassment- and interdiction-type missions. Such missions commonly grew out of armed reconnaissance operations. A Shadow gunship was assigned to patrol a "box"—an area bounded by precise coordinates.[†] It navigated to and within the box area by TACAN with ground-radar backup. Shadow kept a terrain clearance of 500 feet as it pressed an unrestricted search for the target with the night observation device or visually by means of the flares/illuminator. When a target was identified, the gunship plotted the coordinates and called the controlling agency for clearance to fire. (Often it dropped Mk-6 flares [marker logs] to pinpoint the target's position.) Upon receipt of firing clearance, Shadow climbed to 3,500 feet, usually selected a semiautomatic firing mode, banked into the left orbit, and fired. Sometimes, the gunship dropped flares to illuminate the area and operated one or two guns, often at a slow rate (3,000 rounds-per-minute).[89]

The evaluators had less trouble in assessing the results of the close air support missions than the harassment and interdiction strikes. The Gunship III used its illuminator and flares many times to assist troops in contact with the enemy. One Shadow was directed to an outpost near Dak To and the ground unit asked for flares and/or use of the illuminator. The enemy had lobbed mortar rounds on the outpost and probed its perimeter but withdrew when the gunship lit up the area. AC-119G firepower was even more telling. A Shadow attack on a suspected enemy troop concentration and storage area north of Pleiku AB touched off 80 secondary explosions. Another Shadow out of Nha Trang aided a U.S. Army unit pinned down by the enemy. The call of the ground unit's radio operator showed that the AC-119G had tilted the balance: "Thanks a lot,

---

*Col. Conrad S. Allman, 14th Special Operations Wing commander (Mar 18, 1968–Mar 5, 1969) supported the negative conclusion on forward air controlling. In his End of Tour Report he noted that the size and speed of the AC-119G made it impossible to maintain either a constant target acquisiton or constant visual contact with the fighters, both essential to direct a fighter strike and adjust ordnance delivery. He flatly recommended discontinuance of the AC-119G's use as a forward air controller. [Kott, *The Role of USAF Gunships in SEASIA*, p 23.]

†Many of the boxes were located west of the cities of Kontum and Pleiku where Cambodia, Laos, and South Vietnam converged.

Shadow, you made my trip home possible."[90] The evaluators concluded that the close air support role was the "most effective" one for the AC-119G.[91]

Shadow attacks in the course of the combat evaluations recorded noteworthy statistics, including 6 enemy killed and another 184 estimated killed. The AC-119Gs silenced five .50-caliber gun positions and destroyed or damaged thirty-one trucks. Many secondary explosions triggered by attacks on ammunition/fuel dumps, vehicles, and base camps were confirmed. Shadow maintained an operational readiness rate of 78.8 percent over the evaluation period.[92]

Up to March 8, 1969, the AC-119G Shadows had reported eighty-six instances of ground fire but suffered only one hit. A Shadow was flying an interdiction mission near Da Nang when fire from an unknown type of small-arms weapon damaged the right wingtip. On several Shadow flights, fighter escort suppressed antiaircraft fire.[93]

As the combat evaluation progressed, more aircraft and crews came to South Vietnam. By March 1, 1969, all eighteen aircraft* of the 71st Special Operations Squadron† were in the combat theater.[94] The squadron gained combat-ready status on March 11, 1969.[95] The complete deployment of this unit, commanded by Lt. Col. James E. Pyle, and the promising combat debut of the AC-119G (called a "flying anachronism" by one authority)[96] marked the fruition of the months of arduous development and sharp debate over the gunship force.

Meantime, work on the AC-119Ks went on. WRAMA told AFLC on August 13, 1968, that the modification pace was slowed by adjustments on the cockpit configuration and by nonreceipt of the forward-looking infrared and the 20-mm gun system.[97] The holdup of the FLIRs from Texas Instruments created the more acute problem. In June 1968 WRAMA had proposed fixing aircraft schedules to the availability of the infrared system and delivery of the first few AC-119Ks to TAC and PACAF without FLIRs. These aircraft would be fitted with the FLIR in the field later.[98] In August WRAMA remained confident that four K models, minus the delayed FLIRs, would be ready in November for deployment to Southeast Asia.[99]

The FLIR delivery problems were not so easily nor quickly resolved. Fall came and Texas Instruments let WRAMA know it could not meet FLIR schedule deadlines. The priority afforded the installation of the first eight FLIRs in the AC-130As drew out the delivery delay. By the first few days of October 1968, it was clear the first eighteen AC-119Ks coming out of modification would have simply the basic components to accommodate and support the infrared sensor.[100]

Frustrated by the delays in the mission-essential FLIR, WRAMA complained that Texas Instruments had vastly "over committed" itself in agreeing to the delivery schedule. It thought of canceling Fairchild-Hiller's

---

*This included sixteen unit-equipment aircraft plus two not operationally active.
† Later designated 17th Special Operations Squadron.

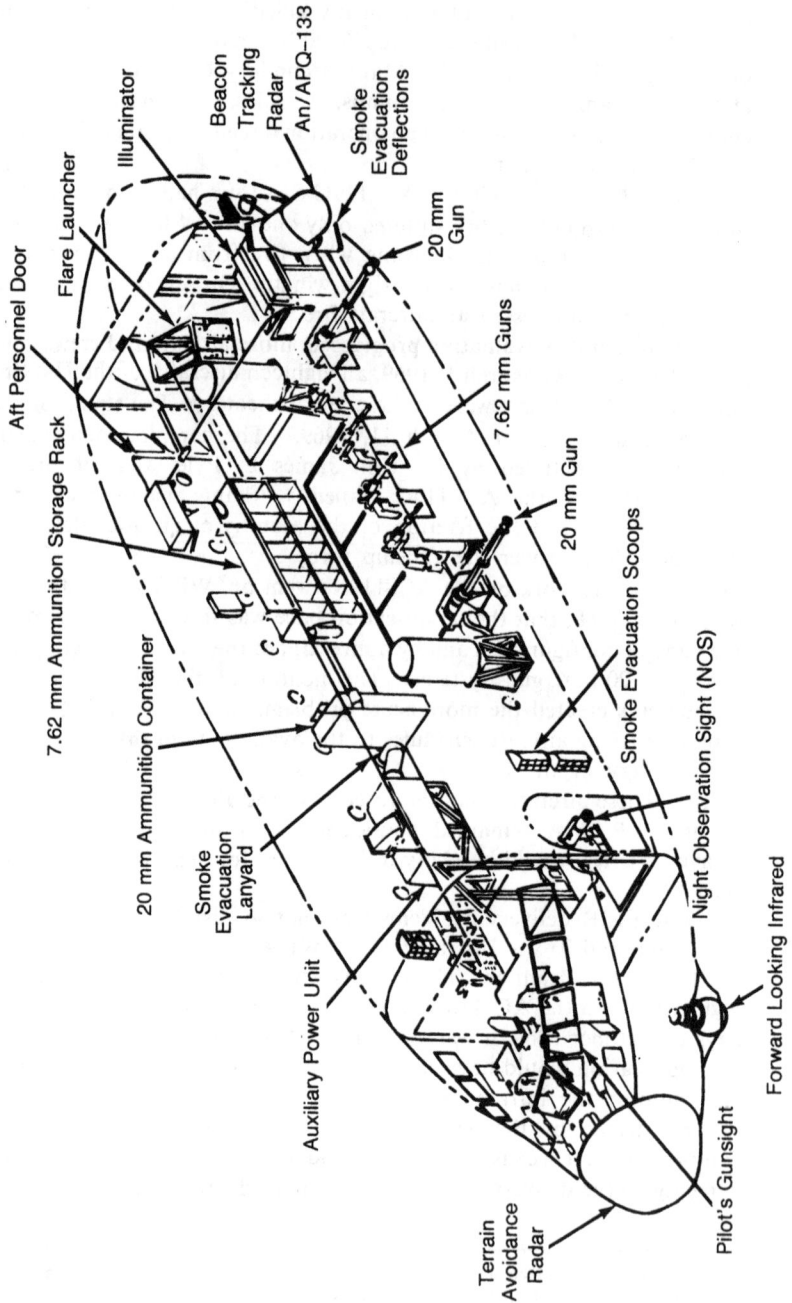

AC–119K Fuselage Arrangement

Aft Personnel Door

Flare Launcher

Illuminator

Beacon Tracking Radar An/APQ–133

Smoke Evacuation Deflections

20 mm Gun

7.62 mm Guns

20 mm Gun

7.62 mm Ammunition Storage Rack

20 mm Ammunition Container

Smoke Evacuation Lanyard

Smoke Evacuation Scoops

Night Observation Sight (NOS)

Forward Looking Infrared

Auxiliary Power Unit

Pilot's Gunsight

Terrain Avoidance Radar

subcontract with the Texas firm but dropped the idea upon realizing Texas Instruments was the one company capable of filling the order within a reasonable time. Hughes Aircraft, the only serious competitor, was at least a year away from delivery of a comparable system.[101]

To expedite the FLIR delivery, a WRAMA Tiger Team* went to the Texas Instruments plant on December 2, 1968. A revised schedule for FLIR-equipped AC-119Ks resulted:

	FY 1969					FY 1970		
	Feb	Mar	Apr	May	Jun	Jul	Aug	Sep
TAC	1	2	1	0	0	0	1	3
PACAF	0	0	4	4	5	4	1	0

WRAMA estimated that the sensor could be installed in the AC-119K in the field within one day, if necessary, utilizing thirty-two man-hours (four men, eight hours each).[102]

Despite the new schedule, doubt persisted about FLIR deliveries. It was by no means certain that Texas Instruments had the "bugs" out of the equipment. This became a fact when the company notified the Air Force on January 24, 1969, it was suspending production of the sensors until design problems were licked and the production line changed. In February 1969 the firm reported that it might require eighteen months to complete the contract and need an additional $5 million to cover costs. The Air Force had no choice but to extend the letter contract with Texas Instruments and to push any necessary re-engineering, production, and delivery.[103]

Texas Instruments' production difficulties impeded the AC-130 and AC-119K programs. Troubles beset the air conditioning of the FLIRs in the AC-130s. Early versions of the FLIRs proved hard to maintain, operated below standard and failed often. In the opening months of 1969, a dearth of spare parts made supply and maintenance marginal for the high-priority AC-130s. To lessen these support problems, AFSC proposed a redistribution of the FLIR assets. It would first replace the AC-130 FLIR systems in Southeast Asia and equip the other AC-130s being readied for deployment. AFLC, PACAF, TAC, and the Air Staff approved this plan even though it would further delay the training and deployment of the AC-119Ks. An ASD/contractor team visited Southeast Asia in February 1969 and identified what modifications would improve the FLIR operation and maintenance. These changes were then embodied in Texas Instruments' production models of the sensor.[104]

The first FLIR, originally due at Fairchild-Hiller in June 1968, did not arrive until May 3, 1969.[105] Installed in an aircraft, it underwent initial airborne tests on May 20, 1969.[106] The Air Force received the last FLIR in April 1970, nearly a year later. With this long delay and despite a lengthy hold on AC-119K deployment, three K models reached Southeast Asia

---

*A team that specialized in studying and recommending solutions to contractor production problems.

197

without the FLIR installation. They flew G-model mission profiles until the sensors arrived.[107]

The AC-119K's excessive weight also plagued its modification program. Even before the first roll-out ceremony for the AC-119K (September 24, 1968), the aircraft's estimated weight raised ripples of concern. On August 8, 1968, TAC suggested the weight problem be tackled at an AC-119K performance improvement conference, similar to the one held for the AC-119G. TAC believed "an early meeting would reduce impact upon aircraft modification/deliveries as well as crew training and deployment."[108] WRAMA, however, evaluated the weight problem without recourse to a formal meeting. On August 23 it informed AFLC that "total weight of K model components increased 6946 pounds over initial estimates, thereby decreasing mission duration."* One of the PACAF mission profiles—belatedly sent to WRAMA—showed that in addition to the expected use of the AC-119Ks' jet engines during takeoff and climb, they were used in the attack phase. This would require 950 pounds of added fuel. WRAMA established a weight-reduction goal of 5,079 pounds, of which 1,525 pounds could be cut via the same route as the AC-119Gs' weight reduction. It mounted an all-out effort to trim the remaining 3,554 pounds.[109]

WRAMA sought to slim down the AC-119K by means other than stripping it of selected items. One possibility was a carburetor modification to permit operation of the R-3350 engines at a lean mixture during higher power settings. A structural analysis of the landing gear and nacelle was undertaken to determine if the ground limit of 77,000 pounds could be scaled upward to the inflight limit of 83,000 pounds. As a last resort, WRAMA would recommend to PACAF a cutback in loiter-time requirements from four to three hours and/or elimination of gunship items such as armorplating.[110] Removal of armorplating had been previously avoided because PACAF wanted the AC-119Ks to fly interdiction missions which exposed them to larger-caliber ground fire.†

On September 27, 1968, WRAMA reported a solution to the AC-119K weight problem (see Table 5). With it WRAMA believed the aircraft could fly the most demanding Southeast Asia combat-mission profile and yet return to base with 1,050 pounds of fuel. To drop the weight outlined, the first few production aircraft would recycle. The majority still in modification would do it at St. Augustine.[111]

Moves to organize the AC-119K squadron paralleled the modification, recycling, and testing of the AC-119K aircraft. Unlike the 71st Special Operations Squadron, the new unit would have many aircraft before activation.[112] A deployment conference in mid-December 1968 agreed to

---

*Of this total, 2,825 pounds was common to the AC-119G while 4,121 pounds was equipment peculiar to the AC-119K.

†CINCPACAF stated on August 15, 1968, the "primary role of [the] AC-119K is night interdiction of lines of communication to destroy wheeled or tracked vehicular traffic on roads as well as sampans and other small maritime traffic in the canals." [Msg, CINCPACAF to CSAF, TAC, AFLC, 152344Z Aug 68, subj: Combat Hornet.]

TABLE 5. WRAMA SOLUTION TO THE AC-119 WEIGHT PROBLEM

Action	Pounds Saved
Remove AC-119G weight-reduction items applicable to the AC-119K	1,630.5
Remove armor in the area of the 20-mm guns*	783.0
Raise the maximum gross ramp (ground) weight from 77,000 to 80,400 pounds with minor ground-handling precautions	3,400.0
Total	5,813.0

AC-119K weight after above savings		Pounds
Maximum ramp (ground) weight		80,400.0
Loaded AC-119K less fuel:		
Basic AC-119K weight	57,864.0	
Crew and oil	3,068.0	
Ammunition and flares	4,947.0	
Total		65.879.0
Fuel capacity		14,521.0

*Agreed to after Fairchild-Hiller reported gunners would spend little time at the 20-mm guns and thus could stay in more protected areas.
Source: Msg WRAMA to AFLC, CSAF, TAC, CINCPACAF, 7AF, USAFSOF, subject: AC-119K Weight Reduction, 271400 Sep 68.

retain production aircraft nine through thirteen at St. Augustine awaiting the 18th Special Operations Squadron's activation. TAC said it lacked the people on station to maintain these five extra aircraft until the squadron was formed. A TAC conference at Lockbourne AFB on January 13, 1969, discussed activation of the 18th SOSq and the slow aircraft deliveries.[113] The 18th Special Operations Squadron first operated at Lockbourne in late January. For several months it concentrated on crew training, aircraft familiarization, and development of mission procedures.

The late delivery of AC-119Ks hampered combat crew training. At one time, the first combat crews were to enter Phase I training at Clinton County AFB, Ohio, on October 3 and complete the phase in December 1968.[114] A shortage of aircraft, however, delayed entry dates and created problems for classes moving from one training phase to the next. Moreover, the first AC-119Ks were without FLIRs which further weakened training. TAC finally had to draw upon its AC-130 experience and take special measures to train FLIR operators. The training program nonetheless planned to ready five crews each month, February through May, and four in June 1969.[115] The ten-man crew of the AC-119K consisted of an aircraft commander, pilot, navigator/safety officer, FLIR/radar operator (navigator), NOD operator (navigator), flight engineer, three gunners, and an illuminator operator. Plans envisioned aircrew manning at a 1.5 ratio per assigned aircraft.[116] The experiences of the 71st Special Operations Squadron guided the 18th SOSq's training and deployment.

In mid-March 1969 WRAMA personnel met with those of TAC, 18th SOSq and 4440th Air Delivery Group to complete the AC-119K ferry configuration. The group picked the same route used in deploying the AC-119Gs (except for substituting Malmstrom AFB, Mont., for McClellan AFB) and readied a logistic plan for enroute support.* Three 500-gallon rubberized fuel tanks would be installed in each aircraft, requiring the temporary removal of cockpit/cargo armor, 7.62-mm and 20-mm gun installations, the radar, and the flare launchers. In May 1969 WRAMA advised AFLC that final preparations for the ferry/deployment configuration were over.[117] On May 20 it closed out its AC-119 Gunship Program Office and assigned further management of the gunship program to the Cargo Aircraft Systems Management Division.[118]

In the spring of 1969, the development of the 18th Special Operations Squadron appeared near at hand, but several factors held it up. Finding headroom for the AC-119K squadron plagued planners in early 1969. The transfer of the AC-47s to the Vietnamese air force enabled Seventh Air Force to eke out enough manpower spaces by the end of April. At that time, however, the Secretary of Defense had not approved the deployment adjustment request.[119] More serious in holding up deployment was the slow production of the FLIRs. WRAMA reported on March 12, 1969, that further slippage would result in this delivery/installation schedule:

	FY 1969			*FY 1970*					
	Apr	*May*	*Jun*	*Jul*	*Aug*	*Sep*	*Oct*	*Nov*	*Dec*
FLIRs delivered	1	1	2	6	7	8	3		
FLIRs installed			1	0	3	5	8	7	2

Air Force headquarters proposed a possible May–June deployment without FLIRs. CINCPACAF suggested a squadron deployment in September 1969—without FLIRs if production so dictated. TAC favored an August–September deployment. On April 22, 1969, after weighing the command responses, Air Force headquarters set an early September 1969 target date for deployment with an initial operating capability in Southeast Asia by September 30. The Air Staff knew the FLIR installation was the pacing factor but assumed some AC-119Ks could be entirely equipped by that time. TAC projected in May that the 18th Special Operations Squadron would have two complete aircraft in October, 10 in November, 17 in December, and 18 in January 1970.[120]

Another problem came to light during TAC's test of the AC-119K in April, May, and June. The aircraft's flux-gate compass fed inputs to the fire-control system computer that were up to 40° in error after flying a firing circle. This plus a known error in the computer enlarged the overall error to 1,000 meters.[121] On May 22, 1969, TAC notified the Air Staff and AFLC that the tests verified the AC-119K's current configuration did not "possess a

---

*To support the ferrying of the AC-119Ks: three built-up R-3350 engines, two built-up props, two built-up J-85 engines, and a war readiness kit were prepositioned at McClellan AFB (but later at Malmstrom AFB) to support the aircraft in the United States; a built-up engine, a built-up prop, and a war readiness kit were prepositioned at Clark AB and a war readiness kit located at Hickam AFB, to support the aircraft in the PACAF theater.

Organization and Dispersal of Gunships (Nov. 1969)

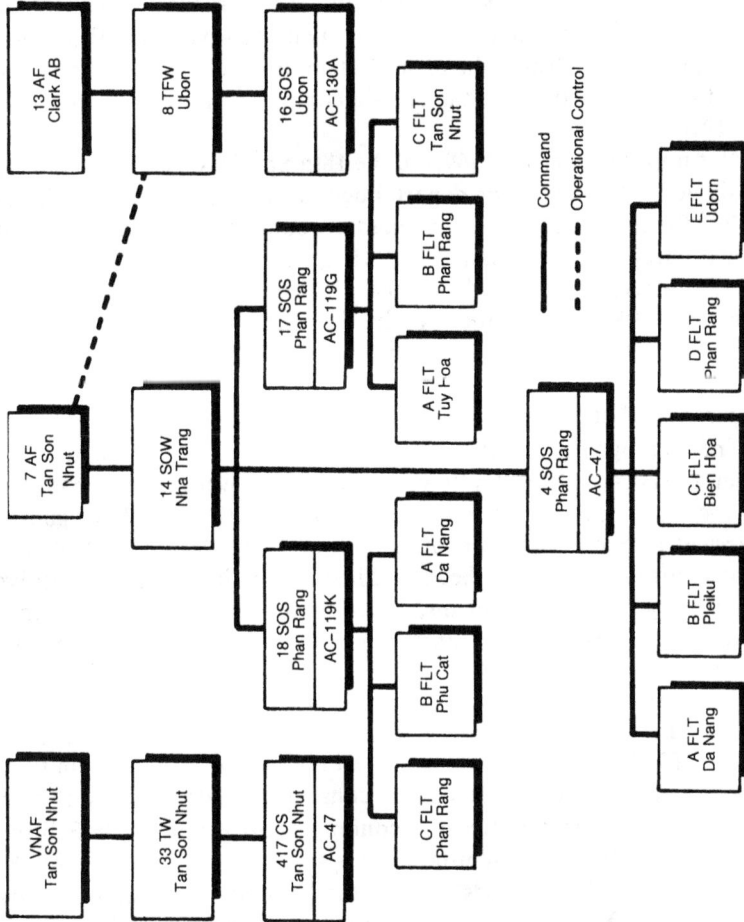

13 AF Clark AB	8 TFW Ubon	16 SOS Ubon / AC-130A
VNAF Tan Son Nhut	33 TW Tan Son Nhut	417 CS Tan Son Nhut / AC-47
7 AF Tan Son Nhut	14 SOW Nha Trang	

17 SOS Phan Rang / AC-119G — A FLT Tuy Hoa, B FLT Phan Rang, C FLT Tan Son Nhut

18 SOS Phan Rang / AC-119K — A FLT Da Nang, B FLT Phu Cat, C FLT Phan Rang

4 SOS Phan Rang / AC-47 — A FLT Da Nang, B FLT Pleiku, C FLT Bien Hoa, D FLT Phan Rang, E FLT Udorn

——— Command
- - - - Operational Control

NOTE: 1. VNAF and USAF gunship effort in-country coordinated in 7AF TACC.
2. USAF gunship effort out-country coordinated in 7AF Command Center (BLUE CHIP).

201

reliable offset-fire capability." TAC said it could not "in good conscience recommend employment of the existing AC-119K in the offset-mode in close air support role."[122] New tests revealed that replacement of the flux-gate compass with a two-axis gyro system could shrink the error to 400 meters. This in turn could be cut to 50 meters by giving the AC-119K a "complete solution" analog computer. AFLC recommended retrofitting the whole AC-119 fleet with the new compass and computer at an approximate cost of $4.5 million.[123] TAC agreed if 50-meter accuracy would result.[124] Previous to the AC-119K deployment, the Air Staff assented to the installation of the two items. When the two-axis-gyro modifications were through, a recheck termed the offset system satisfactory.[125] WRAMA teams would fit the AC-119s with the analog computer in Southeast Asia during June 1970.

Not until October 21, 1969, did the 18th Special Operations Squadron's first six AC-119K gunships depart Lockbourne AFB for South Vietnam. Lt. Col. Ernest E. Johnson, the squadron commander, and the rest of the advance party reached Phan Rang AB on the 11th of October. The first AC-119K arrived there on November 3,[126] and by the close of the year twelve AC-119Ks were in the theater. The final contingent of six aircraft deployed on December 27, the eighteenth, and last, AC-119K ending its transpacific flight on January 25, 1970.[127] All aircraft were combat-configured by February 4, 1970.[128]

The deployment of the 18th SOSq signaled the close of Combat Hornet, the AC-119G/K development program. Over 2½ years had gone by from the moment Secretary Brown decided to use the C-119 as a gunship to the arrival in South Vietnam of the 18th SOSq's last AC-119K. A long arduous project, it had been riddled with indecision, controversy, technical/engineering problems, contractor/subcontractor equipment-development delays, and competition with higher-priority weapons systems.[129]

In addition, the Combat Hornet program had met with stiff cost over-runs. On June 18, 1969, Air Force headquarters singled out the AC-119 program to AFLC as a prime example of an undesirable cost-overrun trend.[130] These costs caught the eye of economy-conscious Senator William Proxmire, chairman of the Subcommittee on Economy in Government. On February 3, 1970, he asked Philip N. Whittaker, Assistant Secretary of the Air Force (Installations and Logistics) why the twenty-six-aircraft program's estimated costs began at $50 million and climbed to $158 million. "I wonder if you would verify these facts and explain why there has been such a large increase in the modification costs," said the senator.[131] The Air Force replied that the 52 AC-119G/K modification program was first pegged at $81.2 million with a new estimate of $141.4 million. It attributed this sizable rise to numerous changes in design and equipment and a greater quantity of spares.[132] Not offered in rebuttal to Senator Proxmire were the delays in defining the contract and the premium overtime pay dictated by the project's urgency. Inflation, too, appeared to have played a part.[133]

The long-delayed arrival of the AC-119Ks wound up a major realignment of gunship forces in South Vietnam. The Nha Trang Proposal, approved earlier in the year, had called for the relocation from Nha Trang to Phan Rang of the 14th Special Operations Wing headquarters, the 71st Special Operations Squadron and the 18th Special Operations Squadron (yet to arrive).[134] When the 18th SOSq left the United States, it went directly to Phan Rang AB. The 71st SOSq suffered more turmoil. It not only moved its headquarters to Phan Rang and its Flight A to Tuy Hoa AB but underwent a major reorganization as well. The 17th Special Operations Squadron, activated on June 1, replaced the 71st SOSq which returned[135] to Bakalar AFB, Ind., for inactivation.[136] The 17th Squadron absorbed about two-thirds of the 71st's personnel. The remainder were reservists who departed South Vietnam for the United States on June 6 and reverted to inactive status by June 18, 1969.[137] This drain of skilled men imposed stringent training demands. Nevertheless, by the end of June, the 17th SOSq, commanded by Lt. Col. Richard E. Knie, had trained replacements and reestablished routine operations. With the two AC-119 squadrons in place, the Air Force inactivated the 3d and 4th SOSqs and transferred their AC-47s to the VNAF or RLAF. Thus the AC-119 units became the sole USAF gunship force based in South Vietnam.

At the close of 1969, the AC-119s were deployed as follows.

	Aircraft Assigned	Aircraft Planned
17th Special Operation Squadron		
A Flight, Tuy Hoa Air Base	4 AC-119G	6
B Flight, Phan Rang Air Base	7 AC-119G	6
(Main Support Base)		
C Flight, Tan Son Nhut Air Base	5 AC-119G	6
18th Special Operations Squadron		
A Flight, Da Nang Air Base	6 AC-119K	6
B Flight, Phu Cat Air Base	3 AC-199K	6
C Flight, Phan Rang Air Base	3 AC-119K	6
(Main Support Base)		

The distribution of AC-119 aircraft reflected early gunship concepts and experience and an effort to respond rapidly to Army close air support needs. Its soundness would be open to question should the AC-119K be largely used for interdiction in the Steel Tiger area of Laos. This seemed to be the case, for the Da Nang and Phu Cat contingents of the 18th SOSq were already heavily out-country oriented. Their aircraft were scheduled daily by the Seventh Air Force against vehicle traffic on the Laotian roads.[139] CINCPAC had told the Joint Chiefs of Staff that twelve AC-119Ks of the 18th Squadron would supplement other self-contained night attack systems in Laos.[140] These facts and concern over keeping the more sophisticated AC-119K at a number of forward locations impelled the 14th Special Operations Wing to propose another look at AC-119K deployment. The wing recommended that the Seventh Air Force locate twelve AC-119Ks at Da Nang and six at Ubon RTAFB. This would put the

TABLE 6. COMBAT EVALUATION OF THE AC–119K
(3 November 1969–28 February 1970)

Attacks on	Number	Destroyed	Damaged
Suspected enemy locations	144		
Known enemy locations	137		
Trucks	1,290	302	271
Sampans	27	26	1
Storage areas	42		
Bridges	4		
Other targets	23		

Positive target results: 538 secondary explosions and 186 secondary fires.
Target illumination: 178.1 hours with illuminator; 115 Mk–24 flares expended.
Rounds of ammunition fired: 1,354,846 of 7.26-mm and 595,519 of 20-mm.
Flying time: 2,417.2 hours of which 2,117.3 were combat hours.

Type of Sortie	Number
Armed reconnaissance in support of U.S. and other friendly ground forces or against LOCs along major enemy land/waterway supply routes	638*
Support	85†
Check flights	36
Training	19
Total	778

*410 flown outside and 228 inside South Vietnam.
†52 for troops in contact with the enemy.
Source: TAC OPlan 120 subj: Final Report Combat Introduction/Evaluation AC–119K. Gunship III (Combat King), August 1970, pp 41–61.

AC–119Ks closer to the target area and let them use the special maintenance equipment at Ubon—equipment common to both AC–130s and AC–119Ks. The Seventh Air Force rejected the proposal in the main, but on February 17, 1970, activated Flight D at Udorn RTAFB with three AC–119Ks and four aircrews taken from Flight B at Phu Cat AB.[142]

The 18th SOSq's combat operations commenced side by side with the AC–119K's combat evaluation (known as Combat King). The initial cadre of the 18th Squadron entered training and theater indoctrination with the 17th SOSq. On November 13, 1969, barely ten days after the first AC–119Ks arrived, the first combat mission was flown.[143] During the combat evaluation (November 3, 1969–February 28, 1970), eighteen AC–119Ks flew a total of 778 of the 865 sorties scheduled, a ninety percent rate. The type of sorties ranged from armed reconnaissance to check flights (see Table 6). On February 1 the 18th Special Operations Squadron began flying the full rate of ten sorties a day as directed by the Seventh Air Force.[144] After all this activity, the Combat King evaluators concluded that "the AC–119K effectively supported the PACAF mission requirements by flying its assigned combat missions. It was capable of destroying trucks and attacking targets as assigned."[145] By the end of 1969, MACV had judged the AC-119K a successful system.[146]

The nearly four-month combat evaluation of the AC-119K did disclose certain deficiencies. Maintenance manning, made difficult by decentralization, was found inadequate to properly support the forward operating locations. Likewise, squadron manning did not provide for a commander and operations officer at the FOLs so full-time crewmembers had to discharge these duties. Aerospace ground equipment was short and logistic support in general needed reevaluation. The forward-looking infrared, rated an essential and effective sensor, was kept operational only through contractor maintenance support. The final evaluation report recommended the four 7.62-mm miniguns be removed and one additional 20-mm gun be installed. As currently configured, the AC-119K needed to carry more 20-mm ammunition, since it expended an average of 655 rounds on each truck. Furthermore, the high failure rate of the 20-mm system, due chiefly to the ammunition-feed system, created concern. The beacon-tracking radar was not evaluated because of little utilization during the test period.[147]

The AC-119K had been into the combat evaluation almost a month when it received a new call sign and thus a new nickname. The 18th Special Operations Squadron reviewed a list of available calls including Gun Shy, Poor Boy, and Charlie Brown. The men of the squadron dejectedly picked Charlie Brown as the "least of these evils" but strongly asserted they deserved better. It turned out later the 366th Tactical Fighter Wing at Da Nang had an unused tactical voice call sign—Stinger. The 18th SOSq, backed by the 14th Special Operations Wing, put in a claim for it. The 18th saw Stinger as slightly off the gunship tradition but a satisfactory compromise, a sign around which unit pride could be built and a continuation of the "S" alliteration of gunship call signs.[148] The Seventh Air Force approved the call-sign transfer and the AC-119K became Stinger on December 1, 1969.[149] Stinger now joined Spectre in armed reconnaissance of enemy supply lines in Laos and Shadow in a variety of missions in South Vietnam. Spooky was also around, carrying the flag of allied nations.

The AC-119Gs were in combat virtually a year before the AC-119Ks. The AC-119G squadron solidly buttressed the 1969 war effort although bedeviled by aircraft corrosion/equipment problems,[150] redeployment and reorganization, and ceaseless retraining of aircrew/support personnel. At the time its designation switched to the "17th Special Operations Squadron" (June 1, 1969), the 71st SOSq had flown 1,209 missions (1,516 sorties) and 6,251 combat hours; fired 14,555,150 rounds of 7.62-mm ammunition; dropped 10,281 flares; killed 682 enemy troops (1,104 probables); and destroyed 43 vehicles (eight probables).[151] From June through December 1969, the 17th SOSq's performance exceeded: 2,000 sorties and 8,000 combat hours flown; 20 million rounds of ammunition fired; 12,000 flares expended; 800 enemy killed; 150 sampans destroyed;

and 800 secondary explosions recorded.[152] The 14th Special Operations Wing still proudly claimed that no allied outpost had been overrun while the gunships were overhead.

During 1969 the night observation device and computerized fire-control system of the AC-119 Shadow enabled it to edge ever closer to offensive missions. The AC-47 Spooky largely reacted to enemy strikes but the Shadow actively sought out enemy supply convoys and troop concentrations.[153] The AC-119K Stinger's more sophisticated gear supplied a stronger punch for even more offensive missions.

An attempt to capitalize on Shadow's see-in-the-dark capability occurred in February 1969. Since October 1968, observers had sighted unidentified flying objects of helicopter speed and altitude in the Duc Co area of western II Corps. The matter aroused operational interest because the enemy might be transporting men and equipment by helicopter from Cambodia to strategic locations in South Vietnam. The Seventh Air Force committed Shadows to joint surveillance with the Army Hawk radar element, counter-mortar radar, and Cobra helicopters. On several missions into the area, the AC-119Gs saw UFOs but could not identify and/or intercept them.[154]

Shadow gunships at first joined the AC-47s in protecting friendly outposts. Special Forces camps, district towns, or other fixed military positions under enemy assault. The Spooky Count became the Spooky/Shadow Count. The two gunship types defended 1,296 friendly positions in the first three months of 1969. Not one position fell while the gunships circled above. By December the Shadows had entirely replaced the Air Force Spookies.[155]

Cooperation between Shadow crews and ground personnel during support missions steadily improved. Allied troops and direct air support agencies became more familiar with the AC-119G and what it could do.[156] A typical ground-support episode unfolded on June 7, 1969. Enemy forces tried to overrun 25th Infantry Division fire-support base "Crook," which nestled near an enemy route into Tay Ninh Province. AC-119G/AC-47 gunships and USAF tactical fighters answered the call for assistance. To help turn back the enemy attack, the gunships used flares and miniguns, the fighters napalm and bombs. A sweep of the area afterwards counted 323 enemy killed. The few prisoners questioned told how the aerial firepower surprised and overwhelmed them.[157]

Very early the AC-119G had a small role in an effort to improve air support of ground forces. In September 1968 Air Force headquarters had directed TAC to use Shadow in two evaluations—Combat Cover and Combat Rendezvous.[158] In Combat Cover an OV-10A armed FAC joined the AC-119G in sustaining an Air Force strike presence over an Army unit. The aim was to slash response time to Army requests for air support. Combat Cover's first phase shaped FAC/gunship mission profiles and the second phase rated reaction times. The FAC response averaged 2.4 minutes, the gunship 5 minutes from notification to target area and 3.4

Combat Rendezvous (AC–119/AC–130)

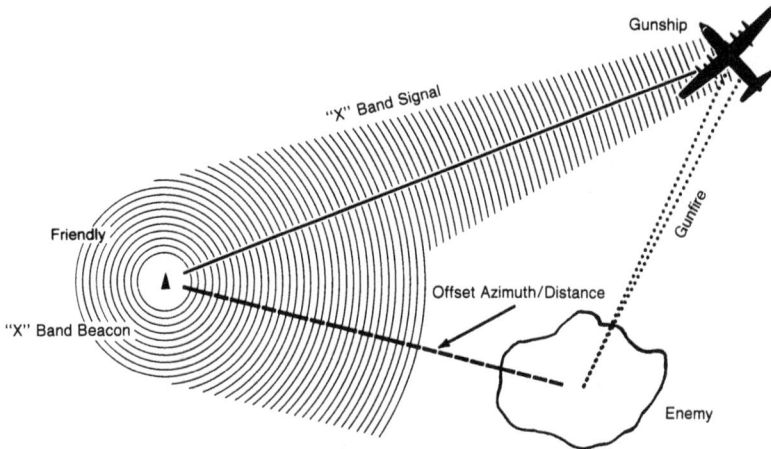

minutes to swing into firing position. TAC evaluators considered the concept feasible but pointed to the discomfort and extra workload of the OV–10A pilot and the "debatable use of the gunship in the close air support role."[159]

General Momyer, TAC commander, informed Air Force headquarters that Combat Cover revealed; no marked improvement in reaction time, the armed FAC (perhaps compromising the FAC role) had little firepower to apply, the OV–10 was too noisy for the strike role, and the gunship was vulnerable to anything larger than .30-caliber fire. The general recommended cancellation of an evaluation of the concept in Southeast Asia. Other organizations did not share these negative views and the Air Staff set the tests for mid-1969.[160] TAC nevertheless went on record as opposed to the allocation of gunships to Army divisions as well as use of the gunship in a phased-response concept.[161] The chief upshot of Combat Cover was the arming of the OV–10s. As to Combat Rendezvous, AC–119s and AC–130s participated in the test at Hurlburt Field, Fla., from November 18 to 22, 1968.[162] The evaluation centered on close air support by means of offset firing, utilizing a ground force's beacon or transponder as a reference point. Combat Rendezvous uncovered concept/equipment potential but also a need for further development.

Arranged visits between gunship crewmembers and U.S. Army unit commanders sought to strengthen air/ground coordination. The visits were designed to widen perspectives and pinpoint requirements for effective operations. Crewmembers of the 17th Special Operations Squadron visited the Americal Division in the last quarter of 1969. A written guide for aiding Army commanders on gunship-employment techniques grew out of these exchange visits.[163]

Shadow flew a far different mission early in 1969. A friendly compound lost electric power during a Viet Cong attack. At that time a doctor was performing a delicate operation on a wounded Vietnamese soldier. Responding to the call for help, an AC–119G from the 71st SOSq

207

hovered over the compound, its one-million-candlepower illuminator pouring light over doctor and patient. Lt. Col. Burl C. Campbell and his crew held the aircraft in a tightly controlled orbit despite the bright beam's marking the gunship for enemy gunners. The Vietnamese trooper lived, his operation and Shadow's a success.[164]

In the last half of August 1969, the 17th Special Operations Squadron put in for relief from at least one AC-119G mission per night due to the strain on aircraft maintenance. Four Shadows incurred battle damage and on August 6 one more took .50-caliber hits in the fuselage and one engine, producing an engine fire and extensive damage. Corrosion-control work, maintenance inspections, and disruptions in the supply of parts (owing to unit movements under the Nha Trang Proposal) aggravated the aircraft problems.[165] The 17th SOSq lost its first aircraft on October 11—Shadow 76 crashed upon takeoff for a mission from Tan Son Nhut AB. Six crewmembers were killed and the aircraft was destroyed.[166] Another AC-119G sustained severe damage on November 10 when its right gear collapsed on landing at Chu Lai AB.[167]

The drop in squadron missions, a decline of enemy activity, and worsening weather slightly altered the "seek and destroy" concept of the first half of 1969 to a "combat air patrol" operation.[168] By mid-December most of the problems afflicting the AC-119Gs had eased and the squadron's posture strengthened. [169]

January 1970 ushered in the second year of Shadow operations. Enemy action had so dwindled within South Vietnam that many missions were directed to border areas with more interdiction targets.[170] Specific strikes zones (Shadow boxes) were designated for armed reconnaissance. Intelligence officers determined each afternoon which boxes would likely prove most lucrative. A box would be assigned to a Shadow for the night mission. Enroute, the navigator secured artillery ("arty") clearances that often required a roundabout approach to the area and a great deal more time to reach the target. The aircraft commonly flew a TACAN radial to a prominent landmark in the box. It acquired the landmark with the night observation device and dropped a ground marker for positive positioning. The Shadow descended to 3,500 feet for the target search. If the aircraft detected a vehicle, for example, it might drop another ground marker for better reference as the attack began. Through study and briefings, the aircrews had to know all roads and trails in the box so Shadow could reconnoiter any new parallel routes.[171] These missions yielded few enemy vehicles destroyed because the AC-119G lacked the weapons punch needed.

The Shadows were at their best in defense of the CIDG camps at Dak Seang and Dak Pek. Aided by Stingers, the Shadows flew one or two sorties a night to cover the besieged posts during the hours of darkness. From April 1 to May 22, 1970, the AC-119 gunships flew 147 sorties and used up 2,380,161 rounds of 7.62-mm ammunition and 21,796 rounds of 20-mm in defense of the two camps. In addition, the Shadows were called upon to

Cambodia

illuminate a drop zone while C–7A Caribous tried to resupply the defenders by air. Three C–7A s had been downed in previous tries. Gunship/Caribou teamwork evolved whereby the gunship would orbit the posts and provide fire support until the Caribou reached the initial point for its drop. At that instant the gunship turned on the illuminator. The cargo away—and upon signal from the C–7A—Shadow switched off the illuminator and the Caribou escaped in the darkness. This tactic worked in a total of sixty-eight drops (April 6–May 1) without a Caribou being hit.[172]

Meantime, Shadows joined in the Duffel Bag Unit Systems Evaluation of new airborne equipment that monitored signals from ground sensors. From April 3 to May 31, AC–119Gs from Tan Son Nhut AB carried a portable UHF receiver. It could receive, decode, and display the sensor signals and audio transmission. Shadow 77 picked up signals on April 18 that signified movement in a sensor field. The gunship fired nearly 6,000 rounds of 7.62-mm ammunition into the area and 28,500 rounds the next night after again detecting the movement. Shadow further assisted an airstrike into the region. A later ground sweep of the zone discovered 150 enemy dead and netted seventeen prisoners, plus nine crew-served weapons as well as sixty-seven individual ones. The final assessment recommended the new equipment be permanently placed in the AC–119.[173]

On May 1, 1970, United States and South Vietnamese forces crossed the border into Cambodia with a dual objective. They were to (1) shore up the weak Cambodian army struggling with North Vietnamese units, and

(2) destroy the enemy forces and the supplies long stored in numerous border base camps. AC–119 gunships flew many missions in close support of this big offensive. In anticipation of support requirements, particularly in the Parrot's Beak* area, gunships had been shifted to Tan Son Nhut and Phan Rang on May 3. These AC–119s soon returned to their permanent bases because the ground force met light enemy resistance.[174]

The Air Force gave first mission priority to support of troops in contact with the enemy in Cambodia, followed in turn by convoy escort and armed reconnaissance. On a number of occasions, the AC–119Gs competently supported friendly units under night attack. At times the assaults were broken off when Shadow appeared overhead. Obtaining a count of enemy dead was difficult due to the fluid offensive. Furthermore, the friendly forces were reluctant to sweep battle areas before daylight, allowing the enemy time to dispose of those killed or wounded.[175]

At the height of Cambodian activity, new artillery clearance procedures speeded up gunship flights to the aid of ground units. The Air Force coordinated artillery clearances from Phan Rang AB to the Cambodian border with the Army before the gunships took off. Formerly, the gunships had secured clearances when airborne which meant more course alterations to avoid guns not shut down. This change slashed reaction time and afforded the gunships more time-over-target.[176]

Both river and road convoy escort missions assumed an early importance because of a critical petroleum shortage in Phnom Penh, the Cambodian capital. The Seventh Air Force controlled an air-cover package of aircraft from three services, put together for armed escort of Navy convoys plying the Mekong River. The Navy generally gave a three-day advanced-planning notice for their river convoys. An AC–119G would circle the convoy for twenty-four hours at 3,500 feet. An Army light fire team† flew coverage at 1,500 feet during daylight. The helicopters cycled between the convoy and their base at Chi Lang for refueling. The Navy employed two UH–1Bs and two OV–10s for low-altitude coverage at night. These planes cycled from their command-and-control vessel anchored in the Mekong River at Tan Chau, across the border in South Vietnam.[177]

Shadows escorted road convoys in Cambodia either alone or with forward air controller aircraft. When paired, the FAC searched for enemy ambush preparations along the convoy's route while the AC–119G flew in a large elliptical orbit overhead.‡ An excellent example of a successful convoy-escort mission occurred a year later when the enemy was aggressively attacking convoys. On June 30, 1971, a fifty-one-truck convoy left Phnom Penh headed southwest on Route 4 for Kompong Som. An

---

*The tip of the Cambodian salient west of Saigon.
†The team contained one command-and-control helicopter, two Cobra helicopter gunships, and two light observation helicopters.
‡The Cambodians often upset convoy-escort planning. They scheduled their own convoys and failed to coordinate the air cover.

escort FAC detected enemy movement north of Route 4 and suspected an ambush in the making. The FAC requested strike aircraft and a diverted AC-119G arrived. A recheck of the area confirming his suspicions, the FAC cleared the Shadow for attack. The gunship poured 7.62-mm fire on the clusters of troops who then answered with ground fire. The AC-119G raked the enemy position until the last truck had rolled safely by the planned ambush site.[178]

Cambodian armed reconnaissance missions zeroed in on trucks and river sampans. The AC-119Gs' 7.62-mm miniguns could do little against these targets and far less when the enemy armored the sampans. In July 1970 the AC-119Ks with their 20-mm cannons undertook this role. Even the Stinger had to use 20-mm armor-piercing incendiaries to sink the sampans when 20-mm high-explosive incendiary rounds could not. The AC-119G picked up punch when it tried a few 7.62-mm armor-piercing incendiaries from the U.S. Army against vehicles and watercraft. Additionally, the sparks of the armor-piercing rounds upon impact helped the pilot gauge his firing accuracy.[179]

This short span of Cambodian operations (May 5–June 30, 1970) saw the AC-119 gunships fly 178 sorties.[180] The U.S. ground operations in Cambodia quickly closed but the gunship continued supporting Cambodian and Vietnamese troops. Over nine months (July 1970–March 1971) the Shadows and Stingers destroyed or damaged 609 vehicles, destroyed 237 sampans and damaged 494, and killed 3,151 of the enemy.[181]

Fortunately, the gunships found the Cambodian area lightly defended. The small-caliber enemy fire inflicted no aircraft losses. On August 1, 1970, the AC-119Gs, joined by a few AC-119Ks, started daytime air interdiction—a further reflection of feeble enemy antiaircraft fire.[182]

On April 28, 1970, the 17th Special Operations Squadron did lose another aircraft. The gunship lost an engine on takeoff from Tan Son Nhut AB, crashed, and killed six of the eight crewmembers. The Air Force then trimmed the AC-119Gs' maximum gross takeoff weight by cutting fuel/ammunition loads to achieve a 150-foot-per-minute rate of climb on a single engine.[183]

While the Cambodian offensive opened a new war area for the gunships, especially the AC-119Gs, operations progressed in the panhandle and Barrel Roll areas of Laos. As 1970 began, an enemy offensive alarmingly succeeded against General Vang Pao's forces in northern Laos. With PACAF's permission, the Seventh Air Force directed a trail deployment of AC-119Ks to Udorn RTAFB in support of Barrel Roll during February's high moon phase. On February 5 Seventh ordered an operational test during February 17–27 from Udorn.[184] On February 15, three AC-119Ks, four crews, and thirty maintenance men deployed to that base from Phu Cat AB. The AC-119K's main mission was armed reconnaissance along Routes 7 and 61 in Barrel Roll and secondarily the support of Lima Sites under attack. The first Stinger mission was flown out of Udorn on February 17.[185]

PLAIN OF JARS

About this time the enemy's offensive crested. The North Vietnamese and Pathet Lao forces captured the Xieng Khouang airfield then rolled west and overran the Royal Laotian Air Force T–28 base at Muong Soui. The key Lima Site 22 gave way after a 2½-hour nighttime assault when no gunship support was scheduled. By February 24, 1970, the enemy again occupied the Plain of Jars with pro-government forces clinging to a defensive perimeter west and south of the Plain.[186] The AC–119K operations intensified to meet the crisis. As the end of Stinger's ten-day operational test neared, the Seventh Air Force stretched it stay at Udorn to July 2, 1970, with reevaluation set at that time.[187]

The Stingers significantly strengthened the effort in northern Laos. In view of the AC–47's anticipated release, the AC–119K's ongoing role in Barrel Roll operations seemed essential.[188] On March 21, 1970, the Thai-based detachment's strength rose to four aircraft, seven crews, and forty-seven support personnel.[189] The total aircraft dropped to three (five crews) on May 20 as bad weather slowed ground operations.[190] In June, the Seventh Air Force asked CINCPACAF to keep the AC–119Ks at Udorn another 120 days, explaining the "AC–119K had been the number one truck killer in Barrel Roll, accounting for 70 percent of all trucks destroyed."[191]

Although Barrel Roll occupied part of the 18th's aircraft, the squadron was chiefly charged with interdiction in Steel Tiger and the adjacent A Shau Valley area. The AC-119Ks shared with the AC-130s a heavy commitment to stop every enemy truck they could. The last Stinger contingent had reached South Vietnam in February 1970. Shortly thereafter, estimates of tonnage trucked by the North Vietnamese through Laos toward Vietnam soared. Pressure on truck-killing paralleled this surge of traffic. Mission reports disclosed 2,321 trucks were destroyed during one month—2,125 of them in Steel Tiger. Gunships claimed sixty percent of these kills.[192] Da Nang-based Stingers flew four sorties per night against heavy truck traffic on Routes 92 and 922.[193] The AC-119Ks at Phu Cat went from two missions a night on January 1 to five a night by February 1.[194] Over the first quarter of 1970, Stingers claimed 406 trucks destroyed and 607 damaged. On April 25, 1970, the 18th Special Operations Squadron operating location at Da Nang—focal point for most squadron interdiction missions—claimed its 1,000th disabled truck.[195]

Support problems and the demand for greater time-over-target soon spurred a further adjustment in 18th Special Operations Squadron basing. The first few interdiction missions from Phu Cat clearly proved that base unsuitable for such out-country sorties. Phu Cat's distance from the target area and the AC-119K's fuel load confined Stinger operations to certain areas in Laos.[196] Even to the closest areas, the Stingers had trouble getting 1½ hours on target. On March 3, 1970, CINCPACAF suggested that Seventh Air Force reappraise the entire 18th SOSq concept if the Udorn operation continued. CINCPACAF felt the current logistical/maintenance headaches pointed up the need to consolidate bases.[197]

On March 16, Seventh Air Force began planning for redeploying the 18th Special Operations Squadron, tailored to the new tactical situation and support requirements. The 14th Special Operations Wing proposed moving B Flight's remaining assets from Phu Cat AB to Da Nang AB, expanding the AC-119Ks there from six to nine. Timed with this move, the A Flight of the 17th SOSq would depart Tuy Hoa AB and occupy the vacated 18th SOSq facilities at Phu Cat. This latter change would permit programmed base-closure actions at Tuy Hoa to progress and at the same time assure a faster gunship response to I Corps support requests.[198] The plan was approved, and the Seventh Air Force authorized the Da Nang buildup on April 5. It was completed on April 23, 1970.[199] The A Flight of the 17th SOSq accomplished its move from Tuy Hoa to Phu Cat on April 12, 1970.[200]

A fresh study in June of Stinger's time-over-target (TOT) led the 14th Special Operations Wing to urge a beddown of twelve AC-119Ks at Da Nang and six at Ubon. This would bring the Stinger force closer to the armed reconnaissance areas. The commander of the 14th SOWg, told the Seventh Air Force commander that in 1,395 hours the AC-119K had destroyed/damaged 1,712 trucks—an average of 1.23 trucks disabled per hour-over-target. "Since there is a direct relationship between TOT and truck

Southeast Asia Air Bases

NVN

Hanoi ★

LAOS

Udorn ●
Nakhon Phanom

THAILAND

Takhli ●
Korat ●
Ubon ●

Da Nang ●

Don Muang ●

Pleiku ●
Phu Cat ●

Tuy Hoa ●

CAMBODIA

RVN

Nha Trang ●

U-Tapao ●

Cam Ranh Bay ●
Bien Hoa ●
Phan Rang

Saigon
Tan Son Nhut ●★

Vung Tau

Binh Thuy ●

kills, increased TOT appears the most readily available potential to exploit in improving effectiveness," he said. The 14th Wing commander offered deployment of the AC–119K force to Da Nang and Ubon as the best way to capitalize on greater target time.[201] He also advocated setting up the main support base for the AC–119Ks at Da Nang and removing Stinger's beacon-tracking radar to reduce weight and allow a greater fuel load.[202]

The Seventh Air Force replied that it favored a move from Udorn to Nakhon Phanom RTAFB rather than to Ubon. Seventh reasoned that the Nakhon Phanom location would add flexibility to both Steel Tiger and Barrel Roll operations. Then too, the projected force cuts at Nakhon Phanom would open up facilities there.[203] Planning for executing a move to Nakhon Phanom pushed ahead but at mid-1970 the AC–119 basing stood as follows:[204]

Location	Aircraft assigned
Phan Rang AB, RVN	7 AC–119G/4 AC–119K
Phu Cat AB, RVN	5 AC–119G
Tan Son Nhut AB, RVN	5 AC–119G
Da Nang AB, RVN	9 AC–119K
Udorn RTAFB, Thailand	3 AC–119K

The beacon-tracking radar figured in discussions of where the AC–119K would be based because its extra weight cut twenty to thirty minutes from the aircraft's time-over-target. Consequently, the AC–119Ks flew without the beacon-tracking set during the early days at Da Nang and Phu Cat. Since it was designed for close support of ground troops, the system was considered nonessential for interdiction missions.[205] Furthermore, the lack of test equipment at the forward operating locations hampered radar maintenance.

The Seventh Air Force received a requirement in January 1970 to support a special operations team equipped with transponders to be inserted into Laos. A maintenance team from Phan Rang AB visited the operating locations and installed the beacon-tracking radar in all AC–119Ks.[206]

Equipping the Stingers with beacon-tracking radar opened the way to test their offset firing. The earlier Combat Rendezvous tests in the United States had underscored the offset firing system's potential, but development of the concept and associated equipment had lagged. The Army Limited War Laboratory offered mini-ponders (5-watt and 400-watt) to the U.S. Army in Vietnam in February 1970 for Southeast Asia evaluation.[207] The 14th Special Operations Wing sent Seventh Air Force a proposed test order on February 21. The test—Combat Rendezvous Phase II—would introduce an all-weather close-support capability for all gunships fitted with the radar.[208]

In the spring of 1970 a ground beacon was placed at Dak Seang under the auspices of the Seventh Air Force Tactical Air Control Office and the II Direct Air Support Center. Using a Stinger from Da Nang, the test firings yielded excellent results. However, a later demonstration for Army commanders was less impressive because the firing was against Army-placed point targets in lieu of the more advantageous area targets. Some all-weather firing with the APQ–133 cued on a ground transponder was successful at Bung Lung, Cambodia. Although the system was relatively impressive in testing situations, it was not fully integrated into AC–119K gunship operation, but was employed in selected high risk tactical situations where ground troops had transponders.[209]

The heavy demand for AC–119K support of ground operations and interdiction of the enemy's dry-season supply effort contributed to some early losses. The first occurred on February 19, 1970, when a Stinger crashed short of the Da Nang runway while returning from a combat mission. The final approach had gone normally until the landing gear and flaps went down about two miles out at 500- to 600-foot altitude. A sudden power loss in the jet and reciprocating engines on the left side, apparently due to fuel starvation, prevented the pilot from maintaining either directional control or altitude. The crash demolished the aircraft but the crewmembers escaped with only minor injuries.[210] Another AC–119K was nearly lost when a 37-mm round shattered the nose section as the aircraft worked a few miles north of Ban Bak, Laos. The crew nursed the Stinger back to Da Nang but damage was extensive.[211]

Concern about AC–119K vulnerability to antiaircraft fire, especially to fire encountered over the Laotian trail and road system, led to use of fighter escorts as developed on AC–130 operations. F–4 Phantoms from the 366th Tactical Fighter Wing at Da Nang flew constant escort and antiaircraft suppression for all Stinger armed reconnaissance flights. At the height of the truck-hunting season the 366th TFWg averaged six escort sorties per night.[212]

The 18th Special Operations Squadron lost a second aircraft on the night of June 6, 1970. Shortly after the plane took off from Da Nang, its left-engine propeller went out of control. The pilot tried to head back to base but the situation deteriorated and the crew bailed out over the South China Sea just east of Da Nang. The empty aircraft kept on seaward, creating a momentary flurry of excitement since it seemed headed for China's Hainan Island. The Stinger crashed at an undetermined spot. All crew members but one were safely recovered.[213]

The night of May 8, 1970, witnessed an extraordinary display of airmanship when a Stinger from Udorn was heavily damaged by antiaircraft fire:

> Capt. Alan D. Milacek and his nine-man crew had been reconnoitering a heavily defended road section near Ban Ban, Laos, when they discovered, attacked and destroyed two trucks. Capt. James A. Russell and Capt. Ronald C. Jones, the sensor operators, located three more trucks. As the aircraft banked into attack orbit, six enemy positions opened up with a barrage of AA fire. The copilot Capt. Brent C. O'Brien, cleared the fighter escort for attack and the gunship circled as the F–4's worked to suppress the AA fire. Amid the heavy enemy fire, Captain Milacek resumed the attack and killed another truck. At 0100, just about 2 hours into the mission, "the whole cargo compartment lit up" as enemy rounds tore into the Stinger's right wing. A "sickening right dive of the aircraft" ensued and Milacek called "Mayday, Mayday, we're goin in." He shouted orders to SSgt. Adolfo Lopez, Jr., the IO [illuminator operator], to jettison the flare launcher.
>
> Captain Milacek directed the entire crew to get ready for instant bailout. As the gunship dropped about 1,000 feet within a few seconds, Captains Milacek and O'Brien pooled their strength to pull the aircraft out of its dive. By using full-left rudder, full-left aileron, and maximum power on the two right engines, they regained stabilized flight. The full-engine power fueled 2- to 3-foot flames—torchlights for enemy gunners as the crippled Stinger desperately headed for friendly territory. The navigator Capt. Roger E. Clancy gave the correct heading but warned they were too low to clear a range of mountains towering between them and safety. What's more, the crew discovered that fuel consumption would likely mean dry tanks before reaching base.
>
> The crew tossed out every possible item to lighten the load and the aircraft slowly climbed to 10,000 feet. TSgt. Albert A. Nash, the flight

engineer, reported the fuel-consumption rate had fallen. Captain Milacek elected to land the damaged plane and when he approached the base area he ran a careful check of controls. He found that almost full-left rudder and aileron would allow him to keep control. With uncertain flap damage, Milacek chose a no-flap landing approach at 150 knots (normally 117 knots). Utilizing every bit of pilot skill he landed the plane. Upon leaving the Stinger, the crew saw about one-third of the right wing (a 14-foot section and aileron) had been torn off.[214]

Captain Milacek and crew received the Mackay Trophy for "the most meritorious flight of the year." General Ryan, Chief of Staff, presented the trophy on August 5, 1971, during a Pentagon ceremony.[215]

In the latter half of 1970, AC-119 gunship operations continued to expand in Cambodia. AC-119Gs from Tan Son Nhut AB interdicted communist supply lines, joined by AC-119Ks at the end of July. In addition, Shadows and Stingers were the chief defenders of Kompong Cham, Kompong Thom, Skoun, and Phnom Penh. Protection of these towns was crucial since they were control points on key highways.[216] The commander of Cambodian forces at Kompong Thom (north of Phnom Penh) reported that 17th Special Operations Squadron gunships played a prominent role in lifting the enemy siege of that provincial capital. From December 12 to 15, 1970, a typical ground-support action took place at Prey Totung. Thirty-two Shadow missions supported the town's defenders, expending 555,800 rounds of 7.62-mm ammunition and 128 flares.[217] AC-119 Cambodian sorties in October were credited with killing 1,400 of the enemy.[218] As the main air interdiction force in Cambodia, the AC-119s were seen as a big reason why Cambodian population centers stayed in the hands of friendly forces.[219]

In August 1970 representatives from the FAC group operating in Cambodia and the 17th Special Operations Squadron met at Bien Hoa AB to refine coordination and procedures for joint operations in Cambodia. They agreed to schedule day-and-night missions and to try a new concept that mated a FAC and 17th/18th SOSq aircraft as a hunter-killer team on selected interdiction missions. AC-119s were fragged as a separate sortie in a night truck/sampan hunter-killer effort. On September 2, 1970, to further refine coordination in Cambodia, an EC-121 served as an extension of the tactical air control center. This aircraft furnished better control of aircraft separation, sharpened airstrike coordination, and speeded up firing clearances. French speaking interpreters went along on night gunship missions to help with air-to-ground communication and to gather intelligence.[220]

On December 7, 1970, the 17th Special Operations Squadron was ordered to fly night support for Laotian forces on the Bolovens Plateau. Three aircraft and four crews accordingly moved from Phan Rang to Phu Cat.[221] Several Lima Sites were surrounded and the situation was deteriorating. Even so, U.S. and RLAF gunship support by night and other attack aircraft by day enabled the Lima Sites to reset their outer defenses in about five days.[222]

AC–119K interdiction operations picked up markedly in December 1970 after a longer-than-usual wet season. On December 16 a Stinger set a new high for truck-kills by a single AC–119 aircraft in one night—29 trucks destroyed and 6 others damaged along Route 92 near Ban Bak, Laos.[223] Collectively, the Stingers recorded 312 trucks destroyed and 196 damaged in the last three months of 1970[224] and 1,845 destroyed/damaged in the first quarter of 1971.[225] The AC–119Ks were also pitted against North Vietnamese tanks as the Stingers shouldered heavy support commitments growing out of the South Vietnamese offensive into Laos (Lam Son 719). On February 28 Stinger destroyed eight PT–76 tanks.[226] The AC–119Ks compiled their interdiction record despite bad weather early in the hunting season and diversions for emergency support of Lima Sites and troops in contact with the enemy.

The AC–119K's truck-killing record rested in part on a mix of 20-mm rounds—armor-piercing incendiary (API) and high-explosive incendiary (HEI). First tested on November 18, 1970,[227] the mixed rounds fully demonstrated their worth against tanks in Lam Son 719.[228] Another plus was the reworking of the 20-mm guns, including new gun barrels. Also, a

concentrated maintenance effort eased the maintenance/operational headaches from these guns over the months of Stinger operations. Moreover, the removal of the beacon-tracking radar had been approved which stretched Stinger's time-over-target up to 30 more minutes. The AC–119K had tested a more advanced fire-control computer in late 1970 but problems prevented its quick use for Stinger operations.[229]

The AC–119 force deployment adjusted to new tactical needs. The Seventh Air Force's recommended shift of the 18th SOSq's D Flight from Udorn to Nakhon Phanom was carried out from October 26 to 29, 1970, with practically no break in mission plans. During October 10–November 27 the 17th SOSq moved more aircraft to Tan Son Nhut from Phu Cat and Phan Rang to satisfy operational demands in Cambodia. On December 29 A Flight of the 17th SOSq was inactivated at Phu Cat, its personnel and aircraft assigned to B Flight at Phan Rang.[230] As 1970 closed, the AC–119s were spread over five bases—Phan Rang (seven AC–119Gs), Tan Son Nhut (nine AC–119Gs), Phan Rang (three AC–119Ks), Da Nang (seven AC–119Ks) and Nakhon Phanom (six AC–119Ks).[231]

Amid expanding AC–119 operations, plans were afoot to turn over the AC–119Gs to the Vietnamese Air Force, consistent with the Nixon administration push for Vietnamization of the war. This spawned proposals for a bigger and better VNAF gunship capability. A plan emerged to activate the Vietnamese Air Force's 819th Combat Squadron at Tan Son Nhut AB on September 1, 1971.[232] On that date the 17th SOSq would turn over the AC–119Gs and specified maintenance and supply support equipment. The VNAF would then schedule all AC–119G missions.[233] The 17th Squadron was charged with VNAF combat crew training in the AC–119G. In Phase I at Clinton County AFB the VNAF pilots were checked out in the C–119. Phase II aircrew training would take place at Phan Rang: three crews to enter training on February 1, 1971; seven, April 3; seven, May 18; and the last seven, June 25.[234] The goal called for the VNAF squadron having twenty-four crews operationally ready by May 1, 1972.[235] Thus as 1971 began, the 17th SOSq got ready to convert from a combat squadron to a training one.

In Southeast Asian combat the AC–119G/K gunships had proven a worthy follow-on for the AC–47. Indeed, the G and K models each had distinct capabilities that assured a far more flexible gunship force. The Shadows could do Spooky's job in South Vietnam and Barrel Roll. Stingers could ably help Spectre interdict enemy supply lines. The AC–119s occupied the middle ground in development and operations between the AC–47 (the "model T" of gunships) and the AC–130E (the ever more sophisticated and potent "Cadillac").

The AC–119s were thrust into the Southeast Asian conflict at a time when the war was moving in new directions. Hostilities had spilled over into Cambodia (a whole new arena for the gunships) and had quickened in the Barrel Roll and Steel Tiger sectors of Laos. AC–119 operations steadily spread over a larger and larger geographic area. Attention fixed more on gunship offensive operations outside South Vietnam than on defensive missions within. These shifts of emphasis forced AC–119 deployment to constantly adjust. In addition, Vietnamization grew in importance, accompanied by the turnover of AC–119Gs to the Vietnamese Air Force and a downturn in U.S. strength. Despite the new operational demands, the AC–119s performed well. They built up their own "Shadow Count," saved Lima Sites from capture, flew cover for troops and convoys, and destroyed enemy trucks and sampans bearing supplies.

The AC–119's road to combat twisted through long-delayed, costly, and difficult development. The aircraft started out in a climate of skepticism and opposition. It endured the higher priority of the AC–130 program. It was overweight. Production of its subsystems lagged, and even when ready for deployment, the AC–119 ran into Southeast Asia "headroom" problems. But despite all the difficulties, the AC–119G/K gunships played a significant and successful role in the war.

VI. Commando Hunt VII and the Enemy's 1972 Offensive—The Final Major American Combat Challenge

In 1971 gunship development and operations proceeded apace. Although Vietnamization edged steadily ahead toward future American disengagement, the North Vietnamese and Viet Cong gave little evidence of weakening their own war effort. They kept on moving troops and equipment south, and went to great effort to resupply soldiers already fighting there. The communists were massing men and supplies for a major offensive in 1972 to be carried out by large conventional infantry, tank, and artillery units, a plan unknown to American and South Vietnamese forces. To impede this southward flow, gunship interdiction remained a high-priority mission. At the same time, enemy advances in Laos and Cambodia imposed ever wider demands upon the gunships. But the big 1972 offensive gave the AC-130s and AC-119s their stiffest test, and they responded in an outstanding manner by helping troops ward off determined communist attacks; operations were similar to those in the early days of the war, when AC-47s blunted the foe's attempts to overrun hamlets, villages, outposts, and forts.

As spring 1971 neared, preparations were under way for yet another intensive dry season attempt at cutting the enemy's Laotian resupply routes. The forthcoming interdiction campaign (Commando Hunt VII) formed the fourth major fall-winter operation since the 1968 cutoff of bombing in North Vietnam.* Allied military leaders believed that continued interdiction of enemy supplies was crucial to the success of Vietnamization and withdrawal of more American forces. "Our aim," President Nixon told Congress on February 25, "is to destroy their supplies and disrupt their planning for assaults on allied forces in South Vietnam."[1] Clearly, Vietnamization needed more breathing room before being put to the hard test by North Vietnamese attacks.

As the gunship girded for Commando Hunt VII, study and activity on the Vietnamization of interdiction gathered momentum. American leaders looked for some reasonable answer to a thorny dilemma. How could the Vietnamese Air Force, already taxed with many missions and their accompanying maintenance support, shoulder the huge interdiction effort

---

*Begun in November 1968, Commando Hunt I was the first campaign to focus on Laos without attacks on related North Vietnamese targets. Subsequent dry-season campaigns carried sequential odd numbers: III, V, and VII.

when the United States withdrew from combat completely?[2] Among the principal solutions proposed was use of a short-takeoff-and-landing aircraft as a mini-gunship, a concept and plan that would become known as "Credible Chase."

Obviously the mini-gunship could not replace the interdiction firepower and other strengths of the AC–119 or AC–130. However, it would be a system that the South Vietnamese could more easily operate and maintain, advantages that were essential.

Before the focus on Vietnamizing interdiction, the short-takeoff-and-landing (STOL) aircraft had been regarded as a possible counterinsurgency mini-gunship for the Thai Air Force. Its proposed role was to augment or substitute for additional helicopter gunships and for T–28 aircraft. Then, in late March 1971, the President expressed fresh interest in helicopter gunships. This led Secretary of Defense Laird to suggest on April 8 that Secretary Seamans have two STOL aircraft tested for Southeast Asia by June 30.[3]

On May 10 Mr. Packard called Dr. Seamans and the other service secretaries to "make detailed investigations of the concept of providing the VNAF with a 'mini-gunship' fleet." He coupled the request with a possible cutback of "dependence on Igloo White." Packard said that "providing a system operable, maintainable, and perhaps even manufacturable by SVN is extremely attractive, if practical." He thought tests of an "available configuration (including some available night vision device) should be conducted expeditiously."[4]

During May an initial mini-gunship evaluation of the Helio Stallion and the Fairchild Peacemaker began at Eglin AFB, Fla.[5] These light STOL aircraft chosen for testing had turboprop engines, high wings, fixed conventional landing gear, and side-by-side seating for pilots. Data from the Eglin tests went to an Air Staff ad hoc group who put together the Credible Chase concept[6]—a plan to give VNAF more mobility and firepower within a short time.

Secretary Laird meanwhile lent his weight to the mini-gunship evaluation. On May 17 he challenged the chairman of the Joint Chiefs of Staff to be more imaginative, broadly hinting that the mini-gunship might be an answer.[7]

Secretary Seamans on June 10 sent Secretary Packard a mini-gunship study spelling out the Credible Chase concept. Many light STOL planes were to operate from austere airfields patrolling a thirty kilometer-wide border strip from the demilitarized zone to the Laos-Cambodia-Thailand boundary. This twenty-four-hour surveillance-attack operation would cover twenty-two border segments of about nine hundred square kilometers each. As many as three aircraft by day and nine at night would patrol every sector. Working with simple sensors, an aircrew would team with highly mobile ground teams to comb a selected area. To strike any targets turned up, the mini-gunship would pack a 20-mm side-firing gun or similar weapon. The strong selling points of Credible Chase were low cost and time saved by training aircrews and maintenance personnel in-country.[8]

Credible Chase edged forward during June and July 1971, as the Helio Stallion and Fairchild Peacemaker underwent combat evaluation in Southeast Asia. The test team discovered quite a few deficiencies in the two aircraft, and recommended further testing after their correction.[9] At this point Secretary Seamans visited Southeast Asia. He found that the combat evaluation had not dispersed the cloud of skepticism hovering over the use of the light planes. "In the field there continue to be reservations," PACAF reported to the Chief of Staff on July 1.[10]

Lukewarm reaction from the field failed to dampen Secretary Laird's support for the mini-gunship concept. On July 2 he ordered the Air Force to design a combat test for the next dry season, and instructed Army and Defense Special Projects Group (DSPG) to assist. "I need not remind you the fate of our national Vietnamization policy rests in part on evolution of a credible South Vietnamese interdiction capability at the earliest possible time," said the secretary. He offered to help in getting Congressional approval for procurement of the STOL aircraft.[11]

General Meyer, Vice Chief of Staff, handed in a combat test plan on July 19.[12] Approving it on the 30th Secretary Laird urged the Air Force to "pursue this effort with the priority and aggressiveness now shown in your successful AC-130 gunship program."[13]

The Air Force's Credible Chase planning group set a February 1, 1972, target date for the joint USAF/VNAF evaluation. Funds for thirty STOL aircraft were still needed, however.[14] To keep the slow legislative pace from delaying the evaluation, dual-source procurement was recommended.[15] Secretaries Laird and Seamans both wrote letters to Senator John Stennis, chairman of the Armed Services Committee, requesting the required $14.5 million.[16] Laird reminded the senator that Credible Chase "would contribute to completing U.S. deployment at an early date."[17]

Meantime a Credible Chase planning conference took place in August 1971 at Tactical Air Command headquarters, Langley AFB, Va. A like meeting followed in September at Headquarters, Tactical Air Warfare Center, Eglin AFB.[18]

Dr. Seamans informed Mr. Laird on October 13 that the Air Force would choose a light STOL aircraft in late FY 1972, if the combat evaluation showed any promise for Vietnamese Air Force use in 1973. Such aircraft would fill future Southeast Asia needs under foreign military sales or the military assistance program "in the interests of minimizing training, support and logistic requirements."[19]

In October 1971 Mr. Leonard Sullivan, Jr., Deputy Director of Defense Research and Engineering, visited South Vietnam to explore Vietnamization of interdiction. He reported a "certain amount of head shaking" on the part of leaders there. They doubted if the Credible Chase aircraft could survive the foe's potent arsenal of antiaircraft guns, surface-to-air missiles, and possible Mig fighters.[20]

In the course of Sullivan's visit, the Chief of Staff of South Vietnam's Joint General Staff (JGS) approved a Credible Chase program of fifty percent Vietnamese pilots and thirty-three percent VNAF maintenance personnel. (Air America* would train the pilots.) The JGS chief further agreed to the proposed tactical area of responsibility for the combat evaluation. Still, MACV sought without success to secure an alternate area of lower threat for the test—in case the primary one should "heat up." Sullivan reported that he had addressed the reservations of the Vietnamese regarding Credible Chase. He told them the STOL aircraft could be diverted to a different use, so long as it freed other VNAF resources for interdiction duty.[21]

By early October 1971, Defense Secretary Laird completed his study of the Combined Interdiction Campaign Plan which the Joint Chiefs had sent him on August 23. The Joint Chiefs approved giving CBU–55 munitions† to the Vietnamese Air Force, but deemed the proposed strategic readout system‡ unrealistic though operationally feasible. They saw the mini-gunship concept generating a need for a thousand more pilots and a sharp rise in ground support personnel. They foresaw serious problems in controlling and deploying so many STOL aircraft, and deplored the mini-gunship cost estimate of nearly $1.7 billion for the first three years. Notwithstanding, the Joint Chiefs went along with a mini-gunship evaluation, including a limited strategic readout system.[22]

Secretary Laird proffered his comments to the Joint Chiefs of Staff on October 8. He faulted the interdiction plan for relying too heavily on U.S. air power, saying "I am establishing the objective of achieving an optimal RVNAF [Republic of Vietnam Armed Forces] interdiction capability by fall 1972 which could, if necessary, be self-sustaining with no more than limited U.S. advisory effort."[23] The secretary proposed to make mini-gunships part of the next year's Improvement and Modernization Program, as one of several suggestions to perfect the interdiction plan. In his view, the mini-gunships could be considered either a part of direct interdiction efforts or a substitute for diverted air assets, such as AC–119s. Laird also directed that the South Vietnamese take over 1972–73 interdiction planning.[24]

Around mid-November the Joint Chiefs responded, asserting that such features as low cost, ease of maintenance, and flexible performance seemed to suit the STOL aircraft for a variety of missions. If the Vietnamese could come up with the needed personnel, the Credible Chase program could be worked into the planned force structure. If not, it would have to be pursued at the expense of the O-1 aircraft or other programs. One or two STOL aircraft squadrons could be ready by late 1972, and four or five added by June 30, 1973. The Joint Chiefs acknowledged that the combat test results would decide the fate of these plans. They nevertheless urged that funding and procurement proceed at once to meet the above timetable.[25]

---

*A contract airline that flew for the Central Intelligence Agency in Southeast Asia.

† Basically, a cluster bomb unit (CBU) consisted of a dispenser filled with small spherical bombs that in turn contained small steel spheres. When the dispenser was ejected from the aircraft, a timer opened it and the bombs were released. The bombs were fuzed to detonate and expel the steel spheres against personnel and materiel.

‡ A system that received pulses from ground sensors, decoding and displaying them for use by the aircraft gunner.

On the 24th of November, Secretary Seamans asked Secretary of Defense Laird to approve five squadrons of STOL aircraft for the Vietnamese Air Force. Seamans said a favorable decision would start action to procure the required personnel.[26] Five days later, Secretary Laird told Admiral Moorer, the Joint Chiefs' chairman, that "review of our manifold efforts to improve the RVNAF interdiction capabilities indicates a clear necessity to proceed immediately with procurement action for STOL aircraft if a mini-gunship force is to become available for the 71–73 dry season." The secretary agreed that final judgment must await results of the "impending field test." He believed that enough facts were known, however, to begin planning for "five operational STOL squadrons (32 aircraft each—200 total aircraft, including command support and initial attrition) for the FY 1973 campaign." Laird underscored the need for the "concerted efforts of all concerned" to reach this goal. He called for confirmation by December 3, 1971, of the military requirement for the Credible Chase aircraft and coordination with the Vietnamese on manning the STOL units.*[27]

The secretary's order created waves of discussion within the Joint Chiefs of Staff, as the search began for common ground on which to base a reply. The Air Force's concern about STOL aircraft in the interdiction role came out during the talks. The Air Force hoped the Army might "soften" the confirmation for the Credible Chase aircraft.[29] These reservations were reinforced by CINCPAC and COMUSMACV. Their messages to the Joint Chiefs of Staff on December 2 asserted that no requirement existed for Credible Chase aircraft in South Vietnam.[30] Jolted by this clear-cut stand, the Air Force proposed that the Joint Chiefs send a message to CINCPAC posing these questions:

> After U.S. air power is withdrawn from SEA, will continued interdiction be required?
> If so, are currently programmed VNAF forces adequate?
> If they are not, what can be done by the fall of 1972?[31]

In a December 2 meeting, the Joint Chiefs decided to delay sending such a message. The next day, Admiral Moorer asked Secretary Laird to give him until December 10 to reply on the Credible Chase program. Moorer said he wanted to get "first hand comments" from General Ryan, Air Force Chief of Staff, who was on an inspection tour in the Western Pacific.[32] Laird granted the delay but cautioned that the issue was "time sensitive." Regardless of Credible Chase, the South Vietnamese had to have interdiction capabilities soon.[33]

Upon his return, the Chief of Staff studied a December 7 paper on Vietnamizing interdiction. In it Brig. Gen. Leslie W. Bray, Jr., Assistant for Vietnamization, stressed that from the outset the Air Force had "explored

---

*An interservice conference convened at Headquarters, Tactical Air Warfare Center during November. The conferees wrote a Credible Chase test plan, issued later in the month as TAWC project 1142.[28]

every potential alternative we could identify, ranging from the addition of F–4Es and the Igloo White System to STOL aircraft." He argued that Credible Chase offered the sole workable solution without major impact on the Vietnamese Air Force. Moreover, the mini-gunship would "alleviate the projected firepower and mobility shortfalls within the time, manpower, training, and lead-time constraints."[34]

General Ryan was convinced that the STOL aircraft could clearly strengthen VNAF interdiction operations. He urged that procurement and manpower actions commence without delay, so as to be ready for a favorable outcome of the Credible Chase combat test.[35] Orders accordingly went out to buy fifteen each of the AU–23A Fairchild Peacemaker and the AU–24A Helio Stallion. Every aircraft had five ordnance stations, a side-firing Gatling gun, and sensor monitoring/recording equipment. A night-vision sight was mounted directly to the top of the Gatling gun.

In their December 10 response to Secretary Laird, the Joint Chiefs of Staff concluded that a military requirement did exist for a South Vietnamese interdiction capability. A question still remained whether the STOL aircraft could fill the bill. The mini-gunship had shown some promise in a low-threat area, but the chiefs believed a final assessment should await combat test results. Additionally, they estimated it would take 2,100 new manpower spaces for a five-squadron STOL force. This would entail difficult, drawn-out changes in the Vietnamese Air Force's plans for training, logistics, and manpower. Hence such a force would have to be balanced against other Vietnamese Air Force programs. In this regard the Joint Chiefs spotlighted the views of CINCPAC and COMUSMACV. The latter saw the Vietnamese Air Force was already overextended, with its plans to form nine new squadrons (not counting the five STOL ones) by December 1972.[36]

Later in the reply, the chiefs shifted somewhat from their "wait and see" position. They said they were ordering field commanders to plan for the personnel to support the debut of the STOL aircraft in case the Credible Chase combat evaluation proved successful. The Joint Chiefs of Staff also mentioned their screening of other options to strengthen Vietnamese interdiction, such as a step-up in F–5E production. The F–5E could interdict in a high-threat area and conduct air defense against Migs. Lastly the Joint Chiefs urged Secretary Laird to seek supplemental funding for Credible Chase rather than saddling Service budgets. They based this appeal on the uncertainties in cost and performance of the STOL aircraft.[37]

As preparations for the combat test continued, a series of episodes in early 1972 clouded the STOL aircraft's prospects. In a January memo to the chairman of the Joint Chiefs of Staff, Adm. Elmo R. Zumwalt, Jr., Chief of Naval Operations, declared it was "increasingly evident" that "accelerated RVNAF interdiction programs are taxing RVN resources." Specifically, he alleged that "any early dedication of RVNAF resources to Credible Chase (before final evaluation)" would hamper the Vietnamese Air Force in assuming "support of the South Vietnamese Navy's coastal surveillance, interdiction and riverine operations."[38]

Besides this growing Navy concern, the Joint Chiefs pondered the conditions in South Vietnam, the "accelerated U.S. redeployment schedule, mission priorities, ceiling constraints, and other considerations," plus delays due to deficiences in the STOL aircraft. Then the chiefs proposed canceling the combat phase of the Credible Chase evaluation in favor of testing at Eglin AFB. The Secretary of the Air Force next agreed,[39] and on February 18 the Air Staff canceled the combat test.[40]

A rash of troubles with the STOL aircraft crimped the operational test and evaluation at Eglin. Three Peacemakers arrived there on January 19. Their testing was soon interrupted, when on February 4 they were grounded because of rudder cracks. The first Stallion reached Eglin on March 4,* and on the 17th a decision was made to test it. On April 3, however, the ASD System Program Office ordered a halt to acceptance of Stallions. It wanted to check closely the quality control procedures of the contractor and the Federal Aviation Administration. The result was that flight restrictions were imposed on the Stallion. In the interim, the test of the AU-23As halted for tail assembly modification, and on March 22 all of them were returned to the factory for correction of the rudder cracks.[41]

Air Force headquarters revised the Credible Chase test directive in March 1972. On the 11th of April, the Tactical Air Warfare Center dispatched a new test plan to TAC headquarters. Testing of the Stallion started eleven days later. Though a brief hold on Stallion deliveries took place on May 3, the Systems Command suggested that the tests push ahead with the planes on hand. By May 22, 1972, the operational tests of the AU-24A were completed.[42]

At the same time, testing of the Peacemaker met with more delay. The crash of one of the planes (the pilot escaped injury) triggered a suspension of flying on May 10 until accident investigation results were known. Power failure was found to have been the apparent cause. The Air Force lifted the grounding on the 22d, but operational tests did not resume until June 7. All testing was finished by the 30th of June. As the Credible Chase project came to a close, the AU-23s and the AU-23As flew to Davis-Monthan AFB in Arizona for temporary storage.[43]

The operational test and evaluation reports for the AU-23A and the AU-24A were similar. The Southeast Asia-seasoned evaluators judged both aircraft to have "marginal capability" in armed escort, close air support, hamlet defense, airlift and supply, armed reconnaissance, area and border surveillance, counterinfiltration, and forward air controlling. They concluded that "the aircraft could perform some of the elements of every mission, but not well when compared to aircraft designed for specific mission capability." The aircraft rated only "a marginal capability to perform a day or night interdiction role in a low threat environment." Significantly, the evaluators noted that in every role "the problem of survivability of the aircraft

---

*On February 22, the Air Force had sent the leased Helio Stallion back to the factory, due to a misalignment of the aircraft structure and the left main landing gear.

is extremely questionable in all combat environments except possibly the pure counterinsurgency (guerrillas armed with light single shot or semi-automatic weapons)." Highlighted were mission-degrading weaknesses such as limited airspeed, range, ordnance capacity, visibility, and the fatiguing strain of heavy control forces on pilots.[44]

In a more positive vein, Credible Chase test personnel said "the VNAF pilots, gunners, and mechanics who participated in the program showed potential of attaining skill level equal to their USAF counterparts once they attain a comparable level of experience." Nevertheless, the Vietnamese detachment commander voiced concern over the survivability of the STOL aircraft, and surmised that the Vietnamese Air Force would use it sparingly. Both evaluation reports made the same recommendation—against employment of the Peacemaker and the Stallion.[45]

Despite all the energy expended in behalf of the Credible Chase project, the operational test and evaluation spelled the end of the STOL aircraft. Events in Southeast Asia also had a hand in its demise. While there was little serious argument over the need for Vietnamizing interdiction upon the removal of American forces, there was a long debate and deliberation over the means of achieving this goal. The Secretary of Defense and some others believed that Credible Chase offered the sole solution, given the constraints of time and Vietnamese capabilities. On the other hand, field commanders remained pessimistic about any Vietnamization of interdiction. They questioned the wisdom of pitting the light STOL side-firing aircraft against the enemy's guns, missiles, and possibly Migs. They likewise doubted if the Vietnamese Air Force could assume added burdens.

The Defense Secretary won the argument momentarily, pending the outcome of the combat test. Meanwhile, the slow delivery of STOL aircraft and their structural troubles impeded test progress and acceptance of Credible Chase. There followed a reassessment of plans to use mini-gunships in Vietnam, in light of the violent fighting stemming from the foe's major offensive in March 1972. Competing demands for money and resources mushroomed. The skeptics then had their day. Credible Chase aircraft headed not to South Vietnam but to U.S. storage.

During the time of debate and test of Credible Chase, operational planning forged ahead for Commando Hunt VII, the 1971–72 interdiction campaign. Interdicting enemy supplies promised to be harder than ever before. The North Vietnamese, by November 1, 1971, had stretched their Laotian route by 400 miles of roads.[46] Since 1966 the communists had expanded the Ho Chi Minh Trail three-fold, from a road net of 820 miles to 2,710. Graveling and corduroying had upgraded many of the roads to all-weather.* Also the enemy's staying in the trail area through the wet season presaged an early push of supplies.

---

*The North Vietnamese also speeded work on a new road that would run through the demilitarized zone to the A Shau Valley. It had not been completed when Commando Hunt VII began.

228

Enemy defenses had registered similar improvement. About 655 antiaircraft weapons ranging from 23-mm to 100-mm were in place at the close of the 1970-71 dry season. It appeared that the guns and the surface-to-air missiles had not been shifted from their sites during the rainy months. The total of antiaircraft weapons was expected to increase 20 percent by the start of the 1971-72 campaign. Besides, the North Vietnamese heavily camouflaged the gun emplacements and moved them about the preplanned sites to escape detection. There were in addition signs that Migs could carry out extended ground-controlled interception against Commando Hunt aircraft.

Over the summer months an overall strategy evolved for interdicting the enemy's supply routes. As in past campaigns, the prime effort would go toward interdiction in southern Laos, with air support supplied elsewhere as necessary. The planners proposed greater use of advanced bombing systems, full utilization of sensors for triggering air strikes, and faster tactical adjustments. A three-phase operation was envisioned.

Enemy interdiction would dominate the first phase with Arc Light B-52 Stratofortresses bombing Mu Gia, Ban Karai, and Ban Raving passes. These attacks were to continue as long as the road system stayed wet. Mig combat air patrols (MIGCAPS), consisting of Iron Hand F-105s and EB-66s* would support and protect the B-52s. Every effort would be concentrated on keeping watch over the passes and dropping area-denial and antipersonnel ordnance to prevent road repairs. As road traffic swelled, Arc Light strikes were to zero in on the southern passes of Ban Raving and the western demilitarized zone. The object was to force the trucks to travel over longer, exposed distances. Tactical aircraft would augment the Stratofortresses by pounding critical mountain points with laser-guided bombs.

Phase two called for the use of blocking belts on selected road segments, as supplies trickled down to the central network. A typical blocking belt comprised aerial mines and sensors implanted across naturally narrow route areas. Sensors would also be embedded over possible bypass routes. Task Force Alpha was to monitor the sensor data, noting enemy exertions to skirt the belts or to clear the mine fields. Gunships and other aircraft would then be directed to attack the hoped-for traffic jam behind the blocking belts. As usual the gunships were to work at night, for their own protection and to strike when the trucks were on the move. By day, fighters were to team with FAC aircraft in searching out supply storage points and truck parks.

The third phase dealt with exit interdiction. Seeing that the final supply gates into South Vietnam opened mainly upon wider terrain, B-52s were specified instead of blocking belts. At the same time, gunships and F-4s would press their strikes against moving trucks and storage and parking areas.

The plan's phases were keyed to the expected pattern of the North Vietnamese logistic effort. The initial heavy movement of supplies wound through the mountain passes early in the dry season with a slow decrease

---

*The F-105s were specially equipped to suppress surface-to-air missiles, and radar-controlled antiaircraft weapons. The EB-66s had several configurations for electronic intelligence or for radiation jamming to protect the strike force.

toward the end. Supplies were next stored along the central route structure, with shuttles working them in the direction of southern Laos and Cambodia. The final push of materiel into South Vietnam built by degrees and usually peaked in March and April.

As the dry season set in, the plan was amended to include Vietnamese air interdiction. The Vietnamese Air Force was assigned areas within South Vietnam and border sections where it could strike trucks and storage points. This marked a first step in readying VNAF to conduct the 1972-73 dry season interdiction campaign on its own.

For the 1971-72 campaign, however, the Seventh Air Force saw that Vietnamese interdiction would be sorely crippled by long-range communication deficiencies, want of adequate maintenance, and shortages in qualified people. Notwithstanding, USAF personnel were to show their Vietnamese counterparts how to collect and collate target information, select targets, figure munitions requirements, and schedule and control aircraft. This training would get under way on November 8, 1971. Moreover, the Vietnamese Air Force Air Operations Center at Tan Son Nhut would begin controlling VNAF interdiction sorties in coordination with the Seventh Air Force.

Due to the drawdown of American forces in South Vietnam, total aircraft for interdiction had declined. The 911 U.S. strike aircraft on hand for the previous dry season campaign had sunk to 535 as Commando Hunt VII opened.* By the same token, the Office of the Secretary of Defense authorized 700 gunship and 10,000 tactical air sorties each month for Commando Hunt VII—a drop of 300 and 4,000 per month respectively from last year's campaign. A boost in South Vietnamese, Laotian, and Cambodian sorties was expected to bridge part of the gap.

Abnormally low rainfall in August and September seemed to signify an earlier than usual start of dry season truck movements. But in October a typhoon and two tropical storms disrupted enemy resupply routes. By November 1 the rain stopped, and that date became the official commencement of Commando Hunt VII. Even then, Ban Karai pass remained flooded and traffic barely resumed through Mu Gia pass.

As foreseen, most enemy activity occurred in the pass areas during the first twenty-two days of November. B-52s and tactical aircraft (including Navy planes) hammered the key interdiction entryways. With the creation of blocking belts on November 23, the first and second phases of the plan ran concurrently. Vehicles backed up by, or trying to get around, the mined belts were pummeled by the gunships. The latter flew eighty-five percent of their sorties against trucks on the move or storage points.

Based at Ubon, Thailand, the AC-130 Spectre gunships worked in the Barrel Roll area of Laos as well as in Cambodia, South Vietnam, and the Laotian panhandle. The lion's share of their strikes took place in the central and southern areas of Steel Tiger. For operational purposes, the Laotian

---

*There were 833 aircraft throughout Southeast Asia on December 31, 1971, compared to 1,584 in October 1970. [Hist, USMACV, 1971, II, F-13, F-15.]

panhandle from the passes south was carved into nine sectors. Gunships covered every one of them until the alarming loss of two AC-130s in March 1972. Whereupon the gunships withdrew from all Steel Tiger areas, save sectors six through nine (roughly Ban Bak southward).

The sixteen AC-119K Stinger gunships staged out of Da Nang, SVN, and Nakhon Phanom, Thailand. The Stingers based in Thailand usually operated in Barrel Roll, while those from Da Nang struck targets in the southern portion of Steel Tiger and in South Vietnam. B-57G strike aircraft joined the AC-119Ks in the night interdiction missions.

Commando Hunt VII gunships used basically the tactics of past seasons, but there were changes. To conserve fighters, gunship escorts had been pared to two in high-threat areas during the early part of the campaign. Gunships operating in Barrel Roll continued with three escorts. However, after the loss of a second AC-130 in March, three escorts again became standard for all gunship operations.[47]

Throughout the 1971-72 campaign, extra emphasis was placed on gunship target acquisition. There were several reasons for this. First, computer accuracy in truck-killing presented less of a problem than in the 1970-71 season. Second, the foe more carefully spaced his trucks to avoid big convoys. He likewise seemed to camouflage better and—most important to the gunships—peaked his truck traffic during dawn and dusk hours. This made the gunships more vulnerable, for in the dim light their fighter escorts had trouble acquiring and attacking ground targets. The North Vietnamese also turned heavily to resupply by water, especially using boats on the Mekong River in Cambodia to move equipment to battle fronts. Some gunship crews spotted on a single sortie more than 200 river craft. Over the entire campaign, gunships destroyed 223 and damaged 142 boats and barges.

Aside from offensive tactical concerns, major attention riveted on the refinement of gunship defensive tactics. Compelling this action were the modernized missiles and guns of communist defenses. The loss of an AC-130 to an SA-2 missile on March 29 underscored the dangers gunships faced in areas populated by surface-to-air missiles.

On May 5 the enemy unveiled a new surface-to-air missile threat—the shoulder-fired, infrared-seeking SA-7 Strela. Five SA-7s were fired in the first attack on an AC-130 in the An Loc area. One missile struck the tail section but the gunship was able to land successfully at Tan Son Nhut AB. The Strela's appearance caught gunship crews by surprise and without a ready countermeasure. The menace of enemy antiaircraft guns also burgeoned. Most were 57-mm mounted on tracked vehicles, but larger 85-mm and 100-mm guns were also detected.[48] Fire-control radar assisted some of the antiaircraft weapons. The concentration of antiaircraft fire cut down the number of gunship "kills." The principal tactic used to counteract the enemy threat was a B-52 strike, a response that was effective on more than one occasion. Nevertheless, aircraft battle damage increased during Commando Hunt VII.

As in past Commando Hunt campaigns, the destruction of trucks remained the key in restricting the enemy's logistic flow into South Vietnam,

Cambodia, and Laos. Every truck disabled or destroyed made the North Vietnamese southward movement more costly and difficult. Most attacks on trucks were part of interdiction or in connection with the blocking belts. The gunship again turned out to be the best weapon system of the total interdiction effort, particularly with the blocking-belt strategy.

Sensor-detected truck movements during Commando Hunt VII fell forty percent from the 1970-71 campaign. The drop evidently stemmed from the enemy's extending his pipeline about fifty-five nautical miles south and from his ability to grow and seize foodstuffs in Laos.[49] Thus the foe could cut truck traffic, for he had to haul less food and petroleum.

The night of January 26, 1972, was one of the most rewarding and spectacular for truck hunting. Spectre 12 slipped into Steel Tiger East at 1905, and at once the LLLTV operator picked up a truck that could serve as a boresight target. The AC-130 destroyed the vehicle. While enroute to another sector, a second sensor operator discovered a line of ten trucks. Spectre 12 rolled into attack orbit and succeeded in destroying four and damaging six. Meanwhile the three fighter escorts were busy suppressing ground fire, eventually wiping out a 37-mm site. Within five minutes after this affair, the infrared operator detected twenty more trucks parked alongside a road. Again the crew laid down sharp fire that crippled twelve trucks before low fuel intervened. The gunship then passed location information to Spectre 18 just entering the area. The latter came upon twenty-four parked trucks, destroying nine and damaging fifteen. Gunfighter 1, its fighter escort, hammered the antiaircraft positions. Later in the evening, Spectre 18 found eight more trucks, but could destroy only one and damage four prior to returning to base for fuel. The two Spectre crews ran up a remarkable score for the night—fifteen trucks destroyed and thirty -seven damaged.[50]

In spite of less traffic on the roads, U.S. aircraft destroyed or damaged* 10,609 trucks in the Steel Tiger area from November 1971 through March 1972. The trucks actually destroyed totaled 4,727. The AC-130 gunships accounted for more than one-half (2,782) of these and were credited with nearly seventy percent (7,335) of the totally destroyed or damaged.[†51] AC-119s added 345 trucks destroyed and 595 damaged. The rest were claimed by B-57Gs or various tactical aircraft. Intelligence analysis estimated that of the 30,947 tons of supplies funneled into Steel Tiger by the North Vietnamese only 5,024 tons (sixteen percent) got through to South Vietnam or Cambodia.

The figures below further reveal why the AC-130 stood out as the premier truck-killer. The AC-119 was next best, the F-4 last.

---

*According to bomb damage assessment criteria for gunships, a truck was "destroyed" if it exploded or suffered a sustained fire. A truck was "damaged" if it received a direct hit from a 40-mm shell but no fire or explosion resulted; or took a direct hit from a 20-mm round, sustained no fire or explosion, but did not move.

†A highlight came in March 1972 when a Pave Aegis AC-130E destroyed twelve trucks in fifteen minutes.

	Trucks Destroyed/Damaged (Per Sortie)	Trucks Destroyed/Damaged (Per Truck Sighted)
AC-130	5.37	.89
AC-119	2.14	.67
F-4	.29	.29

More gunships operated in Commando Hunt VII than in the 1970–71 campaign, but the gunship sorties (1,806) in Steel Tiger were just about the same as the year before. Save for two sorties, all gunship truck-killing took place at night. The AC–130s averaged 3 hours time-over-target, AC–119Ks, 2.2, and B–57Gs,1. Sorties and truck-kills peaked in the latter half of January 1972 then tapered off.

Apart from Steel Tiger, the sole lucrative place for hunting trucks was Barrel Roll (northeastern Laos). The 1,577 trucks disabled there amounted to only twelve percent of the total damaged or destroyed throughout Southeast Asia. The AC–130s claimed more than half of the 1,577 and the AC–119Ks took credit for 417. Both type gunships chalked up far better results per sortie in Steel Tiger. In Barrel Roll they were called upon more often to support troops under fire, leaving less time for truck-hunting. Then, too, there were no sensors employed there. Even so, U.S. aircraft averaged about ten disabled trucks a day in this region.

Fewer than 700 vehicles were knocked out in Cambodia and South Vietnam. A good many of these were disabled in South Vietnam during February–March 1972.[52]

Statistics can not catch the human element in air operations. Through many sorties the emotions of gunship crews ran the gamut from fear, tenseness, exhilaration, confusion, to even a businesslike professional calm. Crews singly or as a team reacted in sundry ways to varying combat conditions. Success of a mission and at times survival hinged on the failings and the greatness of human judgment, and maybe a bit of luck.

The exemplary efforts of Spectre 21's crew on November 14, 1971, were a case in point. The gunship was flying night armed reconnaissance over heavily defended Laotian supply routes when Capt. Charles E. Baertl, aircraft commander, fixed on a moving vehicle. While tracking the "mover," the AC–130 drew heavy antiaircraft fire. About twenty seconds after Spectre 21 swung into attack orbit, a bright flash and muffled explosion suddenly occurred near engines three and four. The plane pitched left and down, Captain Baertl and copilot struggling to regain aircraft control. The navigator furnished altitude and heading data required to reach friendly territory. The flight engineer feverishly checked systems to see if the gunship could stay aloft. Two forward gunners rushed to aid the right scanner, thrown from his position by the blast. Other crewmembers gave the aircraft commander their status and the plane's condition near their stations.

Spectre 21 dropped 2,500 feet before the pilots recovered control. A survey disclosed that the explosion had separated the propellers and forward halves of both number three and four engines. There appeared to be fire close to number three engine, so necessary precautions were taken. A checkout of controls revealed a gradual but constant loss of altitude. Consequently, crewmen not needed at their positions began to jettison 7,460 pounds of ammunition and equipment. Inside of five minutes they finished the task. Once over safer territory, the copilot notified ground personnel of the gunship's plight. Meanwhile, Captain Baertl and the rest of the crew readied the plane for a landing. At a point nearly twelve miles from base, the instruments of number two engine warned of possible turbine failure and imminent power loss. Careful throttle adjustments were therefore made to avoid loss of a third engine. Amid gusty winds the pilots and crew skillfully coaxed the gunship in to a safe landing—averting possible injuries from bailout over rugged Laotian terrain and loss of a $6 million aircraft. Spectre 21's crew had weathered a dangerous crisis.[53]

A similar instance of gunship crew heroics took place on March 30, 1972, during night armed reconnaissance over Laos. Capt. Waylon O. Fulk, commander of Spectre 22, and his crew destroyed or damaged three enemy supply trucks and touched off four secondary fires and explosions. While attacking the third truck to make sure it was destroyed, the gunship flew into a solid barrage of 57- and 37-mm AA fire. One 57-mm round slammed into the right wing and another ripped the right side of the fuselage. Fuel leaking from a pylon tank burst into flames, enveloping the right wing. The spray of burning fuel also set fires on the fuselage's right side.

Captain Fulk ordered all emergency measures to put out the fires. Seeing the seriousness of the situation, he directed the other fourteen crewmembers to prepare for bailout. Fulk steered the Spectre away from the intense antiaircraft fire, while reporting the emergency to controlling radar stations and nearby aircraft. A plane soon came along and advised the gunship crew on the extent of the damage. Steadying the wounded Spectre as best he could, the aircraft commander called for crew bailout and radioed position information. Serving as jumpmaster, the illuminator operator informed Captain Fulk that thirteen of the crew had "hit the silk." Fulk engaged the automatic pilot and placed the gunship in a slight turn to insure a crash-landing heading away from friendly territory. He then joined the illuminator operator at the AC-130's cargo ramp. After checking parachute harnesses, both men jumped. Moments later, the fires and ammunition explosions turned the aircraft into three plummeting fireballs. Next day all fifteen crewmembers were picked up, the largest and most successful mass crew rescue ever recorded.[54]

Night after night on combat sorties most gunship crewmen performed as professionally and courageously as those described above. Many experienced an aircraft shuddering from enemy antiaircraft fire, equipment malfunctions, and target searches frustrated by weather. Some survived combat, some did not. All joined those countless men down through the ages who braved the battle. "What battles have in common is human: the behaviour of men struggling to reconcile their instinct for self-preservation, their sense of honour and the achievement of some aim over which other men are ready to kill them."[53] The gunship successes and failures were inseparable from the individuals involved—the indispensable human element.

Commando Hunt VII came to a close on March 31, 1972. Though truck traffic had somewhat diminished in parts of Steel Tiger, the chief reason for the early ending was the enemy's big spring offensive. The North Vietnamese struck with ferocity and strength on three major fronts. Virtually all aircraft, especially the available gunships, were hard-pressed to satisfy combat demands within South Vietnam.

Plans captured in January 1972 told of an offensive by the North Vietnamese during Tet in mid-February. Reported sightings of tanks and 130-mm guns near the demilitarized zone and the central highlands seemed to confirm this intention. At the same time, there was no letup in the harassment of air bases by the North Vietnamese and Viet Cong. On February 6 the concerned Joint Chiefs of Staff ordered preemptive air strikes. A forty-eight hour, maximum strike was to be made on forces believed poised for attacks on the central highlands. Another forty-eight hours of strikes would follow against troops in the demilitarized zone and Military Region 1 border areas. The chiefs wanted the air operations completed before the close of the Tet holidays on February 17. The gunships played a key part in this intensified effort, flying fifty-eight sorties.

To further brace for the expected onslaught, changes in the rules of engagement created new prevalidated target areas near the highlands (Military Regions I and II of South Vietnam). Inside these specified strike zones, gunships had blanket approval to hit any military target. Hence they could respond more quickly to targets of opportunity.[56]

The enemy failed to loose his offensive during Tet, but the buildup persisted. On March 30 the expected came. The North Vietnamese army rolled across the demilitarized zone in a full-scale conventional attack, strongly supported by artillery and tanks. The objective appeared to be seizure of Quang Tri and the old imperial capital of Hue. Meanwhile, slower-developing drives into the provinces of Kontum in Military Region II and Binh Long in Military Region III left no doubt that the communists had kicked off a massive three-pronged invasion. The crucial test of Vietnamization and possibly the survival of South Vietnam was at hand.

As North Vietnamese infantry, armor, and artillery spilled into Military Region I, the South Vietnamese Joint General Staff ordered general reserve forces to bolster ARVN divisions in the threatened areas. The U.S. response chiefly consisted of naval gunfire and tactical air strikes by Navy, Marine and Air Force aircraft. The gunships flew close air support, armed reconnaissance, and interdiction.

In the first stages of the offensive, marginal weather crimped air operations. Typical weather problems plagued a mission that took place on the evening of March 30. The 8th Battalion of Vietnamese marines at Fire Support Base Holcomb requested a flareship and gunship. An Air Force AC-119K answered the call and orbited the base for 1½ hours. The Stinger could not lock onto a ground beacon despite the yeoman efforts of U.S. Marine

Corps advisors in the teeth of intense enemy artillery fire. The use of an infrared strobe light eventually enabled the gunship to locate the target area, discharge flares, and fire on enemy positions. When the weather worsened, the AC-119K had to break off the mission.[57]

The enemy's large-scale use of artillery—derived no doubt from standard Soviet army strategy and tactics—markedly unnerved the many South Vietnamese defenders in the Quang Tri-Hue areas. Of special concern were the heavy guns such as the 130-mm. Gunship supporters believed their aircraft might be useful in countering the enemy shelling. Colonel Gentzel, Air Staff gunship advocate, headed a team from the Aeronautical Systems Division and 415th Special Operations Training Squadron that visited Ubon in April 1972. The team briefed Spectre crews on gunship tactics for ferreting out and destroying big artillery guns. The design of these tactics had been done earlier to fill a State Department request for aid to Royal Laotian units being shelled by large-caliber pieces near embattled Long Tieng.

The basic antiartillery tactical concept called for AC-130 gunships to approach an area at a specific minimum altitude and search with the infrared sensor for the distinctive heat pattern of enemy guns. The most difficult task, of course, was finding the target. Once it was located, the gunship would go into attack orbit, firing its Pave Aegis 105-mm gun. Or it could request a strike by B-52s or by a F-4 armed with a Pave Sword (laser-guided bomb). Combat Sierra, employing an air-droppable X-band beacon (miniponder), would be put to work if B-52s were involved.

Even though antiartillery tactics with B-52s proved successful in U.S. tests, they were never tried in South Vietnam. The press of the enemy offensive and the rising demand for Stratofortress strikes militated against scheduling B-52s for joint operations with gunships. In addition, communist artillery fire often ceased when AC-130s were in the vicinity.

As gunships were diverted from their role as truck-killers over the Ho Chi Minh Trail, they countered assaults on fire support bases and other defensive points. However, a full fifty-five percent of their sorties through April–June 1972 were in support of troops in contact with the enemy.[58] The majority of gunship actions in Military Region I tended to be nearer Hue. This was due mainly to North Vietnamese attempts to disrupt air attacks, by shifting antiaircraft guns and SAMs closer to the battlefields around Quang Tri.

Of the sundry AC-130 sorties in Military Region I supporting troops in contact, these were typical. On July 27, Spectre 14 received credit for killing six of the enemy. While saturating ten to twelve percent of a target area surrounding a fire support base, a Spectre on August 10 broke an attack by scattering troops and silencing mortar sites. During September 26-27, a Spectre came to the aid of a friendly position under fire. The defenders passed coordinates of enemy troop concentrations to the Spectre and the gunship crew attacked, observing one secondary explosion. Later reports showed that the AC-130 had blown up 2,000 rounds of 60- and 82-mm mortar ammunition, and killed fourteen of the foe.[59]

The growing dependence on AC-119K and AC-130 gunships to assist troops under attack created initial operational difficulties. In the reconnaissance sectors of Steel Tiger, gunship crews had controlled air traffic. But in South Vietnam, control at the scene of engagement fell to a forward air controller in a light observation plane. Inasmuch as these FACs were accustomed to working with fighters, they frequently did not know what the gunship could do. A gunship would be orbiting unable to fire, while the controller directed fighters in air support strikes. In fact, the fixed-wing gunships and other components of tactical air had not kept in close touch with one another over the past few years. This severely sapped the coordination so vital to best operations.[60]

Despite ARVN troop reinforcements along with VNAF and USAF air strikes, the defense of Quang Tri City failed. The South Vietnamese lost many forward bases and retreated toward the threatened cities. Over a span of thirty-three days, the North Vietnamese army captured Quang Tri City and the entire northern province. The defeat triggered changes in RVNAF command structure in Military Region 1. President Nguyen Van Thieu assigned Lt. Gen. Ngo Quang Truong the task of defending Hue and retaking Quang Tri. While work proceeded around the clock to shore up Hue's defenses, the enemy had to move his armor and artillery closer to the old capital.

During the first week of May, the Seventh Air Force and Vietnamese air power went all-out to choke off the enemy's movement and resupply. One group of more than a hundred trucks was isolated between destroyed bridges north of Hue. The air strikes destroyed many of these trucks as well as numerous tanks throughout the area. At the end of the invasion's first ninety days, the defensive approaches to Hue seemed secured, and the regrouped South Vietnamese forces counterattacked. They focused on retaking Quang Tri City in a frontal assault, against the recommendation of U.S. advisors. Bearing the brunt of the bloody and costly fighting, battle-weary South Vietnamese marines retook the Quang Tri Citadel on September 16, 1972.[61] Though the North Vietnamese still held big chunks of territory in the northern provinces of South Vietnam, their offensive had not only been stalled but thrown back in several key areas.

Many military analysts placed the focal point of the enemy offensive in Military Region II. They predicted the capture of Kontum, Pleiku, all of the central highlands, followed by a possible push to the sea to cut South Vietnam in two. The swift loss of South Vietnamese control over Tam Quan, Hoai Nhon, and Hoai An districts of coastal Binh Dinh Province lent credence to this belief. Until mid-May, however, action in the central highlands remained surprisingly minor. Then an upsurge in attacks at Tan Canh/Dak To and smaller fire support bases along Rocket Ridge presaged the major attacks of May 4 and 24 on Kontum City.

Gunship support matched the mounting attacks on forward bases. An AC-119K, for example, helped out Dak Pek Ranger Camp on April 19–20. The ARVN camp commander estimated that Stinger fire left sixty to eighty communist casualties. On April 21 barrages of mortar and artillery fire rocked the Forward Support Base Delta, followed by a ground attack bolstered by three tanks. A Stinger covered the withdrawal of the defenders to Fire Support Base Delta South while a Spectre opened fire on the tanks and reported one hit. The defenders knocked out all three before completing their retreat.

Even though air support to the Tan Canh/Dak To region soared dramatically, the tactical situation worsened as the enemy cut roads and isolated bases. Sightings of tanks grew more frequent. On April 23, 1972, an ARVN 22d Division forward element reported thirty tanks moving south on Route 14 toward Tan Canh. A Pave Aegis AC–130E on station flew to the scene and positively identified ten tanks accompanied by other vehicles. The Spectre raked the tanks with 105-mm cannon fire, destroying one and damaging four.

That same evening, Capt. Russell T. Olson piloted a Spectre to the beleaguered Tan Canh/Dak To area. The Pave Aegis gunship braved 23-mm and 51-caliber antiaircraft fire to break up a concentration of tanks rumbling toward friendly positions. Upon return to Pleiku AB the AC–130E could not find a replacement aircraft, so it made a fast turnaround and was back over the battlefield by dawn. The gunship descended through a thick cloud layer to support ground troops, meeting with 57-mm and other antiaircraft fire. The Spectre drew the fire from two tanks onto itself and away from a helicopter trying to lift out eleven U.S. Army advisors. Though low on fuel, the AC–130E acted as FAC for newly arrived tactical aircraft that could not locate the targets because of the clouds, haze, and smoke. The gunship did not leave the battle until the rescue operation was completed. The Seventh Air Force credited the Spectre with putting at least seven of the tanks out of action.[62]

The performance of the Pave Aegis gunships fired the ground troops with enthusiasm. Whenever a Spectre appeared, they asked if it had "the big gun." The AC–130Es with the 105-mm cannon earned this response. Comprising only 12.5 percent of the fleet, they accounted for 55 percent of the tanks damaged or destroyed. Pave Aegis also got credit for knocking out a major road bridge on Highway 13.[63]

In May the overall military situation in Military Region II became more critical. North Vietnamese forces struck key points northwest of Kontum City, and enemy artillery zeroed in on the city itself. Moreover, the Joint General Staff withdrew 1,000–1,500 airborne troops sorely needed in Kontum and sent them to Saigon.[64] Concern for the capital's safety was apparently behind this move.

On May 5 communist tanks and troops fought their way to the wire of Polei Kleng compound, but strike aircraft and AC–130s helped repel the threat to overrun the camp. At the Ben Het Ranger Camp, a Spectre also beat back attackers. On the 6th the enemy struck Polei Kleng once more, this time with a regiment-size force. The situation grew so serious that U.S. advisors were removed. Air commanders diverted an AC–130E to Military

Region II to aid the camp defenders. Speaking directly with the South Vietnamese ground commander, the gunship crew poured minigun and cannon fire all around his position. The only targets seen from the air were muzzle flashes and a bridge. So far as the AC–130E crew could tell, the night's work amounted to expending a full load of ammunition, including ninety-six 105-mm rounds. Bomb damage assessment totaled one large secondary explosion and fire on the bridge and the silencing of a few mortars.

Not until June did the Spectre crew learn that the Defense Intelligence Agency credited them with killing 350 enemy soliders, repulsing a full-scale attack by a North Vietnamese regiment, and saving the lives of 1,000 friendlies. The episode underscored how hard it was to record results of the gunship's support of troops in battle. Since their truck-killing could be verified quite closely, the gunship crews found the usual absence of specifics from their attacks to aid troops somewhat demoralizing. Nevertheless, the ground report of "situation quiet" as a gunship departed an area was often compensation enough.[65]

In addition to Polei Kleng and Ben Het, the AC–130s and strike air-craft helped score temporary successes at other points on the approaches to Kontum City—Dak Pek, Dak Seang, and Plei Mrong. Still, the tremendous enemy pressure on these outlying defensive positions deepened concern as to how long they could be held. The answer soon came. On May 9 communist troops overran Polei Kleng Camp and the defenders withdrew. Meantime, infantry and tanks breached Ben Het's perimeter. Efforts to heli-lift out the 71st Ranger Battalion failed because of the heavy antiaircraft fire from the surrounding enemy sites. Once again Spectre gunships were called upon to hold the foe at bay by flares and fire. By May 11 the camp was free of the enemy.[66]

More and more enemy tanks and troops appeared near Kontum City. On May 14 the hammer fell. An infantry battalion and eleven tanks attacked the city from the north and northwest. The ARVN 23d Division fought tenaciously, and engaged the tanks with M–72 light antitank weapons. A Spectre lent a hand, and on May 15 reported nine secondary explosions and the possible destruction of a tank north of the city. Spectres likewise assisted C–130 resupply missions at the threatened and bombarded Kontum airport. The gunship flew escort for the Hercules, suppressing antiaircraft fire. Often the mere presence of a Spectre orbiting the airfield silenced communist guns and rockets. The combined actions of ARVN forces, gunships and tactical aircraft, and C–130 resupply missions nevertheless fell short. On May 23 the enemy gained a foothold in Kontum City and, in a related attack to the south, pounded Pleiku AB with rockets.

The crucial and seesaw struggle for Kontum City raged for several days. The Vietnamese Air Force and U.S. tactical air aided the defenders by day, while the B–52s and gunships afforded night protection. A typical action took place on May 26 when a Spectre scattered four tanks, one of which was firing at the city. Air power kept the foe constantly confused from May 27 to 29, even though he held the east end of the city and the south side of the airport runway. The North Vietnamese and Viet Cong failed to advance, and on June 1 the South Vietnamese began clearing out pockets of them in counterattacks. By June 8 there were no enemy left in the city. Communist losses during the campaign for Kontum (May 14–June 6) included 5,688 killed and 38 tanks destroyed, compared to 382 and 3 for the friendlies.[67]

The airpower brought to bear on the enemy proved a major factor in halting his Military Region II offensive. In spite of serious problems in coordinating air strikes, Vietnamese aircraft, U.S. tactical air, B–52s, and gunships severely punished the communists. The initial difficulty in making known what the gunship could do was never entirely overcome, particularly with respect to forward air controllers. All the same, the versatile AC–119Ks and AC–130s were potent mainstays in the defense of the central highlands.

The third prong of the enemy's spring offensive pushed down Highway 13 into Military Region III, piercing Loc Ninh and An Loc of Binh Long Province. The road ran through huge rubber plantations and at times wore a heavy canopy of rain-forest foliage. The chief military position along the way after leaving Cambodia was An Loc, the provincial capital. Some seventy-six kilometers farther south lay the real communist goal—Saigon.

The North Vietnamese and Viet Cong tried to trick the South Vietnamese and Americans into thinking that the main attack would be by way of Tay Ninh. Intelligence data depicted the North Vietnamese Army 7th and Viet Cong 5th and 9th Divisions poised just across the Cambodian border, ready to move out. But in truth, the 5th had the task of capturing Loc Ninh then pressing on to An Loc. The 7th was to cut the highway south of the provincial capital, and prevent reinforcements from reaching it. The 9th would go straight to An Loc. After capturing the city, the divisions would continue on to Saigon.

The Military Region III offensive jumped off in the early hours of April 5, and passed through three distinct stages. The enemy first occupied Loc Ninh, then went on to attack An Loc, which was surrounded and cut off from reinforcement by road. Fierce frontal assaults on the provincial capital's defenses faltered, largely due to air power and especially the gunships. This led to the second stage, a lengthy siege of the city. Finally, when the North Vietnamese and Viet Cong found their strength waning under the constant aerial bombardment around An Loc, they again mounted an all-out attack. From the moment the communists spilled into Binh Long Province, the gunships flew without letup. Their operations figured greatly in the eventual repulse of the enemy's advance.

At the very outset of the furious fighting, Spectre and Stinger gunships supported the South Vietnamese troops. Loc Ninh (a town of about 4,000) bore the brunt of the first major assaults by heavy artillery, tanks, and two regiments. Hemmed in two compounds at opposite ends of the town near the airstrip, the defenders called for gunship support during the first day and night. Many ground attacks were beaten back, but the Viet Cong and North Vietnamese crowded close to the compounds to escape the air strikes. As the defenses bent to the enemy's blows, Capt. Mark A. "Zippo" Smith, U.S. Army (the American advisor) cleared an AC–130 to fire inside his compound. By noon the next day, three large-scale ground assaults had been shattered by fighter-bomber and gunship fire. Communist troops tried to break through the eastside defenses of the command post compound, and the gunships killed many of them on the wires. More attacks followed, backed by 75-mm recoilless and 122-mm rocket fire and spearheded by tanks. On April 8 the flood of enemy engulfed Loc Ninh positions and swept on toward An Loc.

As in Military Regions I and II, the number of aircraft responding to requests for assistance spawned command and control problems. Gunships found themselves shunted aside by forward air controllers, so strike aircraft could make target runs. Sometimes the controllers erred in thinking Spectres were merely flareships, and failed to exploit their full potential. A briefing of FAC pilots by AC-130 crewmen worked out most of the coordination kinks. Moreover, nearly all combatants in the air and on the ground soon realized how accurately the gunships could apply their fearful firepower.

A striking example of such firepower came as the main body of Loc Ninh defenders retreated toward An Loc. Among the wounded left behind were Capt. Marvin C. Zumwalt, U.S. Army (an infantry advisor to the ARVN 18th Division) and fifteen South Vietnamese troops. Spectres continuously circled the small group, placing a ring of covering fire to within 350–400 meters of the wounded men. When one AC-130 returned to base, another took over. Finally on April 8, medical evacuation helicopters whirled in through heavy fire and plucked out the wounded.

The thunder of heavy artillery shelling on April 12 announced the opening of the battle for already encircled An Loc. At 0730 on the 13th, two dozen tanks (T-54s and PT-76s) led to sizable ground assault out of the northeast. At 1015 the communists unleashed a second attack from the northwest. An ARVN relief column tangled with the enemy and was stopped south of the city.[68]

As the onslaught stepped up, the AC-130s operated around the clock. Things turned so critical that the gunship crews worked directly with a U.S Army ground commander. He did not hesitate using the gunships, often calling for fire close to friendly positions. Now and then, Spectres were asked to strike enemy points across the street from South Vietnamese emplacements. Told by spotters to make gun corrections as small as one meter, the gunship crews came to know which street and house they had to destroy. Even the AC-130's 20-mm guns garnered praise, one commander radioing, "Great Spec! There are bodies everywhere. They're stacked up like cordwood." At other times, the Pave Aegis pinpointed fire on dug-in troops. On May 16, for example, a Spectre got credit for wiping out one 75-mm recoilless rifle and two 82-mm mortar sites with its 105-mm cannon.[69]

Overall, the air strikes dealt deadly blows to enemy assaults while South Vietnamese troops fought valiantly. Gunships and tactical air stopped and knocked out tanks, destroyed supply vehicles, and killed many troops. In the face of intense enemy antiaircraft fire, various aircraft helped ground forces splinter still another attack on April 15. By the 16th the first attack phase had ended, and true to President Thieu's word, the An Loc defenses held. Now the siege began.

With the shift to strangulation-starvation tactics, the communists quickened the rhythmic barrages from the 105- and 155-mm howitzers and 122- and 107-mm rockets. Nearly 10,000 civilians (mostly refugees) compounded the problems of water, food, sanitation, shelter, and medical treatment within the besieged city. Aerial resupply became a must to shore up the morale of the defenders, as well as to bring in survival items. However, stiff antiaircraft fire made daylight airdrops difficult and a nighttime confusion of lights caused the loss of dropped materiel.

During the siege the AC–130s and AC–119Ks switched on their two-kw lights to mark drop zones for C–130 supply aircraft. The gunships located the zone with sensors and, upon request of the Hercules, illuminated it an instant before release of the supply bundle. The light gave the C–130 crews a key reference point, but drew lethal antiaircraft fire to the gunships. So in lieu of the lighting, the Spectres and Stingers supplied fire suppression for the airdrops. Fortunately, resupply methods advanced and in turn boosted the spirits of the An Loc defenders. Between May 4–9, U.S. aircraft dropped 492 bundles and ninety-four percent of them were recovered. Given this success, the chance that the enemy could starve the city into submission started to fade.

In the interim the NVA/VC siege sites came under constant air bombardment, disrupting supplies and killing many troops. Their strength ebbing, the communists realized that another all-out attack to take the city had to be made soon. Preceded by a fearsome 7,000-round artillery barrage, a tank-infantry assault hit An Loc on May 11.

The North Vietnamese and Viet Cong drove a wedge into ARVN defenses in both the northeast and western sections of the city. They hoped to split the defenders in two. The South Vietnamese commander swiftly placed his 5th Airborne Battalion between the two salients, allowing time for air power to strike. Gunships, B–52s, and fighter-bombers pounded the troops in the two ruptures. The enemy positions in the northeast were so narrow that only Spectre armament could be applied safely. The AC–130s routed the communists from bunkers with 105-mm fire. On one occasion the foe fled into automatic Claymore mines that had been carefully set out in anticipation of his flight.[70]

Throughout the night of May 12, the fierce fighting persisted. The enemy pressed an attack spearheaded by PT–76 light amphibious tanks. Six B–52 strikes blunted the assault, destroying two tanks and an ammunition dump. When the weather improved, the Spectres took to the air. Maj. Gen. James F. Hollingsworth, U.S. Army, commanding general of the Third Regional Assistance Command, cited Spectre's "magnificent performance" in marginal weather during this difficult phase of the battle.

Over the second day of the renewed attack, the communists sought to offset the U.S. and South Vietnamese air advantage with Strela missiles.

An AC–130 detected five Strela firings. One missile hit the gunship, causing extensive damage, but the gunship limped back to base.

Regardless of Strela's disruption of air operations, the strength of the enemy forces dwindled. The last of the North Vietnamese and Viet Cong were driven from An Loc on June 12, and two days later U.S. helicopters whisked in 1,650 fresh troops. Not until the 23d, however, did the ARVN relief column finally manage to break the cordon around the city. The remnants of Military Region III attacking divisions slowly melted into Cambodia, leaving behind a thoroughly devastated An Loc, but one proudly controlled by South Vietnam.

There were many ingredients in the successful defense of An Loc—B–52s, tactical aircraft, forward air controllers, C–130 supply crews, resolute South Vietnamese troops, and good U.S. Army advisors. Certainly fixed-wing gunships had to be added to this far from complete list. Spectres and Stingers won credit (indeed praise) for splintering enemy attacks, driving communists out of dug-in positions, suppressing anti-aircraft fire, lifting the morale of friendly troops, interdicting trucks and other vehicles, and assisting air cargo deliveries. The senior advisor to ARVN 5th Division cited the gunships as "responsible for breaking up numerous assaults before they got started."[71]

General Abrams, U.S. Army, COMUSMACV, told General John W. Vogt, Jr., Seventh Air Force commander, that three weapons had been unqualified successes—the TOW,* the guided bomb, and the AC–130.[72] The battle for An Loc seemed destined to stand as the classic example of fixed-wing gunship excellence in support of embattled and besieged troops.

The 1972 spring offensive brought the gunships full circle to their original role of supporting troops under attack. In the 1960s the AC–47 first achieved fame for hamlet defense. Now vastly more sophisticated AC–119Ks and AC–130s helped defend fire support bases in Military Region I, Kontum in Military Region II, and An Loc in Military Region III. While the tasks of the early and late gunships stayed strikingly the same with respect to supporting ground forces, the level of warfare changed radically. The AC–47s had operated under counterinsurgency conditions. In the 1972 offensive the communists waged a war of medium intensity with massed infantry, tanks, heavy artillery, and advanced equipment. As the conflict escalated in tactics and weapons, so did the might of the AC–130s and AC–119Ks. Hence 1972 gunship missions harked back to the 1960s, but the battle scenes and combatants were decidedly different.

No doubt the communists had planned in the offensive to offset the U.S. and South Vietnamese airpower edge with wide use of antiaircraft artillery and the new SA–7 Strela missile. They did restrict gunship activity, notably in Military Region I areas, and force changes in tactics.

---

*Tube-launched, optically-tracked, wire-guided missile. Mounted on U.S. Air Cavalry UH-1 helicopters, this weapon destroyed many enemy tanks.

Top: Crewmembers steady a 105-mm howitzer during installation into an AC-130H; bottom: Personnel of the 16th SOS mount a 105-mm howitzer in an AC-130H.

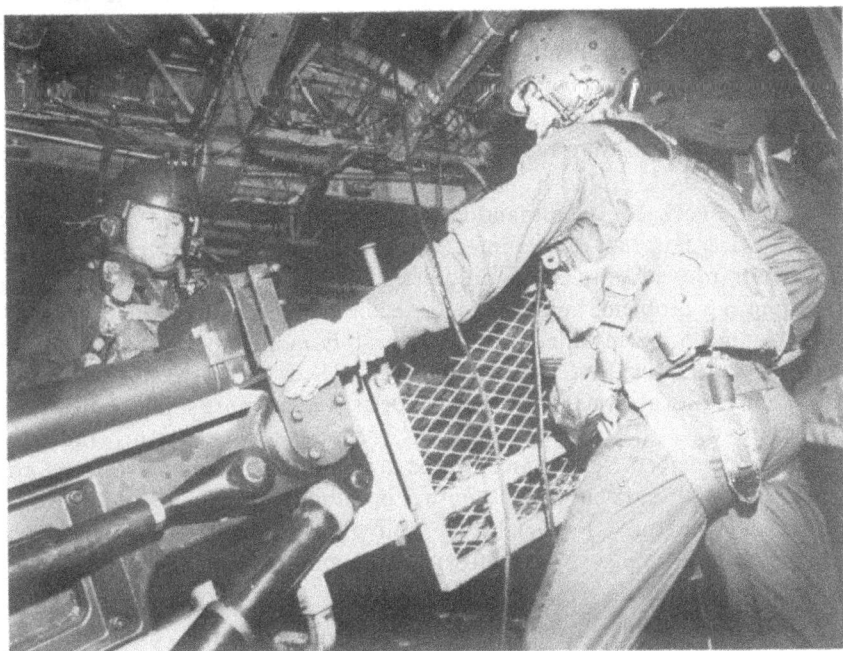

Top left: AC–130 crewman loads shell into the breech of an Army 105-mm howitzer; top right: Close-up of a sensor device and opening for a 40-mm gun on an AC–130; bottom: MSgt. Jacob E. Mercer and Sgt. Lonnie R. Blevins stand near the breech of a 105-mm howitzer, mounted in an AC–130 Gunship, ready to reload.

Overall, however, the North Vietnamese underestimated the strength of that air power and its ability to adjust to fresh tactical challenges. This mistake proved decisive in thwarting the enemy's main goals.

By late summer 1972, the pressure on the gunship squadrons to support embattled troops had eased. Such missions sharply decreased, and more emphasis went to aiding Cambodian forces and to interdicting enemy supply lines. As in past years, preparations began for yet another dry season interdiction effort on the Ho Chi Minh road network.

The cutback in Spectre sorties during the third quarter of 1972 coincided with the onset of bad weather and the return to the United States of six AC–130As for inspection. By September the 16th Special Operations Squadron had but eight AC–130s available for operations: five E and three A models. This weakened force nevertheless destroyed or damaged 180 enemy trucks and 58 boats.

The departure of the six AC–130As created personnel problems, due chiefly to the lack of flying for the A-model crewmembers left behind. An accelerated crew training program commenced, both to keep personnel active and sharp and to upgrade the skills of newcomers to the unit. The excess in A-model members resulted in selected ones being cross-trained into their respective E-model positions. In addition a surplus of aerial gunners led to some tour curtailments. On July 1, 1972, the manning of the 16th Special Operations Squadron shrank by 212, when maintenance functions and men were reassigned to the 8th Organizational Maintenance Squadron.

Spadework for Commando Hunt IX focused mainly on finding a faster flare launcher to counter the SA–7 missile. The LAU–74 flare dispenser proved unreliable for quick reaction against the Strela. After probing the problem, an ASD team recommended that the SUU–25 C/A flare launcher be installed on the A and E models of the AC–130. On September 25 the first wing-mounted SUU–25 C/As were installed.

Aeronautical Systems Division experts studied more sophisticated ways to nullify the SA–7, among them a radar-type detector, radiation intelligence detectors, and an infrared transmitter. Changing the type and color of the aircraft paint was another possibility in reducing the gunship's infrared "signature" (especially by sun glint).[73] As in countering prior enemy defense changes, great effort was devoted to enhancing the gunship and assuring its survival.

Though prime attention was given to AC–130 improvements, AC–119K personnel encountered equally difficult problems afflicting their operations and their aging Stingers. Weapon mechanics and illuminator operators serving as antiaircraft scanners were a case in point. They suffered a rash of colds, ear and throat infections, and back ailments that imposed an extra workload on the well crewmembers. Since the exhaustion and low morale of the scanners threatened to curtail operations, AC–119K experts devised, fashioned, and tested a windscreen for both sides of the gunship. The screens cut crew exposure to the slipstream, and thus slashed time lost to the above ailments by around eighty percent. A dearth of specialists also endangered the sortie rate. The Air Staff responded with a worldwide screening of records to identify men with C-119 experience. Those with needed skills were sent to Southeast Asia on ninety days temporary duty to supplement the Stinger crews. Supervisors emphasized leadership and information programs to help these men with the morale problems inherent in temporary duty tours.

The lack of replacement parts was one more operational headache. The cure flowed from a careful review of parts consumption rates, followed by stock level adjustments and shortening of reordering leadtimes. Lastly, AC-119K squadron personnel matched their AC-130 counterparts in toiling vigorously in solutions to the SA-7 threat.

Meanwhile, combat-mission demands intensified in Cambodia. Communist forces increased the pressure on President Lon Nol's struggling Cambodian troops, and many calls went out for gunship support. The fighting spread over wide areas of Cambodia, but more and more the conflicts centered on roads and towns not far from Phnom Penh. Lon Nol's soldiers sought to keep open the supply routes to several key provincial centers, even resorting to offensive sweeps. On his part, the enemy was obviously intent on isolating cities and positions, and trapping units.

A typical AC-130 support action took place on August 8 in the southern Cambodia-Kampong Trabeck area. A ground forward air guide reported a mass of communist troops advancing on his position with tanks and three 75-mm guns. As ammunition ran low, the forward air guide declared a tactical emergency. Working with the guide's directions, a Spectre destroyed one tank, caused abandonment of the 75-mm weapons, and forced the enemy to retreat. At the time the gunship headed for home base, a forward air controller confirmed that the foe was disorganized and pulling back.[74]

To choke off or disrupt supplies for Phnom Penh, the enemy set up sites on the Mekong River. Serious food shortages by September in the Cambodian capital brought river convoys and rice barges up the Mekong. The AC-130s flew cover for this exposed fleet, orbiting and pouring fire into shoreline attackers. The operation turned out so well that gunship-escorted convoys plied the river during the following months and on into 1973.[75]

Though deeply enmeshed in Cambodia, the gunships assumed a new mission on August 17, 1972. Nagging concern swelled around protection of the Saigon area (the Capital Military District) through the night hours. A number of intelligence analysts and political figures believed that the North Vietnamese and Viet Cong might try a newsmaking attack on Saigon. They expected it to be timed with the peace negotiations and the forthcoming U.S. elections. In the plans for combat air patrol over Saigon, two gunships were to fly overlapping coverage every night. One would stay in orbit while the other landed for refueling and rearming. At first the combat air patrol staged out of Bien Hoa, but this base was open to attack. Operations therefore shifted to Tan Son Nhut AB.[76]

Early on, ARVN units thought the combat air patrol Spectres were merely flareships and used them solely for flaring. Moreover, ground commanders did not understand that these AC–130s could fire without seeing the ground. The matter cleared up considerably after beacons were issued to ARVN troops and briefings explained what the gunship could do. An added boost to the combat air patrol came from a personnel radar detection network. The net passed information on infiltrators through a central command post to the orbiting gunship for attack.

The results of the Capital Military District patrol were somewhat nebulous. Although reports of troops killed by gunships were rare, no rocket attacks on Tan Son Nhut ensued so long as Spectres orbited the area. The combat air patrol lasted until the truce commenced on January 27, 1973.[77]

As 1972 closed, the AC–119Ks and AC–130s still ranged far and wide on diverse missions. Calls for gunships sounded in Laos, Cambodia, and each military region of South Vietnam. The Spectres and Stingers aided troops under attack, and in their familiar interdiction role hit trucks and boats. They protected the rice barges pushing up the Mekong River to Phnom Penh, and orbited the Saigon area to deter rocket and sapper attacks. Their sorties nevertheless fell short of the total at the crest of the enemy's spring campaign. Perhaps this tapering off befitted the post-offensive period. After all, the peace negotiations were moving toward a truce that would end the U.S. combat presence in Laos and South Vietnam.

VII. Aftermath—Expansion in the Employment of Gunships

While American fixed-wing gunships grew more sophisticated and potent, the simplicity of the early gunships, such as the AC-47, appealed to other nations threatened or confronted with guerrilla warfare. The gunship held many advantages for small, less-developed nations struggling to maintain an effective air force. The side-firing weapon system could supply several hours of heavy but accurate airborne firepower even in remote or other inaccessible areas. Guerrillas normally like to attack and move supplies under the cover of darkness. Hence the gunship's night ability to support points under assault and to interdict the insurgent's supplies kindled keen interest. Few of the world's air forces were effective in night air operations. Moreover, the gunship's combat advantages came at a bargain price. Most nations had the aircraft and ordnance suitable for easy conversion to a simple gunship. Gunship tactics and techniques required relatively little training for crews. Existing facilities and the skill-level of support personnel could usually handle gunship maintenance and ground support. In addition, the simplicity of gunship conversion pointed to unusual aircraft flexibility. It was possible, for example, to quickly reconvert the gunship to a transport.

For these reasons, several Latin American countries early showed interest in the gunship concept. In January 1966, representatives from sixteen Latin American air forces attended an Inter-American Air Force Counterinsurgency Symposium hosted by the Air Force Special Air Warfare Center at Hurlburt Field, Fla.[1] At such meetings, the gunship concept information conveyed to these countries triggered further inquiries. In September 1966, for example, Chile asked the United States Air Forces Southern Command (USAFSO) for drawings, specifications, and cost information on installation of machineguns on C-47 aircraft.[2]

The Air Staff pondered various ways for responding to Latin American interest in gunships. The Special Air Warfare Center proposed sending to Chile an AC-47 mobile training team which included one of the finest AC-47 crews. The team could furnish facts on machinegun installation and turn Chile's fully qualified C-47 pilots into AC-47 pilots after ten flying hours and expenditure of 4,000 rounds of ammunition per pilot.[3] On the other hand, the Southern Command wanted its own AC-47s for demonstration and gunship training for Latin American air forces.[4]

In January 1967 the Southern Command studied its requirements for AC-47 aircraft. The conversion of the C-47 into a potent counterinsurgency strike aircraft offered high promise for meeting Latin American needs, especially after Congress passed legislation in 1968 prohibiting U.S. sales of high performance aircraft to countries south of the border to slow an arms race under way there. Furthermore, the simple modification of transports would tend to forestall pressure from other countries for more sophisticated aircraft. The Southern Command hoped to install SUU–11A miniguns or .50-caliber machineguns in the C–47, a dim prospect in view of Vietnam war demands on funds and equipment. Nevertheless, USAFSO later asked the Air Staff to support a project for equipping a C–47 with a .30-caliber machinegun, gunsight, and associated wiring. USAFSO felt this modification well-suited as a demonstration gunship since most Latin American nations had .30-caliber guns on T–6s and other aircraft.[5] The year ended without action on these ideas however.

In January 1968 the Southern Command restated a requirement for C–47s equipped with three .50-caliber machineguns. The command wanted a configuration so simple that the Latin American countries could modify their own aircraft with materials at hand. To render the aircraft more flexible, pallet gun mounts were recommended. The mounts would contain azimuth/elevation vernier adjustments allowing for fine boresight corrections. The mount's elevation scale would cover 10° above to 30° below level to compensate for the extremes in Latin American terrain.[6] Air Force headquarters asked TAC to tap SAWC and 1st Combat Application Group resources to develop, test, and deliver two machinegun kits to USAFSO together with plans and technical data for additional installations.[7]

TAC Test Number 68–201, May 9, 1968, ordered three .50-caliber machineguns placed on pallet mounts built of materials available in Latin America.[8] The idea of putting machineguns on pallets led TAC to consider also pallet-mounting the semi-automatic flare launchers and the emergency ram-air smoke-removal system. Even a palletized day/night target-acquisition system (incorporating a computer and sighting device for gunship application) was investigated.[9] Meanwhile, the 1st Combat Application Group reported in July that flight-testing of the prototype machinegun installation had been successful and that contract modification was proceeding. Delivery of the guns to the Canal Zone was estimated in the latter half of August.[10]

Air Force headquarters authorized four AC–47s in early 1969 toward satisfying the Southern Command's long-standing requirement. Two reasons partly prompted this action: (1) to fill a void left by the withdrawal of the Southern Command's A–26s in 1968, and (2) to help counter moves by U.S. Army forces in the Canal Zone aimed at usurping close air support and training roles assigned to USAFSO.[11] After many years of trying, the Southern Command would get its demonstration/training gunships.

While not forgetting Latin American gunship development the Air Force greatly stressed a gunship capability for allied nations in Southeast Asia. It first focused on supplying AC–47s to the Vietnamese Air Force but in time put gunships in the hands of the Laotians as well.

The Vietnamese Air Force began on July 1, 1955, with thirty-two old planes inherited from the French. In May 1956 the U.S. Air Force first took over French Air Force advisory functions, and a modest program of modernizing the VNAF got under way almost at once. Improvement of the VNAF accelerated as the war in Southeast Asia intensified, and it later became a major program in the Nixon administration policy of Vietnamization.* At first, U.S. aid emphasized equipping the VNAF as a war ally but the Nixon program shifted to preparing the Vietnamese to go it alone.

By 1965 the Vietnamese Air Force had two squadrons of C–47s (each with seventeen aircraft) and thus were quite familiar with the Old Gooney Bird. Furthermore, VNAF C–47s shared the night flare mission role with American C–123s in 1964 because of a sharp rise in June 1963 of Viet Cong night attacks on both outposts and "new life" rural villages.[12] It was not until 1967, however, that a program emerged to give the VNAF a gunship squadron. The program called for converting ten C–47s of the VNAF's 417th Transport Squadron to gunships by September 1, 1967, and six more by January 1, 1968. The Seventh Air Force submitted SEAOR 89 in May 1967 for equipping sixteen AC–47s with SSU–11A guns. Since Air Force AC–47s had new MXU–470/A gun modules, the SUU–11 guns being replaced were expected to be used in the VNAF conversion.[13]

In September 1967 the Air Force Advisory Group in South Vietnam urged headquarters to prod the lagging Air Force coordination of the VNAF AC–47 conversion program: "It would materially aid in coordinating and obtaining the necessary 7AF support including training of the Vietnamese cadre if an expected date of Air Staff approval could be obtained" as "an early VNAF AC–47 capability is desired." The Advisory Group figured it would take about 2½ months to train the Vietnamese instructor cadre.†[14] In the meantime, the Advisory Group and the 14th Air Commando Wing drew up a memorandum of understanding in December 1967 regarding the conduct of VNAF training.[15]

Plans for a Vietnamese Air Force AC–47 squadron nonetheless went awry for several reasons. First, strong enemy attacks on U.S. air bases in 1967 imposed a heavier airbase-defense commitment on the Spookies, and in turn generated requests for more AC–47s. Uncertainty arose whether guns and related equipment would be enough for USAF needs. Second, the Air Force suspended the VNAF conversion in early 1968 when it seemed that the SUU–11 pods on hand would be needed for the AC–119 program. This hold order was brief, but such actions delayed execution of VNAF plans. Moreover, USAF officials stayed troubled over the supply of new 7.62-mm miniguns.

---

*Vietnamization of the war had two phases. Phase I emphasized the Vietnamese in the ground role. Phase II stepped up the use of armored equipment, improved logistics, and began air support. The transfer of gunships fell in Phase II.

†In late 1967 the 14th Air Commando Wing submitted a proposal for training VNAF aircrews in the AC–47. [14th ACWg Training Proposal, Dec 1967.]

The problem of accommodating gunship personnel of the AC–119G deployment under the Southeast Asia manpower ceiling fueled fresh effort toward establishing a VNAF gunship squadron. In December 1968 General Brown, Seventh Air Force commander, ordered a study on the transfer of AC–47s to the VNAF. He wanted quick action with consideration of an "optimum schedule from the VNAF side, even though it results in some degradation of the Seventh Air Force capabilities." From the study the Seventh Air Force concluded the VNAF had the capability and desire to accept the AC–47s.[16] Provisions were again made for a VNAF gunship squadron.

Following months of preparation and aircrew training, the VNAF received the first five AC–47 gunships on July 2, 1969, and the sixteenth and last on August 20.[17] The VNAF 817th Combat Squadron, popularly known as "Fire Dragon," earned a combat-ready (C–1) rating on August 31—one month ahead of schedule.[18] That squadron's AC–47s based at Tan Son Nhut comprised the complete VNAF gunship force until AC–119Gs were turned over to the Vietnamese in September 1971.

The U.S. Advisory Group eyed VNAF combat operations intently, inasmuch as the AC–47s were to supply the main support for an expanding Regional Forces/Popular Forces program.[19] The Vietnamese Fire Dragons would likewise supplement USAF gunships in a number of in-county roles for quite some time. Much hinged on the VNAF success.

The Vietnamese AC–47 squadron swiftly won the praise of American advisors and commanders. As 1969 closed, the Vietnamese were flying all gunship support for the IV Corps Zone. The VNAF put two or three AC–47s on airborne alert from sunset to sunrise while six stood ground alert at Binh Thuy and Tan Son Nhut.[20] One advisor reported the VNAF gunship had "never failed to meet a target commitment."[21] Another, the evaluator of the VNAF unit, declared: "This squadron is better than any USAF AC–47 squadron that was ever over here."

Crew experience was the key ingredient of Vietnamese success. In late 1969 the average Fire Dragon pilot had flown more than 6,000 hours with some having logged over 12,000 hours in the C–47.* This contrasted with USAF crews logging 800 AC–47 hours throughout a one-year tour. What's more, the VNAF crews knew the Vietnamese terrain and could generally spot more on the ground.[22] Deficient night and poor-weather operational capability tempered the high experience level of Vietnamese crews.[23] This was gradually overcome, leading a USAF colonel to comment, "The Vietnamese seem to be able to acquire the target much faster at night"[24] than the Americans.

An instance of the Vietnamese operational progress was an AC–47 mission on October 17, 1969, commanded by Capt. Huynh Van Tong. While on airborne alert over Binh Thuy AB, Captain Tong was directed to a Vietnamese army outpost at Phung Hiep under attack. The VNAF AC–47 fired 63,000 minigun rounds and dropped 150 flares in support of the

---

*Some Vietnamese pilots had flown C–47s since 1958.

defenders. Extra air support was requested and Captain Tong acted as forward air controller, directing the strikes of the USAF F-100s that responded. Captain Tong and his crew flew three sorties in defense of the outpost, returning to Binh Thuy to replenish ammunition and flares. The attack on the outpost was repulsed.[25]

By December 31, 1969, the VNAF gunships had demonstrated a firm grasp of all facets of their mission to include acting as forward air controller for USAF strikes. At year's end they had flown more than twenty-eight percent of the total gunship effort in South Vietnam. The chief of the Air Force Advisory Group reported the VNAF's killed-by-air figures were at least equal to a USAF gunship squadron's.[26]

The VNAF gunship squadron had some problems in maintaining the MXU-470/A gun module which were resolved by degrees with greater experience. Overall AC-47 maintenance proved surprisingly good, reflecting the long acquaintance of VNAF maintenance men with the C-47. The VNAF's rapid expansion, however, caused constant concern. It was obvious the South Vietnamese would have to withdraw some of their best people from the established squadrons to man new units being activated.[27]

Step by step the Vietnamese Air Force took over more of the gunship missions. They extended their AC-47 operations into all four military regions, eventually covering the entire country. The 817th Combat Squadron deployed alert aircraft to Da Nang, Pleiku, and Binh Thuy Air Bases.[28] At the same time, preparations commenced for the VNAF AC-119G squadron.* In the first quarter of 1971, the 17th Special Operations Squadron, 14th SOWg, set about training the VNAF aircrews in the AC-119G. The three-phase program consisted of a week's ground school, then basic flying training with stress on instrument/emergency procedures, and ending with a concentration on combat tactics.[29] In late April 1971, Vice President Nguyen Cao Ky attended a graduation ceremony at Phan Rang AB for the eighteen-member first class of AC-119G crewmen. The graduates—pilots, navigators, flight engineers, gunners, and illuminator operators—would form the cadre of the VNAF's AC-119G unit, the 819th Combat Squadron.[30]

On September 24, 1971, the Air Force announced that the AC-119G Shadow gunships of the 17th Special Operations Squadron had been turned over to the VNAF.[31] Another big milestone in the VNAF Improvement and Modernization Program had been reached. The Vietnamese were able to

---

*At Dr. McLucas' request, the Air Staff examined in August 1969 the possibility of converting excess EC-121 aircraft into gunships for the VNAF. The Air Staff recommended against considering the C-121 because: A previous study of the airframe had rejected it for gunship use (scoring poorly on maneuverability, vulnerability, maneuvering load factor, crew-egress capability, and a suspected tail-section twist resulting from firing of guns in the aft section of the aircraft); high operating/modification costs; the aircraft was sophisticated beyond VNAF capability; VNAF AC-47s were considered adequate; and the long leadtime required for modification. The report concluded: "In the event it becomes necessary to expand the VNAF gunship fleet, recommend the AC-119Gs be given to the VNAF." [Ltr, Gen. John C. Meyer, Vice Chief of Staff to SAFUS (Dr. McLucas), subj: Conversion of EC-121s to Gunships, Aug 30, 1969.]

shoulder even more of the gunship-mission load within their country and free additional USAF gunships for interdiction.

Gunships were provided for the Laotians as well as the South Vietnamese. In 1968 the American Embassy in Vientiane believed the Royal Laotian Air Force desperately needed to improve its C–47 operations. Specifically, the Americans wanted to give the RLAF some night and "weather" capability, sharpen C–47 maintenance, and broaden the training of selected RLAF personnel. The goal was a self-sufficient RLAF with an AC–47 tactical capability.[32] In December 1968 CINCPAC approved and submitted to the Secretary of Defense a request from the Joint United States Military Advisory Group (JUSMAG) Deputy Chief in Thailand to convert four RLAF C–47s to gunships by installing .50-caliber machineguns.[33] Almost simultaneously, the deputy chief of the advisory team asked that a C–47 mobile training team come to Udorn RTAFB and conduct the required RLAF training.[34]

After top-level agreement in Washington, the Air Staff levied the requirement for an AC–47 mobile training team at Udorn on TAC's Special Operations Force (SOF). In February 1969 a team of five officers and nineteen enlisted men ended its planning and left for Thailand.*[35] The team's first increment reached Udorn on February 24 and the second on March 2, 1969. Eighteen Laotians entered training on March 8 utilizing four C–47s from the Military Assistance Program, Laos. Though no AC–47 was on hand for gunship training, the RLAF was nevertheless told to choose men for loadmaster and gunner training. A request for instructors to conduct this special training went to the Special Operations Force. Two SOF loadmaster instructors got to Udorn on June 20. Three days later, the RLAF personnel began loadmaster instruction after which they would receive gunner training if an AC–47 was available. On July 12 two instructor gunners came and the 14th SOWg lent a Spooky for the gunship-training phase. The training, completed on July 31, formed a small nucleus for an RLAF gunship cadre.[36]

The training made headway† but efforts to supply the RLAF with gunships mired down. On March 28, 1969, the Chief of Staff refused funding on the earlier-requested .50-caliber gun modification, due to its

---

*The mobile training team went to Udorn in a temporary duty status. Later Ambassador Sullivan in the Laotian capital reacted negatively to reports that the team was to become a permanent organization at Udorn. He argued that the job could be better done by Special Operations volunteers who were properly motivated to endure the advisory-training frustrations. [Msg, Ambassador Sullivan to General McConnell, subj: C–47 Mobile Assistance Team (no DTG).]

† Success of the mobile training team training brought a follow-on request for the next two training periods. RLAF crews from the first class would augment the follow-on team. (A factor in sending the MTT training team in a temporary duty status was avoidance of trade-offs that seemed necessary to squeeze under the Southeast Asia manpower ceiling.) [Hist, Dir/Ops, I Jan–30 June 69, p 348.]

relatively low priority and a "critical shortage of FY 69 modification funds." Instead, the Air Staff offered in April eight C–47s and a like number of 7.62-mm gun kits to come from VNAF excess. Air Force headquarters believed an extra three aircraft already modified to the gunship configuration, might be turned over to the RLAF in May and June of 1969.[37]

In early June 1969, the Air Force decided the three gunship-configured aircraft would remain in Vietnam but the eight VNAF C–47s, together with 7.62-mm SUU–11 gun kits, would be transferred to "MAP Laos on an expedited basis." The first five aircraft were delivered on July 5 and the last one on October 2, 1969. Only five complete gun kits were furnished from VNAF excess, however. The remainder would have to come from AFLC sources. By the end of September, the U.S. Air Force had modified five of the C–47s as gunships. The American Embassy at Vientiane reported on October 7, 1969, that after the first few operational flights the guns had "hopelessly jammed." U.S. officials asserted that the gun kits "were unserviceable and should have been salvaged and/or overhauled prior to delivery." They definitely felt the "tactical position in-country could be enhanced greatly with good serviceable gunships" but they had not gotten them.[38]

In response to Royal Laotian Air Force gunship difficulties, Air Force headquarters next directed that gun pods and parts be sent from the United States to the Laotians. Headquarters specified that a technician to help in their installation arrive at Udorn by October 14, 1969. Meantime, the Deputy Chief, JUSMAG, Thailand, learned of the impending inactivation of the 4th SOSq which would render AC–47s equipped with MXU–470/A gun pods excess to the Seventh Air Force. The JUSMAG deputy chief asked CINCPAC on October 31, 1969, for immediate transfer of eight AC–47s to the Military Assistance Program (MAP) Laos (at no cost to MAP) "to replace present SUU–11A RLAF equipped C–47 acft." On November 4 CINCPACAF suggested just the SUU–11A guns of the RLAF be traded for the MXU–470 ones. Notwithstanding, after phoning Headquarters PACOM on November 7, G. McMurtrie Godley, American Ambassador to Laos, concluded that CINCPAC could justify the substitution of USAF AC–47s for RLAF C/AC–47 aircraft and urged the exchange be made.[39]

On November 14, PACAF agreed to trade eight 4th SOSq AC–47s (with MXU–470/A gun pods) for five RLAF AC–47s (with SUU–11 guns) and three standard-cargo C–47s. PACAF proposed to reassign three of the 4th SOSq AC–47s to the 432d TRWg at Udorn for ongoing support of Lima Sites and troops in contact with the enemy and three to the VNAF as advanced attrition. PACAF would return to the RLAF C/AC–47s to the United States for storage. CINCPAC concurred in this redistribution plan on November 18, commenting "the one-for-one swap appears the most economically feasible solution." On December 4, 1969, the Chief of Staff approved the CINCPACAF plan. He also authorized retention of the eight RLAF C/AC–47s but stipulated that no more of these aircraft be modified into gunships. Directives were issued specifying delivery of the eight AC–47s to the RLAF by January 5, 1970, expanding the RLAF gunship inventory to thirteen.[40]

Unfortunately, development of a Royal Laotian gunship force experienced continued difficulties. RLAF maintenance capability fell short of the self-sufficiency goals. The Air Force section of the Joint U.S. Military Advisory Group, Thailand, informed Air Force headquarters in June 1970 that "Phase inspections, IRAN, drop-in maintenance and TCTOs (time compliance technical orders) are still accomplished under contract by Thai-Bangkok." In addition, delivery of gunships to the RLAF had fallen behind schedule. The three AC–47s (with MXU–470A guns) turned over to the RLAF in June 1970 raised their total to only nine, with but eight then operational.[41] The Royal Laotian Air Force did in truth have a gunship capability. Nonetheless, its small base of experience with air operations made expansion and progress painfully slow in the face of deeper enemy penetration into the country.

Other countries worked on their own to fit the side-firing concept to their express demands. An Israel Aircraft Industries gunship version of a military transport, displayed at the Hanover Air Show in Germany, afforded a case in point.* The aircraft had .50-caliber machinegun pods on each side of the fuselage in addition to a rear-mounted machinegun and forward-firing guns and rockets.[42] Clearly the United States could no longer claim the gunship concept as its exclusive property.

Despite world interest in the gunship and the steady improvement of the U.S. gunship force, the weapon system was accepted within definite and somewhat narrow limits. In the extended Southeast Asian war, burdened with many indecisive qualities, the gunship proved a most useful but certainly not a major factor in resolving the conflict. The gunship's chief achievements lay in interdiction, hamlet and outpost defense, air base defense, close ground force support, and convoy escort. Yet even with these mission categories, the enemy got supplies through, ambushed troops, bombarded bases, and overran positions. Furthermore, the gunships occupied only a thin band in the wide spectrum of Southeast Asia air activity. U.S. air operations, supplemented more and more by those of the VNAF and RLAF, had grown infinitely complex with a great number and variety of missions, munitions, aircraft, and tactics. At their 1969 peak, however, the gunships totaled only 53 of over 1,800 U.S. aircraft in the war theater.[43]

Also in comparison of sortie totals, the gunship number stood relatively low. The highest monthly average for Air Force gunship attack sorties in South Vietnam crested at 368 during fiscal year 1969. This contrasted sharply with a monthly average of 9,797 USAF fixed-wing tactical air sorties over the same period. In the fixed-wing attack sorties over Laos, the

---

*Discussed in *Aviation Week & Space Technology*, May 1972.

gunship monthly average climbed to 348 in fiscal year 1971, compared to 4,954 for other tactical air sorties.[44]

At one time or another, the gunship virtually ranged the entire war area except North Vietnam, yet was continually confined to less well-defended enemy-held areas. The aircraft always needed friendly control of the skies and even with the flak suppression of a jet-fighter escort its vulnerability remained a nagging worry. In summary, the gunship was a limited weapon even in a limited war.[45]

Nevertheless, the gunship carved a niche for itself in Southeast Asia air operations and in the post-war force. Almost from its first flights over enemy supply routes, the aircraft became the preeminent truck-destroyer, particularly at night. Gunship truck-kill claims were criticized and at times discounted. All the same the gunship was assuredly the most cost-effective aircraft performing interdiction. There was plenty of justified acclaim for its role as an aerial defender of villages, Lima Sites, fortified posts, and troops fighting off enemy attacks. The Spooky count, the number of times the enemy broke off the assault, the reports of gratitude from ground units—these are facts of record. The gunship's presence exerted both a psychological and material impact. Its versatility stretched from the most sophisticated self-contained capability for target search of any Air Force aircraft to such diverse tasks as illuminating a lifesaving surgical operation. Its varied weapons could saturate an area or concentrate fire on a point. In short, the weapon fully displayed in combat the qualities expected of it by its early promoters. General McConnell's 1964 reply to General Sweeney's expressed opposition to the gunship rang hauntingly true: "it certainly is in the Air Force interests to run the program rather than to sit on the sideline commenting."[46]

The gunship had firmly established its role and importance in the Southeast Asian war and in the military assistance programs for other nations. It likewise earned a place in the Air Force plans for postwar tactical forces. In September 1970 Tactical Air Command reported on its "in-depth review" of post-Southeast Asia gunships as requested by Air Force headquarters. TAC concluded that a "self-contained all-weather/night-attack (SCANA) system" capable of destroying mobile surface targets was required. The system would pressure the enemy at all times and keep him from moving men and equipment during darkness and bad weather. "Of many weapon systems developed to accomplish this high priority mission in SEAsia, one, the AC-130A Surprise Package Gunship, has been singularly successful," said the command. The Gunship II, then, supplied the "initial evolutionary" stages of a SCANA capability to meet this post-Southeast Asia need. TAC believed the AC-130As projected to be left over from Southeast Asia operations would take care of gunship force needs to about 1980. TAC cautioned, however, that "past emphasis on gunship development had been stimulated by the AC-130 success and the existence of a favorable environment for employment." Bearing in mind that "cargo type aircraft are suited for low level conflict situations which require a low national involvement profile," TAC preferred to view the post-war gunships as "transitional" until development of an attack-experimental (A-X) aircraft.[47]

Transitional or not, the gunship had definitely met a combat air operations need, albeit in a "limited war." The aircraft had fulfilled its assigned missions better than any other available weapon system. As General Momyer, TAC commander (and former Seventh Air Force commander) put it: "with its multiple sensors, I think it is the best weapon for either air or ground support of a night engagement."[48] Considerable evidence points to "wars of national liberation" (Vietnam-type wars) as being the most acceptable level of conflict by enemy nations in the future. If so, the side-firing concept would continue to be advantageous. John Paul Vann, perhaps one of the most knowledgeable and respected of American advisors in Vietnam until his death in 1972, remarked in the early years of U.S. involvement in Southeast Asia: "This is a political war and it calls for discrimination in killing. The best weapon of killing would be a knife."[49] The side-firing gunship and the helicopter gunship were probably the closest air power could come to Vann's knife. Even when the Southeast Asian war erupted into more conventional battles, the gunship dealt surprisingly well with tanks and other heavy enemy weapons. General Ryan, Air Force Chief of Staff, asserted in the fall of 1971 that "One of the most successful developments arising from our experience in Southeast Asia is the gunship," and "we intend to keep this capability to deliver a tremendous volume of sustained accurate firepower in the tactical force."[50]

The year 1972 marked a climax for gunship operations, but opened amid one more Commando Hunt interdiction campaign. The gunships formed a key element in the blocking belt strategy. They excelled again in destroying vehicles and thus slowing the southward logistic flow. Their success sparked a long and labored debate on ways to Vietnamize interdiction. The Credible Chase concept emerged as the brightest hope but mini-gunship troubles, fears over the small craft's combat survival, and the foe's spring offensive scuttled the project. Defense Secretary Laird, on January 8, 1973, told Congress that "as a consequence of the success of the military aspects of Vietnamization, the South Vietnamese people today, in my view are fully capable of providing their own in-country security against the North Vietnamese."[51] In truth, however, the South Vietnamese had not perfected a strong interdiction punch. This weakness and grave psychological doubts about fighting without American air power finally proved fatal.

Interdiction always continued as an important gunship mission. Still, the strenuous demands put on gunship aircraft and crews in the defense of An Loc, Kontum, and Hue during the spring of 1972 produced operations not previously equaled in intensity. Reports from the ground troops, aircrews, and commanders at all levels attested to the major role of the fixed-wing gunships in turning back enemy forces from their primary goals. Gen. Frederick C. Weyand, U.S. Army, Commander, Military Assistance

Command, as of October 12, 1972, believed it "unlikely that the South Vietnamese forces could have stopped the invasion without the tremendous effectiveness of airpower." He could not "see how anybody in any service, could question the decisive role played by the fixed-wing gunships, TACAIR [tactical air] and the B-52s."[52] Ironically, the response to the enemy's strong, conventional, tank-led attacks brought the gunships back to where they started—aiding troops in defense of fixed positions.

As in the past, the gunship developers and crews struggled to stay ahead of enemy defenses and tactics. Striking advances were registered in the use of the 105-mm cannon ("Big Gun") and the more powerful engines for the AC-130E. The communists countered with an increase in truck operations, massed antiaircraft fire, and the Strela missile.

Development of ground beacons for use in support of ground forces forged ahead but never reached full fruition. The hurdle lay in lack of troop understanding of the beacons and gunship capabilities as well.

While the truce of January 27, 1973, finished American gunship operations in Laos and South Vietnam, support of troops in Cambodia went on. The worsening conditions there, however, presaged an end of combat missions before many months passed. Characteristic of the whole gunship story was the arrival of new aircraft in Southeast Asia as combat neared a close. Painted gray to reduce the infrared signature, these Gray Ghosts pictured the ongoing evolution of a remarkable weapon system. They marked one more chapter in the now familiar story of gunship advances that never ceased contesting the defensive countermeasures of the enemy.

In reviewing the course of the gunship's evolution from painful birth to an accepted, unique, and potent weapon system, certain significant points stand out. First, resourceful, persistent and imaginative men conceived and developed a new aerial weapons concept. They did it in the face of formidable obstacles and almost stifling opposition. Second, the constant growth in gunship effectiveness came from an unusually high art of improvisation, skillful borrowing, and use of available equipment. Ten years of experience with limited war had disclosed that modifying existing aircraft was surely the best way to secure new weapon-system capabilities from the standpoint of both time and money. Third, the innovative management of dedicated men, given free rein within target costs to do whatever was needed to get the job done, developed and produced the more advanced AC-130 gunships on schedule and below the projected expense. This was a miracle in a time of notable cost overruns and production delays.* Fourth, remarkably

---

*On August 12, 1971, General Brown, AFSC commander, addressed a Department of Defense/National Security Industrial Association Symposium on Major Defense Systems Acquisition: "As a creative innovation, the first experimental gunships were delivered to combat units in Southeast Asia in record time. They were so successful that it was decided to make this a regular Air Force program—and it was put into the formal acquisition system. Then, as the Secretary [Packard] pointed out, he found it would take two years to get more gunships to the theater. So we took the program out of the formal system, turned it back to the original small project group, and got them out in six months."

close relations between gunship developers and the combat-zone users strengthened application of state-of-the-art equipment to combat needs. Fifth, the gunship developers constantly sought to keep ahead of the enemy and his defenses. They extended the range and quality of sensors and weapons and worked on electronic countermeasures. This dictated pressure-packed modification of gunships in the United States during the summer months (the wet season in Southeast Asia), so the aircraft could return to combat by the time the dry hunting season began. Sixth, the gunship's combat successes in Southeast Asia, especially in night operations, generated demands for more gunships and their use in a greater variety of missions. This touched off much top-level debate over the "optimum" gunship force and its place in a "balanced" air force. Seventh, gunship tactics changed from strikes by a single aircraft on armed reconnaissance missions to a complex team effort of many aircraft, particularly fighter escort. Fitted with heavier armament like the 40-mm gun and the 105-mm howitzer, the gunship became virtually an escorted aerial artillery platform somewhat analogous to a Navy battleship with a protective screen of destroyers. Proposals and tests even emerged to tie the gunship with such aircraft as the B-52. The relatively small gunship program had surprising impact in many areas, ranging from combat to management of airpower resources.

Appendices

Appendix 1   *Gunship Types*

Gunship	*Spooky* *AC-47*	*Spectre* *AC-130* *(Gunship II)*
Mission	Area defense	Armed recce, interdiction
Area/target	In-country, Out-country/ troops-in-contact	Out-country/trucks, LOCs
Armor	None	5,000 lbs
Armament	3 x 7.62-mm miniguns (MXU–470/A) Fast: 6,000 rds/min Slow: 3,000 rds/min	4 x 7.62-mm miniguns Fast: 6,000 rds/min Slow: 3,000 rds/min
		4 x 20-mm cannon 2,500 rds/min
Ordnance	21,000 rds	15,000 rds 7.62-mm; 8,000 rds 20-mm
Target acquisition	Visual	Night observation device (NOD); Infared (IR); side-looking radar; Black Crow
Fire-control system	None	Computerized; incorporating fully automatic, semiautomatic, manual-fir offset-capable
Illumination	24-56 flares, manually dispensed	Illuminator 1.5 million candlepower variable beam (20 kw); IR filter capability; 24 flares, dispensed from launcher
Reaction airspeed	130K TAS	200K TAS
Operating altitude	3,000 ft AGL (optimum)	————————
One engine out	Unsatisfactory at combat gross weight	400 feet-per-minute climb
Fuel duration	7 hr	6 hr 30 min
Turnaround	30 min	1 hr 30 min
Aircrew	2 pilots, 1 navigator, 2 gunners, 1 loadmaster, 1 flight engineer	2 pilots, 3 navigators (table navigator, NOD operator, radar/IR operator), 1 illuminator operator, 3 gunners, 1 flight engineer (crew members adde later: fire-control officer, electronic warfare officer, two additional gunne
Escorts	None	1 x F-4 (of 3 rotating to tanker)

Maj Richard K. Kott, *The Role of USAF Gunships in SEAsia* (HQ PACAF, Project CHECO, August

Components and Characteristics

Shadow AC-119G (Gunship III)	Stinger AC-119K (Gunship III)
Armed recce	Armed recce, interdiction
In-country/troops-in-contact, mover, etc.	In-country/troops-in-contact, movers, etc.; Out-country/ trucks, LOCs
2,000 lbs	2,000 lbs
4 x 7.62-mm miniguns Fast: 6,000 rds/min Slow: 3,000 rds/min	4 x 7.62-mm miniguns Fast: 6,000 rds/min Slow: 3,000 rds/min
	2 x 20-mm cannon 2,500 rds/min
31,500 rds	31,500 rds 7.62-mm; 4,500 rds 20-mm
Night observation sight (NOS)	Night observation sight (NOS); infrared; side-looking radar
Computerized; incorporating semiautomatic, manual-firing, offset capable	Computerized; incorporating fully automatic, manual-firing, offset-capable
Illuminator 1.5 million candlepower variable beam (20-kw); 24 flares, dispensed from launche	Illuminator 1.5 million candlepower; pencil beam (20-kw); 24 flares, dispensed from launcher
180K TAS	180K TAS
3,500 ft AGL	3,500 ft AGL
Unsatisfactory at combat gross weight	500 feet-per-minute climb
6 hr 30 min	5 hr
30 min	30 min
2 pilots, 2 navigators (table navigator, NOS operator), 1 illuminator operator, 2 gunners, 1 flight engineer	2 pilots, 3 navigators (table navigator, NOS operator, radar/IR operator), 1 illuminator operator), 3 gunners, 1 flight engineer
None	None

69), pp 59-62.

Appendix 2

*Credible Chase Aircraft and Test Items**

1. *AU–23 Fairchild Peacemaker.* The AU–23 is an all-metal, light-weight, high-wing monoplane manufactured by Fairchild Industries. It has a rectangular, strut-braced wing of constant profile over the entire span. The wing has four mechanically and interconnected inboard and outboard double-slotted, electrically operated flaps. The aircraft has a fixed, conventional landing gear. The pitch axis is controlled by a conventional elevator with electrical and manual trim. Aileron trim is electric and rudder trim is manual. The AU–23A is powered by an Airesearch Model TPE331-1-101 turboprop engine, flat-rated at 650 shaft horsepower (shp). The engine is equipped with a 3-bladed, constant-speed, full-feathering Hartzell propeller that has beta and reverse ranges. The aircraft has five ordnance stations, four wing pylons, and a fuselage pylon. The aft cabin is configured to mount the XM–197 20-mm automatic gun system. Maximum gross weight of the aircraft is 6,100 pounds.

2. *AU–24A Helio Stallion.* The AU–24A is a lightweight, single-engine turboprop, high-wing monoplane. It is manufactured by Helio Aircraft Company, a division of General Aircraft Corporation. Except for fabric ailerons, the aircraft is of all-metal construction. The wing is full cantilever and contains long-span, single-slotted flaps, aerodynamically automatic full-span leading-edge slats; and leading-edge interceptors (spoilers). The interceptors augment roll control in slow flight and are mechanically inter-connected to the ailerons. Pitch control is maintained by a stabilator. The aircraft is equipped with electric and manual stabilator trim, electric aileron trim, and manual rudder trim. The AU–24A is powered by a 680-shp Pratt and Whitney turboprop engine and a Hartzell 3-bladed propeller with constant-speed, full-feathering, beta control, and reverse ranges. It has five ordnance stations, four wing pylons, and a fuselage pylon. The aft cabin is fitted to mount the XM–197 (20-mm) automatic gun system. Maximum gross weight is 6,300 pounds.

3. *XM–197 Gun.* The XM–197 is a 3-barrel, 20-mm Gatling gun. It is a lightweight version of the 6-barrel, M–61 Vulcan 20-mm gun, which has

---

*Final Report, *Credible Chase/AU–23A* (TAC Proj 71A–211T/TAWC Proj 1142, USAFTAWC, Aug 1972).

been a reliable Air Force inventory item since 1955. The XM–197 installed in the mini-gunship is pintle-mounted and has two firing rates, 350 and 700 rounds-per-minute. For night use, it is equipped with an AN/TVS–5 night vision sight (NVS). The XM–197 is controlled by the gunner through a range of 20° forward, 60° aft, -6° up, and 55° down. (See NAVAIR Manual 11-85M197-1 and TO 1U-2-1(A)A-101.)

4. *AN/TVS-5 Night Vision Sight.* The TVS–5 was developed by VARO, Inc., for the Army and consists of a night sight with a single-stage image-intensifier tube and weapon-mounting brackets. The fixed sight is mounted directly to the top of the XM–197. It is aligned by munitions maintenance personnel with special equipment before being attached to the gun. Physical characteristics of the sight follow.

Weight—7 pounds
Length—14.5 inches
Diameter—6 inches
Field of view—157 angular mills (8.9°)
Magnification—6.3
Power source—2.7-volt battery, 12-hour life

(See Department of the Army Technical Manual DTM 11-5855-214-12.)

5. *Sensor Equipment.* The following is a list and description of the sensor and readout equipment that was used during the revised Credible Chase evaluation:

a. *Portatale III (AN/USQ-46).* The Portatale III is a militarized, portable VHF receiver that receives and decodes sensor activations. It can be set to receive any one of the 1,919 possible sensor channels and will decode and display activations from 64 sensor identification codes (IDs) on that channel. An output connector provides a means of connecting an auxiliary display, event recorder (RO–376), to the Portatale. Power for the Portatale III is furnished by the aircraft 28–VDC electrical system. The unit weighs 17.5 pounds and measures 4 by 13 by 10.25 inches. (See Department of the Army Technical Manual 11-5820-790-12, Radio Frequency Monitor Set AN/USQ-46, July 1970.)

b. *Event Recorder (RO-376A/USQ).* The event recorder is a militarized, 30-channel, strip-chart recorder that provides a permanent record of sensor activations received by the Portatale III. Each time a valid sensor message is received by the Portatale III, one of the 30 pins makes a mark on a paper strip chart moving at 12 or 24 inches per hour. At the slow rate, 40 minutes of data are visible at any given time. A roll of chart paper is sufficient for 36 or 72 hours of continuous operation. The event recorder is powered by the aircraft 28–VDC power supply through the Portatale. The recorder measures 4 by 18 by 15 inches and weighs 20 pounds. Both the Portatale and event recorder are operated and interpreted by the aircraft gunner. (See Department of the Army Technical Manual 11-5895-725-35, Recorder, Signal Data, January 1971.)

c. *Ground Sensors.* The ADSID III is an air-deliverable seismic intrusion detector designed for hand-launch from low-speed, light, fixed-wing aircraft or helicopters. (See Interim Technical Manual SM–MA33–1.) The MINISID III is a hand-emplaced seismic intrusion detector. The normal life expectancy after implant is approximately 100 days. The detectors are channelized to operate from 163 to 174 megahertz, and there are 64 separate IDs available on each channel. Each sensor is assigned a unique identifier which is composed of a channel and an ID code. (See Department of the Army Technical Manual 5–6350–225–13, MINISID AN/GSQ–154, June 1970.)

Bibliographic Note

Source material for this study falls into four general categories: official records (largely Air Force); manuscript histories; information derived from interviews and other direct personal contacts; and various published works.

Official Records

Messages and papers generated by the Joint Chiefs of Staff proved particularly enlightening with respect to strategy, force deployments, and other high-level decisions—touching at times on foreign relations. Most current JCS documents relating to gunship matters were in the files of the Directorate of Plans, Headquarters USAF. Non-current JCS material, plus a limited number of Military Assistance Command, Vietnam records pertaining to gunships are retired at the National Federal Records Center, Suitland, Maryland, and were examined there.

By far the largest portion of the author's research involved Air Force records. These were voluminous but uneven in quality. The papers of the Secretary of the Air Force (mostly at the Pentagon but non-current ones at the Suitland Records Center) afford valuable insights into the decision-making process and the rationale behind certain decisions. These papers frequently include memos and letters from and to the Secretary of Defense.

Records produced or held by the Air Staff were consulted at the Pentagon and the Suitland Records Center. The Pentagon office charged with gunship/special operations under the DCS/Plans and Operations possessed the richest lode of documents. Messages, letters, and miscellaneous correspondence (involving major commands and other organizations below Headquarters USAF) were obtained from the Air Force archives at the Albert F. Simpson Historical Research Center, Maxwell AFB, Alabama, or directly from the unit. The Gunship Program Office, Aeronautical Systems Division, Air Force Systems Command, Wright-Patterson AFB, Ohio, proved an especially worthwhile source of materials relating to gunship research and development. The Air Force archives at Maxwell AFB holds important operational records of the gunship squadrons, the 14th Special Operations Wing, Seventh Air Force, and other commands in Southeast Asia or the Pacific. Quite often, the more significant records were appended to various command or unit histories as supporting documentation.

Manuscript Histories

Project CHECO (Contemporary Historical Examination of Current Operations) Reports, first narratives written during the war by Air Force historians in the field, have greatly simplified and aided research into South-east Asia combat operations. The following have been most valuable: *First Test and Combat Use of AC-47, The Role of USAF Gunships in SEASIA,* and *Fixed Wing Gunships in SEA (Jul 69–Jul 71)*. Others can be noted in the citations. Likewise, Project Corona Harvest Reports, studies, and evaluations relating to the Southeast Asia war supplied gunship data and "lessons-learned" material. Fortunately, both Projects CHECO and Corona Harvest collected, compiled, and preserved supporting documentation, much of which is now on microfilm. These sources are available either at the Office of Air Force History or the Maxwell AFB archives.

Also helpful were the semiannual histories of Headquarters USAF directorates, the major commands (chiefly Pacific Air Forces, Tactical Air Command, Air Force Logistics Command, and Air Force Systems Command), plus relevant air force, wing, and squadron histories. Warner-Robins Air Materiel Area historical studies and accompanying documents set the background for the trials and tribulations growing out of the AC-119G/K modifications. Histories of the Commander in Chief, Pacific Command (CINCPAC), and MACV offered rich detail and a deeper insight into the broader aspects of the Southeast Asian war—strategic plans, objectives, and armed services/allied country roles and missions. Most of the above histories are in the Office of Air Force History. Those below major command level (air force, division, wing, squadron, and detachment) are in the Air Force archives. Squadron or detachment histories were usually incorporated into wing semiannual histories. Unit history quality varies considerably according to the writer's training and dedication.

Other history manuscripts consulted included monographs, commonly called "bluebooks" or "blue covers," prepared by the Office of Air Force History personnel. These studies cover a wide range of subjects. The series on Headquarters USAF Plans and Policies and those on different aspects of the Southeast Asia war proved most profitable to this work.

Personal Contacts

Considerable background material, particularly concerning the origin and early trials of the gunship concept, was obtained by personal interviews. The author visited Wright-Patterson AFB, Ohio; Eglin AFB, Florida; the Air Force Academy, Colorado; and Maxwell AFB, Alabama, to discuss gunship development and operations with men who played key roles in the gunship's evolution. The tapes and transcripts of these interviews are in the Office of Air Force History. In addition, the oral history branch of the Maxwell AFB archives has conducted interviews, the transcripts of which supplement those by the author.

While at Eglin AFB, the author flew with an AC-119 crew on a live-firing, night training mission over the Eglin-Hurlburt Field range. This flight provided a first-hand look at crew coordination and gunship operations.

Published Works

Published works reviewed were chiefly of a general nature, bearing on opinions and perceptions about the Southeast Asia war or the strategic/ tactical setting for gunship operations. For example, David Halberstam's *The Making of a Quagmire* offers a striking portrait of the deteriorating military situation in the early 1960s and the increasingly desperate need for a gunship capability. Similarly, *The Pentagon Papers* provides the author greater understanding of the political considerations affecting the waging of the war. The periodicals, newspapers, and Congressional publications (appropriation hearings) used can be found in the study's notes. A number of official manuals, RAND studies, and Air War College or Air Command and Staff College theses contributed data or differing viewpoints on subjects usually more narrow in scope. Most of the above published material may be found in the Air Force Studies and Analysis Library and the Pentagon's Army Library. The theses are in the Air University Library at Maxwell AFB.

Notes

Chapter I

1. Ltr, Ralph E. Flexman, Asst Ch Engr, Sys Spt Dept, Bell Aerosystems Co, Div of Bell Aerospace Corp, to Dr. Gordon A. Eckstrand, Ch/Tng Rsch Br, Behavioral Sci Lab, WPAFB, Ohio, Dec 27, 1962.

2. Col John A McCann, "The Ugly Duckling of Air Power," *The Air Power Historian,* V (Jan 1958), 54–61.

3. *Wings of Praise and Prayer* (Los Angeles), May 1953; Martin Cole, "The Ingenious Handiwork of Nate Saint, MAF Pilot," *Journal of the American Aviation Historical Society,* 17, (Summer 1972), 96–98.

4. Intvw, author with Ralph E. Flexman, Wash, DC, Sep 7, 1971.

5. Ltr, 1st Lt G. C. MacDonald, 95th Coast Artillery (AA), to National Inventors Council, Wash, DC, Apr 21, 1942.

6. Ltr, Capt G. C. MacDonald, Ord Dept to R&D Svc Sub-Ofc (Rocket), Dover Army AB, Dover, Del, subj: Transverse Firing of Rockets from Liaison Type Aircraft, May 2, 1945.

7. Memo, Lt Col G. C. MacDonald to Limited War Committee, subj: Transverse Firing of Rockets and Guns, Sep 14, 1961. MacDonald turned in a number of other ideas to the Limited War Committee at this time in response to an Air Force-wide call for ideas on counterinsurgency warfare.

8. Suggestion, Lt Col G. C. MacDonald to Tac Warf Application Proj, subj: Transverse Firing from Aircraft, Sep 19, 1961.

9. Intvw, author with Gilmour C. MacDonald, Eglin AFB, Fla, Sep 27, 1971.

10. Intvw, author with Ralph E. Flexman, Wash, DC, Sep 7, 1971; "Side-Firing C–47 Conceived by AF Psychologist," *Dayton Daily News* (Dayton, Ohio), Nov 29, 1965.

11. Ltr, Ralph E. Flexman to Capt John Simons, Engrg Psych Lab, WPAFB, Ohio, Apr 16, 1963.

12. Intvw, author with Lt Col John C. Simons, AMRL, WPAFB, Ohio, Mar 2, 1971.

13. Memo, Telephone Conversation between Ralph E. Flexman and Capt John C. Simons, Apr 29, 1963.

14. Handwritten note on DD Form 95 (Memo Routing Slip), Capt John C. Simons, Ch/Crew Stns Br, Human Engrg Div, 6570th AMRL, WPAFB, Ohio, to Dr Julien M. Christensen, Ch/Human Engrg Div [undated].

15. Telecon/Trip Report, Ralph E. Flexman, Apr 29, 1963.

16. Ltr, Stuart M. Schram, Jr., Asst Ch/Avionics Div, Dir/Def & Trnsp Sys Engrg, ASD, WPAFB, Ohio, to Capt John C. Simons, sub: Evaluation of Bell Aerosystems Company Proposal (Apr 16, 1963), May 8, 1963.

17. Encl, Ballistics of Laterally Fired Weapons, to ltr, Ralph E. Flexman to Capt John C. Simons, Engrg Psych Lab [sic], WPAFB, Ohio, Apr 16, 1963.

18. Narrative, Recommendation for awarding the Distinguished Service Medal to Capt John C. Simons, in AF Forum 642 (Recommendation for Decoration), 6570th AMRL (MRHEU), WPAFB, Ohio [undated]; intvw, author with Lt Col John C. Simons, AMRL, WPAFB, Ohio, Mar 2, 1971.

19. Simons intvw, Mar 1971.

20. Ltr, Capt John C. Simons, Ch/Crew Stns Br, Human Engrg Div, to Dep/Engrg, ASD, subj: Request for Support of Limited War Study, May 20, 1963.

21. Simons intvw, Mar 2, 1971.

22. Lt Col John C. Simons, Sgt Estell P. Bunch, Ralph Flexman, and Lt Col T. E. Rickelman, *Project Tailchaser: Development of a Lateral Firing Concept,* AMRL–TR–66–202 (AMRL, WPAFB, Ohio, Nov 1967); Lt Col John C. Simons and B. C. Dixon, *Long-Loiter: Improvement of Some Free-Fall and Circling-Line Techniques,* ASD–TR–69–95 (ASD, WPAFB, Ohio, Sep 1969), I, 1.

23. See note above.

24. Memo, Capt John C. Simons, Ch/Crew Stns Br, Human Engrg Div, Dr Julien M. Christensen, Ch/Human Engrg Div, subj: Lateral Sighting Study [ca Jul 2, 1963].

25. Memo, Dr. Julien M. Christensen, Ch/Human Engrg Div, ASD, to Lt Col Parrish, Ch/Behavioral Sci Lab, and Dr. Walter F. Grether, Tech Dir, Behavioral Sci Lab, Jul 2, 1963.

26. Simons intvw, Mar 2, 1971.

27. Simons, *et al, Project Tailchaser: Development of a Lateral Firing Concept,* AMRL–TR–66–202, pp 12–14.

28. *Ibid.*

29. Memo, Simons to Christensen [ca Jul 2, 1963].

30. Ind, Lt Col J. L. Hight, Ch/Pers Subsys Div, Dir/Crew Subsys Engrg, to 6570th AMRL, Jul 3, 1963.

31. Flight Test Plan ASNM-63-1, Project Tailchaser—Lateral Sighting Study, Oct 28, 1963.

32. Ibid.

33. Msg, Capt John C. Simons to Ralph E. Flexman, subj: Lateral Gun Firing Program, Nov 11, 1963.

34. Narrative, Recommendation for awarding the Distinguished Medal to Captain John C. Simons [undated]; Simons intvw, Mar 2, 1971.

35. Memo attached to file material.

36. Simons intvw, Mar 2, 1971; narrative Recommendation for awarding the Distinguished Service Medal to Captain John C. Simons [undated].

37. See note above.

38. The team was headed by Brig Gen David M. Jones. See AFSC COIN R&D Past, Present, Future, Sep 23, 1964, pp 1-10.

39. Intvw, author with Lt Col Ronald W. Terry, Gunship Prgm Dir, ASD, WPAFB, Ohio, Mar 1, 1971.

40. Ibid.

41. Simons intvw, Mar 2, 1971.

42. Flight Test Plan ASNM 63-1 (Addendum 1), Project Tailchaser—Lateral Sighting Study, Aug 29, 1964.

43. Hist, APGC, Jan 1-Jun 30, 1965, I, 61-73. The prototype SUU-11A gun pods (length 84″ and diameter 12″) averaged 325 pounds when fully loaded with 1,500 rounds of 7.62-mm ammunition.

44. Intvw, author with MSgt Estell P. Bunch, Gunship Prgm Ofc, ASD, WPAFB, Ohio, Mar 3, 1971.

45. Simons, et al, Project Tailchaser: Development of a Lateral Firing Concept, AMRL-TR-66-202, pp 14-15.

46. Ibid.

47. Terry intvw, Mar 1, 1971.

48. Ibid.

49. Simons, et al, Project Tailchaser: Development of a Lateral Firing Concept, AMRL-TR-202, p 16.

50. Ibid, pp 16-17. Simons suggested some ancillary advantages of a loitering-type aircraft such as: enhanced air-to-ground visual communication, improved aerial-delivery possibilities, using long-line technique to suppress flak or SAM installations by remote TV guidance, illuminating targets by sliding flares along a line, and suspending speakers at a fixed height on a long line. Flexman suggested also the idea of "sonar dipping" by long-line, loitering technique in antisubmarine operations.

51. Terry intvw, Mar 1, 1971.

52. Ibid.

53. Memo, telephone rprt from Lt Edwin Sasaki to Walter F. Grether, Tech Dir/Behavioral Sci Lab, AMRL, Nov 2, 1964.

54. Jacob Van Staaveren, USAF Plans and Policies in South Vietnam and Laos, 1964 (USAF Hist Div Liaison Ofc, Dec 1965), pp 15, 22, 36.

55. Interestingly, "An ad hoc committee was formed at Detachment 2 Alpha [Second ADVON] in early 1962 to recommend the features of a ground support aircraft/weapons system optimized to the South Vietnam environment." [Hist, 2d ADVON, Nov 15, 1961-Oct 8, 1962, p 138.]

56. Msg, CSAF (Dir/Ops) to PACAF, AFXOP 86983, 031944Z Sep 64; Kenneth Sams, First Test and Combat Use of AC-47 (HQ PACAF, Project CHECO, Dec 8, 1965), pp 1-2.

57. Msg, MACV to CINCPAC, MAC JRATA 9858, 180911Z Sep 64.

58. Ltr, Lt Gen James Ferguson, DCS/R&D, to Maj Gen Joseph H. Moore, Comdr, 2d Air Div, Nov 12, 1964.

59. Ibid.

60. Msg, 2d Air Div to 34th TAC Gp, Bien Hoa AB, Dec 1, 1964.

61. Msg, CINCPACAF to 13th AF, C00012, 092142Z Nov 64. General Sweeney cautioned that Vietnam combat tests might "appear to be successful due to several reasons resulting in a lack of accurate, concentrated enemy ground fire during the test." [Sams, First Test and Combat Use of AC-47, p 2.]

62. Msg, CINCPACAF to 2d Air Div, AFCVO 97373, 142350Z Dec 64; Sams, First Test and Combat Use of AC-47, p 3.

63. Msg, MACV to CSAF, MAC JRATA 18669, 290955Z Dec 64; hist. 2d Air Div. Jun-Dec 1964, II, Doc 10. The crew for the first series of flights out of Bien Hoa included: Capt Ronald W. Terry and Sgt Thomas Ritter of ASD; 1st Lt Edwin H. Sasaki and Sgt Estell P. Bunch of AMRL; and 1st Lt Ralph D. Kimberlin, A1C James H. Schmeisser, and A1C Allan W. Sims of Eglin AFB.

64. Hist, MACV, 1965, Annex K, pp 439, 442.

65. Hist, 13th AF, 1964, I, 119.

66. Msg, MACV to CSAF, MAC JRATA 18669, 290955Z Dec 64; hist, 2d Air Div. Jun-Dec 1964, II, Doc 10.

67. Bunch intvw, Mar 3, 1971.

68. To avoid confusion, the designation

was revised to AC–47 in late November 1965. [Hist, ASD, Jan–Dec 1965, 1-A (Narrative), 26; Terry intvw, Mar 1, 1971.]

69. Terry intvw, Mar 1, 1971.

70. Lt Col T. E. Rickelman, "Overseas Firing Tests," App II, *Project Tailchaser: Development of a Lateral Firing Concept,* AMRL-TR-66-202, Nov 1967. Lt Col Rickelman was with the 1st ACSq, Bien Hoa AB, Vietnam.

71. *Ibid.*

72. *Ibid.*

73. PACAF Tactics and Techniques Bulletin 56, Feb 13, 1967.

74. Robert F. Futrell, *Chronology of Significant Airpower Events in Southeast Asia, 1954-1967* (USAF Hist Div, ASI, Dec 1967), p 49.

75. Terry intvw, Mar 1, 1971.

76. Sams, *First Test and Combat Use of AC-47,* pp 4-5.

77. Extract from 2d Air Div U-55 Report, DC 00932, 23-24 Dec 64, Report 55, in Lawrence J. Hickey, *Night Close Air Support in RVN (1961-1967)* (HQ PACAF, Project CHECO, Mar 15, 1967), p 36.

78. Terry intvw, Mar 1, 1971.

79. Hist, 2d Air Div, Jan–Jun 1964, V, 6. At this time the pacification plan was referred to as the "strategic hamlet" plan, the "oil stain" concept, or "new life" village program.

80. *Ibid.,* p 7; Hickey, *Night Close Air Support in RVN (1961-1966),* p 32.

81. Futrell, *Chronology of Significant Airpower Events in Southeast Asia, 1954-1967, p 25;* Hickey, *Night Close Air Support in RVN (1961-1966),* p 32.

82. "No Vietnamese outpost which was supported by aerial flares dropped from a C-47 at night was ever over-run by the Viet Cong guerrillas during the period. Whether or not the strike aircraft arrived in time to punish the guerrilla, the presence of the C-47 flare ship, as in the case of the unarmed L-19 convoy escort aircraft, intimidated the Viet Cong and kept him from gaining a victory." [Hist, 2d ADVON, Nov 15, 1961–Oct 8, 1962, p 150.]

83. Maj James R. Wolverton, "Gunships and Guerrilla Warfare," *USAF TAWC Quarterly Report,* Sep 1970, p 24.

84. Msg, MACV to CSAF, MAC JRATA 18669, 290955Z Dec 64; hist, 13th AF, 1964, I, 119.

85. *Ibid.*

86. MR, JRATA, subj: Night Mission in Side-Firing FC-47, Dec 29, 1964; Sams, *First Test and Combat Use of AC-47.*

87. Extract from 2d Air Div U-55 Report,

DC 0483, 8 Feb 65, Report 65-6, in Hickey, *Night Close Air Support in RVN (1961-1966),* p 38. This successful mission was later referred to in message, AFSC to CSAF, SCGV 14747, 231338Z February 65, which urged certain gunship development actions.

88. Rickelman, "Overseas Firing Tests," App II, AMRL-TR-66-202, Nov 1967.

89. MR. JRATA, Dec 29, 1964.

90. Rickelman, "Overseas Firing Tests," App II, AMRL-TR-66-202, Nov 1967.

91. *Ibid.*

92. *Ibid.*

93. Terry intvw, Mar 1, 1971.

94. MR, JRATA, Dec 29, 1964.

95. Terry intvw, Mar 1, 1971; Sams, *First Test and Combat Use of AC-47,* p 6.

96. Msg, PACAF to 2d Air Div, DO 50059, 150004Z Jan 65.

97. Msg, PACAF to 2d Air Div, DORQ 00052, 272259Z Jan 65. This was information given 2d Air Div from a CINCPACAF to CSAF message. [Sams, *First Test and Combat Use of AC-47.*]

98. See note 97.

99. Msg, CSAF (DCS/Prgms & Resources) to PACAF, AFODC RQ 81937, 012049Z Feb 65.

100. JRATA Proj 3T-753.0, *Final Report Evaluation of Side Firing Capability in C-47 Type Aircraft,* Aug 2, 1965.

101. Terry intvw, Mar 1, 1971.

102. JRATA Proj 3T-753.0, Aug 2, 1965.

103. Terry intvw, Mar 1, 1971.

104. Msg, AFSC to CSAF, TAC. PACAF, SCGV14747, 231338Z Feb 65.

105. *Ibid.*

106. AFLC Historical Study 374, *AFLC Support of Forces in Southeast Asia: Special Aircraft Projects, 1965-1968* (AFLC, Feb 1971), p 36.

107. Lt Col Terry says that even during these early tests they thought about equipping a future gunship with sensors, armor, and heavier armament. [JRATA Proj 3T-753.0), Aug 2, 1965.]

108. Msg, CINCPACAF to CSAF, VC 30673, subj: Side-firing Aircraft Requirements, Mar 20, 1965.

109. Document CH 0001708, FC-47, AF Archives. Maxwell AFB, Ala.

110. Msg, CSAF (Dir/Opl Rqmts & Dev Plans) to AFLC, AFRDQ RA-2 71840, May 12, 1965.

111. Msg, CINCPACAF to CSAF. DOP 31024, 180117Z Jun 65.

112. Document CH 0001708, FC-47, AF Archives, Maxwell AFB, Ala.

113. *Ibid.*

Chapter II

1. Leonard Bridgman, ed and compiler, *Jane's All the World's Aircraft, 1947* (London, 1947), p 221C.

2. Illustrating the adaptability of the C–47s to the Vietnam conflict was the statement of Gen Emmett O'Donnell, Jr., PACAF Commander, to CINCPAC on February 21, 1962: "SVN has, or will soon have, more than 150 airstrips of varying capability. . . .It is estimated that C–47s could operate in and out of about 60 of these airstrips."

3. Hist, 2d Air Div, Jan–Jun 1965, II, 27–28.

4. Terry intvw, Mar 1, 1971.

5. Hist, WRAMA, Jan 1, 1965–Mar 31, 1968, III, 2.

6. AFLC Historical Study 374, Feb 1971, pp 37–38.

7. *Ibid.*, pp 45–46.

8. MR 1445 (FS–1729/C–47), Dir/Opl Rqmts & Dev Plans, Modification Requirement for C–47 Aircraft, Jul 17, 1965; hist, Dir/Opl Rqmts & Dev Plans, Jul 1–Dec 31, 1965, p 51.

9. See note 5 and Chapter I of this study.

10. See note 5 and Chapter I of this study.

11. The August 12 amendment listed this equipment: AN/ARC–44 VHF/FM radio, AN/ARC–XXX VHF radio (Wilcox 807), AN/AIC–10A interphone, AN/APX–6 IFF, AN/ARN–18 glide slope receiver, AN/APN–70 Loran, HF–103 (618T–3 single sideband transceiver), AN/ARA–31 homing adapter, AN/ARC–27 UHF radio, AN/ARN–6 radio compass, AN/ARN–14 VOR, AN/ARN–21 TACAN, marker beacon. [AFLC Historical Study 374, Feb 1971, p 39; MR 1445–1 (FS–1729/C–47), Dir/Opl Rqmts & Dev Plans, Amendment to a Modification Requirement for C–47 Aircraft, Aug 12, 1965.]

12. See note 5.

13. Msg, CSAF (Dir/Ops) to TAC, AFXOPF 86010, 121326Z Jul 65, subj: Additional Air Force Unit Deployment to SVN.

14. Hist, USAFSAWC, Jul 1–Dec 31, 1965, pp 44–45.

15. Msg, TAC to SAWC, DORF–SW 30555, 132131Z Jul 65, subj: Additional Auxiliary Field Requirement.

16. Msg, SAWC to TAC, DOTR 00412, 162200Z Jul 65, subj: FC–47 Squadron for SEA; msg, SAWC to TAC, DOTR–AT 00427, 211630Z Jul 65, subj: Deployment of Additional AF Units to SVN; msg, SAWC to TAC, DOTR–AT 00434, 271645Z Jul 65, subj: Deployment of Additional AF Units to SVN.

17. Msg, TAC to SAWC, DPLPR 37748, 272145Z Jul 65, subj: Training Location for New SAW Units.

18. Hist, USAFSAWC, Jul 1–Dec 31, 1965, p 112.

19. *Ibid.*, pp 14, 50.

20. SAWC OpOrd 16–65, Appendix 1–Annex N, subj: Personnel Requirements—Det 8–1 ACW, Jun 65.

21. Msg, CSAF (Dir/Ops) to TAC, AFXOPF 90290, 311629Z Jul 65, subj: ANG U–10 Instructor Pilot; hist, USAFSAWC, Jul 1–Dec 31, 1965, p 51. The code name "Big Shoot" was often coupled with "Quick Speak" (psychological warfare training, using U–10s and C–47s) which occurred simultaneously.

22. Hist, USAFSAWC, Jul 1–Dec 31, 1965, pp 15, 52.

23. Activity Reports, Det 8, 1st ACWg.

24. Hist, USAFSAWC, Jul 1–Dec 31, 1965, p 53.

25. Msg, USAFSAWC to TAC and WRAMA, DMM 22370, 221230Z Sep 65, subj: Deficiencies of FC–47D, Serial Nos. 45–0919 and 43–49124; hist, USAFSAWC, Jul 1–Dec 31, 1965, pp 91–92.

26. Msg, Det 8, 1st ACWg, to TAC and SAWC, subj: Survival Equipment Shortages, Oct 5, 1965; msg, OOAMA to TAC, subj: Cal .30 MG Ammo for FC–47 Training at Forbes, Aug 27, 1965.

27. Hist, USAFSAWC, Jul 1–Dec 31, 1965, p 52.

28. *Ibid.*, p 53.

29. Msg, 4440th Acft Delivery Gp to SAWC, DPL 06007, 062030Z Aug 65, subj: Movement Directive for Four C–47s, Hurlburt AFB, Florida, to Nha Trang AB, Vietnam; msg, 4440th Acft Delivery Gp to TAC, DPL 06969, 202022Z Oct 65, subj: Sixteen Buck–Big Shoot.

30. Hist, ASD, Jan–Dec 1965, I–A, 47.

31. Msg, 6251st TFWg (Bien Hoa AB) to CSAF, subj: Red Sea: Marriage of Forward Looking IR Set with the FC–47 Side-Fire System, Sep 18, 1965; hist, USAFSAWC, Jul 1–Dec 31, 1965, pp 79–80.

32. Hist, ASD, Jan–Dec 1965, I–A, 48–49.

33. Gen John D. Ryan, "Airpower in Southeast Asia," *Air Force Policy Letter for Commanders*, Mar 1, 1971.

34. Hist, 2d Air Div, Jul–Dec 1965, I, 5–6.

35. Hickey, *Night Close Air Support in RVN (1961–1966)*, p 55.

36. Msg, CSAF (Ofc of Info) to TAC and AFSC, SAF–OIPC 93843, 222304Z Nov 65, subj: Release of Story on AC–47. It was assumed at this time that the Viet Cong and North Vietnamese knew of the gunship.

37. Hist, PACAF, Jan–Dec 1966, pp 354–55.

38. Hist, 6250th CSGp, Jul 1–Dec 31, 1965, I, 15–16. Upon its arrival in Vietnam,

the 4th Air Commando Squadron was assigned to the 6250th Combat Support Group. The 6250th CSGp (formerly the 33d Tactical Group) was organized July 8, 1965.

39. Hist, PACAF, Jan–Dec 1966, p 354.

40. It was May 1966 before each of the Squadron's aircraft had its three guns installed. [Hist, PACAF, Jan–Dec 1966, p 354.]

41. Hist, 14th ACWg, Jul 1–Sep 30, 1966, p 47.

42. Hist, 6250th CSGp, Jul 1–Dec 31, 1965, I, 17.

43. Msg, CINCPACAF to TAC, DPL 52276, 040004Z Aug 65, subj: Additional AF Deployments to SVN; msg, CINCPACAF to CSAF and TAC, OPL 52265, 290312Z, Jul 65, subj: Psychological Operations Augmentation.

44. Warren A. Trest, *Control of Air Strikes in SEA, 1961–1966* (HQ PACAF, Project CHECO, Mar 1, 1967), p 68.

45. See note 42.

46. Memo, Maj Cline, 7th AF (DOPR-PL), to Gen Momyer, subj: AC–47 Aircraft [undated]; Maj Richard F. Kott, *The Role of USAF Gunships in SEASIA* (HQ PACAF, Project CHECO, Aug 30, 1969), p. 77.

47. *Ibid.*

48. Jacob Van Staaveren, *USAF Deployment Planning for Southeast Asia, 1966* (USAF Hist Div Liaison Ofc, Jun 1967), p 1.

49. The Headquarters of the 4th Air Commando Squadron was inactivated on 31 May at Tan Son Nhut and activated 1 June at Nha Trang. [Hist, 4th ACSq Jan q–Jan 30, 1966.]

50. Hist, PACAF, Jan–Dec 1966, p 355.

51. Hickey, *Night Close Air Support in RVN (1961–1966)*, p 57.

52. Hist, 4th ACSq, Jan 1–Jun 30, 1966, p 16.

53. Hickey, *Night Close Air Support in RVN (1961–1966)*, p 68.

54. *Ibid.*, p 69.

55. Warren A. Trest and SSgt Dale E. Hammons, *Air Operations Thailand, 1966* (HQ PACAF, Project CHECO, Oct 31, 1967), pp 88–89.

56. Hist, 4th ACSq, Jan 1–Jun 30, 1966, p 20.

57. Hist, 14th ACWg, Jul 1–Sep 30, 1966, pp 54–57.

58. *Ibid.*

59. *Ibid.*

60. *Ibid.*

61. *Ibid.*; memo, Maj Cline, 7th AF (DOPR-PL), to Gen Momyer, subj: AC–47 Aircraft [undated]. For the Army report on the AC–47 support see: After Action Report—The Battle for A Shau, Detachment C-1, 5th Special Forces Group (Abn), 1st Special Forces, March 28, 1966.

62. Kenneth Sams, *The Fall of A Shau* (HQ PACAF, Project CHECO, 18 Apr 66), pp 3–4.

63. Hist, 14th ACWg, Jul 1–Sep 30, 1966, pp 59–60. During this attack on A Shau, Maj Bernard F. Fisher became the first USAF individual honored with the Medal of Honor. He landed an A–1E on the pot-holed runway during an attack, rescuing a downed airman. For an interesting account of the AC–47 being downed in defense of A Shau see: Jim G. Lucas, *Dateline: Vietnam* (New York, 1966) pp 302–304.

64. Hist, 4th ACSq, Jan 1–Jun 30, 1966, p 17.

65. *Ibid.*

66. Hist, 14th ACWg, Jul 1–Sep 30, 1966, p 50.

67. *Ibid.*

68. Hickey, *Night Close Air Support in RVN (1961–1966)*, pp 62–63.

69. Ltr of Commendation from Comdr, 2d Bn, 35th Inf, 25 Inf Div, to Comdr, 4th ACSq, Oct 22, 1966.

70. Hists, 14th ACWg: Jan 1–Jun 30, 1966, p 60; Oct 1–31, 1966, p 19.

71. Hist, 14th ACWg, Nov 1–Dec 31, 1966, I, 25.

72. Hist, MACV, 1965, p 445.

73. Hickey, *Night Close Air Support in RVN (1961–1966)*, p 58.

74. Futrell, *Chronology of Significant Airpower Events in Southeast Asia, 1954–1967*, p 117.

75. Hist, 4th ACSq, Jan 1–Jun 30, 1966, p 18.

76. Maj Gordon L. Eells, *Advanced Aircraft for the Forward Air Controller*, ACSC thesis, Jun 1967, p 20. Major Eells assesses the AC–47 as an FAC aircraft this way: "The area between the two pilots is too cramped, visibility is very poor for the FAC due to the small cockpit, the wing blocks the target area most of the time, and since there is no radio jack for the FAC, he cannot use the aircraft radios."

77. Hist, 4th ACSq, Jan 1–Jun 30, 1966, p 2.

78. Melvin F. Porter, *Night Interdiction in Southeast Asia* (HQ PACAF, Project CHECO, Sept 9, 1966), pp 44–45.

79. Hist, PACAF, Jan–Dec 1966, p 356.

80. *Ibid.;* Porter, *Night Interdiction in Southeast Asia*, p. 45. Some AC–47s based at Pleiku flew armed reconniassance missions in support of Tiger Hound. [Trest *Control of Air Strikes in SEA, 1961–1962*, p 68.]

81. Hist, 4th ACSq, Jan 1–Jun 30, 1966, p 19.

82. Ltr, Lt Col Frederick A. Roll, 7th AF Chief/Strike Plans Br, to Col Horne, Current Ops Div, 7th AF, subj: Flare/Gunship Support, Jul 15, 1966.

83. Trest, *Control of Air Strikes in SEA, 1961–1966*, p 69.

84. Intvw, Kenneth Sams with Col John F. Groom, Dir/Tiger Hound TF, May 29, 1966, quoted in Kenneth Sams, AC–47 Operations, Jan 1–Jun 30, 1966 [undated], p 8 [Project CHECO report draft].

85. Hist, 4th ACSq, Jan 1–Jun 30, 1966, p 21.

86. Trest & Hammons, *Air Operations Thailand, 1966*, pp 104, 110.

87. See note 83.

88. Memo, Maj Cline, 7th AF (DOPR-PL), to Gen Momyer, subj: AC–47 Aircraft [undated]; Sams, AC–47 Operations, Jan 1–Jun 30, 1966 [undated], p 1 [Project CHECO report draft]. With the two losses in late 1965, the total now stood at six.

89. Hist, PACAF, Jan–Dec 1966, p 357.

90. Msg, 7th AF to PACAF, DO 08195, Jun 15, 1966.

91. Hist. 14th ACWg, Jul 1–Sep 30, 1966, pp 48–49.

92. See note 89.

93. Msg, CSAF to PACAF, AFCCS 91575, Feb 18, 1966.

94. Hist, PACAF, Jan–Dec 1966, p 359.

95. Trest, *Control of Air Strikes in SEA, 1961–1966*, p 69; hist, 315th Air Div (Combat Cargo), Jul 1–Dec 31, 1965, pp 42, 58. The 4th Air Commando Squadron had six C–47 aircraft assigned as flareships.

96. Hist. CINCPAC, 1966, II, 540.

97. Msg, CSAF (Dir/Aerosp Prgms) to CINCPACAF, AFOAPBB 91752, 251950Z May 66, subj: AC–47 Aircraft.

98. *Ibid.*

99. Hist, Dir/Opl Rqmts & Dev Plans, Jan 1–Jun 30, 1966, p 66.

100. Msg, 7th AF to CINCPACAF, DPL 73417, Sep 7, 1966; msgs, 7th AF to PACAF: PL 73730, Oct 9, 1966 and PL 74066, Nov 23, 1966; msg, 7th AF to CSAF, PL 199, Oct 31, 1966.

101. Msg, CINCPAC to JCS, 220554Z Oct 66.

102. Msg, JCS to CSAF, JCS 2000, Dec 22, 1966.

103. Hist, 14th ACWg, Jul 1–Sep 30, 1966, p 49.

104. Msg, CSAF to PACAF, subj: Deployment of USAF Units to Thailand, 1 Jul 66. To comply with Ambassador Sullivan's desires, PACAF requested in February 1966 the addition of eight AC–47s to the "Lucky Tiger" Squadron for night armed reconnaissance in Laos. [Data Book, VCS, USAF, Conference— CINCPACAF, Apr 25–26, 1966.]

105. AFLC Historical Study 374, Feb 1971, p 81.

106. *Ibid.*, p 85.

107. Porter, *Night Interdiction in Southeast Asia*, App 5.

108. Hist, 14th ACWg, Nov 1–Dec 31, 1966, I, 21, 32.

109. *Ibid.*, p 35.

110. Hist, 4th ACSq, Jun 30–Sep 30, 1966, p 1.

111. *Ibid.*, p 2.

112. Ltr, ALO/Tay Ninh Province to 14th ACWg, subj: Close Air Support by AC–47s, Nov 11, 1966.

113. Hist, 14th ACWg, Nov 1–Dec 31, 1966, I, 35.

114. Two replacement aircraft were received in May and two more in July. [Memo, Maj Cline, 7th AF (DOPR-PL), to General Momyer, subj: AC–47 Aircraft [undated].]

115. Hist, 14th ACWg, Jul 1–Sep 30, 1966, p 59; hist, 4th ACSq, Jun 30–Sep 30, 1966, p 5. Lt Col Max F. Barker discusses this in his End of Tour Report.

116. Hist, 14th ACWg, Oct 1–31, 1966, p 19.

117. *Ibid.*, pp 27–28.

118. Hist, 4th ACSq, Jan 1–Jun 30, 1966, p 9.

119. Hist, 14th ACWg, Oct 1–31, 1966, p 28.

120. Hists, 14th ACWg: Jan 1–Jun 30, 1966, pp 46–49; Jul 1–Sep 30, 1966, p 98.

121. Hist, 4th ACSq, Jun 30–Sep 30, 1966, p 8; ltr, Capt Russel R. Young, Armt Off, 4th ACSq, to Mr. Kenneth K. Cobb, Dir/ Armt Dev, Eglin AFB, Fla, subj: Armament Memo Report 65–36, Oct 26, 1965.

122. Rprt, Ballistics Div, AFATL, *Ballistics* [undated].

123. Hist, 14th ACWg, Jan 1–Jun 30, 1966, p 46. With the 12° declination the aircraft bank angle on a standard firing pass was 30°.

124. Hist, 4th ACSq, Jan 1–Jun 30, 1966, p 9.

125. *Ibid.*, p 10. Having given some attention to the safety of flare operations, WRAMA recommended in March 1966 that pneumatic mechanisms then used in launchers be eliminated. WRAMA contended this would reduce the lanyard length from 42 inches to 10 inches and would require only manual-pulling while the flare was in the launch tube. The SAWC recognized that this was a simpler procedure. It nevertheless objected to the WRAMA proposal, believing safety might be sacrificed if a malfunction occurred while the flares were still in the tubes. [AFLC Historical Study 374, Feb 1971, p. 47.]

126. Hist, 4th ACSq, Jan 1–Jun 30, 1966, p 3.

127. Hist, 14th ACWg, Jan 1–Mar 31, 1967, pp 13–15.

128. *Ibid.*, p 15.

129. *Ibid.*, p 16.

130. Msg, Lt Gen Robert Cushman, Jr, CG, III Marine Amph Force, to 4th ACSq, Sep 26, 1967.

131. Hist, 14th ACWg, Jan 1–Mar 31, 1967, p 14.

132. Hist, 14th ACWg, Apr 1–Jun 30, 1967, p 18.

133. Msg, COMUSMACV to Comdr, 14th ACWg, Sep 7, 1967.

134. Hist, PACAF, Jan 1–Dec 31, 1967, Annex 1, Chronology, p 15.

135. Hist, MACV, 1967, I, 416.

136. Ltr, Lt Col Francis E. Wilkie, Dir/SP, 7th AF, to Dir/Ops, 7th AF, subj: 26 Feb 67 Attack on Da Nang Air Base, Mar 4, 1967.

137. *Ibid.*

138. Msg, CSAF (Dir/Ops) to CINCPACAF, AFXOPFI 88928, 282157Z Feb 67.

139. Msg, CINCPACAF to CSAF, DO 31430, 082147Z Mar 67.

140. Msg, 7th AF to PACAF, DPLG 82642, 200630Z Mar 67. This message noted that an increase of fifteen AC–47s was previously submitted in the CINCPAC CY 66/67 requirements document as line number HO 110, but was disapproved by SECDEF Program 4.

141. *Ibid.*

142. Staff Summary Sheet, Ch/Current Plans, 7th AF, Flare Support of 7AF Bases, Mar 11, 1967.

143. Msg, CINCPACAF to CSAF, PPL 50052, 070325Z Apr 67.

144. Msg, CINCPAC to JCS, 080715Z Apr 67.

145. Msg, CINCPACAF to CSAF, DOP 52148, 130319Z Apr 67.

146. Hist, MACV, 1967, I, 416–417.

147. Msg, COMUSMACV to CINCPAC, 210223Z May 67; hist, PACAF, Jan–Dec 1967, p 475.

148. Hist, MACV, 1967, I, 417.

149. Msg, CINCPACAF to CSAF, 2420–25Z May 67, subj: Increased AC–47s for Air Base Defense.

150. Staff Summary Sheet, 7th AF, Base Defense Seminar, May 27, 1967.

151. *Ibid.*

152. Staff Summary Sheet, 7th AF, Increased AC–47s for Air Base Defense, May 31, 1967.

153. Msg, CSAF (Dir/Ops) to CINCPACAF, AFXOPF 89998, 031434Z Jun 67, subj: Increased AC–47s for Base Defense.

154. Msg, TAC to CSAF, 081450Z Jun 67, subj: Increased AC–47s for Base Defense.

155. Msg, CSAF (Dir/Ops) to TAC, AFXOPF 91872, 132030Z Jun 67, subj: Increased AC–47s for Base Defense; msg, CSAF (Dir/Ops) to CINCPACAF, 242242Z Jun 67, subj; Increased AC–47s for Air Base Defense.

156. Msg, CINCPACAF to CSAF, DMM 47006, 300148Z Jun 67, subj: Increased AC–47s for Base Defense.

157. Futrell, *Chronology of Significant Airpower Events in Southeast Asia, 1954–1967*, p 138.

158. A change to USAF Program Document 69–3 accomplished the unit realignment. [Msg, CINCPACAF to 7th AF, 062128Z Sep 67, subj: Change to USAF PD 69–3.]

159. Msg, CSAF (Dir/Maint Engrg) to AFLC, 091446Z Sep 67.

160. Msg, CSAF (Dir/Ops) to PACAF, Sep 9, 1967.

161. Staff Summary Sheet, 7th AF, AC–47 Realignment, Sep 16, 1967.

162. On August 19, 1967, the 14th Air Commando Wing Commander had recommended establishment of a gunship FOL for airbase defense support. [Ltr, Comdr, 14th ACWg, to 7th AF (DCO), subj: Airborne Base Defense Support, 19 Aug 67.] Establishment of a FOL at Da Nang would require construction of billeting for 24 officers and 71 airmen at an estimated cost of $140,000. A target date for FOL operation was Feb 1968. [Staff Summary Sheet 7th AF, Da Nang Beddown, Oct 10, 1967.]

163. Staff Summary Sheet, 7th AF, AC–47 Realignment, Sep 16, 1967.

164. *Ibid.*

165. Msg, 7th AF to PACAF, subj: SEA Deployment AC–47, Sep 18, 1967.

166. Hist, 7th AF, Jul 1–Dec 31, 1967, I, XV.

167. The MACV History declared that at the end of 1967 the Gunship II evaluation indicated a threefold improvement over the AC–47. [Hist, MACV, 1967, I, 11.]

168. Hist, 14th ACWg, Jan 1–Mar 31, 1967, p 13.

169. *Ibid.*, pp 20–21.

170. *Ibid.*, p 13.

171. Final Report, 14th ACWg, Evaluation of AC–47 Mini-Gun Problems, Sep 30, 1967.

172. Hist, 14th ACWg, Apr 1–Jun 30, 1967, p 14.

173. AFLC Historical Study 374, Feb 1971, pp 47–48.

174. Hist, 14th ACWg, Jul 1–Sep 30, 1967, p 20.

175. Hist, 14th ACWg, Oct. 1–Dec 31, 1967, p 22.

176. Hist, 14th ACWg, Jul 1-Sep 30, 1967, p 19.

177. Hists, 14th ACWg: Jan 1-Mar 31, 1967, p 15; Apr 1-Jun 30, 1967, p 16.

178. Jacob Van Staaveren, *The Air Force in Southeast Asia: Toward a Bombing Halt, 1968* (Ofc/AF Hist, Sep 1970), p 7.

179. *Ibid.*, p 14.

180. *Ibid.*

181. Ltr, Col Paul C. Watson, Comdr, 366th TFWg, to Comdr, 14th ACWg, subj: Defense of Da Nang, Mar 14, 1968.

182. Hist, 14th ACSq, Jan 1-Mar 31, 1968, pp 48-50.

183. *The Air Commando*, Mar 15, 1968; hist, 14th ACWg, Jan 1-Mar 31, 1968, pp 27-28.

184. *Ibid.*

185. *Ibid.*

186. Hist, 14th SOWg, Jul 1-Sep 30, 1968, p 23.

187. Taped intvw of participants at Duc Lap; hist, 14th SOWg (formerly 14th ACWg), Jul 1-Sep 30, 1968. *The New York Times* September 2, 1968, told of the gunship role in the battle at Duc Lap. The heading was "Spooky the Plane Hailed in Vietnam."

188. DAF SO GB-260, Jun 13, 1968.

189. Newspaper clippings in hist, 14th ACWg, Apr 1-Jun 30, 1968, I, atch 3.

190. *Ibid.*

191. Msg, CINCPACAF to 7th AF, subj: Redesignation of 14th Air Commando Squadron, Mar 21, 1968.

192. Hist, 14th SOWg, Jul 1-Sep 30, 1968, p 3.

193. Msg, 14th SOWg to DASC Victor Hue Phu Bai, I DASC Da Nang, II DASC Pleiku, III DASC Bien Hoa, IV DASC Can Tho, subj: Spooky Operations, Sep 3, 1968.

194. Ltr, 4th SOSq to 14th SOWg, subj: Night Hawk Mission Report, Sep 25, 1968.

195. *Ibid.* Paragraph VI of the report contained this comment: "Some investigation could be warranted as to the feasibility of using a night observation device in conjunction with the AC-47 pilot gunship. This capability would allow a more direct approach to the basic mission outlined in the concept of operations." At this same time, of course, Gunship II was so equipped and the Gunship IIIs would include this capability.

196. Msg, USAFSAWC to TAC, 012204Z Mar 68, subj: Semi-Automatic Flare Launcher and Eraser System.

197. Msg, 7th AF to PACAF, subj: SEAOR 152 FY 68 Class V Mod-Installation of Special Equipment in AC-47 Gunship, Oct 22, 1968. Air Force Systems Command considered still another palletized fire-control system for test in the latter half of 1968. A company had developed a computerized day/night fire-control system which appeared to offer advantages in quick conversion of cargo aircraft into gunships. In July AFSC proposed to TAC that a joint test be arranged. [Msg, AFSC to TAC, subj: Evaluation of Palletized Day/Night Fire Control System for AC-47 and other Applications, Jul 19, 1968.]

198. Msg, 7th AF/13th AF to 7th AF, subj: AC-47 Gunship Employment in Barrel Roll, May 15, 1969; Kott, *The Role of USAF Gunships in SEASIA*, p 16.

199. Msg, 7th AF to PACAF, 131230Z Mar 69, subj: AC-47 Deployment.

200. Briefings, Col William H. Ginn, Jr., Dep Comdr/Ops, 14th SOWg, to SAF Robert C. Seamans, Jr., subj: [Defense of Lima Sites] [undated].

201. Msg, CINCPACAF to CINCPAC, 152125Z Mar 69, subj: AC-47 Gunship Operations. This became Detachment E, 4th SOSq.

202. Kott, *The Role of USAF Gunships in SEASIA*, p 17.

203. Ltr, 4802d JLD to 7th/13th AF, subj: "Spooky" BDA, 19 Mar 69.

204. Hist, SOWg, Jan 1-Mar 31, 1969, p 26.

205. The Air Attache's congratulatory remarks are quoted in message, 7th AF to 14th SOWg, 130230Z May 1969, subject: AC-47 Gunship in Barrel Roll.

206. Hist, 14th SOWg, Jan 1-Mar 31, 1969, p 26.

207. Msg, 7th AF/13th AF to 7th AF, subj: AC-47 Deployment, May 8, 1969.

208. *Ibid.*

209. Msg, CINCPACAF to 7th AF, 010320Z Jul 69, subj: Gunship Support in Barrel Roll.

210. Hist, 14th SOWg, Apr 1-Jun 30, 1969, p 24 and p 1 of Gunship Operations.

211. Hist, CINCPAC, 1969, p 208.

212. Kott, *The Role of USAF Gunships in SEASIA*, p 19. The transfer of AC-47s to VNAF was contained in VNAF Conversion Plan 69-15. [Msg, 7th AF to 14th SOWg, subj: AC-47 Transfer, Jun 6, 1969.]

213. Hist, 14th SOWg, Apr 1-Jun 30, 1969, p 3.

214. Hist, 14th SOWg, Jul 1-Sep 30, 1969, p 13.

215. Hist, CINCPAC, 1969, III, 209.

216. Hist, 14th SOWg, Jul 1-Sep 30, 1969, p 1 of Gunship Operations. Briefly in 1969, the 4th SOSq was given supervision of the Seventh Air Force C-47 Theater Indoctrination School. When the 4th SOSq was later inactivated the school was transferred to the 9th SOSq.

217. This was done by PACAF Movement Order 26, July 10, 1969. Also, see: History,

14th SOWg, Oct 1–Dec 31, 1969. A total of thirty-two tons of equipment, four aircraft, and ninety personnel were involved in the move.

218. Hist, 14th SOWg, July 1–Sep 30, 1969, p 3 of Gunship Operations. On October 12 the 4th SOSq acquired two C–47 Moonshine aircraft (one each from the 5th and 9th SOSqs) and began using them on flareship missions out of Bien Hoa and Pleiku.

219. Hist, 14th SOWg, Jan 1–Mar 31, 1969, p 31.

220. *Ibid.*, p 2; hist, 14th SOWg, Apr 1–Jun 30, 1969, p 2.

221. Msg, 14th SOWg to 7th AF, Jan 18, 1969.

222. Hist, 14th SOWg, Jan 1–Mar 31, 1969, p 1. The 14th SOWg had become the largest fighting wing in Vietnam. It was unusual in flying 9 types of aircraft from 11 operating locations. On March 8 the 14th Wing ended its third year in the Southeast Asian war.

223. For a fast-moving detailed account of this gunship episode, see Capt Gary A. Guimond, "Hot Flare! Hot Flare!" *Airman* XIV (June 1970), 28-30.

224. *Ibid.*, A1C Levitow became the lowest ranking airman ever to receive the Medal of Honor.

225. Hist, 14th SOWg, Oct 1–Dec 31, 1969.

226. Hists, 14th SOWg, Apr 1–Jun 30, 1969, p 22; Jul 1–Sep 30, 1969, p 3. Action was again taken in September to economize on ammunition by minimizing its expenditures.

227. Hist, 14th SOWg, Jan 1–Mar 31, 1969, p 21.

228. *Ibid.*

229. Hist, 14th SOWg, Apr 1–Jun 30, 1969, p 18. In eighteen months of operation, the 3d SOSq had to give in-country indoctrination and training to over 400 combat crewmembers. This illustrates the magnitude of the continuous training problem. [Ltr, 14th SOWg to 7th AF, subj: Recommendation for Award of Unit Decoration, May 21, 1969.]

230. Hist, 14th SOWg, Jan 1–Mar 31, 1969, p 19. In December 1968 General Brown, Seventh Air Force commander, proposed to PACAF that Nha Trang AB be returned to the VNAF and USAF units be relocated. Many messages passed between PACAF and Air Force headquarters before approval was given. [Hist, PACAF, Jan 1–Jun 30, 1969, pp 43-49.]

231. Msg, CINCPAC to 7th AF, subj: Clearance for AC–47 Aircraft, Oct 22, 1969.

232. Hist, 14th SOWg, Jul 1–Sep 30, 1969 p 2 of Gunship Operations.

233. Msg, 14th SOWg to 7th AF, subj: AC–47/AC–119G Deployment, Oct 24, 1969.

234. See note 232.

235. Hist, 14th SOWg, Oct 1–Dec 31, 1969, p 18.

236. Hist, 14th SOWg, Oct 1–Dec 31, 1969, pp 4–6. Inactivation of the 4th SOSq was effective December 15, 1969.

237. ROC PACAF–6–69, PACAF, subj: Gunship Program for Air Base Defense, Apr 7, 1969.

238. *Ibid.*

239. Hist, WRAMA, Jul 1, 1969–Jun 30, 1970, part II, 44; Hearings before the House Subcommittee of the Committee on Appropriations, 92d Cong, 1st sess, Apr 6, 1971, p 661. A cost figure of $5.3 million was stated in these Hearings.

Chapter III

1. Proj Little Brother Planning Doc, Dir/ Alft Planning, Dep/Adv Sys Planning, ASD, Jul 1, 1966.

2. Maj Ronald W. Terry and Capt Terry R. Jorris, "Gunship II, A Study of In-House Response to a Unique Operational Requirement," *Proceedings of the 1968 Air Force Science and Engineering Symposium*, USAFA, Oct 30–Nov 1, 1968, IV, U-10.

3. Memo, Dr V.V. McRae to Dr Donald F. Hornig, subj: Case Study for the Vietnam Development Group: Night Vision for Aircraft Systems, Dec 13, 1967.

4. *Ibid.*

5. *Ibid.*; memo, Sp Asst to the Pres on Sci & Tech, Dr Lee DuBridge, to SAF Robert C. Seamans, Jr., Jul 1, 1969.

6. Hist, Dir/Dev, Jul 1–Dec 31, 1966, pp 93–98; Herman S. Wolk, *USAF Plans and Policies R&D for Southeast Asia, 1965–1967* (Ofc/AF Hist, Jun 1969), pp 59–61.

7. *Ibid.*

8. This title had a definite nautical sound and was evidently chosen to distinguish it from Army armed helicopters. [Terry intvw, Mar 1, 1971.]

9. Ltr, Dir/Dev (AFRDD-S) to AFSC, TAC, AFLC, ATC, PACAF, subj: Shed Light Guidance, Nov 17, 1966.

10. Hist, Dir/Dev, Jul 1–Dec 31, 1966, pp 76–77.

11. See note 9.

12. Hist, Dir/Dev, Jan 1–Jun 30, 1967, p 98.

13. *Ibid.*, p 80.

14. Terry and Jorris, "Gunship II, A Study of In-House Response to a Unique Operational Requirement," p 118.

15. Hist, Dir/Dev, Jan 1-Jun 30, 1967, p 80.

16. AFLC Historical Study 374, Feb 1971, pp 92-93; hist, ASD, Jul 1968-Jun 1969, I, 132.

17. Hist, ASD, Jul 1968-Jun 1969, I, 132.

18. Hist, Dir/Ops, Jan 1-Jun 30, 1967, p 219.

19. Hist, Dir/Dev, Jan 1-Jun 30, 1967, p 81.

20. Hist, Dir/Dev, Jul 1-Dec 31, 1967, p 180.

21. Hist, MACV, 1967, II, 871.

22. Hist, Dir/Dev, Jul 1-Dec 31, 1967, p 181.

23. Hist, ASD, Jul 1968-Jun 1969, I, 132. Headquarters AFLC assigned the nickname Loggy Stinger with a precedence rating of 1-7 to the program to aid in its support. [AFLC Historical Study 374, Feb 1971, p 93.]

24. Terry and Jorris, "Gunship II, A study of In-House Response to a Unique Operational Requirement," p U-26.

25. *Ibid.*, p U-28.

26. Hist, 7th AF, Jul 1-Dec 31, 1967, I, 135-36. Page XV of this history's Chronology indicates that the prototype arrived at Nha Trang AB on September 26, 1967.

27. Kott, *The Role of USAF Gunships in SEASIA*, p 25.

28. TAC OPlan 6, Final Report Gunship II, Feb 1968.

29. Hist, 7th AF, Jul 1-Dec 31, 1967, I, 136.

30. Gunship II Flight Test and Combat Evaluation Interim Report, TAC, Dec 11, 1967, p 3.

31. Ltr, USA Vietnam (AVHGC-DST), to Dep CG, USA Vietnam, subj: Letter Report— Army Evaluation of USAF Gunship II, Jan 10, 1968, p 9.

32. Ltr, USA Vietnam to CG, USA Combat Development Command, Fort Belvoir, Va, subj: Army Evaluation of USAF Gunship II, Jan 15, 1968.

33. Hist, 7th AF, Jul 1-Dec 31, 1967, I, 53.

34. Hist, Gunship II Proj Div, ASD, Jul 1-Dec 31, 1968, p 4.

35. Release, ASD, Aug 16, 1968.

36. AFLC Historical Study 374, Feb 1971, pp 93-94.

37. Terry intvw, Mar 1, 1971.

38. Hist, Gunship II Proj Div, ASD, Jul 1-Dec 31, 1968, p 4. There were also: 13 secondary fires, 23 secondary explosions, 3 gunsights destroyed, and an average of 94 flying hours per month. Of the total 53

missions (94 sorties) flown, 20 missions supported friendly forces engaging the enemy.

39. Hist, MACV, 1967, I, 11.

40. Kott, *The Role of USAF Gunships in SEASIA*, pp 25-26.

41. Hist, 7th AF, Jul 1-Dec 31, 1967, I, 136.

42. MR, Lt Gen William D. Momyer, Comdr 7th AF, subj: CHC Meeting (2 Dec 67), Dec 3, 1967.

43. Hist, ASD, Jul 1968-Jun 1969, I, 133. To expedite the prototype's return, the original TAC/AFSC task force was to return with the aircraft for temporary duty of 179 days. Permanent crew replacements were expected in SEA by March 1968. At this time the task force personnel would return to the United States to assist in the follow-on gunship development and training. [Msg, CSAF to CINCPACAF, TAC, AFSC, ASD, USAF-MPC 102046Z Jan 68, subj: Gunship II Deployment.]

44. Terry intvw, Mar 1, 1971.

45. The Detachment 2 Commander was Lt Col Ross E. Hamlin. [Hist, 14th ACWg, Jan 1-Mar 31, 1968, pp 23-25.]

46. Hist, 14th ACWg, Jan 1-Mar 31, 1968, p 23.

47. Hist, Gunship II Proj Div, ASD, Jul 1-Dec 31, 1968, p 4. On March 19, 1968 General Momyer passed along to the 14th ACWg the following message from General Westmoreland: "Have noted with pleasure the continuing impressive accomplishments of Gunship II." General Momyer added: "I deeply appreciate the spectacular accomplishments of Gunship II." [Msg, 7th AF to 14th ACWg, subj: Congratulatory Message, General Momyer to Col Patton, Mar 19, 1968.]

48. Staff Summary Sheet, 7th AF, Employment of AC-130 (Gunship II), Jun 15, 1968.

49. Staff Summary Sheet, 7th AF (DPLG), AC-130 Gunship II, Jun 19, 1968; Ltr, 7th AF to 14th ACWg, subj: Gunship II (AC-130) Temporary Deployment, Jun 19, 1968.

50. Kott, *The Role of USAF Gunships in SEASIA*, p 27.

51. Staff Summary Sheet, 7th AF (DPLG), AC-130 Gunship II, Jun 19, 1968. The execution order was message, 7th AF to 834th Air Div, 14th ACWg, 8th TFWg, 460th TRWg, 377th CSGp, 210355Z June 1968, subject: Employment of AC-130 (Gunship II).

52. Hist, 14th SOWg, Jul 1-Sep 30, 1968, p 12.

53. Hist, Gunship II Proj Div, ASD, Jul 1-Dec 31, 1968, p 4. Ammunition expenditures for February through November were: 565,900 rounds of 20-mm and 423,400 rounds

of 7.62-mm. A total of 1,610 illumination flares and 66 marker flares were used.

54. Kott, *The Role of USAF Gunships in SEASIA*, p 27.

55. Hist, Gunship II Proj/Div, ASD, Jul 1–Dec 31, 1968, p 3; hist, Dir/Dev, Jul 1–Dec 31, 1968, p 166.

56. The 14th ACWg strongly urged the prototype be returned to the United States with the substitution of production models. [Msg, 14th ACWg to 7th AF, 240641Z Apr 68, subj: AC-130 Gunship; msg, 7th AF to CINCPACAF, 120220Z Sep 68; subj: Gunship II Prototype Replacement; msg, 14th SOWg to 7th AF, 070947Z Sep 68; subj: AC-130 Aircraft Transfer.] The extent of the prototype's equipment problems was revealed by message, 7th AF to CINCPACAF, 200200-Z September 1968, subj: Gunship II and message, TAC to AFSC, AFLC, CSAF, 011805Z October 1968, subj: Gunship II. The items with difficulty included: APS-42 radar, doppler radar, weather-avoidance radar, flare launcher, illuminator, fire-control safety display, and infrared target acquisition.

57. The Directorate of Development at Air Force headquarters reported different cost figures. It listed total cost of the prototype program as $3,701,222; average cost per operating hour, $3,459; and average cost per kill, $5,676. [Hist, Dir/Dev, Jul 1–Dec 31, 1968, p 167.]

58. Air Staff Summary Sheet, Use of C-130s in Shed Light Program, Oct 24, 1967.

59. Memo, SAF Harold Brown to Chief of Staff, subj: Use of C-130s in Shed Light Program, Nov 7, 1967.

60. Msg, CSAF (Dir/Ops) to CINCPAC-AF and TAC, AFXOPF 84039, May 6, 1967. This message asked the addressees to submit comments on a follow-on gunship aircraft by May 10, 1967.

61. Msg, CSAF to CINCPACAF, subj: Follow-on Aircraft for AC-47 and SEAOR 50/Hunter/Gunship, Jun 8, 1967.

62. Memo, SAF to Vice Chief of Staff, subj: C-119 G/K Gunship Phase-in, Jun 8, 1967.

63. Msg, CSAF to CINCPACAF, subj: Follow-on Aircraft for AC-47, Jun 24, 1967; hist, Dir/Ops, Jan 1–Jun 30, 1967 p 291.

64. Msg, Gen Momyer, Comdr, 7th AF, to Gen Ryan, CINCPACAF, subj: Follow-on Aircraft for AC-47, Jun 30, 1967. In a handwritten note, General Momyer commented: "We have too many worn out aircraft in the theater now. For the future, we should seek quality improvements."

65. See note 61.

66. Msg, CSAF (Dir/Dev) to AFSC, AFRDDH 81350, Aug 1, 1967. This message

noted that "7AF and TAC prefer the AC-130 for the Gunship II role while DOD and SECAF actions indicate selection of the C-119K." Later, the message reported: "Results of the 60- to 90-day combat evaluation of Gunship II starting in September 1967 may have some influence on future replacement aircraft." This was a hint that the matter might be reconsidered.

67. Hist, Dir/Dev, Jul 1–Dec 31, 1967, p 182.

68. Gunship II Flight Test and Combat Evaluation Interim Report, Dec 11, 1967.

69. Ltr, Gen John P. McConnell, Chief of Staff, to SAF, subj: Additional Gunship II Aircraft for Night Operations, Dec 13, 1967.

70. Memo, Gen John P. McConnell, Chief of Staff, to SAF Harold Brown, subj: Gunship II Aircraft, Dec 13, 1967. General McConnell added a postscript to his memo: "It should turn out to be highly complementary to Muscle Shoals concept."

71. See note 69.

72. Memo, SAF Harold Brown to Chief of Staff, subj: Gunship Aircraft Dec 20, 1967. As a corollary to the Gunship II development, the self-contained night attack (SCNA) aircraft program (AP-2H) was canceled on December 11, 1967. The Black Spot, Gunship, and Tropic Moon programs seemed to offer more immediate operational capability. [Hist, Dir/Dev, Jan 1–Jun 30, 1968, pp 168–170.]

73. *Ibid.*

74. Msg, 7th AF to CINCPACAF, DPL 3920, Dec 26, 1967, subj: Mixed Force of Gunships in SEA; Kott, *The Role of USAF Gunships in SEASIA*, pp 4–5.

75. Msg, 7th AF to CINCPACAF, 180318Z Nov 67.

76. Msg, 7th AF to CINCPACAF, 310815Z Dec 67, subj: Gunship II Requirements; hist, 7th AF, Jul 1–Dec 31, 1967, I, 143.

77. Msg, PACAF to 7th AF, 150030Z Dec 67.

78. Msg, 7th AF to CINCPACAF, 310815Z Dec 67, subj: Gunship II Requirements.

79. Msg, Gen Ryan, CINCPACAF, to Gen McConnell, CSAF, subj: Gunship II Requirements, Feb 12, 1968; Kott, *The Role of USAF Gunships in SEASIA*, p 26.

80. Ltr, CSAF to SAF, subj: Gunship Aircraft, Jan 5, 1968; Air Staff working paper, subj: Gunship Aircraft, Jan 5, 1968, in Doc 220, AFLC Historical Study 374, Feb 1971.

81. *Ibid.*

82. Memo, Dep SECDEF Paul H. Nitze to SAF, subj: AC-119 Gunship Force, Feb 24, 1968. Secretary of the Air Force Brown informed the Secretary of Defense on February 1, 1968 of plans for BIAS/Hunter aircraft: 8 AC-130s, 16 AC-119Gs, and 16 AC-119Ks.

He added: "I believe we should make these forces additive to the AC-47s already in SEA . . ." [Memo, SAF Harold Brown to SECDEF, subj: AC-130 Gunship II and C-130 BIAS/Hunter Aircraft, Feb 17, 1968.]

83. Msg, TAC to CINCPACAF, AFSC, USAFTAWC, USAFSAWC, ASD, AFLC, subj: Gunship II Follow-on Aircraft, Feb 6, 1968.

84. Msg, CINCPACAF to TAC, 200538Z Feb 68, subj: Gunship II Follow-on Aircraft.

85. Msg, CSAF to AFLC, TAC, AFSC, ATC, CAC, PACAF, 251854Z Mar 68.

86. Hist, Dir/Dev, Jan 1–Jun 30, 1968, p 168.

87. Msg, AFLC to CINCPACAF, 151440Z Jan 68; msg, CINCPACAF to CSAF, 202035Z Jan 68, subj: Gunship Program.

88. Air Staff Summary Sheet, Maj Gen Andrew J. Evans, Jr., Dir/Dev, Third Study "Increased Gunship Force," Apr 22, 1968

89. *Ibid.*

90. *Ibid.*

91. Memo, SAF to CSAF, subj: Increased Gunship Force, Apr 29, 1968.

92. Seventh Air Force was especially concerned about a reported cost study of 208 gunships including possibly C-97 aircraft. [Msg, 7th AF (DPL) to CINCPACAF, subj: Mixed Gunship Force for SEA, Apr 5, 1968; Kott, *The Role of USAF Gunships in SEASIA,* p 5.] The Seventh Air Force reaction can be found in Staff Summary Sheet, 7th AF (DPLR) Gunship Force, Apr 15, 1968.

93. Ltr, 7th AF Dir/Manpower & Orgn, to 7th AF DCS/Ops, DCS/Plans, DCS/Personnel, subj: AC-130 Gunships, Jul 28, 1968.

94. Staff Summary Sheet, 7th AF (DPLR) Gunship Force, Apr 15, 1968.

95. Hist, Gunship II Proj Div, ASD, Jul 1–Dec 31, 1968, p 1.

96. Memo, Hugh E. Witt, Dep/Sup & Main, Asst SAF (Instls & Logs), to Robert H. Charles, Asst SAF (Instls & Logs), subj: Estimated Cost to Destroy/Damage a Truck in Laos, May 2, 1968.

97. Hist, Dir/Dev, Jul 1–Dec 31, 1968, pp 167–68.

98. Hist, Gunship II Proj Div, ASD, Jul 1–Dec 31, 1968, p 1.

99. Hist, Dir/Dev, Jul 1–Dec 31, 1968, pp 168–169. This reference contains the statement: "The Air Force will continue its efforts to secure the concurrence of OSD in modifying additional Gunship aircraft when the new political administration comes into office."

100. Staff Summary Sheet, 7th AF (DPLG) AC-119 Gunships, Jul 9, 1968; Knott, *The Role of USAF Gunships in SEASIA,* p 7.

101. Msg, Gen W. W. Momyer, 7th AF Comdr, to Gen B. K. Holloway, VCS, USAF, subj: AC-119 Gunships, Jul 10, 1968; Kott, *The Role of USAF Gunships in SEASIA,* p 7.

102. Msg, 7th AF C/S to CINCPACAF DCS/Plans, subj: Gunship Force Adjustments, Sep 11, 1968.

103. Modification Program Directive 1885 (FS-2209/JC-130A), Dir/Opl Rqmts & Dev Plans, Dec 14, 1967; hist, ASD, Jul 1968–Jun 1969, I, 135-136.

104. Modification Program Directive 1885-1 (FS-2209/JC-130A), Dir/Opl Rqmts & Dev Plans, Install Gunship Equipment in JC-130 Aircraft, Feb 13, 1968.

105. Study, AFSC, Gunship II Program Management: A Study of Its Management Success, [undated], p 2.

106. AFLC Historical Study 374, Feb 1971, p 95.

107. Msg, CSAF to AFSC and AFLC, 060135Z Jan 68, subj: Gunship Programs.

108. See note 106.

109. Trip report, Louis A. Benavides, HQ AFLC (Visit to LTVE, Greenville, Tex., Jan 10-13, 1968), Gunship II/BIAS/Hunter I, Jan 23, 1968; AFLC Historical Study 374, Feb 1971, p 98.

110. Because of support problems, AFLC very early recommended that the prototype be modified into contractor-modified Gunship II configuration. [AFLC Historical Study 374, Feb 1971, p 100.]

111. Msg, ASD to CINCPACAF, 13th AF, subj: Gunship II Logistic Support in SEA, Feb 12, 1968.

112. Msg, CINCPACAF to CSAF, May 8, 1968.

113. Msg, AFLC to CSAF, subj: Logistic Support of AC-130A Gunship II Program, May 10, 1968.

114. AFLC Historical Study 374, Feb 1971, p 102.

115. Hist, Gunship II Proj Div, ASD, Jul 1–Dec 31, 1968.

116. AFLC Historical Study 374, Feb 1971, p 103.

117. *Ibid.,* pp 106–09. Too often the extent of the logistical effort remains in the background and is not full appreciated.

118. See note 116.

119. Hist, ASD, Jul 1968–Jun 1969, I, 137.

120. AFLC Historical Study 374, Feb 1971, pp 103–04.

121. *Ibid.*

122. Amendment to Modification Program Directive 1885-2 (FS-2209/JC-130A), Dir/Opl Rqmts & Dev Plans, Install Gunship Equipment in JC-130 Aircraft, Mar 5, 1968.

123. AFLC Historical Study 374, Feb 1971, pp 104–06, CINCPACAF proposed use of air-

craft 1, 2, and 3 for initial training and delivery of 4, 5, 6, and 7 to PACAF. [Msg CINCPACAF to CSAF, 091921Z Sept 68, subj: AC-130 Gunships.] Despite logistic problems, TAC insisted on using aircraft number 4. [Msg, TAC to AFLC, subj: Revised AC-130 Delivery Schedule and Proposed Deployment, Jun 26, 1968.

124. Hist, Dir/Opl Rqmts & Dev Plans, Jul 1-Dec 31, 1967, p 51.

125. Msg, ASD to AFSC, TAC, 212309Z Jun 68, subj: Gunship II Delivery Schedule. Monitoring of LTVE's effort by Gunship II Project Division personnel had led to a belief LTVE was "unrealistic."

126. Msg, TAC to CINCPACAF, 122316Z Apr 68, subj: AC-130 Gunship Training/ Development.

127. AFLC Historical Study 374, Feb 1971, p 106.

128. *Ibid.*, p 109.

129. Hist, ASD, Jul 1968-Jun 1969, I, 136.

130. AFLC Historical Study 374, Feb 1971, p 99; Modification Program Directive 1885-1 (FS-2209/JC-130A), Dir/Opl Rqmts & Dev Plans, Install Gunship Equipment in JC-130 Aircraft, Feb 13, 1968.

131. Hist, ASD, Jul 1968-Jun 1969, I, 137.

132. *Ibid.*, p 138.

133. AFLC Historical Study 374, Feb 1971, pp 110-111; Hist, 8th TFWg, Jan-Mar 1969, p 24.

134. Hist, Gunship II Proj Div, ASD, Jul 1-Dec 31, 1968, p 12.

135. AFLC Historical Study 374, Feb 1971 pp 111-12.

136. End of Tour Report, Col William M. Fagan, Comdr, Det 6, ASD (AFSC) (AFSC-LO), Nov 10, 1969.

137. *Ibid.*, AFLC Historical Study 374, Feb 1971, p 112.

138. Hist, Dir/Dev, Jan 1-Jun 30, 1969, p 188. Amendment to MR 1885 (FS-2209/JC-130A) June 23, 1969, revised total cost upward from $37,728,835 to $47,069,555. [Hist, Dir/Opl Rqmts & Dev Plans, Jan 1-Jun 30, 1969, p 245.]

139. Ltr, 14th ACWg to 7th AF, subj: Command Relationship Thailand Based AC-130 Gunships, Jul 17, 1968.

140. Ltr, 7th AF to 14th ACWg, subj: Command Relationship Thailand Based AC-130 Gunships, Jul 30, 1968. USAF Program Document (PD 70-2) called for the 16th ACSq to be assigned to the 8th TFWg. The problems involving the Royal Thai government were also expressed to General Momyer in message, CINCPACAF to 7th AF, 130327Z June 1968.

141. *Ibid.*

142. Although proposing it control all gunships, the 14th Air Commando Wing urged in August that the transfer of command and control to the 8th Tactical Fighter Wing be expedited. Seventh Air Force said expediting was impossible since the transfer required PACAF, PACOM, and State Department approval. In October the 14th Special Operations Wing (formerly Air Commando Wing) reiterated its original position that it control the AC-130s. [Msg, 14th SOWg to 7th AF, subj: Beddown and Operational Control of AC-130 Aircraft, Oct 10, 1968.]

143. Kott, *The Role of USAF Gunships in SEASIA*, p 27. Even the one aircraft was in South Vietnam at the time.

144. 7th AF OpOrd 543-69, Jul 1968, p 1.

145. *Ibid.*, pp 2-3.

146. Hist, 8th TFWg, Jan-Mar 1969, p 15.

147. Msg, 8th TFWg to 7th AF, subj: On Dec 13 an AC-130 was diverted by ABCCC, Dec 26, 1968; Kott, *The Role of USAF Gunships in SEASIA*, p 29.

148. Rprt 69-4, *The Interdiction Campaign 1 April-31 October 1968*, ASI, Jul 69, p 22.

149. Maj Louis Seig, *Impact of Geography on Air Operations in SEA* (HQ PACAF, Project CHECO, 11 Jul 70). The following sentence from a message report of prototype operations reflects the effect of terrain and vegetation: "It must be pointed out that due to terrain, forest canopy, etc., we quite often get only one shot at a target before we lose his precise location." [Msg, Det 2, 14th ACWg, to 14th ACWg, Apr 2, 1968.]

150. Seig, *Impact of Geography on Air Operations in SEA*, pp 2-9.

151. Scientific Advisory Group Working Paper 16-67, CINCPAC, Evaluation of Laos Interdiction Program October 1965 through June 1967, Sep 5, 1967, p 2.

152. Trends, Indicators, and Analyses, Dir/Ops, Aug 1968, pp 2-12.

153. Rprt 69-3, *Air Operations in Southeast Asia, August 1967-January 1969*, ASI, Jul 1969, p 22. The 388th TFWg at Korat RTAFB, Thailand, commented on this point: "Repairing interdicted roads most certainly indicates that the enemy repairing is well prepared to cope with our more or less stereotyped system of interdiction, i.e., road repair crew base camps at strategic locations based on our repeated bombing of specified targets." [Msg, 388th TFWg to 7th AF, 131145Z Aug 68.]

154. In 1967 an analysis of the interdiction effort contained this statement: "Overall trend indicates daytime oriented strike sorties and predominantly nighttime Roadwatch reported truck movements." [Scientific

Advisory Group Working Paper 16-67, CINCPAC, Evaluation of Laos Interdiction Program October 1965 through June 1967, Sep 5, 1967, p 29.]

155. Rprt 69-5, *The Interdiction Campaign 1 April-31 October 1968*, ASI, Jul 69, p 2.

156. Rprt 70-14. *Development of All-Weather and Night Truck Kill Capability*, ASI, Jan 70, p 12.

157. *Ibid.*, pp 12-17. There was high-level interest in the interdiction effort. At midyear the Military Aircraft Panel of the President's Scientific Advisory Committee reported its concern with the development of a "truck interdiction plan for the fall of 1968." The Panel wanted to see the intergraded use of such developments as Igloo White sensors, gunships. and aerial-delivered mines. It pointed to the urgent necessity for limiting truck-flow through Laos in the critical October-April period. On July 12, 1968 Clark Clifford (Secretary of Defense), Paul H. Nitze (Deputy Secretary of Defense), Dr John S. Foster, Jr. (Director of Defense Research and Engineering), and Dr Donald F. Hornig (Special Assistant to the President for Science and Technology), met to discuss anti-infiltration systems and a truck-killing campaign. This concern was in turn passed to Seventh Air Force by Gen Creighton W. Abrams, Jr., MACV commander. He requested a study of the "entire truck infiltration problem" with a report of findings by August 31. [Msg, COMUSMACV to 7th AF, 300238Z Jul 68, subj: Anti-Truck Infiltration.] Also, the Air Force Chief of Staff had requested (on July 20, 1968 through Air Force channels) the development of an intensified truck-interdiction plan. [Msg, CSAF to CINCPACAF, 201449Z Jul 68.] In response to General Abrams' request for a report by August 31, 1968, Seventh Air Force briefed him on Commando Hunt plans. The MACV commander had reservations about the force commitment, allocation of Igloo White sensors (the Marines needed some on the DMZ), and command and control. He refused to commit a fixed level of force, saying it would have to come under continuous review depending on the tactical situation. Further, General Abrams was greatly concerned about the effect on operations by the review authority of Ambassador Sullivan in Laos. General Brown, Seventh Air Force commander, told General Nazzaro, PACAF commander, that he had detected an "air of suspicion" in his discussions of Commando Hunt with General Abrams and the MACV senior staff. General Brown suggested that—with the "clarity of hindsight"—the requirement for planning the interdiction effort "might better have been levied on MACV by the JCS." This would have made it General Abrams' plan and assured his unqualified indorsement. [Msg, Gen Brown, 7th AF Comdr, to Gen Nazzaro, CINCPACAF, 311130Z Aug 68.] The Air Force's desire to control the Commando Hunt planning stemmed from a fear it might develop into a joint operation and thereby threaten the Tactical Air Control System. [Ltr, Maj Gen George B. Simler, Dir/Ops, USAF, to Maj Gen Gordon F. Blood, 7th AF DCS/Ops, Jul 26, 1968.]

158. Wolk, *USAF Plans and Policies R&D for Southeast Asia 1965-1967*, p 78.

159. Rprt 69-7, *Air Interdiction Campaign, Nov 1, 1968-May 31, 1969*, ASI, Dec 69. Interdiction points were sometimes called "choke points" or "traffic control points."

160. Rprt 70-14, *Development of All-Weather and Night Truck Kill Capability*, pp 14-16. The emphasis on interdiction points "down-graded the previous technique of 'armed reconnaissance,' wherein strike aircraft sought out and attacked targets of opportunity although this technique was still authorized." [Hist, MACV, 1968, I, 409.]

161. Hist, MACV, 1968, I, 409. This included more than 20 B-52 strikes.

162. Msg, 7th AF to CSAF, CINCPACAF, CINCSAC, TAC, 140930Z Nov 68, subj: Impact of 7AF Summer Interdiction Campaign—July 14 through October 31, 1968.

163. Msg, 7th AF to PACAF, 191055Z Nov 68, subj: AC-130 Gunship Employment.

164. *Ibid.;* 7th AF OpOrd 543-69, Gunship II (AC-130), Aug 1968.

165. Rprt 69-7, *Air Interdiction Campaign, 1 Nov 68-31 May 69*, p 6.

166. Msg, 7th AF to 14th ACWg, 317th TAWg, 261415Z Feb 59, subj: FAC Schooling for C-130 Gunship Crews.

167. 7th AF OpOrd 543-69, Aug 1968.

168. This mission narrative is taken from AC-130 Mission Report, Mission 1316/17 Detachment 2, 14th ACWg, December 30, 1968.

169. Rprt 70-14, *Development of All-Weather and Night Truck Kill Capability*, p 14.

170. Hist, 8th TFWg, Apr-Jun 1969, III, 12.

171. *Ibid.*, 16-18.

172. *Ibid.*, 18-20.

173. *Ibid.*, 20-23.

174. Air Staff Summary Sheet, AFRDP, Use of C-130s in Shed Light Program, Oct 24, 1967.

175. *Ibid.*

176. Msg, 14th ACWg to 7th AF, 221009Z Jun 68, subj: Gunship II.

177. Lt Col Monte D. Wright, *USAF Tactics Against Air Ground Defense in SEA*

November 68-May 70 (HQ PACAF, Project CHECO, 25 Sep 70), pp 4, 10.

178. Msg, CSAF to CINCPACAF, 171941Z Jun 68, subj: Gunship II.

179. Msg, Det 2, 14th ACWg to HQ USAF, AFSC, TAC, ASD, TAWC, SAWC, AFATL, 7th AF, 14th ACWg, PACAF, 211001Z Mar 68, subj: Gunship II Report of Operations Feb 22 thru Mar 20, 1968.

180. Report of Project Moonwatch, 16th SOSq, Jun 69, pp 2-3.

181. DOA Working Paper 68/18, Dir/Tac Analys, 7th AF, Flak Suppression with F-4s for AC-130 Missions Against Trucks, Dec 10, 1968.

182. Hist, 8th TFWg, Oct-Dec 1968, p 35.

183. Wright, *USAF Tactics Against Air Ground Defense in SEA November 68-May 70*, pp 38-39; End of Tour Report, Col Wendell L. Bevan, Jr., Comdr, 432d TRWg (Sep 3, 1968-Jun 7, 1969); Kott, *The Role of USAF Gunships in SEASIA*, pp 41-42.

184. *Ibid.*

185. Kott, *The Role of USAF Gunships in SEASIA*, p 41.

186. Egan, End of Tour Report, Nov 10, 1969, p 4.

187. *Ibid.*, p 3.

188. *Ibid.*, p 6.

189. Msg, USAFTAWC to TAC, 052150Z Feb 68, subj: Gunship II.

190. AFSC recommended larger caliber guns in August 1968. [Msg, AFSC to CSAF, 011815Z Aug 68, subj: Gunship II.]

191. Hist, 8th TFWg, Jan-Mar 1969, p 16.

192. Msg, 8th TFWg to 13th AF, 251041Z May 69, subj: AC-130 Battle Damage Accident, May 24, 1969; AC-130 Mission Report, 16th SOSq, 24 May 69.

193. *Ibid.*

194. *Ibid.*

195. Kott, *The Role of USAF Gunships in SEASIA*, p 31.

196. *Gunship II Program Management: A Study of Its Management Success*, AFSC, undated, p 2.

197. Kott, *The Role of USAF Gunships in SEASIA*, figs 18, 20.

198. Msg, 7th AF to 8th TFWg, 080425Z May 69, subj: Spectre Operations.

199. *Ibid.*

200. Msg, American Emb, Laos, to Sec of State, subj: Critique of Effectiveness of AC-130 Gunship Against Enemy Trucks, May 6, 1969.

201. Msg, Gen Brown, Comdr, 7th AF, to 8th TFWg, 090207Z Jun 69.

202. Memo, Air Ops Div, 7th AF/13th AF, to Dep Comdr, 7th AF/13th AF, subj: AC-130 Gunship II Support in Barrel Roll, Jan 10, 1969.

203. Msg, Maj Gen Seith, 7th AF/13th AF Dep Comdr, to Maj Gen Jones, 7th AF DCS/Ops, subj: Night Coverage in Barrel Roll, Mar 5, 1969; Kott, *The Role of USAF Gunships in SEASIA*, pp 33-34.

204. Hist, 8th TFWg, Apr-Jun 1969, pp 30-31.

Chapter IV

1. Msg, CINCPACAF to AFSC, 260608Z Jun 68.

2. Msg, AFSC to CSAF, 011815Z Aug 68, subj: Gunship II.

3. Msg, CSAF to CINCPACAF, 051417Z Sep 68.

4. Nomination for USAF Harold Brown Award, General Technical Area: Improvement for Combat Operations, [ca Jan 1970].

5. *Ibid.*

6. *Ibid.* C-130A (56-490) had completed IRAN at LTVE, Greenville, Tex., and was delivered to Wright-Patterson AFB on May 10, 1969. [Hist, Gunship Proj Br, ASD, Jan 1-Jun 30, 1969, p 2.]

7. AFSC Activity Input . . . on AFSC Support to Southeast Asia, April 1-December 31, 1969, ASI, Case Hist 5, p 54.

8. See note 4.

9. Msg, CINCPACAF to AFSC, 140347Z Aug 69, subj: Surprise Package. On August 4, 1969 General Momyer, TAC commander, indicated he supported General Ferguson. On August 14, 1969 TAC alerted

the Special Operations Forces at Eglin AFB to identify AC-130 qualified aircrew personnel for possible use in the project. [Msg, TAC to USAFSOF, Eglin AFB, 141317 Aug 69, subj: Project Surpise Package.]

10. Combat Evaluation Surprise Package, 7th AF, Jun 1970, p 2.

11. Msg, CSAF to AFSC, 022058Z Sep 69, subj: Project Surprise Package.

12. See note 4.

13. See note 4.

14. See note 4.

15. The presentation was made at a ceremony in Washington, D.C. on September 17, 1970. [Release 70-244, ASD Info Ofc, Sep 17, 1970.]

16. Hist, TAC, Jul 1969-Jun 1970, p 356.

17. See note 4.

18. Hist, Dir/Ops, Jul 1-Dec 31, 1969, p 298.

19. Tech rprt TAC OPlan 132, Final Report Combat Introduction/Evaluation (Coronet Surprise), Aug 1970, p i.

20. *Ibid.,* p iii; hist, 8th TFWg, 1 Oct–Dec 31, 1969, p 32. See final report for a list of key task force participants.

21. Hist, 8th TFWg, Oct 1–Dec 31, 1969, p 32.

22. Tech rprt TAC OPlan 132, Aug 1970, pp iii, 24.

23. *Ibid.*

24. Combat Evaluation Surprise Package, 7th AF, Jun 1970, p A-1. AFSC Activity Input . . . on AFSC Support to Southeast Asia, April 1, 1968–December 31, 1969 lists 680 trucks destroyed and 256 damaged.

25. Unfortunately, statistics vary on comparisons of aircraft effectiveness. Page 52, *The Air War in Vietnam, 1968-1969,* puts the average trucks destroyed or damaged per sortie at 5.4 for Surprise Package, 2.62 for Spectre, and .36 for tactical fighters. [Kenneth Sams, et al, *The Air War in Vietnam, 1968-1969* (HQ PACAF, Project CHECO, Apr 1, 1970.] Commando Hunt III Report, Seventh Air Force, May 1970, states the Surprise Package record was 7.34 trucks destroyed or damaged per sortie compared to 4.34 for Spectre. Also see: Combat Evaluation Surprise Package, 7th AF, June 1970.

26. AFSC Activity Input . . . on AFSC Support to Southeast Asia, April 1, 1968–December 31, 1969, p 443.

27. Combat Evaluation Surprise Package, 7th AF, Jun 1970, pp iii, 7.

28. Maj James R. Wolverton, Maj Richard E. Willes, and Lt Col Bradford W. Parkinson, The Genesis and Development of Gunship II, ASD/USAFA, [undated working copy], pp 15–19.

29. Hist, 8th TFWg, Jan 1–Mar 31, 1970, pp 3–4.

30. Cole, *Fixed Wing Gunships in SEA (Jul 69–Jul 71),* pp 77–78. In 1965–66 the development of a LLLTV camera led to the use of such equipment on aircraft to aid reconnaissance, navigation, and strike missions under low-light-level conditions. The Air Force began experiments with LLLTV on aircraft in early 1967 with Project Tropic Moon.

31. Tech rprt TAC OPlan 132, Aug 1970, pp 4, 9.

32. Hist, 8th TFWg, Apr–Jun 1969, III, 3, 38–39.

33. Msg, 8th TFWg to 13th AF, subj: AAD-4 Update (Forward Looking Infrared) for AC-130A, Jun 1, 1969.

34. Cole, *Fixed Wing Gunships in SEA (Jul 69–Jul 71),* pp 64, 75.

35. Hist, 16th SOSq, Jun-Sep 1970, App A.

36. MR, Lt Gen William W. Momyer, 7th AAF Comdr, subj: CHC Meeting (December 2, 1967), Dec 3, 1967.

37. Msg, Det 2, 14th ACWg, to 14th ACWg [ca Apr 3, 1968].

38. Msg, 8th TFWg to 7th AF, 160400Z Mar 70, subj: AC-123K/AC-130 Bomb Damage Assessment.

39. Bevan, End of Tour Report, (Sep 3, 1968–Jun 7, 1969).

40. Intvw, author with Lt Col Charles F. Spicka, Dir/Ops, Mar 13, 1972. Colonel Spicka was a member of the 16th SOSq at this time.

41. See note 39.

42. Msg, 7th AF to 7 ABCCC, 8th TFWg, 432d TRWg, 101120Z May 69, subj: Documentation of AC-130 Truck Kills by RF-4C Night Recon; hist, 8th TFWg, Apr–Jun 1969, p 37.

43. See note 39.

44. Hist, Dir/Opl Rqmts & Dev Plans, Jan 1–Jun 30, 1969, p 254.

45. Spicka intvw, Mar 13, 1972.

46. Hist, 8th TFWg, Apr–Jun 1969, I, 32.

47. Hist, 8th TFWg, Apr–Jun 1969, III, 37–38.

48. See note 46.

49. See note 47.

50. Cole, *Fixed Wing Gunships in SEA (Jul 69–Jul 71),* p 68; Spicka intvw, Mar 13, 1972.

51. Msg, 7th AF to CINCPACAF, 100550Z Mar 70, subj: SEAOR 180.

52. Msg, 7th AF to PACAF, 031114Z Aug 69, subj: Offset Firing with AC-130.

53. Intvw, author with Lt Col Bradford W. Parkinson, USAFA, May 5, 1971. Col Roger R. Bate, Professor and Head of the Department of Astronautics and Computer Science, confirmed on November 17, 1969 the continued participation of Air Force Academy personnel in gunship development. He did this with an informal statement, "Support for ASD on Project Surprise Package." Lt Col Bradford W. Parkinson was designated as "gunship project officer for the Department of Astronautics, USAFA."

54. Hist, Dir/Opl Rqmts & Dev Plans, Jan 1–Jun 30, 1969, p 246.

55. Hist, Dir/Opl Rqmts & Dev Plans, Jul 1–Dec 31, 1969, p 209.

56. Combat Evaluation Surprise Package, 7th AF, Jun 1970, p B-2.

57. Tech rprt TAC OPlan 132, Aug 1970, p 3.

58. Combat Evaluation Surprise Package, 7th AF, June 1970, p 7.

59. Tech rprt TAC OPlan 132, Aug 1970, p iii.

60. Hist, 8th TFWg, Oct–Dec 1969, p 10. On May 17, 1969 the 16th SOSq formally requested a change from three to five 462XO weapons mechanics per crew. [Ltr, 16th SOSq

to 8th TFWg, subj: Gunship A462XO Requirements, May 17, 1969.]

61. Spicka intvw, Mar 13, 1973; ltr, PACAF to HQ USAF, subj: Request for Aircrew Composition Change, Jun 4, 1970; ltr, PACAF to HQ USAF, subj: Request for Aircrew Composition Change (AC-130 EWOs), Jul 6, 1970.

62. *Ibid.*

63. Memo, Col W. Y. Smith, Mil Asst to SAF, to Asst AF VCS, subj: Gunship Truck Kills, Mar 17, 1970.

64. Ltr, Lt Gen John W. Carpenter III, Asst AF VCS, to SAF, subj: Gunship Truck Kills, Mar 25, 1970.

65. Hist, Dir/Opl Rqmts & Dev Plans, Jan 1-June 30, 1970, p 207.

66. Msg, ASD/ASG to AFSC, 012144Z May 70.

67. Msg, 7th AF to PACAF, 060800Z May 70.

68. Msg, PACAF to CSAF, 200670Z May 70.

69. Msg, CSAF (Dir/Dev & Acq, Dir/Opl Rqmts & Dev Plans) to AFSC, AFLC, PACAF, 211358Z May 70.

70. Memo, SAF Robert C. Seamans, Jr., to SECDEF, subj: Trip Report, Far East Trip (January 10-21, 1970), Jan 23, 1970.

71. Chronology, 16th SOSq, Jan 1-Mar 31, 1970, in hist, 8th TFWg, Jan 1-Mar 31, 1970, III, 3.

72. Hist, Dir/Opl Rqmts & Dev Plans, Jan 1-Jun 30, 1970, p 204.

73. Memo, Under SAF to CSAF, subj: Surprise Package, Jan 19, 1970.

74. See note 70.

75. Msg, 7th AF to CSAF, 190730Z Jan 70.

76. Hist, TAC, Jul 1969-Jun 1970, I, 354-55.

77. *Ibid.*

78. Ltr, Lee A. DuBridge, Science Adviser to the President, to SECDEF Melvin R. Laird, Jun 26, 1969.

79. Air Staff Summary Sheet, Maj Gen Sam J. Byerley, Dir/Ops, Increased Use of Gunships, Aug 14, 1969.

80. Ltr, AF VCS to SAF, subj: Status of Gunship Program, Jul 23, 1969. This letter responded to Dr McLucas' July 15, 1969 request for the status of gunship procurement.

81. Ltr, Gen John D. Ryan, AF VCS, to AFSC, subj: Additional Gunship II Aircraft, Jul 28, 1969.

82. Memo, SAF Robert C. Seamans, Jr., to SECDEF, subj: Increased Use of Gunships, Oct 9, 1969.

83. JCS 2344/157-13 (Memo), subj: Aircraft for Laos, Jan 27, 1970; Dr. Elizabeth H. Hartsook, *The Air Force in Southeast Asia: The Role of Air Power Grows, 1970* (Ofc/AF Hist, Sep 1972), p 56.

84. Memo, Dep SECDEF David Packard to SAF, subj: Gunship Plans for the 1970's, Dec 3, 1969.

85. Memo, SAF Robert C. Seamans, Jr., to Dep SECDEF, subj: Gunship Plans for the 1970's, Feb 13, 1970.

86. Msg, CSAF (Dir/Main Engrg, Dir/Opl Rqmts & Dev Plans) to AFSC, AFLC, 221515Z Jan 70; hist, Dir/Opl Rqmts & Dev Plans, Jan 1-Jun 30, 1970, p 205.

87. Hist, ASD Gunship Prgm Ofc, Jan 1-Dec 31, 1970, p 8.

88. *Ibid.*, p 5.

89. Msg, TAC to CSAF, 240921Z Feb 70, subj: Surprise Package.

90. Hist, Dir/Opl Rqmts & Dev Plans, Jan 1-Jun 30, 1970, p 205.

91. Msg, CSAF (VCS) to PACAF, TAC, 292341Z Jan 70. General Meyer, Vice Chief of Staff, notified the Air Force Secretary in a January 29 memo that more information was needed from PACAF. [Ltr, Gen Meyer to SAF, subj: Surprise Package, Mar 2, 1970.]

92. Msg, PACAF to CSAF, 171200Z Feb 70, subj: Surprise Package.

93. Hist, Dir/Opl Rqmts & Dev Plans, Jan 1-Jun 30, 1970, p 206.

94. Hist, Dir/Opl, Jan 1-Jun 30, 1970, p 285.

95. Hist, ASD Gunship Prgm Ofc, Jan 1-Dec 31, 1970, p 7.

96. Hist, Dir/Ops, Jan 1-Jun 30, 1970, p 285.

97. Ltr, Gen Meyer, AF VCS, to SAF, subj: Surprise Package Gunshps, May 11, 1970. Maj Gen A. J. Beck, WRAMA commander pressed strongly for in-house modification at WRAMA. [WRAMA Historical Study 25, *The AC-130E Aircraft (Gunship) (Project Pave Spectre), 1970-1971* (WRAMA, Jan 1972, I, 12.]

98. Air Force Council Decision AFC4/140, Apr 30, 1970.

99. Msg, CSAF (Dir/Main Engrg, Dir/Opl Rqmts & Dev Plans, Dir/Dev & Acq) to AFSC, AFLC, 071249Z May 70. AFSC Program Direction 0000-1-70-300, Jun 17, 1970, implemented the program.

100. Memo, Lee A. DuBridge, Science Adviser to the President, to SAF, May 1, 1970.

101. Air Staff Summary Sheet, Maj Gen Joseph J. Kruzel, Dep Dir/Ops, 11 May 70; Hartsook, *The Air Force in Southeast Asia: The Role of Air Power Grows, 1970*, p 57.

102. PACAF called attention to these factors when it was evaluating requirements for new AC-130s. [Msg, CINCPACAF to CSAF, 171200Z Feb 70, subj: Surprise Package.]

103. Memorandum on Briefing to the Secretary of the Air Force, subj: Surprise Package, May 14, 1970.

104. *Ibid.*; hist, Dir/Opl Rqmts & Dev Plans, Jan 1–Jun 30, 1970, p 206.

105. Msg, CSAF to TAC, 172138Z Jun 70, subj: Post-SEASIA Gunship Force Structure.

106. Memo, SECDEF to CJCS, subj: Interdiction of NVN Supplies, May 20, 1970.

107. Commando Hunt III Report, 7th AF, May 1970; hist, MACV, 1970, I, Annex A, VI–95, VI–96.

108. *Ibid.*

109. JCSM-232-70 to SECDEF, Jun 15, 1970.

110. Memo, Under SAF John L. McLucas to SAF Seamans, subj: Secretary Packard's Call on Gunships and Laser-Guided Weapons, Jun 17, 1970.

111. Memo, Under SAF John L. McLucas to SAF Seamans, subj: PSAC and Surprise Package, Jun 12, 1970.

112. *Ibid.*

113. MR, Ofc/Under SAF, subj: Meeting on Gunships and Laser-Guided Bombs, Jun 19, 1970.

114. Air Staff Summary Sheet, Dep Dir/Ops, Additional AC-130 Gunships for the CY 70–71 Dry Season, Jul 2, 1970.

115. Msg, Dir/Mat Mgt, Robins AFB, Ga., to AFLC, 252220Z Jun 70, subj: Additional AC-130 Gunships.

116. Msg, Gen Momyer to Lt Gen Robbins (513th TAWg (RAF), Mildenhall, England, to TAC), 111700Z May 70.

117. Memo, SAF to Dep SECDEF, subj: Additional AC-130 Gunships for CY 70–71 Dry Season, Jul 2, 1970.

118. Memo, SAF to Dep SECDEF, subj: Acquisition of Additional Gunships, Jul 10, 1970.

119. Msg, CSAF to AFSC, AFLC, TAC, ATC, ASD, USAFMPC, WRAMA, CINCPACAF, 7th AF, 13th AF, 141731Z Jul 70, subj: Additional AC-130A Gunships.

120. MR, ASD, subj: Pave Pronto Conference (22-25 July 1970), Jul 25, 1970.

121. Hist, ASD Gunship Prgm Ofc, Jan 1–Dec 31, 1970, p 11.

122. See note 120.

123. Hist, Dir/Dev & Acq, Jan 1–Jun 30, 1970, p 160.

124. Memo, Dep SECDEF to SAF, SECNAV, CJCS, Jul 11, 1970.

125. Memo, SECDEF to Assistant to the President for National Security Affairs, Jul 23, 1970.

126. Ltr, CSAF to SAF [forwarding AF reply to Dep SECDEF], Jul 29, 1970.

127. Memo, CJCS to SECDEF, subj: JCSM-367-70, Jul 30, 1970.

128. Gunship Weekly Status Report to Secretary of the Air Force, Aug 6, 1970.

129. Hist, ASD Gunship Prgm Ofc, Jan 1–Dec 31, 1970, p 6.

130. *Ibid.*, Pave Pronto Conference Report, 22-25 Jul 70, ASD, 25 Jul 70, p 5.

131. *Ibid.*, p 7.

132. Hist, Dir/Ops, Jan 1–Jun 31, 1971, pp 294-96.

133. Ninth Gunship Weekly Status Report to the Secretary of the Air Force, Oct 1, 1970.

134. Seventh Gunship Weekly Activity Report to the Secretary of the Air Force, Sep 10, 1970.

135. Air Staff Summary Sheet, Dep Dir/Ops, SAF Visit to Ling-Temco-Vought Electrosystems, Sep 9, 1970.

136. Air Staff Summary Sheet, Dep Dir/Ops, Demonstration of Surprise Package Aircraft for SAF, Sep 3, 1970.

137. Minutes of Meeting 70-22 SAF Program Reviews, Program Reviews (Gunship, Program 647, F-111, B-1), Sep 22, 1970.

138. Memo, SAF to Dep SECDEF, subj: Acquisition of Additional Gunships, 1 Oct 70. Consideration had been given to contracting the optional aircraft with Hayes Aircraft Company or Fairchild-Hiller. [Memo, Philip N. Whittaker, Asst SAF (Instls & Logs), to SAF Seamans, Oct 2, 1970.]

139. Hist, Gunship Prgm Ofc, ASD, Jan 1–Dec 31, 1970, p 8.

140. *Ibid.*

141. See note 138.

142. WRAMA Historical Study 25, Jan 1972, I, 20.

143. *Ibid.*, p 22. A total of $14,859,525 was approved for modification of the prototypes.

144. Fifteenth Gunship Weekly Status Report to Secretary of the Air Force, Nov 20, 1970.

145. WRAMA Historical Study 25, Jan 1972, I, 21.

146. *Ibid.*, p 34.

147. Twelfth Gunship Weekly Status Report to Secretary of the Air Force, 28 Oct 70; hist, 8th TFWg, Jul 1–Sep 30, 1970.

148. Ltr, CSAF to SAF, subj: Twentieth Gunship Weekly Status Report, Dec 28, 1970.

149. Cole, *Fixed Wing Gunships in SEA*, pp 51-52; Air Operations Review, Dir/Ops, 1971, Vol 7, 1–5 to 1–8.

150. Twelfth Gunship Weekly Status Report to Secretary of the Air Force, Oct 28, 1970.

151. *Ibid.*

152. Trends, Indicators, and Analyses, Dir/Ops, Dec 1970, p 1–4.

153. Memo to SECDEF, subj: AC–130 Gunship Program Status, Jan 4, 1971.

154. Seventeenth Gunship Weekly Status Report to Secretary of the Air Force, Dec 3, 1970.

155. Memo, SAF to SECDEF, subj: AC–130 Gunship Program Status, Jan 4, 1971.

156. Msg, TAC to CSAF, 240921Z Feb 70, subj: Surprise Package.

157. Hist, 8th TFWg, Jul 1–Sep 30, 1970. To compensate for the absence of the AC–130s from Ubon; the 374th TAWg, Naha AFB, loaned two C–130As to the 16th SOSq for pilot proficiency training.

158. Ltr, Gen John D. Ryan, CSAF, to SAF, subj: Twentieth Weekly Status Report, Dec 28, 1970.

159. Ibid.

160. See note 153.

161. Memo, SAF to SECDEF, subj: AC–130 Gunship Program Status, Jan 4, 1971.

162. Sixth Gunship Weekly Status Report to Secretary of the Air Force, Sep 2, 1970.

163. Hist, ASD Gunship Prgm Ofc, Jan 1–Dec 31, 1970.

164. Daily Staff Digest 8, HQ USAF, Jan 13, 1971.

165. Col Bradford W. Parkinson, Significant Concepts from the USAF AC–130 Gunship Program, Naval War College thesis, Jan 28, 1972, p 63.

166. Ibid.

167. AFSC Newsreview XVI (March 1972), 4.

168. Ibid.

169. Hist, MACV, 1970, I, Annex A, VI–105.

170. Ibid., VI–95.

171. Memo, SAF to SECDEF. subj: Far East Trip (October 29–November 11, 1970), Nov 19, 1970.

172. Cole, Fixed Wing Gunships in SEA, p 47. It was pointed out this mission was exceptional and not typical inasmuch as conditions were nearly ideal, crew experienced, and all sensors operating well.

173. OPREP-5 (Commando Hunt/Igloo White).

174. USAF Management Summary Southeast Asia, Aug 18, 1971, p SEA 23.

175. Ibid.; USAF Management Summary Southeast Asia, May 21, 1971, p SEA 21.

176. Air Operations Review, Dir/Ops, 1971 (thru Aug 71), Vol 8, 2–10. Deputy Secretary of Defense David Packard told a press briefing that the "gunships are getting 80 percent of the trucks" in the interdiction campaign in Laos. [Air Force Policy Letter for Commanders, Apr 15, 1971.]

177. Cole, Fixed Wing Gunships in SEA, p 47.

178. Air Operations Review, Dir/Ops, 1971, Vol 9, 2–10. These are peak figures.

179. Ibid., p 2–12.

180. Air Force Magazine, Feb 1972, p 9.

181. Air Operations Review, Dir/Ops, 1971, Vol 9, 2–7.

182. The Baltimore Sun, Feb 24, 1971, pp 1–2.

183. MR, Spec Ops Div, Dep Dir/Strike Forces, Dir/Ops, subj: [regarding briefing for Dir/DIA], Apr 7, 1971.

184. Cole, Fixed Wing Gunships in SEA, pp 55–60.

185. See note 184. Revelations concerning the 1969 National Security Study Memorandum 1 in the April 1972 newspapers bared a long-standing split between optimistic and pessimistic groups on the effectiveness of SEA policies. The U.S. Embassy, the Military Command in Saigon, and the JCS held the more positive views; some DOD offices, the CIA, and the State Department appeared more skeptical. This division of views or outlook was apparent on the matter of enemy infiltration and the interdiction of supplies. [The Baltimore Sun, Apr 27, 1972, p A1.]

186. USAF Management Summary Southeast Asia, Aug 18, 1971, p SEA 23.

187. Ibid.

188. Col J. F. Loye, Jr., et al, Lam Son 719: The South Vietnamese Incursion Into Laos, Jan 30, 1971–Mar 24, 1971 (HQ PACAF, Project CHECO, 24 Mar 71), p 15.

189. Ibid., p 20.

190. Ltr, Gen L. D. Clay, Jr., 7th AF Comdr, to CSAF, subj: Lam Son 719 Operations: Lessons Learned, May 13, 1971, p 12.

190. Loye, et al, Lam Son 719: The South Vietnamese Incursion Into Laos, Jan 30, 1971–Mar 24, 1971, p 15.

191. Ibid., pp 51–52.

193. Ibid., p 105. The number of sorties flown in support of ground troops in contact with the enemy helped generate renewed interest in the gunship offset-firing capability. A meeting on the subject was held at PACAF Headquarters in July 1971. The conferees agreed that the gunship offset-firing system was accurate and when properly maintained could provide dependable night, adverse weather, close air support. [Minutes of Offset-Firing Capability Meeting, Jul 20–22, 1971.] The Air Force established Project Combat Rendezvous in August 1968 to support U.S. Army tests and evaluation of ground transponders for use by Air Force gunships. Ironically, this project had been placed in a hold status in December 1970 after receipt of an Army letter stating they had no requirements for transponders in SEA. The

project was canceled on March 9, 1971. [Hist, Dir/Ops, Jan 1–Jun 30, 1971, p 313.]

194. Commando Hunt V Report, 7th AF, May 71, pp 93, 181–82. Col Bradford W. Parkinson points out some defensive advantages of position, velocity, and acceleration resulting from the firing orbit of the gunship. At the AC–130 operating altitude, slant range of 10,000 to 14,000 feet, the antiaircraft gunner must lead the gunship up to ½ mile. "This is a formidable problem, especially when it is realized that the gunship is a target roughly 10 mils by 1 mil at 10,000 feet." The continuous turn (accelerated flight) would cause fire-control computers to be in error because of positioning based on an assumption of constant velocity. Multiple orbits would allow a ground gunner to adjust his fire, however. [Parkinson, Significant Concepts from the USAF AC–130 Gunship Program, Jan 28, 1972.]

195. Msg, CINCPACAF to HQ USAF, 200105Z May 71; hist, Dir/Ops, Jan 1–Jul 30, 1971, p 197.

196. MR, Spec Ops Div, Dep Dir/Strike Forces, Dir/Ops, subj: Air Staff Gunship Review, Feb 26, 1971.

197. WRAMA Historical Study 25, Jan 1972, I, 82.

198. Chief of Staff Decision Letter, subj: Additional AC–130E Gunships, Mar 22, 1971.

199. WRAMA Historical Study 25, Jan 1972, I, 82–83.

200. WRAMA on Apr 6, 1971 before the House Subcommittee of the Committee on Appropriations, *Department of Defense Appropriations for 1972*, 92d Cong, 1st sess, pt 2, pp 659–665.

201. Memo, SECDEF to the President, subj: Gunships in Southeast Asia, Mar 10, 1971.

202. Msg, 7th AF to CSAF, 031100Z Mar 71, subj: AC–130 Gunships.

203. Hist, Dir/Ops, Jan 1–Jun 30, 1971, pp 98–99.

204. Msg, CSAF to AFSC, ASD, 201912Z Aug 71, subj: Improved ECM for Gunships (CROC 6–71).

205. Msg, CSAF to AFSC, ASD, 091617Z Jul 71, subj: QRC 72–2 Chaff Cartridge.

206. Air Operations Review, Dir/Ops, Jan 1972, I, 1–4, Aircraft 54–1626 was used as the test bed.

207. Intvw, author with Capt John J. Russell, Dep/Engrg Mechanics, USAFA, May 6, 1971.

208. Msg, CSAF to AFSC, 192249Z Nov 71, subj: 105 mm Cannon for AC–130 Gunships.

209. Air Operations Review, Dir/Ops, Jan 1972, I, 1–2.

Chapter V

1. Requirements Action Directive 7–2108–(1), Dir/Opl Rqmts & Dev Plans, C–119G/K Gunship Program, Jun 28, 1967; AFLC Historical Study 374, Feb 1971, pp 122–123.

2. *Ibid.*

3. Msg, CSAF to CINCPACAF, TAC, CAC, AFLC, WRAMA, SAWC, 7th AF, USAFMPC, 222107Z Aug 67, subj: Follow-on Aircraft for AC–47.

4. Msg, CSAF (Dir/Ops) to CINCPACAF, AFXOPF 85469, 22 Aug 67; WRAMA Historical Study 18, *AC–119G/K Gunship Program, 1967–1970, (Project Combat Hornet)* (WRAMA, Mar 1971), pp 6–7.

5. AFLC Historical Study 374, Feb 1971, p 125.

6. Modification Program Directive 1851 (FS 2150/C–119G), Dir/Opl Rqmts & Dev Plans, 20 Oct 67; WRAMA Historical Study 18, Mar 1971, pp 10–14.

7. *Ibid.*

8. Air Staff Working Paper, subj: Gunship Aircraft, Jan 5, 1968; ltr, CSAF to SAF, subj: Gunship Aircraft, Jan 26, 1968.

9. Ltr, Gen J. P. McConnell, CSAF, to SAF, subj: Gunship Aircraft, Jan 26, 1968.

10. Memo, SAF to CSAF, subj: Gunship Aircraft, Feb 2, 1968.

11. Memo, SAF to SECDEF, subj: AC–119 Gunship Force, Feb 8, 1968. Secretary Brown commented: "Events in SVN during the past few days have dramatically emphasized the requirements for enhancing our gunship posture to cope with increased enemy infiltration and attacks at night against population centers and military installations."

12. Msg, CSAF to AFLC, 100058Z Feb 68, subj: AC–119 Gunship Program.

13. AFLC Historical Study 374, Feb 1971, pp 129–130; msg, WRAMA to AFLC, 091600Z Feb 68.

14. Msg, WRAMA to AFLC, 111730Z Feb 68. The AC–130 program had a 1–6 precedence rating.

15. Msg, WRAMA to AFLC, 150111 Feb 68, subj: Gunship Program.

16. Msg, WRAMA to AFLC, 091600Z Feb 68.

17. AFLC Historical Study 374, Feb 1971, pp 130–31.

18. Msg, CSAF to AFLC, 212007Z Feb 68. WRAMA had recommended Dragon II for the AC–119G and Dragon III for the AC–119K. [WRAMA Historical Study 18, Mar 1971, pp 30–31.]

19. *Ibid.*

20. WRAMA Historical Study 18, Mar 1971, p 31.

21. Memo, Dep SECDEF to SAF, subj: AC–119 Gunship Force, Feb 24, 1968.

22. Msg, CINCPAC to JCS, 032255Z Mar 68.

23. Msg, CSAF to CINCPACAF, 251647Z Apr 68, subj: Deployment of Mixed Gunship Force to SEA.

24. *Ibid.*

25. Hist, Dir/Plans, Jan–Jun 1968, pp 81–82.

26. AFLC Historical Study 374, Feb 1971, p 130.

27. Msg, CAC to TAC, 162200Z Feb 68.

28. AFLC Historical Study 374, Feb 1971, p 130; hist, TAC, Jul 1969–Jun 1970, I, 339.

29. Hist, Dir/Dev, Jan 1–Jun 30, 1968, p 169.

30. AFLC Historical Study 374, Feb 1971, pp 132–34.

31. *Ibid.,* pp 134–38; msg, CSAF to PACAF, AFLC, 202022Z Feb 68, subj: SUU–11 Assets.

32. Msg, WRAMA to AFLC, 122321Z Mar 68, subj: Combat Hornet. Earlier, there had been hope of borrowing guns from the Army but negotiations were necessary before approval was secured.

33. Msg, WRAMA to CINCPACAF, 181800Z Mar 68, subj: SUU–11A Assets.

34. AFLC Historical Study 374, Feb 1971, p 138.

35. WRAMA Historical Study 18, Mar 1971, pp 104–111.

36. *Ibid.,* pp 138–141.

37. *Ibid.,* p 141.

38. Hist, TAC, Jul 1969–Jun 1970, I, 340.

39. Hist, SAWC, Jan 1–Jun 30, 1968, pp 16–17.

40. *Ibid.,* p 33.

41. Msg, 1st Cmbt Applications Gp to TAC, 162130Z Jun 68, subj: Combat Hornet Progress Report Number One. The reduction was to 3.5 or lower.

42. Msg, 7th AF to 1st Cmbt Applications Gp, 200900Z Jul 68, subj: Combat Hornet. Seventh Air Force stated: "This headquarters feels it is necessary to maintain the specified 200 feet/minute rate of climb capability at 103 degrees, 80 percent humidity."

43. Hist, USAFSOF, Jul 1–Dec 31, 1968, pp 33–34.

44. Msg, TAC to CSAF, 012143Z Jul 68, subj: Combat Hornet.

45. Msg, TAC to CSAF, 112115Z Jul 68, subj: AC–119G; hist, TAC, Jul 1969–Jun 1970, I, 341.

46. Msg, CSAF to TAC, CINCPACAF, AFLC, WRAMA, 162213Z July 68, subj: AC–119G Operational Test.

47. *Ibid.*

48. AFLC Historical Study 374, Feb 1971, p 142.

49. Msg, WRAMA to AFLC, 232015Z Aug 68.

50. Minutes, AC–119G Weight Reduction/Increased Performance Conference, WRAMA, Jul 30, 1968.

51. AFLC Historical Study 374, Feb 1971, pp 143–45.

52. See note 50.

53. Msg, CSAF to TAC, AFLC, CINCPACAF, WRAMA, 021448Z Aug 68.

54. Msg, CINCPACAF to CSAF, TAC, AFLC, 152344Z Aug 68, subj: Combat Hornet.

55. Msg, WRAMA to AFLC, 232015Z Aug 68.

56. Msg, CSAF to CINCPACAF, 7th AF, TAC, 131614Z Jul 68, subj: AC–119 Deployments.

57. Msg, 7th AF to CSAF, 171913Z Jul 68, subj: AC–119 Gunships.

58. Msg, 7th AF to 1st Cmbt Applications Gp, 200900Z Jul 68, subj: Combat Hornet.

59. Cost Reduction Review, 7th AF, AC–119 Gunship Force, Jul 10, 1968.

60. Msg, CSAF to CINCPACAF, 7th AF, TAC, 131641Z Jul 68, subj: AC–119 Deployments.

61. Increased Gunship Force, Feasibility Study, Supplemental and Summary Report, Dir/Ops, Apr 1968.

62. AFLC Historical Study 374, Feb 1971, pp 151–52.

63. *Ibid.,* pp 150–51; contract AF 096303–69–C–0144.

64. *Ibid.,* p 152.

65. Hist, 14th SOWg, Oct 1–Dec 31, 1968, II.

66. Msg, 14th ACWg to 7th AF, 110635Z May 68.

67. Hist, 14th SOWg, Jul 1–Sep 30, 1968, p 59.

68. Hist, 14th SOWg, Jan 1–Mar 31, 1969, p 34.

69. Msg, CSAF to MAC, TAC, CAC, AFLC, USAFMPC, AFSC, AFCS, USAFSS, ATC, HQ COMD, NGB, 120025Z Apr 68, subj: Mobilization of Air Reserve Forces Units.

70. Intvw, author with Col Joe T. Pound, Dir/Aerosp Prgms, Jun 27, 1972. Colonel Pound commanded the 930th TAGp(CAC) at the time of mobilization. He reported that 250,000 pounds of equipment was moved, largely in war readiness kits and valued at about $3 million. Also, see: WRAMA Historical Study 18, March 1971, pages 43 and 44; history, SAWC, January 1–June 30, 1968, page 17

71. Msg, CSAF to CAC, MAC, TAC, AFLC, AFSC, HQ COMD, NG-AF, USAFMPC, AWS, 092217Z May 68, subj: Mobilization of Reserve Forces.

72. Msg, CSAF to CINCPACAF, 161327Z Sep 68, subj: AC-119 Deployment.

73. *Ibid.*

74. Staff Summary Sheet, 7th AF (DPLG), AC-119 Deployment, Sep 17, 1968.

75. Msg, 7th AF to CINCPACAF, subj: Gunship Force Adjustment [ca Sep 17, 1968.]

76. Msg, CINCPACAF to CSAF, 250545Z Sep 68, subj: AC-119 Deployment.

77. Staff Summary Sheet, 7th AF (DPLG), Combat Hornet (AC-119G) Deployment, Oct 16, 1968. COMUSMACV reported to the JCS on October 12, 1968 that the total Air Force strength in RVN was 61,435 (U.S. military strength: 538,876). [Msg, COMUSMACV to JCS, 120604Z Oct 68, subj: Weekly Strength Report.]

78. Staff Visit Notebook, Lt Gen Robert G. Ruegg, DCS/Sys & Logs, Nov 1968.

79. Memo, Paul H. Nitze, Dep SECDEF, to SAF and Chairman of the JCS, subj: Deployment Adjustment Request (AF-68-123), Nov 27, 1968. Change 41 of CINCPAC plans reflected the Deputy SECDEF's approval for deployment of the 71st SOSq. [Hist, CINCPAC, 1969, III, 18.]

80. WRAMA Historical Study 18, Mar 1971, p 44.

81. Msg, USAFSAWC to TAC, 032235Z Jul 68, subj: AC-119G Fire Control System Computers.

82. See article on "Hoosier" reservists of the 71st SOSq. [*The Air Reservist*, Apr 1969, pp 6, 7.]

83. Msg, TAC to WRAMA, 122119 Nov 68, subj: AC-119G Ferry.

84. Msg, 7th AF to 14th SOWg, 200940Z Nov 68, subj: AC-119G Employment. The basic operations document for the deployment and employment of AC-119Gs in SEA was 7th AF Operation Order 538-69.

85. AFLC Historical Study 374, Feb 1971, p 153.

86. WRAMA Historical Study 18, Mar 1971, pp xxxi-xxxii; TAC OPlan 120, Final Report Combat Introduction Evaluation AC-119G Gunship III (Combat King), Aug 1970.

87. PAD 68-115, 7th AF, Jun 6, 1968.

88. TAC OPlan 118, Report of Gunship G Deployment and Combat Evaluation-Combat Guard, Mar 22, 1969. In addition to assessing combat-mission effectiveness, considerable data was collected on the operational readiness rate, sorties flown versus sorties scheduled, maintenance on special equipment and subsystem operation, and aircraft maintenance.

89. TAC OPlan 118, Mar 22, 1969.

90. Kott, *The Role of USAF Gunships in SEASIA*, p 24.

91. TAC OPlan 118, Mar 22, 1969. This judgment was reinforced by the 7.62-mm armament's greater effectiveness against personnel than vehicles or storage areas.

92. Hist, Dir/Ops, Jan 1–Jun 30, 1969, p 281.

93. *Ibid.*

94. WRAMA Historical Study 18, Mar 1971, p xxxiv. The 18th and last aircraft arrived March 1, 1969.

95. Hist, 14th SOWg, Jan 1–Mar 31, 1969, pp 1, 21. To be rated fully combat ready (C-1), a unit had to possess at least 85 percent of its authorized aircraft with 71 percent combat ready and 90 percent of its authorized personnel with 85 percent combat ready.

96. SSgt Robert J. Lessels, Jr., "Shadow," *Air Force*, Nov 1971, pp 38–40. Other names associated with the C-119 were: Pregnant P-38, Dollar Nineteen, Gun-Toting Guppy, and USAF's Flying Battleship. Some of these were carryovers from C-119 days. [Maj William R. Casey, "AC-119: USAF's Flying Battleship." *Air Force/Space Digest*, Feb 1970, pp 48–50.]

97. WRAMA Historical Study 18, Mar 1971, p xxv.

98. Msg, WRAMA to AFLC, TAC, CINCPACAF, 071515Z Jun 68, subj: Combat Hornet Schedules.

99. See note 97.

100. AFLC Historical Study 374, Feb 1971, pp 147–48.

101. *Ibid.*, p 148.

102. *Ibid.*

103. AFLC Historical Study 374, Feb 1971, p 149.

104. Ltr, Dir/Main Engrg to DCS/Sys & Logs, subj: Personal Summary, Jul 3, 1969.

105. WRAMA Historical Study 18, Mar 1971, p 112.

106. Hist, Dir/Main Engrg, Jan 1–Jun 30, 1969, p ix.

107. AFLC Historical Study 374, Feb 1971, p 149.

108. Msg, TAC to CSAF, 081945Z Aug 68, subj: Combat Hornet.

109. Msg, WRAMA to AFLC, 232015Z Aug 68. Figures on some of the weights vary somewhat. AFLC Historical Study 374 lists 5,124 pounds as the excess weight.

110. *Ibid.*

111. Msg, WRAMA to AFLC, CSAF, TAC, CINCPACAF, 7th AF, USAFSOF, 271400Z Sep 68, subj: AC-119K Weight Reduction.

112. WRAMA Historical Study 18, Mar 1971, p 48.

113. *Ibid.*, p xxxiii.

114. Hist, 14th SOWg, Jul 1–Sep 30, 1968, p 19.

115. Msg, TAC to CSAF, subj: Combat Hornet [ca Oct 15, 1968].

116. TAC OPlan 120, Final Report Combat Introduction/Evaluation AC-119K Gunship III (Combat King), Aug 1970, p 103.

117. WRAMA Historical Study 18, Mar 1971, pp 50–51.

118. *Ibid.*, p xxxv.

119. Ltr, 7th AF to 14th SOWg, 3d, 31st, 35th, 37th, & 366th TFWgs, 460th TRWg, 1st CEG, AFAG, subj: 7AF PAD 68-115, Gunships, Progress Report, Apr 30, 1969.

120. Msg, TAC to CSAF, CINCPACAF, AFLC, 082214Z May 69, subj: AC-119K Deployment.

121. Msg, TAC to CSAF, AFLC, ASD, 222331Z May 69, subj: AC-119K Deficiencies.

122. Hist, USAFSOF, Jan 1–Jun 30, 1969, pp 40–41; msg, AFLC to TAC, 061936Z Jun 69.

123. Msg, TAC to CSAF, 131943Z Jun 69, subj: Gunship Offset Fire Deficiencies.

124. Hist, Dir/Ops, Jul 1–Dec 31, 1969, pp 147–48; TAC TR-68-209, SOC 15-28, AC-119K Operational Test and Evaluation (Combat Hornet K), Supplemental Report, Jan 1970.

125. Ltr, Dir/Main Engrg to DCS/Sys & Logs, subj: Personal Summary, Dec 12, 1969.

126. Hist, 14th SOWg, Jul 1–Sep 30, 1969; Movement Order 20, TAC, Aug 5, 1969. Approximate strength was 125 officers and 441 airmen.

127. TAC OPlan 120, Aug 1970, p 70. One AC-119K damaged the right landing gear while landing at Malmstrom AFB, Mont. TAC reported the brakes locked on the right side, the right tires blew, and the right main gear scissor-swiveled. Since the gear required depot repair, a replacement AC-119K departed Lockbourne AFB on 22 October.

128. *Ibid.*, p 36.

129. WRAMA Historical Study 18, Mar 1971, p 156.

130. *Ibid.*, p 68.

131. Ltr, Senator William Proxmire, Chairman, Subcommittee on Economy in Government, to Philip N. Whittaker, Asst SAF (Instls & Logs), Feb 3, 1970.

132. Ltr, Philip N. Whittaker, Asst SAF (Instls & Logs), to Senator William Proxmire, Chairman, Subcommittee on Economy in Government, Mar 2, 1970. Secretary Whittaker reported the cost of spares alone "resulted in an increase of $20.9 million."

133. WRAMA Historical Study 18, Mar 1971, p 196.

134. PAD 69-101 7th AF. See Chapter II for more discussion on Nha Trang Proposal.

135. PACAF Movement Order 16, Mar 27, 1969. Also governed by PACAF PAD 69-6 ANG/AFRES/USAF Deployment, Dec 1968.

136. Hist, 14th SOWg, Apr 1–Jun 30, 1969, pp 34–35.

137. *Ibid.*, pp 20, 34–35. The number included 27 pilots, 16 navigators, 17 flight engineers, 18 illuminator operators, and 151 other personnel [p 20]. Hist, Dir/Ops, Jan 1–Jun 30, 1969, p 344.

138. Hist, 14th SOWg, Oct 1–Dec 31, 1969. Some 166 aircrew personnel had arrived. The governing plan for the deployment was 7th AF PAD 68-115 (revised).

139. Hist, 14th SOWg, Oct 1–Dec 31, 1969.

140. Msg CINCPAC to JCS, 010130Z Jan 70, subj: Aircraft for Laos; hist, Dir/Ops, Jul 1–Dec 31, 1969, p 297.

141. See note 139.

142. TAC OPlan 120, Aug 1970, pp 36–37.

143. See note 139.

144. TAC OPlan 120, Aug 1970, pp 41–61.

145. *Ibid.*, p iii. The Combat King Task Force commander was Lt Col R. W. McCartan.

146. Hist, MACV, 1969, III, XII-12.

147. TAC OPlan 120, Aug 1970, pp 64–69.

148. Msg, 14th SOWg to 7th AF, 200730Z Nov 69, subj: Command Assistance (Request for Tactical Voice Call Sign, Gen Brown from Col Cheney).

149. Msg, 7th AF to 14th SOWg, 230755Z Nov 69, subj: Change in VCS Assignment.

150. Hist, 14th SOWg, Apr 1–Jun 30, 1969, p 67. Extensive corrosion damage was found on the underside of the fuselage, on hydraulic plumbing, and on many other areas of the aircraft. "The reciprocating power plant and the propeller system caused the majority of the AC-119 aborts."

151. Hist, 14th SOWg, Apr 1–Jun 30, 1969, p 3.

152. Hist, 14th SOWg, Jul 1–Sep 30, 1969; hist, 14th SOWg, Oct 1–Dec 31, 1969.

153. Hist, 14th SOWg, Jan 1–Mar 31, 1969, p 22.

154. *Ibid.*, p 24.

155. *Ibid.*, pp 2–3. For a description of an AC-119G mission, see: Capt Robert P. Everett, "Just a Shadow of Its Former Self," *Airman*, XIV (February 1970), 11–14.

156. Hist, 14th SOWg, Apr 1–Jun 30, 1969, p 33.

157. Elizabeth H. Hartsook, *The Air Force in Southeast Asia: The Administration Emphasizes Air Power, 1969* (Ofc/AF Hist, Nov 1971), p 38.

158. Msg, TAC to WRAMA, 162252Z Sep 68, subj: Combat Hornet.

159. Hist, TAC, Jul 1968–Jun 1969, 86–87; Hartsook, *The Air Force in Southeast Asia: The Administration Emphasizes Air Power*, p 45.

160. *Ibid.*

161. *Ibid.*

162. Hist, USAFSOF, Jul 1–Dec 31, 1968.

163. Hist, 14th SOWg, Oct 1–Dec 31, 1969.

164. "To Help An Ally," *The Air Reservist*, Jun 1969, p 15. Colonel Campbell's crew consisted of: Lt Col James H. Kirke, Maj Harold R. Crawford (navigator), Capt John I. Parish (copilot); MSgt Ronald E. Wheeler (flight engineer); SSgt Robert C. Johnson (illuminator operator); Sgt Robert Baum and Sgt James R. Boyd (aerial gunners). One author declared the illuminator of a Shadow flying at 5,000 could provide sufficient light to "read *Stars and Stripes* easily on the darkest night." The illuminator's beam adjusted from 20 to 40 degrees. [Maj William R. Casey, "AC-119: USAF's Flying Battleship," *Air Force/Space Digest*, Feb 1970, p 4.]

165. Hist, 14th SOWg, Jul 1–Sep 30, 1969.

166. Hist, 14th SOWg, Oct 1–Dec 31, 1969, p 8. A replacement for the lost aircraft was requested. [Ltr, 14th SOWg to 7th AF, subj: Acquisition of Replacement Aircraft, Oct 23, 1969.]

167. *Ibid.*

168. Hist, 17th SOSq, in hist, 14th SOWg, Jul 1–Sep 30, 1969.

169. Hist, 14th SOWg, Oct 1–Dec 31, 1969, p 19.

170. Hist, 14th SOWg, Jan 1–Mar 31, 1970, p 10.

171. AC-119G Gunship Tactics, in hist, 14th SOWg, Apr 1–Jun 30, 1969.

172. Hist, 14th SOWg, Apr 1–Jun 30, 1970, p 13. AC-119Gs flew 135 sorties and AC-119Ks 12.

173. Hist, 14th SOWg, Apr 1–Jun 30, 1970.

174. *Ibid.*, p 14.

175. Cole, *Fixed Wing Gunships in SEA (Jul 69–Jul 71)*, p 22.

176. Hist, 14th SOWg, Apr 1–Jun 30, 1970, p 14.

177. Cole, *Fixed Wing Gunships in SEA (Jul 69–Jul 71)*, p 20.

178. *Ibid.*, pp 21–22.

179. *Ibid.*, pp 19, 23.

180. Hist, 14th SOWg, Apr 1–Jun 30, 1970, p 14.

181. Cole, *Fixed Wing Gunships in SEA (Jul 69–Jul 71)*, pp 22–23.

182. Hist, 14th SOWg, Jul 1–Sep 30, 1970, p 2. AC-119Gs were based at Tan Son Nhut AB. Some AC-119Ks were sent there as weather severely limited Barrel Roll and Steel Tiger missions.

183. Hist, 14th SOWg, Apr 1–Jun 30, 1970, p 23.

184. Msg, 7th AF to CINCPACAF, 051405Z Feb 70, subj: AC-119K Temporary Forward Operating Location.

185. Hist, 14th SOWg, Jan 1–Mar 31, 1970, Chronology.

186. Ltr. Maj Gen Ernest C. Hardin, Jr., DCS/Ops, PACAF, to Maj Gen Sam J. Byerley, Dir/Ops, USAF, Mar 17, 1970.

187. Msg, 7th AF to 14th SOWg, 161250Z Mar 70.

188. Hist, 14th SOWg, Jan 1–Mar 31, 1970, p 4.

189. *Ibid.*, Chronology. "The military situation in the Barrel Roll area, as reviewed at the meeting at Udorn on 20 March, required the augmentation of the AC-119K FOL at Udorn with a fourth aircraft as soon as possible to support Laotian forces." [Msg, 7th AF to PACAF, 221100Z Mar 70, subj: AC-119K FOL.]

190. Hist, 14th SOWg, Apr 1–Jun 30, 1970, p 13.

191. Msg, 7th AF to CINCPACAF, 210945Z Jun 70, subj: AC-119K FOL.

192. See note 186.

193. Hist, 366th TFWg, Jan–Mar 1970, I, 17.

194. Atch to 18th SOSq hist, in hist, 14th SOWg, Jan 1–Mar 31, 1970.

195. Hist, 14th SOWg, Apr 1–Jun 30, 1970, Gunship Operations section.

196. *Ibid.*, p 10.

197. Msg, CINCPACAF to 7th AF, 032147Z Mar 70, subj: AC-119K Temporary FOL.

198. Hist, 14th SOWg, Apr 1–Jun 30, 1970, p 9.

199. *Ibid.*, Gunship Operations section.

200. *Ibid.*, Chronology.

201. Ltr, Comdr, 14th SOWg, to Comdr, 7th AF, subj: Improving AC-119K Gunship Effectiveness, Jun 26, 1970.

202. *Ibid.*, hist, 14th SOWg, Apr 1–Jun 30, 1970, p 16.

203. Msg, 7th AF, to CINCPACAF, 210945Z Jun 70, subj: AC-119K FOL; hist, 14th SOWg, Apr 1–Jun 30, 1970, Gunship Operations section.

204. Hist, 14th SOWg, Apr 1–Jun 30, 1970, p 16.

205. See note 201.

206. Hist, 14th SOWg, Jan 1–Mar 31, 1970, Gunship Operations section.

207. Hist, Dir/Ops, Jan 1–Jun 30, 1970, pp 168–170. The Air Force urged action in the testing since leadtimes for the gunship AN/APQ-133 beacon-tracking radar would require early procurement action.

208. Hist, 14th SOWg, Jan 1–Mar 31, 1970, pp 9–10.

209. Hist, 14th SOWg, Apr 1–Jun 30, 1970, Gunship Operations section.

210. Hist, 14th SOWg, Jan 1–Mar 31, 1970, Gunship Operations section.

211. *Ibid.*

212. Hist, 366th TFWg, Jan–Mar 1970, I, 17.

213. Hist, 14th SOWg, Apr 1–Jun 30, 1970, p 24.

214. 1970 Mackay Trophy Award citation; release 7-6-71-447, Air Force News Service, Jul 6, 1971; intvw, author with Capt Alan D. Milacek and crew, Aug 5, 1971.

215. Release 629-71, Ofc/Asst SECDEF (Public Affairs), Jul 20, 1971.

216. Hist, 14th SOWg, Jul 1–Sep 30, 1970, 18th SOSq historical data, p 2.

217. *Ibid.*

218. Hist 14th SOWg, Oct 1–Dec 31, 1970, chap III, p 5.

219. *Ibid.,* Gunship Operation section.

220. Hist, 14th SOWg, Oct 1–Dec 31, 1970, 17th SOSq section.

221. Hist, 14th SOWg, Oct 1–Dec 31, 1970, pp 6–7.

222. *Ibid.,* p 7.

223. Hist, 14th SOWg, Oct 1–Dec 31, 1970, p 8.

224. *Ibid.*

225. Cole, *Fixed Wing Gunships in SEA (Jul 69–Jul 71),* p 32.

226. *Ibid.*

227. Hist, 14th SOWg, Oct 1–Dec 31, 1970, p 9.

228. See note 225.

229. Hist, 14th SOWg, Oct 1–Dec 31, 1970, p 9.

230. *Ibid.,* p 7 and Wing Plans section.

231. Ltr, Maj Gen C.M. Talbott, Dir/Ops, to CSAF, subj: Response to Gunship Questions Asked by Gen Ryan, Feb 11, 1971.

232. Cole, *Fixed Wing Gunships in SEA (Jul 69–Jul 71),* p 24.

233. Hist, 14th SOWg, Apr 1–Jun 30, 1970, p 9.

234. Hist, 14th SOWg, Oct 1–Dec 31, 1970, Wing Plans section; Cole, *Fixed Wing Gunships in SEA (Jul 69–Jul 71),* p 25.

235. Hist, 14th SOWg, Apr 1–Jun 30, 1970, p 9.

Chapter VI

1. Dr E. H. Hartsook, *The U.S. Air Force in Southeast Asia: Shield for Vietnamization, 1971* (Washington, 1974), p 5.

2. Memo, Dep SECDEF Packard to Service Secretaries and Dir DSPG, subj: Vietnamization of Interdiction Efforts, May 10, 1971.

3. Memo, SECDEF to SAF, Jul 30, 1971. See also Hartsook, *The U.S. Air Force in Southeast Asia; Shield for Vietnamization, 1971,* App 1.

4. Memo, Dep SECDEF Packard to Service Secretaries and Dir, DSPG, subj: Vietnamization of Interdiction Efforts, May 10, 1971. Secretary Packard's memo also called for investigations of providing CBU-55 ordnance to the Vietnamese Air Force, expanded use of small airborne raiding parties on infiltration routes, feasibility of a "strategic read-out system" for RVNAF to measure infiltration, and appraisal of RVNAF needs for additional border surveillance equipment.

5. ASD Evaluation Report, *Armed Light Utility* STOL Aircraft, Jun 71. Details of U.S. and combat phases can be found in USAFTAWC Final Report, *Pave Coin Combat Evaluation,* TAC Test 71B-137T, Sep 71. A test of these aircraft in a pure utility role was also conducted by USAF Special Operations Force in 1965 (TAC Test 65-25).

6. Final Report Credible Chase/AU-23A, Aug 72, USAF Tactical Air Warfare Center, Eglin AFB, Fla., TAC Project 71A-211T and TAWC Project 1142, p 289.

7. Memo, SECDEF to CJCS, subj: I&M of RVNAF, May 17, 1971.

8. Hartsook, *Shield for Vietnamization,* App 1. An intelligence annex to the plan cautioned against unilateral success of South Vietnam interdiction if North Vietnam's buildup of Migs and AA/SAM defenses continued.

9. USAFTAWC Final Report, *Pave Coin Evaluation,* Sep 71, TAC Test 71B-137T.

10. Msg, PACAF to Air Force Chief of Staff, Jul 1, 1971.

11. Memo, SECDEF to Service Secretaries CJCS, and D/DSPG, "RVNAF Interdiction Alternatives," Jul 2, 1971.

12. Ltr, AFVCS, Gen John C. Meyer to SAF, Jul 19, 1971.

13. See Note 3.

14. Ltr, AFVCS to SAF, 6 Aug 71.

15. Air Staff Summary Sheet, "Credible Chase Combat Test," Aug 20, 1971.

16. Ltr, SECDEF to Sen. John Stennis, Jul 30, 1971, and ltr, SAF to Sen. John Stennis, Aug 2, 1971.

17. Ltr, SECDEF to Senator Stennis, Jul 23. 1971.

18. Final Report Credible Chase/AU-13A, TAC Project 71A-211T and TAWC Project 1142, Tactical Air Warfare Center, Eglin AFB, Fla., Aug 72.

19. Memo, SAF to SECDEF, "Final Report on Air-Ground C1 Aircraft for SEA Allies," Oct 13, 1971.

20. See Mr. Leonard Sullivan's SEA Trip Report #14, Interdiction Vietnamization, Oct 26, 1971, in JCS files.

21. *Ibid.* Also, see Hartsook, *The U.S. Air Force in Southeast Asia: Shield for Vietnamization, 1971,* May 1974, App 1, p 121.

22. Memo, JCS to SECDEF, "RVNAF Interdiction Alternatives," Aug 23, 1971.

23. Memo, SECDEF to CJCS, Oct 8, 1971.

24. *Ibid.*

25. Memo, JCS to SECDEF, Nov 12, 1971, subj: Interdiction.

26. Memo, SAF to SECDEF, Nov 24, 1971.

27. Memo, SECDEF to CJCS, "Credible Chase Program," Nov 29, 1971.

28. Final Report, Credible Chase/AU-23A, Annex G, Aug 72, USAF Tactical Air Warfare Center, Eglin AFB, Fla., TAC Project 71A-211T and TAWC Project 1141, p 289.

29. Memo, Col Jack Elliott, Dir/Plans, to Chief of Staff, "Credible Chase Program," Dec 2, 1971.

30. CINCPAC msg 020603Z Dec 71 to JCS, subj: Credible Chase Program, and COMUSMACV msg 020115Z Dec 71 to JCS, subj: Credible Chase Program.

31. Proposed draft msg to CINCPAC from JCS, 2 Dec 71, in Air Staff Briefs to JCS. See also Hartsook, *The U.S. Air Force in Southeast Asia: Shield for Vietnamization, 1971,* App 1, p 124.

32. Memo, Admiral Moorer to SECDEF, Dec 3, 1971, in JCS files.

33. Memo, SECDEF to CJCS, Dec 6, 1971, in JCS files.

34. Talking Paper, Asst for Vietnamization to CSAF, Dec 7, 1971, in Air Staff Briefs to JCS.

35. See Hartsook, *Shield for Vietnamization, 1971,* App 1, p 126.

36. Memo, JCS to SECDEF, Dec 10, 1971.

37. *Ibid.*

38. Memo, CNO to CJCS, Jan 17, 1972. 1972.

39. Memo, SAF to SECDEF, "Credible Chase Combat Evaluation," Feb 16, 1972.

40. Final Report, "Credible Chase Combat Evaluation," Feb 16, 1972.

41. Final Report, Credible Chase/AU-23A, Aug 72, TAC, USAF Tactical Air Warfare Center, Eglin, Fla., TAC Project 71-A-211T and TAWC Project 1142, Annex G, p 291.

42. *Ibid.*

43. *Ibid.,* p 292.

44. Final Report, Credible Chase/AU-24A, TAC USAF Tactical Air Warfare Center, Eglin AFB, Fla., TAC Project 71A-211T and TAWC Project 1142, Jul 72, and Final Report Credible Chase/AU-23A, TAC, USAF Tactical Air Warfare Center, Eglin AFB, Fla., TAC Project 71A-211T and TAWC Project 1142, Aug 72.

45. *Ibid.*

46. Hartsook, *Shield for Vietnamization, 1971,* p 5.

47. Commando Hunt VII, 7AF, Jun 72, pp 7, 14-16, 18-20, 44, 59, 71-72, 201.

48. Commando Hunt VII, 7AF, Jun 72, p 227.

49. Commando Hunt VII, Hq 7AF, p 67.

50. Hist, 8th TFWg, Jan 1-Mar 31, 1972, p 35.

51. Col Harry G. Canham, End of Tour Report, Jan 31, 1973, p 15.

52. Commando Hunt VII, 7AF, pp 19, 76-83, 85-86.

53. Ltr, 8th TFWg to 13th Air Force/DPSP, subj: Hist, 8th Tactical Fighter Wing, Jan 1-Mar 31, 1972.

54. Citation for award of the Air Force Cross to Capt Waylon O. Fulk contained in Hist, 8th TFWg, Jan 1-Mar 31, 1973.

55. John Keegan, *The Face of Battle* (New York), 1976, p 297.

56. Commando Hunt VII, 7AF, Jun 72, pp 164, 167.

57. Capt David K. Mann, *The 1972 Invasion of Military Region I: Fall of Quang Tri and Defense of Hue* (HQ PACAF, Proj CHECO, Mar 15, 1973), pp 1-2, 14.

58. Hist, 8th TFWg, Apr 1-Jun 30, 1972, pp 26-28, 44.

59. Hist, 8th TFWg, Jul 1-Sep 30, 1972, pp 3-5, 11-12.

60. Hist, 8th TFWg, Apr 1-Jun 30, 1972, pp 45-46.

61. Capt David K. Mann, *The 1972 Invasion of Military Region 1: Fall of Quang Tri and Defense of Hue,* (HQ PACAF, Proj CHECO, Mar 15, 1973), pp 50, 57, 69-70.

62. Capt Peter A.W. Liebchen, *Kontum: Battle for the Central Highlands, 30 Mar-10 Jun 72,* (HQ PACAF, Proj CHECO, 27 Oct 72), pp 16-17, 20-21.

63. *Ibid.,* p 21.

64. *Ibid.,* pp 35-36.

65. Hist, 8th TFWg, Apr 1-Jun 30, 1972, pp 50-51.

66. Liebchen, *Kontum: Battle for the Central Highlands, 30 Mar-10 Jun 72;* Col John A. Doglione, *et al, Airpower and the*

1972 Spring Invasion, (USAF SEA Monograph Series, Vol 3, 1976), p 72.

67. Liebchen: *Kontum,* pp 43, 50, 67-70; Doglione, *Airpower and the 1972 Spring Invasion,* p 73.

68. Maj Paul T. Ringenbach and Capt Peter J. Melly, *The Battle for An Loc,* Apr 5-Jun 26, 1972 (HQ PACAF, Proj CHECO, Jan 31, 1973), pp 5, 6-12, 16-17.

69. Hist, 8th TFWg, Apr 1-Jun 30, 1972.

70. Ringenbach and Melly, *The Battle of An Loc,* pp 19-20, 24-25, 31-38, 41-42, 45-46; Gerald J. Till and James C. Thomas, *Pave Aegis Weapon System* (AC-130E Gunship), (HQ PACAF, Proj CHECO, Jul 30, 1973), pp 23-24.

71. *Ibid.;* hist, 8th TFWg, Apr 1-Jun 30, 1972, p 58.

72. *Ibid.*

73. Hist, 8th TFWg, Jul 1-Sep 30, 1972, pp 6, 9-10, 23-26; End of Tour Report, Lt Col Robert G. Mathews, comdr, 18th Spl Operations Squadron, Dec 16, 1971-Nov 13, 1972, pp 2-4.

74. Hist, 8th TFWg, Jul 1-Sep 30, 1972, p 11.

75. End of Tour Report, Col John E. Davis, cmdr, 16th Spl Ops Sqdn, Jun 12, 1972-Apr 8, 1973, p 30. Also, Hist, 8th TFWg, Jul 1-Sep 30, 1972, p 17.

76. Hist, 8th TFWg, Jul 1-Sep 30, 1972, p 28; *The Washington Post* on Sep 19, 1972, p A14, reported the use of gunships for the defense of Saigon. The paper indicated the prime reason for the gunship patrol was to prevent headline grabbing rocket attacks.

77. Hist, 8th TFWg, pp 28-29.

Chapter VII

1. Hist, USAFSAWC, Jan 1-Jun 30, 1966, p 31.

2. Msg, USAFSAWC to TAC, DOTR AT 00542, 071930Z Sep 66.

3. *Ibid.*

4. Hist, USAFSAWC, Jan 1-Jun 30, 1968, pp 33-34.

5. Msg, USAFSO to CSAF, subj: Install SUU-11 and .50 cal. Machine Guns, C-47 Aircraft, Jul 10, 1967.

6. Hist, USAFSAWC, Jan 1-Jun 30, 1968, pp 33-34.

7. Msg, CSAF to TAC, 132042Z Jan 68.

8. TAC Test 68-201, 1st Cmbt Applications Gp (TAC), TAC Test Order: Side Fire C-47 Machine Gun Installation, May 9 1968.

9. Hist, TAC, Jul 1969-Jun 1970, I, 337.

10. Msg, 1st Cmbt Applications Gp to USAFSO, subj: Status Report, C-47 Machine Gun Installation, Jul 4, 1968.

11. Hist, Dir/Ops, Jan 1-Jun 30, 1969, pp 359-360. USAF Program Guidance (PG)-71-1 reflected programming action which revised USAFSO's 24th SOWg force authorization effective third quarter, fiscal year 1969, as follows: three UH-1s and four AC-47s authorized in the Special Forces program; and two Special Operations Squadrons (vice one) authorized in the 24th SOWg.

12. Hist, 2d Air Div, Jan-Jun 1964, pp 7-10. History of the 2d Air Division, November 15, 1961-October 8, 1962, states that the best available information places the first VNAF night flaredrop on February 5, 1962.

13. Hist, Dir/Opl Rqmts & Dev Plans, Jul 1-Dec 31, 1969.

14. Msg, AF Advisory Gp, Tan Son Nhut AB, to CSAF, Sep 16, 1967.

15. Memo of Understanding, 14th ACWg and AF Advisory Gp, Dec 1967, AC-47 Acft (VHAF) file, AF Archives.

16. Kott, *The Role of USAF Gunships in SEASIA,* p 7.

17. *Ibid.* PACAF reassigned the following AC-47D aircraft from the 14th SOWg to MAP Vietnam effective Jan 30, 1969: SNs 45-0919, 44-76722, 43-48801, 43-48701, and 42-49770. [Msg CINCPACAF to 7th AF, AFLC, 14th SOWg 281920Z Jun 69.]

18. Cole, *Fixed Wing Gunships in SEA (Jul 69-Jul 71),* p 5.

19. James T. Bear, *VNAF Improvement and Modernization Program* (HQ PACAF, Proj CHECO, Feb 5, 1970), p 78.

20. *Ibid.,* p 79.

21. See note 18.

22. Bear, *VNAF Improvement and Modernization Program* p 79.

23. John L. Frisbee, "USAF's Changing Role in Vietnam," *Air Force,* Sep 1971, p 44.

24. See note 22.

25. Cole, *Fixed Wing Gunships in SEA (Jul 69-Jul 71),* pp 6-7.

26. Bear, *VNAF Improvement and Modernization Program,* p 82.

27. *Ibid.*

28. Cole, *Fixed Wing Gunships in SEA (Jul 69-Jul 71),* p 6.

29. See comments on the training program in *Air Force Times,* Mar 31, 1971, p 20.

30. *Air Force Times,* Apr 28, 1971, p 20.

31. Release 9-24-71-614, Air Force News Service, "Air Force 'Shadows' transferred to

VNAF," Sep 24, 1971. The VNAF renamed the AC–119s Hac Long or Black Dragons.

32. Rprt, Det 1 Comdr, 56th SOWg/C–47 MTT, to Dep Ch, JUSMAG, Thailand, subj: C–47 MTT Final Report, Aug 10, 1969.

33. Hist, CINCPAC, 1969, III, 208; hist, Dir/Opl Rqmts & Dev Plans, Jan 1–Jun 30, 1969, pp 246–47.

34. See note 32.

35. The deployment of a USAFSOF C–47 MTT was labeled Combat Wombat. [Hist, Dir/Ops, Jan 1–Jun 30, 1969, p 347.]

36. See note 32. The 56th SOWg supervised the MTT since that Wing's mission was to create a reasonably self-sufficient Laotian air arm. Also, see: Bevan, End of Tour Report, September 3, 1969–June 7, 1969.

37. Hist, CINCPAC, 1969, III, 208.

38. *Ibid.,* 209.

39. *Ibid.,* 210.

40. *Ibid.*

41. Ltr, Dep Ch, JUSMAG, Thailand, to CSAF, subj: Military Assistance Program Report, Jun 27, 1970.

42. *Aviation Week & Space Technology,* May 1, 1972, p 17.

43. USAF Management Summary Southeast Asia, Jul 9, 1969, p 28.

44. USAF Management Summary Southeast Asia, Feb 22, 1972, pp 47–48.

45. *Ibid.*

46. Quote referred to in message, CINCPACAF to 2d Air Div, 142357Z Dec 1964.

47. Final rprt, TAC, Gunships Post-SEAsia, An In-Depth Review, Sep 1, 1970.

48. Address, Gen William W. Momyer, TAC commander, to students of Army Command and General Staff College, Ft Leavenworth, Kans., Oct 13, 1971.

48. Address, Gen William W. Momyer, TAC commander, to students of Army Command and General Staff College, Ft Leavenworth, Kans., Oct 13, 1971.

49. David Halberstam, *The Making of a Quagmire* (New York, 1964), p 167.

50. Gen John D. Ryan, "Transitional Adjustments in Air Force Structure," *Aerospace Commentary,* III (Fall 1971), 11.

51. *The Washington Post,* Jan 10, 1973, p A22.

52. Capt David K. Mann, *The 1972 Invasion of Military Region I; Fall of Quang Tri and Defense of Hue,* HQ PACAF, Proj CHECO, Mar 15, 1973), p 71.

Glossary

AC–47	The C–47 transport converted into a gunship by adding the General Electric SUU–11A minigun; the AC–47 had several nicknames—Puff the Magic Dragon, Dragon Ship, and Spooky
AU–23A	Fairchild light STOL aircraft tested as a mini-gunship under the Credible Chase program; nicknamed Peacemaker
AU–24A	Light STOL aircraft built by Helio Aircraft Company. Nicknamed Stallion, it was tested under the Credible Chase program.
AAA	antiaircraft artillery
AB	Air Base
ABCCC	airborne battlefield command and control center
ACSq	Air Commando Squadron
ACWg	Air Commando Wing
ADF	Automatic direction finder; it automatically and continuously measures the direction of arrival of the received signal; data are usually displayed visually
ADSID III Ground Sensor	Air-deliverable seismic intrusion detector designed for hand-launch from low-speed, light, fixed-wing aircraft, or from helicopters
AF	Air Force
AFAL	Air Force Avionics Laboratory
AFATL	Air Force Armament Laboratory
AFB	Air Force Base
AFLC	Air Force Logistics Command
AFSC	Air Force Systems Command
Air America	Contract airline that flew for the Central Intelligence Agency in Southeast Asia
AMRL	Aerospace Medical Research Laboratory
Arc Light	B–52 operations in SEA; initially, missions were flown from Anderson AFB, Guam, Kadena AB, Okinawa, and U-Tapao RTAFB, Thailand; later, all Arc Light missions were flown from U-Tapao
ARVN	Army of the Republic of Vietnam
ASAP	as soon as possible
ASD	Aeronautical Systems Division
B–52	High-speed, high-altitude, land-based heavy bomber; designated Stratofortress
B–57	Strike aircraft developed by Martin Company for night intruder missions; nicknamed Canberra
Barrel Roll	Interdiction and close air support operations in eastern Laos (beginning Dec 14, 1964), later reduced to the area of northern Laos (Apr 13, 1965); the operations were under 2d Air Division and later, Seventh Air Force control; most recently, Barrel Roll refers to strikes against personnel and equipment from North Vietnam
BDA	Bomb damage assessment; the term encompasses the determination of the effect of all air attacks on targets (e.g., bombs, rockets, or strafe); also referred to as "battle damage assessment"
BIAS	battle illumination airborne system
Bias Hunter	C–130 aircraft equipped with a BIAS and other sensor equipment (e.g., infrared devices) to locate the enemy
Black Crow	A sensor used on AC–130 and AC–123 Black Spot aircraft
Black Spot	Converted C–123 transport (AC–123 equipped with FLIR, LLLTV, forward-looking IR detector, laser ranger, advanced navigation system, weapon dispensers (CBUs)

Blind Bat	Nickname of C–130 FAC/flareship aircraft operating in southern Laos; eventually Blind Bat became the nickname of all C–130 flare missions [see Lamplighter]
Blue Chip	The Seventh AF command and control center (7AFCCC) which controlled out-country combat operations
boresight line	An optical reference line used in harmonizing guns, rockets and other weapon launchers
C–119	Twin-boom transport nicknamed Flying Boxcar; modified into AC–119G Shadow and AC–119K Stinger gunships
C–123	Fairchild Provider transport used in airlift and as a FAC/flareship; call sign Candlestick when used in latter mission
C–130	Multi-engine transport developed for the Air Force by Lockheed; nicknamed Hercules
Canberra	The B–57 strike aircraft
Candlestick	The call sign for the C–123 FAC/flare aircraft in Laos
CBU	Cluster bomb unit. Basically, the CBU consisted of a dispenser filled with small spherical bombs containing small steel spheres. When the dispenser was ejected from the aircraft, a timer opened it and the bombs were released. The bombs were fuzed to detonate and expel the steel spheres against personnel and materiel.
CCT	Combat Crew Training
CIDG	Civilian Irregular Defense Group
CINCPAC	Commander in Chief, Pacific Command
CINCPACAF	Commander in Chief, Pacific Air Forces
CJCS	The Chairman, Joint Chiefs of Staff
Claymore	Directional antipersonnel mine.
Commando Bolt	Task Force Alpha-controlled airstrike on moving trucks in a specified area, using sensor activations
COMUSMACV	Commander, United States Military Assistance Command, Vietnam
CONAC	Continental Air Command
cookoff	Ammunition firing as a result of being allowed to rest in the chamber of an overheated weapon
counterinsurgency	Those military, paramilitary, political, economic, psychological, and civic actions taken by a government to defeat subversive insurgency
Covey	Call sign of O–2 and OV–10 FACs of the 20th TASq operating in North and South Vietnam and Laos
Credible Chase	The concept and plan to use a short-takeoff-and-landing aircraft as a mini-gunship
Cricket	Operations in Laos of O–1E and AC–47 FAC aircraft and the C–130 ABCCC
CS	Chief of Staff
CSAF	Chief of Staff, United States Air Force
CSGp	combat support group
CTZ	corps tactical zone
DASC	direct air support center
DCS	Deputy Chief of Staff
DDR&E	Director, Defense Research and Engineering, Office of the Secretary of Defense
DIA	Defense Intelligence Agency
DSPG	Defense Special Projects Group
EB–66	The former B–66 tactical bomber, it had several configurations for electronic intelligence or for radiation jamming to protect strike forces.
ECM	electronic countermeasures
ETA	estimated time of arrival
ETR	Eastern Test Range

F-4	Strike aircraft nicknamed Phantom
F-5	Strike aircraft nicknamed Freedom Fighter
F-105F	Tactical fighter specially equipped to suppress surface-to-air missiles and radar-controlled AA weapons
FAC	forward air controller
Farm Gate	A detachment of USAF air commandos from the Special Air Warfare Center, Eglin AFB, Fla., which entered South Vietnam in November 1961 at President Diem's request; its two-fold mission was training and combat operations.
fire arrow	Could be made of many materials; metal gas cans filled with gasoline-soaked sand were often used; ignited it was easy to see at night; hamlet defenders relayed to flare/strike aircraft the enemy's position with reference to the fire arrow
flak	Bursting shells fired from antiaircraft guns
FLIR	forward-looking infrared
Flying Boxcar	Nickname of the C-119 twin-boom transport
FM	frequency modulation
FOB	forward operating base
FOL	forward operating location
frag	Fragmentation operations order; the daily supplement to standard operations order governing the conduct of the air war in Southeast Asia; it contained mission number and function type of ordnance, time on target, and other instructions; "to frag" means to issue a fragmentation operations order covering the details of a single mission
FSB	fire support base
FY	fiscal year
GCI	ground-controlled intercept
Gooney Bird	Nickname of the C-47 aircraft
gunship	Any of several modified fixed-wing transport aircraft equipped with side-firing machineguns and/or cannons; the fixed-wing side-firing aircraft of the U.S. Air Force
Gunships I, II, III	Specially modified USAF transport aircraft equipped with side-firing machineguns and/or cannons: Gunship I (AC-47s called Spooky); Gunship II (AC-130s called Spectre); Gunship III (AC-119Gs called Shadow and AC-119Ks called Stinger)
hangfire	A delay in the explosion of the charge of a gun after the primer has been fired; the temporary failure of a primer or igniter
headroom	Availability of spaces under manpower ceilings
IFF	Identification, friend or foe; a method for determining the friendly or unfriendly character of aircraft and ships by other aircraft or ships, and by ground forces using electronic detection equipment and associated IFF units
Igloo White	A surveillance system consisting of hand-implemented and air-delivered sensors, relay aircraft, and an infiltration surveillance center; Igloo White was formerly Muscle Shoals
I&M	inventory and management
in-country	That part of the Southeast Asia conflict within South Vietnam
interdict	To prevent or hinder (by any means) enemy use of an area or route
Interdiction Boxes	Refers to four specified strike zones on the main routes and passes from North Vietnam into Laos; the Air Force allocated intensive sorties against these boxes during Commando Hunt V
IR	infrared
IRAN	inspection and repair as necessary
Iron Hand	Suppression of surface-to-air missiles and radar-controller antiaircraft weapons by F-105F aircraft

JCS	Joint Chiefs of Staff
JGS	Joint General Staff, Republic of Vietnam Armed Forces
JRATA	Joint Research and Test Activity; the Commander, JRATA, advised COMUSMACV on research, development, testing, and evaluation
JUSMAG	Joint United States Military Advisory Group
KC–135	Tanker aircraft used for air refueling
karst	A limestone region marked by sinks and interspersed with abrupt ridges, irregular protuberant rocks, caverns, and underground streams
Lamplighter	Nickname of C–130 aircraft operating in northern Laos; eventually Blindbat became the nickname for all C–130 flare missions
laser	Light amplification by stimulated emission of radiation; laser light is most often invisible and infrared; it differs from ordinary light in that its individual light rays are all the same wave length and all are in step; hence its energy is not dissipated as the beam spreads out—thus permitting an intense concentration of light energy
LAU–74	4-tube flare launcher that carried 24 flares. Compatible with cargo aircraft only, it was mounted to the aircraft floor. The launcher's chief drawback was the tendency of flares to hang up after being partially ejected from the tubes
LIMA sites	Aircraft landing sites (dirt strips) in Laos used as resupply points
LLLTV	low-light-level television
LOC	lines of communication
loran	Long-range electronic navigation system that uses the time divergence of pulse-type transmissions from two or more fixed stations; also called long-range navigation
loran C	Extremely accurate long-range system of navigation similar to loran, giving accuracy within a few hundred feet for up to 1,000 miles out to sea
loran D	Tactical loran system that uses the coordinate converter of low-frequency loran C and can operate independently of ground facilities and without radiating radio-frequency (RF) energy that could reveal the aircraft's location
LTVE	Ling-Temco-Vought/Electrosystems, Greenville, Tex.
LUU–2/B	Flare used by AC–130 gunships as a heat decoy for SA–7 surface-to-air missiles. It had a burning time of 5 minutes (2 million candlepower).
Mk–6	White flare marker/marker-log used to mark ground targets
Mk–24	Parachute flare that could also be rigged as a ground target marker; dropped at 5- or 10-second intervals. The MK–24 illuminated an area ½-mile across for 3 minutes.
MAC	Military Airlift Command
MACV	Military Assistance Command, Vietnam
MAP	Military Assistance Program
Mig	Term applied to Soviet-built jet fighters used by North Vietnam, including the Mig–15 (of Korean War vintage), the Mig–17, and the Mig–21 all-weather jet fighter
MIGCAPS	Combat air patrols conducted by F–105F and EB–66 aircraft against Migs.
Military Assistance Program	The U.S. program for providing military assistance under the Foreign Assistance Act of 1969, as amended, as distinct from Economic Aid and other programs authorized by the Act: includes the furnishing of defense articles and defense services through grant aid or military sales to eligible allies as specified by Congress
miniponder	Small (5 watt and 40 watt) portable transponder carried by ground troops; used with the AC–119K's beacon-tracking radar to provide offset-firing ground support
MINISID III Ground Sensor	A hand-emplaced seismic intrusion detector. (See App 3.)

Misch-metal	Resembling cigarette flints, Misch-metal was highly pyrophoric on impact. The Naval Weapons Laboratory, Dahlgren, Va., developed Misch-metal.
MJU-3B	A modified LUU-2/B flare. The AC-130 gunships found it a faster-acting heat decoy for SA-7 surface-to-air missiles.
MOB	main operating base
monsoon	A seasonal wind in Southeast Asia which blows from the southwest from April to October and from the northeast during the rest of the year.
MR	memorandum for record
MTI	moving target indicator; a radar presentation which shows only targets in motion; signals from stationary targets are subtracted out of the return signal by the output of a suitable memory circuit
MTT	mobile training team
Nail	Call sign of OV-2 and OV-10 FACs of 23d TASq
NOD	Night observation device; an image intensifier using reflected light from the stars or moon to identify targets
NOS	night observation sight
NSC	National Security Council
NVA	North Vietnamese Army
NVN	North Vietnam
O-2	FAC aircraft nicknamed Skymaster
OV-10	FAC aircraft nicknamed Bronco
OASD	Office of the Assistant Secretary of Defense
OCAMA	Oklahoma City Air Materiel Area
Offset firing	A firing procedure employing a reference or aiming point other than the actual target
OL	operating location
OOAMA	Ogden Air Materiel Area
OSD	Office of the Secretary of Defense
P-2E	Navy patrol plane (Neptune)
PACAF	Pacific Air Forces
PACOM	Pacific Command
Pave Aegis	105-mm gun system of the AC-130E gunship
Pave Phantom	The loran-equipped F-4 aircraft
Pave Spectre	The AC-130E gunship, featuring a bigger fuel load, more armorplate, digital fire control, and integrated inertial navigation
Pave Sword	The F-4's laser-seeker pod; it detected the laser beam from a gunship's laser target designator, giving the fighter pilot steering information to the laser cone ("basket") for release of a laser-guided bomb
Pave Way	The F-4 aircraft using various guidance devices: Pave Way I (laser); Pave Way II (electro-optical); Pave Way III (infrared). Used also for the guidance system itself.
Phantom	F-4 tactical aircraft
pipper	The center or bead of a gunsight
Plain Jane	An unmodified AC-130A gunship
PMD	program management directive
POL	petroleum, oil, and lubricants
Portable III (AN/USQ-46)	A militarized, portable VHF receiver, decoded sensor activations. (See App 4)
Project Moon Watch	A study of the effects of lunar illumination on combat operations; conducted by the 16th SOSq from February 1 to May 31, 1969
PSAC	President's Science Advisory Committee
Pylon turn	An aircraft turn around an object or reference point on the ground
RAF	Royal Air Force (United Kingdom)
R&D	research and development

RDT&E	research, development, test and evaluation
real time	The absence of delay, except for the time required for the transmission by electromagnetic energy, between the occurence of an event and reception of the data at some other location
recce	reconnaissance, to reconnoiter
recon	reconnaissance
Red Horse	Rapid engineering deployment and heavy operational repair squadron, engineering; the Red Horse squadrons handled engineering and construction projects in Southeast Asia.
reticle	A system of lines, dots, crosshairs, or wires in the focus of an optical instrument
RF	radio frequency
RHAW	radar homing and warning
RLAF	Royal Laotian Air Force
ROK	Republic of Korea
Rolling Thunder	Nickname assigned to airstrikes against selected targets and lines of communication in North Vietnam (Mar 1965–Oct 1968)
RTAFB	Royal Thai Air Force Base
rules of engagement	Directives issued by competent military authority delineating the circumstances under which U.S. forces will begin and/or continue combat engagement with other forces met
RVN	Republic of Vietnam
RVNAF	Republic of Vietnam Armed Forces
SA–7	Shoulder-fired, infrared, surface-to-air missile (Strela)
SAAMA	San Antonio Air Materiel Area
SAC	Strategic Air Command
SAF	Secretary of the Air Force
SAM	surface-to-air missile
SAWC	Special Air Warfare Center
SCANA	self-contained all weather/night attack
scenario	An outline plan of the action to be undertaken during a projected exercise or maneuver
SCNA	self-contained night attack
SEA	Southeast Asia
SEAOR	Southeast Asia Operational Requirement
SECAF	Secretary of the Air Force
SECDEF	Secretary of Defense
SECNAV	Secretary of the Navy
Shadow	Call sign of AC–119G gunship
shadow boxes	A number of specific strikes zones designated throughout South Vietnam for AC–119 operations
Shed Light	The overall USAF program to improve night attack/interdiction capability
short rounds	Inadvertent or accidental delivery of ordnance, sometimes resulting in death or injury to friendly forces or noncombatants
single-source contract	A contract let with a single firm without bidding or under circumstances that dictate the contract be given to a single firm
slant range	The line-of-sight distance between two points not at the same elevation
SOF	special operation force
sortie	One aircraft making one takeoff and landing to conduct the mission for which it was scheduled
SOSq	Special Operations Squadron
SOWg	Special Operations Wing
Special Forces	Military personnel with cross-training in basic and specialized military skills, organized into small multiple-purpose detachments with the mission to train, organize, supply, direct and control indigenous forces in guerrilla warfare and counterinsurgency operations and to conduct unconventional warfare operations

special operations	Secondary or supporting operations which may be adjuncts to various other operations, and for which no one Service is assigned primary responsibility
special operations forces	Forces specifically organized, trained and equipped to conduct special operations
Spectre	Call sign of AC–130 gunship
Spooky	Call sign of AC–47 gunship
Spooky Count	Running totals kept by the 4th Air Commando Squadron of its successes in defending outposts/hamlets
Standoff weapon	Offensive weapon fired from a distance sufficient to allow attacking personnel to evade defensive fire from the target area
starlight scope	An image intensifier using reflected light from the stars or moon to identify targets
Steel Tiger	The geographic area in southern Laos designated by Seventh Air Force to facilitate planning and operations; the term also referred to\ strikes in southern Laos against personnel and equipment from North Vietnam.
Stinger	Call sign of AC–119K gunship
STOL	short takeoff and landing
Strategic readout system	A system that received pulses from ground sensors, decoding and displaying them for use by the aircraft gunner (See App 4)
Super Chicken	A nickname applied to Surprise Package by some crewmembers
Surprise Package	An enhanced AC–130A gunship aircraft with improved offensive and survival capabilities due to the addition of special ASD equipment; the aircraft became a test bed for improved techniques and equipment
SUU–11A	Minigun used on the AC–47 gunship
SUU–25/A	A modified LAU–10 "Zuni" rocket launcher; it carried eight Mk–24 flares, two in each of its four tubes
SUU–25C/A	A 4-tube flare dispenser that carried eight flares. The SUU–25C/A could be wing-mounted on both high- and low-speed aircraft. Its better intervalometer and improved tubes rendered it more reliable than the LAU–74 flare launcher
SUU–42	A wing-mounted flare dispenser for both high- and low-speed aircraft. It contained 8 tubes and carried 16 flares. The flares could be launched singly or rippled off. Follow-on AC–130E gunships were to receive this system in lieu of the SUU–25C/A
SVN	South Vietnam
TAC	Tactical Air Command
TACAIR	aircraft sorties other than B–52 and strategic airlift
TACAN	A tactical air navigation system consisting of short-range UHF radio stations; in the form of a readout on the instrument panel the pilot continuously receives accurate distance and bearing information from the station tuned
TAOR	Tactical area of responsibility
target acquisition	Detection, identification, and location of a target in sufficient detail to permit the effective employment of weapons
Task Force Alpha (TFA)	A filter point for sensor information received under the Igloo White/Commando Hunt concept; organized in 1967 under command of Seventh Air Force at Tan Son Nhut AB, South Vietnam, and deployed to Nakhon Phanom AB, Thailand
TCTO	time compliance technical orders
TDY	temporary duty
testbed	A stand at which some mechanism or engine is tested out
Tet	The Vietnamese New Year holiday
TF	task force
TFR	Terrain-following radar; this radar provides a display of terrain ahead of a low-flying aircraft to permit manual control, or signals for automatic control, to maintain constant altitude above the ground

TIARA	Nickname for a chemi-luminescent material which the U.S. Army tested for possible use in bombs or mortar projectiles; when released in the air, TIARA glows rather than flames and gives off little light; since tests proved TIARA undependable, the Army did not put it in bombs or other projectiles
Tiger/Tiger Hound	Southern Steel Tiger south of 17° north latitude, for FAC employment (1965-1968)
TOT	time-over-target
TOW	Tube-launched, optically tracked, wire-guided missile. Mounted on UH-1 helicopters of the U.S. Air Cavalry, this weapon destroyed many enemy tanks
transponder	Radio transmitter-receiver which transmits identifiable signals automatically when the proper interrogation is received
Tropic Moon I	Night-strike A-1E aircraft using LLLTV and CBU or napalm munitions (1968)
Tropic Moon II	Westinghouse LLLTV in the B-57 (1968)
Tropic Moon III	Follow-on B-57 program for night attacks in high-threat areas, forerunner to the B-57G
truck park	A localized area within which trucks were concealed, unloaded, repaired, serviced, and loaded; supplies were stored and personnel obtained food, rest, and medical attention; truck parks were typically located under dense jungle foliage, within villages, or in caves; they were often extensively camouflaged and revetted.
UE	unit equipment
UK	United Kingdom
USA	United States Army
USAF	United States Air Force
USAFA	United States Air Force Academy
USAFSO	United States Air Forces Southern Command
USMC	United States Marine Corps
VC	Viet Cong
VCS	Vice Chief of Staff
Very pistol	A pistol used to fire signal flares
VNAF	Vietnamese Air Force
Wolf	Call sign of the F-4 FACs of the 8th Tactical Fighter Wing, Ubon RTAFB, Thailand
WPAFB	Wright-Patterson AFB
WRAMA	Warner Robins Air Materiel Area
xenon	A heavy colorless inert gaseous element used in specialized electric lamps
XM-197	A 3-barrel, 20-mm Gatling gun
Z	Zulu Time (Greenwich Mean Time)

Index*

AC-47 mobile training team: 249, 154, 154n
ADSID III: 266
AN/TV-5: 266
APQ-133: 215
A Shau Special Forces Camp: 40–41, 71
A Shau Valley: 40–41, 213, 228n
Abrams, Creighton W., Jr. (*see also* Commander, United States Military Assistance Command, Vietnam): 99, 188, 243
Adak: 192
Advanced Research Project Agency. *See* Defense, Office of the Secretary of
Aerospace Medical Research Laboratory (AMRL): 3, 5, 8, 9
Aeronautical Systems Division (ASD): 4, 6, 7, 8, 9, 29, 78, 86, 100, 101, 103, 104, 127, 128, 129, 138, 140, 142, 146, 147, 148, 150, 153, 156, 159, 172, 173, 178, 185n, 197, 236, 246
    Gunship Program Office: 104, 126, 140, 147, 158, 163–164
    Limited War Office: 8, 9, 82, 156
Air America: 45, 224, 224n
Air Commando Squadrons (ACSq) (*see also* Special Operations Squadrons)
    1st: 16–17, 37n
    3rd: 63
    4th: 32, 33, 34, 34n, 35, 36, 37n, 40, 42, 44–45, 47, 49, 50, 51, 52, 55, 56–57, 58, 59, 63
    A Flight: 51, 52, 56
    B Flight: 51, 56
    C Flight: 51, 56, 57
    D Flight: 51, 56
    E Flight: 52
    5th: 32, 32n
    14th: 55, 56–57, 59
    A Flight: 56
    B Flight: 56
    C Flight: 56
    D Flight: 56
    16th: 105–106
Air Commando Wings (ACWg) (*see also* Special Operation Wings)
    1st: 30, 32, 185n
    14th: 36, 42, 47, 48, 56, 63, 90, 92, 105, 135, 178, 189, 251, 251n
Air Delivery Group
    4440th: 199–200
Air Divisions
    2d: 12, 25, 34, 35, 44
    2d/Thirteenth Air Force: 40, 45
    834th: 90
    838th: 32
Air Force, Secretary of (*see also* Brown, Harold; Seamans, Robert C.): 92, 94, 95, 97, 98, 126, 140, 142, 143, 144, 146, 147, 148, 152, 157, 162, 163, 166, 167, 172, 176, 178, 179, 180, 183, 202, 222, 227
Air Force, Under Secretary. *See* McLucas, John L.
Air Force Academy: 138, 140, 157, 158, 173

---

*Numerals in italic indicate an illustration of the subject mentioned.

☆U.S. GOVERNMENT PRINTING OFFICE: 1982-327-157